God's Continent

The Future of Christianity Trilogy

The Next Christendom: The Coming of Global Christianity, Revised and Expanded Edition

The New Faces of Christianity: Believing the Bible in the Global South

God's Continent: Christianity, Islam, and Europe's Religious Crisis

Decade of Nightmares: The End of the Sixties and the Making of Eighties America

Dream Catchers: How Mainstream America Discovered Native Spirituality

The New Anti-Catholicism: The Last Acceptable Prejudice

Images of Terror: What We Can and Can't Know about Terrorism

Beyond Tolerance: Child Pornography on the Internet

Hidden Gospels: How the Search for Jesus Lost Its Way

Mystics and Messiahs: Cults and New Religions in American History

The Cold War at Home: The Red Scare in Pennsylvania 1945–1960

Synthetic Panics: The Politics of Designer Drugs

Moral Panic: Changing Concepts of the Child Molester in Modern America

A History of the United States

Hoods and Shirts: The Extreme Right in Pennsylvania 1925–1950

Pedophiles and Priests: Anatomy of a Contemporary Crisis

Using Murder: The Social Construction of Serial Homicide

Intimate Enemies: Moral Panics in Contemporary Great Britain

A History of Modern Wales 1536–1990

Crime and Justice: Issues and Ideas

The Making of a Ruling Class: The Glamorgan Gentry 1640–1790

GOD'S CONTINENT

Christianity, Islam, and Europe's Religious Crisis

Philip Jenkins

OXFORD
UNIVERSITY PRESS

OXFORD
UNIVERSITY PRESS

Oxford University Press, Inc., publishes works that further
Oxford University's objective of excellence
in research, scholarship, and education.

Oxford   New York
Auckland   Cape Town   Dar es Salaam   Hong Kong   Karachi
Kuala Lumpur   Madrid   Melbourne   Mexico City   Nairobi
New Delhi   Shanghai   Taipei   Toronto

With offices in
Argentina   Austria   Brazil   Chile   Czech Republic   France   Greece
Guatemala   Hungary   Italy   Japan   Poland   Portugal   Singapore
South Korea   Switzerland   Thailand   Turkey   Ukraine   Vietnam

Copyright © 2007 by Philip Jenkins

Published by Oxford University Press, Inc.
198 Madison Avenue, New York, New York 10016

www.oup.com

First issued as an Oxford University Press paperback, 2010

Oxford is a registered trademark of Oxford University Press

Library of Congress Cataloging-in-Publication Data
Jenkins, Philip, 1952–
God's continent : Christianity, Islam, and Europe's religious crisis /
Philip Jenkins.
p. cm.
Includes bibliographical references and index.
ISBN 978-0-19-538462-8
1. Christianity—Europe—21st century. 2. Islam—Europe—21st
century. 3. Europe—Religion—21st century. 4. Christianity
and other religions—Islam. 5. Islam—Relations—Christianity. I. Title.
BR735.J46 2007
200.94'090511—dc22
2006038654

Printed in the United States of America
on acid-free paper

Contents

Note

Several words and terms used throughout this book need explanation. Particularly contentious are the words used to describe Muslims of extreme or radical views. Though the word "extremist" usually refers to hard-line political militants, Muslims reasonably ask whether the term condemns all faithful believers. If Islam is a good religion, they might argue, it is only right to be zealous and radical in its interests. An "extreme Muslim" might be one who, inspired by the faith, devotes his or her whole life to works of charity. Was not Francis of Assisi a radical or extreme Christian? And does "Islamist" mean anything more than a good Muslim? Some Muslim writers retort that if their zealots are Islamists, then devoted Christians with a political orientation must be Christianists.

While acknowledging these objections, I believe that the words "Islamist" and "extremist" do refer to important concepts for which no convenient alternative term exists. As used here, the word "Islamist" refers to activists who seek to establish Islamic political power, to reorganize society according to their vision of Islamic law. As for extremists, I will borrow the definition offered in a thoughtful report by the U.S. National Intelligence Council: "We define *Muslim extremists* as a subset of Islamic activists. They are committed to restructuring political society in accordance with their vision of Islamic law and are willing to use violence."[1]

Another word requiring explanation is "liberal," which refers to quite different political values on either side of the Atlantic. Generally, an American liberal favors expanding personal rights and civil liberties while using state intervention to achieve socially progressive causes, to advance traditionally underprivileged groups. Hence, liberals are on the political left. In Europe, in contrast, liberalism usually means a belief in laissez-faire economics and small government, combating the growth of the over-mighty state: liberals are thus opposed to socialist or communist advances. In American terms, then, European "liberals" are thus on the political right. In the present book, though, I will use the progressive American sense of "liberalism."

Finally, I often refer in this book to the European Union, a phrase that has over the years referred to quite different realities. Though I do not need to offer a detailed history here, we should note changes both of name and of composition. From 1957 to 1973, six nations composed the European Economic Community, which would also be referred to as the European Community. The Community grew steadily, until today it includes twenty-five nations, with several others in line for membership. Since the signature of the Maastricht treaty in 1992, the Community has become the European Union, EU. In speaking of recent European history, I use the term European Union to refer to the various stages of unifying Europe without precisely identifying what that grouping was called at a particular historical point.

Acknowledgments

I would like to thank Jonathan Brockopp and Christopher Darlington for their advice and support.

Abbreviations

BMF	British Muslim Forum
BNP	British National Party
CFCM	Conseil Français du Culte Musulman
FEERI	Federación Española de Entidades Religiosas Islámicas
FNMF	Fédération Nationale des Musulmans de France
GIA	Groupe Islamique Armé
GICM	Groupe Islamique Combattant Marocain
GSPC	Groupe Salafiste pour la Prédication et le Combat
HT	Hizb ut-Tahrir al-Islami
JI	Jamaat-i-Islami
MCB	Muslim Council of Britain
RCCG	Redeemed Christian Church of God
RnS	Rinnovamento nello Spirito
UCOII	Unione delle Comunità e Organizzazioni Islamiche in Italia
UOIF	Union des Organisations Islamiques de France

God's Continent

1

Your Religion Tomorrow

If Europe were a woman, her biological clock would be rapidly running down. It is not too late to adopt more children, but they won't look like her.

Philip Longman

In 1989, the clerical regime of Iran issued a fatwa ordering the death of author Salman Rushdie for his allegedly blasphemous novel *The Satanic Verses*. In several European nations, the controversy spurred mass protests by Muslim residents hitherto known for their political quiescence. Some demonstrators carried placards reading "Islam—Our Religion Today, Your Religion Tomorrow," a slogan that was at once shocking, aggressive, and above all, eye-catching.[1]

Over the past few years, serious scholars have debated whether there might be some truth to this piece of bumper sticker futurology. European nations are presently undergoing historic transformations that mark a real crisis for the continent's traditional religious alignments. Many indices suggest a sharp decline of religious practice among old-stock white Europeans, whose ancestors would conventionally have described themselves as Christian. Timothy Garton Ash describes Europe as "now the most secular continent on earth." Further depleting Christian numbers, religious decline coincides with dramatically falling birth rates among old-stock Europeans. The decline of a religion, or even its death, will not necessarily alarm those who do not belong to the faith in question, nor need it have damaging policy consequences. Liberal or leftist Europeans see no tragedy in the emergence of a fully secular, progressive society.[2] Yet the process of dechristianization, if that is what it really is, coincides not with the growth of scientific humanism,

1

but rather the dramatic expansion of other religions of a traditionalist or fundamentalist bent, especially Islam.

As European Christianity recedes, so Islam offers a plausible rival for the loyalty of future generations; and at least in recent years, the most conspicuous form of that religion appears militant, intolerant, and deeply reactionary. As Bruce Bawer remarks, "when Christian faith had departed, it had taken with it a sense of ultimate meaning and purpose—and left the continent vulnerable to conquest by people with deeper faith and stronger convictions." It is almost too easy to find convenient images of the decay of Christianity, and the growth of Islam. Any traveler in modern European cities has noticed the new mosques, the abandoned and secularized churches, some transformed into museums. In the words of former film star Brigitte Bardot, who these days is a controversial anti-immigration activist, "From year to year, we see mosques sprout up pretty much everywhere in France, while church bells are becoming silent because of a lack of priests."[3]

This would not be the first time that a region regarded as a heartland of Christianity had lost that role, had abandoned the faith. In the early middle ages, Christian thought and practice reached their finest flowering in Near Eastern nations such as Egypt, Syria, and Iraq, which would later become overwhelmingly Muslim. But could such a fate really overcome *Europe*, which for many people symbolizes the roots of the faith, the setting of the great cathedrals and abbeys, the scene of so many critical Christian movements and debates—the center, in short, of what was once Christendom? The symmetry is convincing. In the Middle Ages, the fading Christianity of the Near East had been supplanted by the brash faith of rising Europe; now, as European Christianity itself waned, so it would in its turn witness the religion's center of gravity shift to the global South.[4]

Such a change would have implications far beyond the sentimental. Traditionally, what we call "the West" found what unity and common purpose it had in the assumptions of culture and religion shared by both Europe and North America, and the eclipse of Christianity in one region would drive an enormous wedge between the two halves of the Atlantic alliance. If transatlantic cultural and political divisions seem vast now, what would they be when some leading European powers possess Muslim minorities of 20 percent of the population, and of the electorate?

Undoubtedly, European nations are changing culturally and socially, acutely so in such critical countries as France and Germany. Across the religious spectrum, we see forces pushing toward progress and reaction, assimilation and separatism, secularism and fundamentalism, tolerance and violence. Yet before writing the obituary of European Christianity, before consigning the continent to the fringes of the Muslim world, a reality check is in order. While nobody can pretend that

Christian religious practice is thriving in most of Europe, the situation is nothing as grim as some recent accounts suggest, nor do the population statistics justify the portrait of a wholesale barbarian invasion from Muslim lands. Certainly, European nations face difficult decisions about integration and assimilation, and the fundamental issues of cultural identity upon which such policies must be founded, and failure could provoke disorder or civil conflict. Yet other societies have negotiated these debates quite successfully in the past, not least the United States.

Visions of imminent European collapse contain a fundamental contradiction. European cultural and social arrangements have, it seems, gutted the continent's Christian heritage; yet prophets of Muslim dominance in Europe assume that Islam will somehow be immune to these same overwhelming pressures. In fact, both Christianity and Islam face real difficulties in surviving within Europe's secular cultural ambience in anything like their familiar historic forms. But instead of fading away, both have adapted to Eurosecularity (to use Peter Berger's term), and they are continuing to adapt. The fate of Islam in contemporary Europe must be understood in the wider religious context, so that both Islam and Christianity are considered together in terms of maintaining their hold on believers, and in their relationship with the secular order.

"We're Going to Outbirth You"

In 1938, Anglo-French author Hilaire Belloc wrote, "The future always comes as a surprise, but political wisdom consists in attempting at least some partial judgment of what that surprise may be. And for my part I cannot but believe that a main unexpected thing of the future is the return of Islam." He continued,

> Millions of modern people of the white civilization—that is, the civilization of Europe and America—have forgotten all about Islam. They have never come in contact with it. They take for granted that it is decaying, and that, anyway, it is just a foreign religion which will not concern them. It is, as a fact, the most formidable and persistent enemy which our civilization has had, and may at any moment become as large a menace in the future as it has been in the past. . . . Anyone with a knowledge of history is bound to ask himself whether we shall not see in the future a revival of Mohammedan political power, and the renewal of the old pressure of Islam upon Christendom.[5]

At the time of the Munich crisis and Stalin's great purges, such concerns seemed eccentric, but by the start of the twenty-first century, Belloc's opinions have acquired remarkably mainstream status, and by no means just among Catholics of reactionary bent. Bernard Lewis, one of America's most notable scholars of Middle Eastern history, famously remarked in an 2004 interview with the German newspaper *Die Welt*, "Current trends show Europe will have a Moslem majority by the end of the twenty-first century at the latest. . . . Europe will be part of the Arab west—the Maghreb." Other writers have made similar religious prophecies. Already in 1996, French demographer Jean-Claude Chesnais asserted that "there will be an overall mingling of cultures and civilizations that may lead, as far as France is concerned, to the emergence of a predominantly African population and to rapid Islamization."[6]

This view has been much echoed. Spanish journalist Silvia Taulés notes that "many people say that it is predestined. That Spain will once again be Muslim, centuries after the splendor that *al-Andalus* possessed in its time." In 2004, European Commissioner Frits Bolkestein forecast a global future in which "the USA will remain the only superpower. China is becoming an economic giant. Europe is being Islamicized." Contemplating this Muslim future, he continued, "If this comes about, the liberation of Vienna in 1683 will have been in vain." Even moderate Muslim scholar Bassam Tibi wrote that "either Islam gets Europeanized, or Europe gets Islamized. . . . The problem is not whether the majority of Europeans is Islamic but rather which Islam—sharia Islam or Euro-Islam—is to dominate in Europe."[7]

Some observers see Europe making a wholesale transition into the Muslim world, becoming part of Eurabia, a word that provides a concise shorthand for an array of cultural and ethnic nightmares. The word originated in the 1970s as the title of a journal designed to promote Euro-Arab integration and solidarity, but it was later appropriated by harsh critics of such a vision. Egyptian-born Jewish writer Bat Ye'or envisages Eurabia as an emerging Muslim-dominated subcontinent, in which the remaining Christians and Jews might enjoy some tenuous kind of second-class status, of dhimmitude. Journalist Mark Steyn suggests that

> much of what we loosely call the Western world will not survive this century, and much of it will effectively disappear within our lifetimes, including many if not most Western European countries. There'll probably still be a geographical area on the map marked as Italy or the Netherlands—*probably*—just as in Istanbul there's still a building called St. Sophia's Cathedral. But it's not a cathedral; it's merely a designation for a piece of real estate.

George Weigel contemplates "a Europe in which the muezzin summons the faithful to prayer from the central loggia of St. Peter's in Rome, while Notre Dame has been transformed into Hagia Sophia on the Seine—a great Christian church become an Islamic museum."[8]

Journalist Joachim Güntner notes how thoroughly Germans have internalized such warnings of *überfremdung*, of being overwhelmed by foreigners. Such warnings have promoted urban legends, usually heard via a "friend of a friend":

> There's news of Catholic parishioners in Duisburg that were being sent across the street by Turks claiming that one sidewalk belonged to them and their mosques; one hears tales of women in headscarves threatening "We're going to outbirth you." ["Wir gebären euch kaputt"] Becoming a minority in one's own country is a frightening thing because there's no hope of returning to the homeland—an illusion that immigrants can at least harbor.[9]

If the Islamic future is so assured, then so is the likelihood of chaos and bloodshed leading to its foundation. Following the nationwide rioting by Arab and African youths in France in 2005, the cover of the British *Spectator* portrayed a giant crescent looming over a map of western Europe, under the headline "Eurabian Nightmare." Mark Steyn saw the French riots as an "early skirmish in the Eurabian civil war." A photograph of cars burned in these events adorns the cover of Claire Berlinski's book *Menace in Europe*, directly above the subtitle *Why the Continent's Crisis Is America's, Too.*[10]

For decades, a political consensus held that Muslims would be drawn into Europe's overwhelmingly secular social order, but in the past five years the notion of assimilation has suffered a series of heavy blows. In 2004, bombing attacks at Madrid subway stations killed two hundred civilians, and in the process helped decide the course of a national election. In the Netherlands, filmmaker Theo van Gogh was assassinated by a Muslim activist who had once been held up as a model of integration into Dutch society. On July 7, 2005—7/7—terrorist bombings in London drew attention to a subculture of utterly disaffected second-generation British Muslims, who were prepared to kill and die for their beliefs. The following year, a similar group of young men was reportedly plotting the mass destruction of British and U.S. airliners in a massacre that would have rivaled the September 11 attacks. Also in 2006, the ferocious international response to various perceived insults to Islam suggested the gulf that separates the values of many European Muslims, their attitudes to individual liberty, from those of the secular mainstream. At best, Europe, far more than the United States, faces decades of culture wars, rooted in religious allegiances, while nightmare scenarios for the European future are all too easy to imagine. For recent European writers, Islam threatens *Jihad in Europe, the War in Our Cities*; for one author, France stands on the cusp *Between Jihad and Reconquista*. Two best-selling Danish authors argue that Europeans who fail to acknowledge the lethal seriousness of the Islamist threat are members of the self-deluded tribe of the Naivists.[11]

Visions of doom have become thoroughly familiar, to the point of cliché. As Matthew W. Maguire writes, "To hear many American

Christians talk of Europe, the minarets are all but fitted onto the spires
of Chartres and Notre Dame." The date of Islamization has also moved
steadily closer to the present. Conservative Danish politician Morten
Messerschmidt warns that "Europe will—maybe not in twenty, but
rather thirty to forty years from now—have a Muslim majority of population, if nothing is done. That'll mean the end of our culture and the
end of European civilization." A parody widely circulated on the Internet depicts a map labeled "Europe 2015," in which the various countries have been ominously relabeled. Britain has become North Pakistan. France is the Islamic Republic of New Algeria, Spain the Moorish
Emirate of Iberia, Germany is New Turkey, Belgium is Belgistan, while
Italy and Albania are merged into a new Albanian Federation. Also in
the realm of satire, the *National Review* published an advertisement for
a "Farewell to Europe" tour as early as the year 2010, a last chance to
visit before the borders were closed to infidel visitors and total Islamic
law imposed. "We'll relax in a famous German Biergarten with glasses
of sweet mint tea!" The Islamic Republic of the Netherlands provides a
highlight of the trip: "For this special two-day event, females traveling
with our party will be allowed to disembark the plane *without a veil!*"[12]

The Birth Dearth

If Islam is indeed advancing, then according to many recent accounts,
it has little opposition that it need overcome. Writers stress the collapse
of older religious values—especially Christianity—and link that directly
to the demographic crisis. Niall Ferguson agrees that Europe's Muslims
"may well outnumber believing Christians, given the collapse of
church attendance and religious faith in Europe." Charles Krauthammer
portrays "a cocooned, aging, post-historic Europe," a society waiting
for the barbarians. For conservative Pat Buchanan, the West is approaching calamity, as "dying populations and immigrant invasions
imperil our country and civilization."[13]

In demographic terms, modern Europe seems to have embarked
on a self-destructive social experiment unprecedented in human history, what some have called slow-motion autogenocide. For a society
to maintain its existing level of population, it needs a total fertility rate
of 2.1 children per woman, the extra fraction needed to compensate
for losses through infant mortality. Across Europe, social change over
the past three decades has been reflected in a steep decline in family
size and a growth in single-parent households. Today, western European
nations report some of the lowest birth rates ever recorded. The Italian
birth rate fell below 1.5 in 1984, and is now about 1.28; so is Spain's.
Eastern European rates are comparable, generally around 1.2 or 1.3.
The German birth rate is 1.39 overall, but actually falls below 1.0 in
some German regions, lower than the rate for the horrific last year of

the second world war. Between 25 percent and 30 percent of German women will remain childless: the figure for college graduates is over 40 percent. The situation pointedly recalls Günter Grass's 1982 novel *Headbirths,* which portrays a worldly young couple just too engaged with career and material prosperity ever to consider children. His book's subtitle: *The Germans Are Dying Out.* Projections of European population over the next thirty years or so suggest an absolute decline in European population worse than that inflicted by Hitler's war. Italy could lose a fifth of its population by 2050.[14]

And matters are scarcely improving, despite some claims to see an encouraging rebound in birth statistics: in France, the rate is now above 1.8 and rising, making France the most fertile society in Europe, except for Ireland. Actually, such rosy figures are misleading because they present an average that combines the still very low rates of old-stock white French people, *les français de souche,* with the much higher rates of their immigrant neighbors. If we just focus on old-stock populations, the birth dearth becomes ever more apparent. At the same time, improvements in medical care and the standard of living mean that the people who have had the good fortune to be born are living significantly longer than in bygone eras.[15]

Putting these trends together, we find societies with far fewer children and more old people, so that the median age of a nation rises dramatically. In a typical Third World nation, the proportion of people aged below 14 is about a third, while perhaps 4 percent or 5 percent are over 65. In most western European nations the over-65s currently represent at least a sixth of the population—a quarter in Italy—while the under-14s make up 16 percent to 20 percent. As the low birth rates show no sign of growing, the proportion of old Europeans will increase, and at least for a few decades, the nations will become more elderly. By 2050, by some predictions, 40 percent of Italians will be over the age of 60. For Europe as a whole, the median age will rise in the same period from 37 today to 52.3. The U.S. median at that point, for comparison, will be about 35, roughly what it is today. Old and New Worlds, graying Europe and impetuous young America, will contemplate each other with quite the mutual bafflement that they did in Henry James's day.[16]

This demographic situation poses real difficulties in both the short and long term. If those older people are to survive, someone has to carry on working to pay the taxes to provide their services. This need becomes all the more imperative if older Europeans hope to keep on receiving the high level of social benefits to which they have become accustomed, and many plan to retire in their mid-fifties. As Mark Steyn observes, "The design flaw of the secular social-democratic state is that it requires a religious-society birthrate to sustain it."[17]

If the labor force cannot be found among old-stock white Europeans, then that shortage has to be met from elsewhere, and since the

1960s, that has meant heavy immigration, from Africa, Asia, the Middle East, and the Caribbean. Such immigrants usually come from lands with fertility rates higher than Europe's, countries that cannot cope with the numbers they already have: new inhabitants will desperately wish to migrate somewhere. In the Arab world as a whole, the population over the past fifty years has grown from 80 to 320 million, and half of those are under 20 years of age. Demographic factors provide a powerful force driving migration from North Africa. At the end of its revolution in 1962, Algeria had around 10 million people, but that figure today has risen to 33 million, and almost 30 percent of those are below the age of 14. Morocco's 33 million people have an even younger age profile, with around a third aged 14 or lower. The median age of these populations is around 24, compared with 39 in France, 40 in Spain, 42 in Italy and Germany.[18] The demographic contrast is even more marked when we look at some other countries that have served as major sources of migrants: almost 40 percent of Pakistanis are 14 or younger, and the country's median age is below 20. As Fouad Ajami writes, in contrast to Europe, "fertility rates in the Islamic world are altogether different: they are 3.2 in Algeria, 3.4 in Egypt and Morocco, 5.2 in Iraq and 6.1 in Saudi Arabia. This is Europe's neighborhood, and its contemporary fate . . . nemesis is near." As we will see, these figures need closer examination, but the difference in fertility rates is significant.[19]

The fact of immigration is itself usually associated with large families, because people who move between continents are normally in the prime years for begetting and bearing children. In the European context, this fact means the rapid expansion of non-European populations, especially of people from Muslim countries, whose values often differ substantially from those of old-stock Europeans. In France, less than a third of women born in the early 1960s have three or more children, but these women produced more than half the children born to their particular cohort. And the women with high birth rates are disproportionately likely to be either conservative Catholics or, more commonly, Muslims.[20]

As old-stock Europeans despair of the future, so some Muslims rejoice. Libya's Muammar Qaddafi dreams that "there are signs that Allah will grant Islam victory in Europe without swords, without guns, without conquests. The fifty million Muslims of Europe [*sic*] will turn it into a Muslim continent within a few decades." Another would-be prophet of an Islamic Europe is the Norwegian-based Islamist leader Mullah Krekar, who crows, "Look at the development of the population in Europe, where the number of Muslims increases like mosquitoes. Each Western woman in the E.U. produces, on average, 1.4 children. Each Muslim woman in these same countries produces 3.5 children. By 2050, thirty percent of the European population will be Muslim."[21]

Europe's Failure

In his powerful book *The Cube and the Cathedral,* George Weigel uses Europe as an awful warning for the United States, a disturbing object lesson in how Christianity dies, and the destructive effects of secularism. A Godless Europe, he argues, may for a few years appear pleasantly tolerant and nonjudgmental, but without commitment to faith and family, evaporating moral standards and plummeting birth rates create a society that is literally unsustainable. A society that rejects the supernatural turns instead to short-term hedonism, with the only real criterion for actions being the pleasure and fulfillment of the individuals concerned. Why, in such an atomized world, should individuals make the commitment to posterity implied by the decision to bear and nurture children? Yet demographic destiny ensures that a secular utopia must of necessity be a temporary phenomenon. In a generation or two, the sparse descendants of those liberal hedonists would be heavily outnumbered by the children and grandchildren of those prolific communities that maintained their belief in faith and family. And those grandchildren would legislate for the kind of society they wanted to create.[22]

Fellow-conservative Michael Novak offered a similar analysis following the 2005 French riots, suggesting that the problem was rooted in the continent's abandonment of God:

> the images we recently saw on the TV news suggest that Europe has, once again, lost its way. It looks as though Europe is set to repeat in the twenty-first century the disasters of the 20th. . . . But having turned away from Jewish and Christian faith, a Europe based solely upon the Enlightenment cannot long survive. The Europe that is declining in population is a Europe more rational than Europe has ever been, more scientific, less religious, less pious, more mundane, wealthier, more consumerist, more universally close to living *etsi Deus non daretur* (as if God does not exist). A very large part of the "European crisis" is the crisis of the Enlightenment. On that ground, a civilization cannot be built, a civilization can only burn down to the last waxed threads of its wick.[23]

Though jeremiads about Christian decline are not necessarily linked to dark visions of Eurabia, the different concepts become linked, so that prognostications about the Christian future are bleak. Niall Ferguson argues, "The greatest of all the strengths of radical Islam . . . is that it has demography on its side. The Western culture against which it has declared holy war cannot possibly match the capacity of traditional Muslim societies when it comes to reproduction." German Lutheran scholar Jobst Schoene has said, "I fear we are approaching a situation resembling the tragic fate of Christianity in Northern Africa in Islam's early days," and that analogy deserves closer examination. In Roman times, the lands that today comprise Algeria and Tunisia were Christian heartlands, which produced such paladins of the faith as Tertullian and Augustine, and this Christianity still seemed to be flourishing when Muslim forces arrived at the end of the seventh century. Two centuries later, Christianity was extinct here. And the distant descendants of North Africa's former Christian communities—now solidly Muslim—today make up the largest single share of Europe's contemporary immigrants.[24]

The apparent decline of older Europe and its culture fits easily into familiar intellectual frameworks. At least in the popular historical imagination, most Europeans and Americans have a stereotype of the decline of the Roman Empire, a society of vast wealth and power, that fell prey to decadence and excess, only to be supplanted by the vigorous barbarians from across the frontiers. In the words of one of G. K. Chesterton's characters, "the great destiny of Empire" comprised four acts: "Victory over barbarians. Employment of barbarians. Alliance with barbarians. Conquest by barbarians." Muslims too know a similar pattern, as initially proposed by the pioneering social theorist Ibn Khaldun. Initially, in his view, tribal societies succeed because they possess a strong degree of organic solidarity, of 'asabiya. Over time, though, as they settle down in cities and develop complex economies, 'asabiya fades and social bonds become weaker, until finally the society is taken over by newer and sturdier tribal communities. In modern Europe, too, the loss of cohesion leaves a society open to the expansion of newer peoples who still care for bonds of family and religion. As in the barbarian analogy, Europe's economic successes contribute mightily to its social crisis.[25]

Agendas

Having said this, many of the contemporary alarms about the fate of Europe carry a powerful sense of déjà vu. This does not necessarily invalidate the warnings, but it should make us examine them more closely. A century ago, for instance, European thinkers were deeply disturbed about the racial degeneration of their populations, as population decline among the best stock threatened to leave the future to outsiders and lesser breeds. Prophecies that Islam would overwhelm Christian Europe also have a long history, and the predictions carry heavy ideological agendas. They are prophecy in the biblical sense, that is, they are less concerned with predicting that events will occur at any particular future time than they are intended to warn listeners about horrible developments that will punish the crying sins of contemporary society. While the agendas are diverse, both right and left have strong reasons for making Islam in Europe seem as menacing as possible, while Christianity is almost painted out of the picture. Once this contrast is established, it is possible to dismiss virtually any policy position held by Europe as a whole, or of individual states, as a manifestation of denial or dhimmitude, collaboration or appeasement.

In the past, like today, warnings of Islamic Europe, of Eurabia, had a powerful moral and political content. In the early twentieth century, racial theorist Lothrop Stoddard called for white racial unity in the face of an imminent Muslim threat. He was especially concerned by Islamic advances into Africa: "Pan-Islamism, once possessed of the Dark Continent and fired by militant zealots, might forge black Africa into a sword of wrath, the executor of sinister adventures." So great was the danger that Europeans should bury their petty differences: unity, literally, was a matter of life and death.[26]

For other writers, the success of Islam offered vital lessons for Christianity. For Belloc, what made Islam so formidable was that it had avoided the evils of the European Enlightenment, which had so overwhelmed the glories of traditional Christianity: "In Islam there has been no such dissolution of ancestral doctrine—or, at any rate, nothing corresponding to the universal break-up of religion in Europe" (and he was using that phrase as far back as 1938). Accordingly, "the whole spiritual strength of Islam is still present in the masses of Syria and Anatolia, of the East Asian mountains, of Arabia, Egypt and North Africa."[27]

Chesterton also used Islam as a means of denouncing leftist and liberal secularists. In his fantasy *The Flying Inn* (1914), England's secular elites delude themselves into seeing Islam as progressive: they see it as intellectual and rational rather than ritualistic, and (appealing to their own prohibitionist creed) it is militantly anti-alcohol. Islam thus knows what is right, and has the willpower to enforce it. In every way, then, it is superior to superstitious Christianity. Britain gradually falls under the power of Islam, Islamic law is enforced and alcohol banned. Chesterton's point is that secularism, whatever its adherents think, is itself a religion and a rigidly intolerant one, which leads naturally to new forms of authoritarianism. The book concludes with a successful revolution by English Christians, who rediscover their religious and cultural identity just in time to cast off the Muslim power. At the final battle,

> there flew the green standard of that great faith and strong civilization which has so often almost entered the great cities of the West; which long encircled Vienna, which was barely barred from Paris; but which had never before been seen in arms on the soil of England. . . . Something in that last fact of being crushed by the weapons of brown men and yellow, secretly entrenched in English meadows, had made the English what they had not been for centuries.[28]

While few modern conservatives would explicitly use such racial terminology, the grim prognosis for European societies offers a wonderful

counterargument in American debates over social policy or moral legislation. Yes indeed, one could say, Dutch laws do reflect wonderfully
tolerant attitudes about sexuality—but in fifty years, the Netherlands
could be an Islamic Republic with no compunction about executing
sodomites or stoning adulterers, and women will once again know their
place. Secular liberalism, it seems, is a self-limiting project; unlimited
libertarianism brings its own destruction. The overarching argument is
that a successful society cannot exist without some kind of commitment
to faith, and that militant secular attempts to exclude religion from the
public sphere run the risk of promoting a worse fate in the long term.
The message: let Americans beware.

Such an argument would be anathema to leftist or liberal writers,
but they too frame the Islamic threat as part of a general collapse of
European values, which urgently need to be reasserted. The difference
is that some frame the concept of "European values" in ambitious libertarian terms, which would not be widely acknowledged even by
many Europeans. In 1997, Dutch sociologist Pim Fortuyn published
the book *Against the Islamicization of Our Culture,* in which he warned
that the influx of religiously ultraconservative Muslims posed a massive danger to Europe's values, which he described as liberal, secular,
feminist, and democratic. At their worst, claimed Fortuyn, Muslims,
or at least Muslim religious leaders, consistently flout these values, in
matters as critical as the tolerance of homosexuality, acceptance of
women's equality, and openness to a free and critical discussion of
religion.[29]

Bruce Bawer's book *While Europe Slept: How Radical Islam Is Destroying the West from Within* also presents gay rights and same-sex marriage
as fundamental components of European values. Bawer's concept of
radical or fundamentalist Islam includes all Muslim groups that oppose
sexual libertarianism, which prefer to preserve "the tyranny of their
subculture." After describing the glories of wide-ranging Dutch social
libertarianism, with same-sex marriage and soft policies on drugs, he
complains that "Dutch Muslims kept that society at arm's length, de-
spising its freedoms and clinging to a range of undemocratic traditions
and prejudices." For such liberal writers, the threat of intolerant Islam
provides a rhetorical weapon against social conservatism of any kind,
which they present as shading easily into the repressive thought-world
conjured by words like ayatollahs and Taliban. Bawer himself previously attacked Christian conservatism or "fundamentalism" in terms
almost identical to those he directed against contemporary Islam, and
says that Europe's Muslims constituted a Religious Right on the model
he detested in the United States. ("The main reason I'd been glad to
leave America," he writes, "was Protestant fundamentalism.") Like
Fortuyn, he does not grant the existence of any religious or conservative moral critique that is not stigmatized as "fundamentalist." Unless

we take "fundamentalist" as synonymous with "practicing," we cannot understand Bawer's extravagant claim that in the Netherlands, "most people of non-Dutch origin were fundamentalist Muslims."[30]

Both conservative and liberal critics freely compare the modern era to the morally gutted Europe of the 1920s and 1930s, which collapsed in the face of totalitarianism. When general Muslim intolerance was combined with violent rhetoric and paramilitary organization, Europe seemed to be facing a danger comparable to those years, with a surging Islamofascism confronting secular democracy. Bruce Bawer complains of European appeasement in the face of Muslim aggression, and speaks of a Weimar moment. Warning of the rise of white racist movements, he warns, "If European governments don't stop being dhimmis and appeasers, there'll be more and more movement in the direction of such parties. A Europe torn between nativist fascism and Islamofascism is a grim prospect, all too reminiscent of the situation in Europe in the 1930s." Denouncing European multiculturalism, Oriana Fallaci said that "the situation is politically substantially the same as in 1938 with the pact in Munich, when England and France did not understand a thing. With the Muslims we have done the same thing. Islamism is the new Nazi-Fascism." Mogens Camre of the Danish People's Party said that "Islam is threatening our future. . . . That faith belongs to a dark past, and its political aims are as destructive as Nazism was." Bat Ye'or writes of the Euro-Arab Axis. Writing in *Die Welt* in 2005, publishing magnate Mathias Döpfner directly compared the Islamist challenge to Nazism, and warned of appeasement: the article bore the title "Europe—Thy Name Is Cowardice."[31]

Berlinski's *Menace in Europe* also draws Nazi analogies. She argues that "there is an important tradition in the Netherlands—as there is throughout Europe—of bargaining with depravity. The Dutch response to Islamic terror has much in common with the Dutch posture towards Nazi terror." Berlinski suggests that the collapse of Christianity has forced Europeans to find a substitute religion, leading many to the pseudo-religious ideology of a vitriolic anti-Americanism, which she compares to the totalitarian ideologies of bygone years. Arguments about European appeasement in the face of aggressive Islam gain power for an American audience by their association with the defense of familiar Western liberties—of women's rights, gay rights, and freedom of speech.[32]

In terms of international politics too, forecasts of a Eurabian future have contemporary political consequences, often strongly conservative. The language of Eurabia implies a need for resistance, possibly by restricting Muslim immigration, but also the need to confront Arab or Muslim aggression worldwide. References to appeasement and to a new Axis carry special weight for Jews, who recall the dreadful experiences of Europe in the 1930s and the subsequent collaboration with

Nazi rule. In the modern world, it is easy to draw parallels with attitudes toward the Middle East, to conflicts in Israel or Iraq. If European nations fail to support hard-line American or Israeli positions in the region, they can be accused of bowing to Muslim pressure, of accepting dhimmitude.

By portraying the rise of European Islam as part of a global threat, conservative writers can also link domestic problems in the Netherlands or Germany to struggles around the world. Observing the 2005 riots in French cities, conservatives crowed openly. The French would not support Israel fighting Islamists in the streets of Gaza or Americans struggling in Baghdad, and in consequence, they know they must face an intifada in their own cities. As Lowell Ponte writes in the ultra-conservative *Front Page Magazine*, "A courageous European stand against that nest of Islamist vipers and their atomic eggs in Teheran would be a good place for Europe to demonstrate to itself and to the world that it has the will and skill to survive."[33]

In Search of Europe

Across the political spectrum, then, a diverse range of activists find it in their rhetorical interests to stress the inevitable coming of an Islamicized Europe, sooner rather than later, and to present matters in the grimmest possible terms. They foresee ruinous religious violence, with Muslim minorities set against secular states and Muslim communities against Christian or Jewish neighbors. Yet although it may be approaching the status of a truth universally acknowledged, the vision of a predominantly Muslim Europe nearby on the historical horizon demands serious qualification. Nor should we necessarily accept assertions about the coming triumph of "radical Islam."

That Europe is acquiring much greater ethnic and cultural diversity is certain, but the religious implications are less clear. Visions of an Islamicized Eurabia sliding into Third World status rely upon a number of questionable assumptions not only about demography but also about the condition of Europe's major religions, both Islam and Christianity. If these assumptions are incorrect, Christian-Muslim interactions could develop quite differently, and more benevolently. Europe could yet become the birthplace of a liberalized and modernized Islam that could in turn influence the religion worldwide.[34]

From the heated coverage of European affairs since 2003 or so, Americans might imagine that visiting that continent might involve an encounter with Islamic fanatics on every street corner. In fact, while Muslim numbers have grown dramatically since the 1960s, the numbers of obvious ethnic minorities are still small compared to what one might see in a U.S. metropolis. In most west European nations, Muslims constitute around 4 percent of the population, which is scarcely a human deluge. The relatively small scale of Muslim numbers might surprise Americans, for whom their key minority issues involve an African-American population that has never been less than 10 percent of the national total, and sometimes much larger, while other minorities have also grown in recent years. Counting Latinos and Asians, in addition to African-Americans, the United States today deals with "minorities" of perhaps 30 percent of the national population, probably rising to almost half the population by 2050.

When trying to understand the issue of Muslims in Europe, both the words "Muslims" and "Europe" demand closer examination. Now, the search for precise definition can lead to a kind of casuistry. Testifying to a Grand Jury, President Bill Clinton once notoriously remarked, "It depends upon what the meaning of the word 'is' is." But a lack of definition goes far in explaining visions of new Muslim populations swarming over venerable Europe.

The term "Europe" has shifted its meaning in recent years. During the Cold War era, Americans became accustomed to using the term just in the context of the democratic nations of western Europe, and thus excluding the large and populous Eastern bloc; and discussions of "Muslim Europe" generally refer to the continent in this more limited sense. It is in western portions of Europe, the older regions of the European Community, that Muslims have established themselves in recent years. This was and remains the economic heartland of modern Europe, and it has for some decades served as the principal magnet for immigration. Even here, though, only in France is the Muslim share of the population sufficiently large—currently 8 or 10 percent, and growing—to raise immediate concerns about the cultural hybridization of the society. Even if we assume, controversially, that Islamization represents a deadly menace, then it is presently not an urgent prospect outside France or, conceivably, the Netherlands, which has a Muslim minority of 6 percent.

And despite what French political leaders have assumed for some centuries, there is a great deal more to Europe than just France. We cannot simply project the conditions prevailing here to the whole continent, which stretches from the Atlantic at least to the borders of the former Soviet Union, and arguably beyond. A realistic estimate, allowing for illegal immigration, is that wider Europe, from Ireland to the Carpathians, presently has about 24 million Muslims, or 4.6 percent of the overall population, but by no means all of those represent new immigrants. Over a third of that Muslim population represents old-established communities in the south-eastern quadrant of the continent, in Albania, Bulgaria, and the nations that comprised the former Yugoslavia, together with the island of Cyprus. Outside that area, Muslims are rare in most of the eastern lands that Donald Rumsfeld characterized as the New Europe. In former communist lands such as

Table 1.1 Muslims in the European Union

Nation	Population (millions)	Muslims (millions)	Percentage
Older Member States			
France	60.4	5	8.3
Germany	82	3.5	4.3
United Kingdom	58.6	1.6	2.7
Italy	57.6	1	1.8
Spain	39.4	1	2.4
Netherlands	15.8	1	6.3
Belgium	10.2	0.4	3.9
Sweden	8.9	0.4	4.4
Austria	8.1	0.35	4.4
Switzerland	7.2	0.31	4.3
Denmark	5.3	0.27	5
Norway	4.6	0.08	1.8
	358.1	**15.3**	**4.3**
Newer Member States and Accession States through 2007–2008			
Poland	38.7	0	
Portugal	10.8	0	
Greece	10.6	0.14	1.3
Czech Republic	10.3	0	
Hungary	10.1	0	
Slovakia	5.4	0	
Finland	5.2	0	
Ireland	3.7	0	
Lithuania	3.7	0	
Latvia	2.4	0	
Slovenia	2	0.05	
Estonia	1.4	0	
Cyprus	0.9	0.16	18
Malta	0.4	0	
Luxembourg	0.4	0	
Romania	22.3	0.2	0.8
Bulgaria	7.5	0.9	12.2
	135.8	**1.45**	**1.1**
Membership currently under negotiation, or candidate countries (excluding Turkey)			
Croatia	4.5	0.2	4.4
Macedonia	2.1	0.6	17
Albania	3.6	2.5	70
Serbia and Montenegro	10.8	2.2	19
Bosnia and Herzegovina	4.1	1.6	40
	25.1	**7.1**	**28.2**
European TOTALS			
	521	**23.8**	**4.6**
Turkey	70	70	99.9

Note: Swiss membership was frozen after a referendum in 1992; Norway's membership was withdrawn after a 1994 referendum.

Source: CIA Factbook, online at www.cia.gov/cia/publications/factbook/index.html.

Poland, Hungary, or the Czech Republic, Muslims are as scarce as they have been for centuries and mosques all but unknown. In large areas of the continent, "Muslim Europe" still does not exist. Now, the zeros listed in Table 1.1 should not be taken literally, since Muslim populations have established themselves in recent years, but the numbers are still tiny.[35]

This observation is still more true if, as might happen within a decade or so, the European Union expands its boundaries to include the former Soviet states of Ukraine, Belarus, and Moldova, and formally pushes Europe's borders eastward beyond the Dnieper. Such a move would add 60 million more new Europeans, virtually none of whom are Muslims, further diluting the Muslim presence within the European political community.

Defining Muslims

Furthermore, without defining "Muslims," we can scarcely know their numbers today or how many there will be in future. Undeniably, over the past forty years, European populations have become vastly more diverse ethnically and racially, but it is not obvious how those new communities should be viewed. Some recent accounts portray Europe's Muslims as uniformly pious, primitive, fundamentalist, and docile to clerical whims, an absurd picture for anyone familiar with the vast diversity of the continent's ethnic minority populations. In one wide-ranging passage, Bawer decries Europe's "Muslim enclaves":

> The people outside of them were living in a democracy, but the people in them were living in a theocracy, ruled by imams and elders who preached contempt for the host society and its values. They were against secular law, against pluralism, against freedom of speech and religion, against sexual equality. Husbands believed it was their sacred right to beat and rape their wives. Parents practiced honor killings and female genital mutilation. Unemployment and crime rates were through the roof.

We could probably find representatives of all these patterns somewhere, though female genital mutilation is something that the vast majority of European Muslims know about only from television documentaries, and it is scarcely reasonable to suggest that crime or unemployment are Muslim traits. As Bawer's final sentence indicates, it is often difficult to distinguish between the problems arising from issues of class and poverty, and those inherent in the religion itself. Nor should other social problems, such as honor killings, properly be laid at the door of Islam as a religion, rather than in the social structures of the countries from which migrants stemmed.[36]

We must ask whether Europe's current problems are religious, rather than social, economic, and cultural: are they problems of religion, race, or class? Throughout the early history of that immigration, European governments and media assumed they were dealing with a new racial diversity that bore many analogies to the U.S. situation, and that analysis might still be more accurate than the current perception of a religious confrontation. Some radical groups today continue to see the plight of minorities in racial and ethnic rather than religious terms; but unfortunately, the religious angle has proved too rhetorically useful to such diverse interest groups and commentators. Now, racial conflicts are no more palatable than religious ones, and in extreme cases, they have just as much potential to devastate a society. But the question of perception is important for policy makers—for instance, in identifying community leaders with whom they can negotiate, or in making laws to help integrate minorities. Viewing a minority in religious terms can become a self-fulfilling prophecy, as officials focus on religious grievances and cultivate religious leaders as the presumed voices of their respective communities.

The definition of "Muslims" is also critical for issues of statistics. Imagine two young men, both born in Europe and speaking only the language of their country of birth: call them Tony and Tariq. Tony, of white European stock, was baptized Catholic but very rarely sets foot inside the precincts of a church, except possibly for a wedding or funeral, and his knowledge of Christian doctrine or history is close to nonexistent. Tariq is of ethnic Pakistani or Moroccan origin, but his connection to the faith of Islam is just as tenuous. He drinks, fails to observe Ramadan, is not careful about observing dietary laws, and is as sexually opportunistic as Tony. He has a vague idea that his father attends a mosque but is not sure where it is. Tariq is, in short, anything but a good Muslim.

In compiling religious statistics, however, agencies would almost certainly count an "ethnic" individual like Tariq as a Muslim, and part of Europe's Muslim population. This casual attitude toward religious classification would not matter if agencies applied the same standards across the board, but they do not. Tony, our hypothetical man of Catholic origins, might be counted as a Christian in some statistics but not others. When estimating religious communities, both agencies and scholars tend to accept the very broad definition of Islam offered by that religion itself, which defines as a Muslim anyone brought up in a Muslim community, or whose father is a Muslim. (Honest demographers speak more vaguely of counting "potential Muslims.") Christians, in contrast, are defined in terms of self-identification or religious practice—for instance, by regular church attendance. *Muslim* is an ethnic label loosely applied; *Christian* is a religious classification that demands some knowledge of the individual's personal belief system. If we are to count as Christians only those individuals who have demonstrated allegiance to the faith, then logically we should apply the same more stringent standards to Muslims. But if we apply to Christians the loose cultural/ethnic definition used for Muslims, then Europe's Christians presently outnumber Muslims by over twenty to one, and will continue to form a substantial majority for the foreseeable future.[37]

Discussions of European "Muslims" tend to merge ethnic, cultural, and religious divisions. Bernard Lewis was correct to predict that a larger share of Europeans would be of Arab or Middle Eastern stock, but that fact says little about the religious tone of the future society. We could imagine a western Europe late in the present century in which 20 percent of the people were of newer, nontraditional stock but largely shared the values and outlook of their white European neighbors. A continent with several million Tariqs would not be a spiritual powerhouse, but neither would it be a cauldron of religious hatred. This would be a future quite different from the implied squalor and fanaticism of the Western Maghreb, and need cause little of the same apprehension.

Forces for Change

The core issue, then, is less the ethnic character of a future Europe than its religious tone, and that question remains very open. Over time, Islam has come in many shades of practice, some much more open and tolerant than others. Everything depends on how people of Muslim origin will be affected by the secularizing climate of Europe, and one way to predict likely trends is to understand the recent experience of Christian populations. As Weigel and others have pointed out, Christian loyalties and practice certainly have declined in recent decades, to the extent that recent books bear titles like *The Death of Christian Britain*. Largely, secularization has resulted from potent social and economic pressures, from greater individualism, and the dominance of new values about family, gender, and sexuality. Sociologist Grace Davie argues that these forces have made Europe an exceptional case in global terms, an area of painfully weak religious adherence in striking contrast to the power of religious values in virtually all other parts of the world—in African and Asian societies but also in the United States.[38] Yet this does not mean that Christianity has vanished or is approaching extinction, and there are intriguing signs of growth within that secular framework. The recent experience of Christian Europe might suggest not that the continent is potentially a graveyard for religion but rather that it is a laboratory for new forms of faith, new structures of organization and interaction, that can accommodate to a dominant secular environment.

The obvious question is whether Islam on the European continent might be subject to the same trends. And despite all the publicity justifiably accorded to Islamist extremists, there is already widespread evidence of accommodation to European norms. Historically, neither Christianity nor Islam is any more prone than the other to fanaticism, intolerance, or political activism, and no evidence suggests that Islam is any more immune to secularizing forces. Pessimists about the future of Europe ask, reasonably, whether any society has survived long with a sizable Muslim minority without religious tensions spilling over into civil conflict. The question is legitimate. But we should also point out that none of these apparent precedents involved societies with anything like the enormous pressures toward individualism, feminism, public secularism, and privatized religion that we see in contemporary Europe.

These changes affect communal identity and attitudes to other religions. Indeed, even strained contacts between religions produce a familiarity that is much more positive in its results than a prejudice born of ignorance. In 2006, the Pew Global Attitudes Project survey found many sources of tension and hostility dividing Muslims around the world from the West, but one positive development was in inter-religious attitudes. In Muslim nations, only small minorities held favorable attitudes toward Christians: views were most negative in Turkey and Pakistan, with favorable attitudes rising to 64 percent in Indonesia, the most moderate country. European Muslims, though, felt overwhelmingly positive about Christians in general, at a rate of 91 percent in France, 82 percent in Spain, 71 percent in Britain, and 69 percent in Germany. And although European Muslims were much less favorably disposed to Jews, their attitudes were far more positive than those prevailing in Muslim nations. The European Muslim community least sympathetic to Jews—that of Spain—still had friendlier views than those found in the most favorable Muslim nation, Indonesia.[39]

Apart from the implications for religious practice, Muslim accommodation to European norms is critical for all future demographic projections. Barring major new immigration, visions of Muslims achieving majority status in Europe within this century assume extraordinarily high and continuing rates of population growth. Moreover, the very high birth rates of "Muslim" communities would have to continue steadily on this incredible up-slope through the end of the century, despite all the pressures for cultural assimilation, particularly as they affect women. A growth of individualism and feminism would radically change demographic projections, since Muslim women dedicated to professional and personal fulfillment are much less likely to want large families, helping to bring ethnic birth rates into line with old-stock European figures. Education and literacy—especially for girls and women—also contribute mightily to lowering birth rates. Illustrating this point are the changing fertility rates for Muslim societies around the world (Table 1.2).

Earlier, I quoted Fouad Ajami's ominous remarks from 2004 about birth rates in Muslim societies—"3.2 in Algeria, 3.4 in Egypt and Morocco." As Table 1.2 suggests, though, he was using high and rather

Table 1.2 Fertility Rates in Muslim Nations

Nation	Population (millions)	Total fertility rate 2006
Somalia	9?	6.76
Afghanistan	31	6.69
Yemen	21	6.58
Sudan	41	4.72
Iraq	27	4.18
Pakistan	166	4
Saudi Arabia	27	4
Syria	19	3.4
Libya	6	3.28
Bangladesh	147	3.11
Malaysia	24	3.04
Uzbekistan	27	2.91
Egypt	79	2.83
Morocco	33	2.68
Jordan	6	2.63
Indonesia	246	2.4
Turkey	70	1.91
Algeria	33	1.89
Iran	69	1.8
Tunisia	10	1.74

Nations with fewer than five million people have been omitted
Source: CIA Factbook, online at www.cia.gov/cia/publications/fact book/index.html.

dated estimates, understandably enough, as actual fertility rates are dropping so fast that it is difficult to keep track of them. Several Muslim nations are already below replacement, and others are rapidly approaching that situation. Incidentally, while it is not a hard and fast rule, it is difficult to avoid an impressionistic correlation between extremely high fertility rates (Somalia, Afghanistan, Sudan, Iraq) and a country's tendency to social chaos and internecine strife, with combatants often claiming religious motivation. The Palestinian fertility rate is 5.78 in the Gaza Strip, 4.28 in the West Bank.[40]

There is of course no such thing as a "Muslim birth rate," since actual figures depend on social and economic settings. Moreover, some of the lowest rates are found in the western regions of the Muslim world, those that have the closest relationships to Europe, whether through migration patterns or mass media. While Italians worry about being swamped by Albanian Muslims, the Albanian fertility rate now stands at 2.03 and is falling precipitously; Bosnia's is 1.22. If current trends continue, it would be only a few years before all the nations of the

Maghreb—Algeria, Morocco, and Tunisia—reached the very low Spanish or Italian birth rates, and this region would find it ever harder to serve as a source of migrants. In that situation, Europe would have to dip ever deeper into Africa to find its labor force; and the further south it reaches, the more likely it is to draw in as many Christians as Muslims.[41]

The spread of subreplacement fertility has other implications. As I will argue, traditional and fundamentalist religion tends to flourish more successfully in societies with large extended families and many children, and declines along with family size. That is part of the explanation for the steep decline of institutional Christianity in Europe. But if that projection is correct, it has fascinating implications for the survival of extremist and clerical forms of Islam in the Maghreb, in Turkey and—surprisingly—in Iran itself. Between 1986 and 2000, Iran's fertility rate plummeted from 6 to 2, and the country now has a fertility rate lower than that of the United States. At first glance, one might think that this phenomenon reflects the impact of the Iran-Iraq war of 1980–1988, and the massive loss of young men; but identical conditions did nothing to stem the very high birth rate of neighboring Iraq. The changing fertility patterns of North Africa and the Near East constitute a vastly important phenomenon that would receive more attention from media and policy makers, if it did not prove so inconvenient for so many rhetorical purposes.

If in fact fertility rates in Europe's neighborhood portend its contemporary fate, then that destiny could be very different from either swamping or Islamization. And even if Islam threatens (or promises) to overwhelm Europe, then Europe could well, in its turn, transform Islam. Instead of Europe merging with the Arab Maghreb, we might equally imagine the Maghreb itself joining the southern portions of Europe.

Two Paths

In contemplating such a benevolent scenario, a U.S. analogy comes to mind. A hundred years ago, Protestant Americans were deeply concerned about the cultural and religious implications of mass immigration, and the rhetoric of the time had many resemblances to contemporary warnings about the rise of European Islam. Then as now, immigrants were believed to pose a direct threat of revolution and subversion. In addition to the customary charges derived from anti-Semitic tradition, America's new Jewish immigrants reputedly included a high proportion of radicals and revolutionaries who taught ideologies of anarchism and revolutionary socialism.

Native-born Americans feared Roman Catholics still more intensely, many seeing them as a non-Christian influx into a once-Christian land. They applied the Catholic label indiscriminately, seeing few distinctions between Catholics of very different national or ethnic origin. And people from Catholic countries were labeled Catholic, no matter how religiously indifferent or indeed militantly anti-clerical a given individual might be. Protestants feared Catholics because of the immigrants' high birth rates, their authoritarian religious structures, and their insistence on segregating children in separate school systems. While conservatives condemned the racial contamination of the American people, liberals detested Catholics because of their outmoded gender attitudes, their slavish subservience to clerical authority, and their frequent challenges to the freedom of the press. Both sides bemoaned the political hold that Catholic religious structures had acquired over the nation's cities, not to mention immigrant control of organized criminality. Fears that the nation would be swamped by immigrants, perhaps by revolutionary force, provoked Protestants to mobilize in some of the largest mass movements ever seen in American history, above all, the Ku Klux Klan of the early 1920s. Not until 1960, a century after the great influx of Irish Catholics, was a Catholic president conceivable.[42]

Catholics reputedly maintained dual loyalties inconsistent with American democracy or patriotism. Some ethnic groups in particular, such as the Italians, belonged to movements and societies closely connected to the governments of their countries of origin. Many Italian-Americans sympathized with Fascist movements, while by the 1930s, several ethnic groups had their distinctive "shirt" or fascist movements emulating the Italian Black Shirts. The upsurge of anti-Jewish activism by the (Irish) Christian Front and the German Bund suggested to some that American hopes of integration lay in ruins.[43]

In retrospect, we have to say that many nativist fears proved quite justified. Catholic numbers would indeed increase substantially, to the point that Catholics would soon represent around a quarter of the U.S. population, roughly the same level that Muslims are projected to reach in some European nations by the mid-twenty-first century. In the American context, though, neither the Jewish nor the Catholic presence would remain controversial, as both groups established their credentials as patriots, indeed, as super-patriots. The cultural and political markers separating Catholics from non-Catholics have diminished steadily over the decades, to the point that values and social attitudes have become closely harmonized. So, of course, have birth rates. And the process of assimilation has had a global impact, as the pluralistic values of American prelates and scholars have transformed the wider Catholic Church.

Though in retrospect we regard the assimilation of American Catholics as inevitable, it would have appeared incredible in the 1920s or 1930s, quite as astonishing as any modern suggestion that Europe's Muslims would within a few decades share many of the values of their old-stock neighbors. The decades-long story of American integration provides a rather different perspective on contemporary laments about Europe's alleged failure to integrate its own new ethnic minorities in a far shorter time span. Let us make a fair comparison: just how well was the United States doing with assimilation in 1925 or so?[44]

At present, such an "American" outcome seems a distant dream, and there are key differences from the current European situation. The process of integration in the United States benefited hugely from the long hiatus in new immigration from 1924 through 1965; and the experience of shared national effort in World War II undoubtedly helped Americanization. Europeans cannot assume any parallel developments in their own situation. In modern Europe, moreover, many of Muslim origin find themselves at the bottom of the social and economic order, suffering what they believe to be systematic racism and police discrimination. These grievances led to the outburst of rioting in France in 2005, and in various forms have provoked disturbances elsewhere. Also, while long-term demographic trends favor stability, European societies will have to live for some years with the large cohort of young people born before the recent decline in fertility, the youth bulge that will not shrink until after 2020. The intervening years could well provide a bumpy ride. If the poor and deprived come to link their condition to their religious identity—if the young, poor, and Muslim overtly confront the old, well-off, and Christian—then Europe would face a quite different, and far grimmer, future, which we could term Lebanese rather than American.

In her optimistic survey of *The Islamic Challenge*, Jytte Klausen rightly notes that most Muslim political leaders in Europe are "looking for ways to build institutions that will allow Muslims to practice their religion in a way that is compatible with social integration." Moreover, an "overwhelming majority of European Muslims are as appalled by the ranting of [ultra-radical] clerics as are Christians"; but dissidents need not command an absolute majority before they can bring a society to the verge of ruin. The same Pew survey that seemed to promise a new era of interfaith tolerance also reported that 15 or 16 percent of British, French, and Spanish Muslims felt that violence against civilian targets was sometimes justified in the defense of Islam, a level of radical sympathy comparable to that in Pakistan. Only 17 percent of British Muslims believed that Arabs carried out the September 11 attacks, again a figure parallel to that in Pakistan; 6 percent of British Muslims approved of the suicide bombings on the London subway; and so on. The jihad nightmares of the pessimists could yet come true.[45]

European states face real dangers, demanding innovative and imaginative approaches that at many points challenge assumptions about "European values." Moreover, governments are handicapped in this task by a pervasive secularism that finds it difficult to treat seriously religious concerns, motivations, or sensitivities. Increasingly, as governments try to adapt to accommodate Islam, they find that their policies and legal solutions also have much wider implications, for Christianity as well as for new and emerging religions. Far from being dead, Christian churches and movements also pose continuing difficulties for the secular European project.

When the Soviet Union collapsed, some academics spoke confidently of the End of History, the final resolution of ideological conflicts. Democratic capitalism had won, globally. Less than twenty years later, it seems, not only are rival ideologies once more locked in seemingly permanent struggle, but just as in the Cold War, Europe again represents a critical theater for rivalry—this time, between competing forms of religious belief, between and among Christianity, Islam, and secularism. New specters are haunting Europe.

2

Godless Europe?

Eldest daughter of the church, what have you done with your baptism?

Pope John Paul II

When American Christians discuss the moral state of their nation, especially if they are from the conservative or evangelical end of the religious spectrum, they commonly assume that the Christian faith is in steep decline in the United States. Such an approach amazes American liberals, who worry instead about trends to theocracy, and it staggers Europeans, who are constantly impressed by the vigor of American faith, no less than its confident public expression. In Europe, in contrast, it is tempting to conclude that Christianity is sick or dying. Though ancient churches stand as visible monuments, defining the landscape of cities and villages, most have lost their traditional role as thriving centers of community. At least in its institutional form, and that is an important distinction, European Christianity seems to be terminally ill.

Recessional

A local analogy might help Americans to understand the extent of the crisis. Just imagine that in the United States, Christianity was represented almost exclusively by the liberal mainline churches—Lutheran, Methodist, Episcopal, Congregational, and the rest, and no other bodies existed to compensate for their shrinking membership or attendance figures. In such circumstances, it would be tempting to graph the accumulating statistics of decline to determine just when, in a few decades, the sole surviving parishioner would be forced to turn out the lights on the last church. Of course, Americans have, besides the mainliners, a plethora of thriving and well-attended alternative churches: most European countries do not.

Any number of indices demonstrate the weakness of European Christianity. In terms of belief, most simply, several different surveys regularly ask people in various nations how important religion is to them. In some Muslim nations, around 90 percent declare that religion "plays a very important role" in their lives, while the U.S. figure in 2002 was about 60 percent. The average figure for Europeans was 21 percent, though of course with national variations. The figure for Italy was 27 percent, Germany 21 percent, and France and the Czech Republic 11 percent. Unlike the United States, moreover, religious disaffection is not merely expressed in nonparticipation in church activities. A significant number of Europeans declare themselves atheist or nonreligious. A survey of British respondents in 2004 found only 44 percent admitting to belief in God, with 35 percent denying that belief, and 21 percent "don't knows." Among those aged 18 through 34, atheist respondents rose to 45 percent. Between 1973 and 1994, the proportion of French people claiming no religion grew from 11 percent to 34 percent.[1]

In terms of specific Christian doctrines also, surveys trace a sharp decline in belief. In 1957, 71 percent of British respondents declared that Jesus was the Son of God, but by 2001, the figure had fallen to 38 percent. Breaking such responses down by age group suggests the speed with which Britain is moving toward a post-Christian society. Asked whether Jesus ever lived, which is scarcely a major concession to Christian orthodoxy, 80 percent of those over 65 said that he had, while only 54 percent of those aged 18–24 agreed. And that survey preceded the phenomenal impact of Dan Brown's *Da Vinci Code*, which has since 2003 popularized the idea of a Jesus who existed but whose teachings had nothing in common with any traditional concept of Christianity.[2]

Low levels of religious belief are reflected in figures for attendance, though the enormous disparity in reported rates for Christian loyalties means that we have to use this evidence cautiously, always asking what exactly is being measured. Combining separate surveys can yield puzzling results: surveys taken within a couple of years of each other by equally competent firms apparently showed that while 72 percent of British people claimed to be Christians, only 44 percent of the nation claim any religious affiliation. Similarly, when we read a despairing comment that only some tiny fraction of a given population attends church, that does not necessarily mean that Christianity is near extinction in that society. The figure cited might well refer to those reporting weekly attendance, rather than "regular" or occasional attenders, who still profess Christian loyalties.[3]

With that caveat in mind, though, European levels of church attendance fall far short of American, and the situation is deteriorating fast. Around 40 percent of Americans report visiting a place of worship weekly, compared to less than 20 percent in most of Europe. According to some estimates, the British attendance figure is 15 percent, with 12 percent in Germany, and Scandinavia below 5 percent. If those figures seem low, then the news for Christians is still more depressing. Those rates include attendance at any place of worship, whether church, mosque, or synagogue, so the European figures include Muslim believers. At the other end of the scale of religious practice are those who never or "practically never" attend a place of worship. The American figure for seldom or never attending a place of worship is 16 percent. As of 2000, though, such absentees made up 60 percent of French respondents, 55 percent in Britain, and between 40 percent and 50 percent in Scandinavia and the Low Countries. Young people are much more likely to be never-attenders than regulars. The number of young British people attending Anglican services has halved just since 1979, and only 6 percent of those aged 15 to 29 attend. Between 1900 and 1960, half of those baptized in the Church of England later went on to confirmation: that figure is now 20 percent. In 2005, the English Church Census reported that, since 1998, half a million people stopped going to a Christian church on Sundays.[4]

Such figures would be troubling enough for church leaders if they represented a steady level of low activity, but they do not: the trends are clearly downward and have been so since the 1960s. In Britain, Callum Brown argues that "quite suddenly in 1963 something very profound ruptured the character of the nation and its people, sending organized Christianity on a downward spiral to the margins of social significance." During the 1960s, "the new media, new gender roles and the moral revolution dramatically ended people's conception that they lived Christian lives." Decline accelerated in the post-1975 decade, when most of Britain's Christian churches lost around 20 percent of their adult membership, and matters have deteriorated still further since then. In the words of conservative British writer Danny Kruger, "More than 70 per cent of us claim to be Christian. But only four per cent of us go to church on Sundays. Church membership has fallen by a quarter over the past quarter-century: extrapolate forward and the prognosis is not good." Former Archbishop of Canterbury George Carey has suggested that if the Church of England were a human being, "the last rites would be administered at any moment." He sees the church "as an elderly lady who mutters away to herself in a corner, ignored most of the time." Cardinal Cormac Murphy-O'Connor, Archbishop of Westminster, has said that "Christianity, as a sort of backdrop to people's lives and moral decisions—and to the government, the social life of the country—has now almost been vanquished."[5]

In Germany similarly, the Evangelical Church, EKD, which includes most Protestants, has lost over half its membership in the past half-century. Though in theory the church claims the loyalty of around a third of the population, some 28 million notional members, only a million or so demonstrate any regular religious participation. The proportion of babies born in Switzerland who were baptized was 95 percent in 1970, but 65 percent in 2000.[6]

As we will see, the picture of religious indifference is not uniform, and Christian adherence remains strong in parts of New Europe, especially Poland and Slovakia. Yet eastern and central Europe also have their bastions of secularism. In the closing years of European communism, the churches generally flourished on the strength of their opposition to repressive regimes, but matters changed when the old dictatorships collapsed, and the public gained access to secret police files. In some countries, it became painfully obvious how thoroughly the state apparatus had penetrated the churches, recruiting clergy as spies and propaganda agents.[7]

Such scandals were not inevitably fatal, at least where the structures of belief were secure. The Polish Catholic Church, for instance, has survived a scandalous claim that perhaps a tenth of its priests cooperated with the secret police, while the faith of Slovak Catholics has not been visibly dented by charges that their archbishop collaborated. In other countries, though, like the former German Democratic Republic, such scandals administered the coup de grâce to already weakened churches. Today, some regions of the former Soviet bloc look as secular as the Netherlands, if not more so: Hungary, the Czech Republic, Estonia, and the former East Germany all register very high percentages of adults reporting no religion. According to the European Values Study, "fewer Czechs claim allegiance to organized religion than any other people in Europe, except Estonians." Only a third of Czechs belong to a religious denomination and about 12 percent attend services once a month or more. Today, over 60 percent of Czechs identify themselves as atheists, compared to just 19 percent who believe in God.[8]

Generally, decline has been far more marked in formerly Protestant areas, such as Britain or Denmark, than in nations with a strong Catholic heritage, and that difference is as marked within particular nations. Looking at the former Czechoslovakia, the mainly Protestant Czechs secularized rapidly, while their Catholic Slovak neighbors did not. Yet Catholics can take little comfort from this distinction, which might indicate not a qualitatively different fate, but rather a cultural delay of a decade or two.

Catholic Crisis

Across western Europe, religious nonparticipation is now marked among Roman Catholics, who until fairly recently maintained a high level of practice. In theory, of the ten nations with the largest Catholic

Table 2.1   **The World's Largest Catholic Communities**

Nation	Number of Catholics (millions)
Brazil	145
Mexico	94
Philippines	69
USA	64
Italy	58
France	45
Colombia	38
Spain	35
Poland	34
Argentina	34
TOTAL	616

Source: www.catholic-hierarchy.org/country/sc1.html.

populations, no less than four are European, namely France, Spain, Italy, and Poland (see Table 2.1). Yet figures for regular church attendance must raise questions about the degree of involvement. Around a third of Italian Catholics claim to attend mass weekly, though other estimates suggest a rate closer to half this. This compares to 18 percent in Spain and 12 percent in France. The figures for Germany, Austria, and the Netherlands run between 10 and 15 percent. Between 1975 and 1990, the number of Catholic baptisms in Europe fell by 34 percent, the number of weddings by 41 percent. Changing social attitudes are reflected by the impressive drop in fertility rates and family size from the 1970s onward. According to one comparative study of European nations, in the 1970s, fertility rates in strongly Catholic countries exceeded those in other countries by "almost a half child per woman" (a curiously phrased measure!). By the 1990s, however, fertility had so dropped in these Catholic countries that they "averaged the lowest rates in Europe, about half a child lower than that of the strongly Protestant countries." Today, as German sociologist Ulrich Beck notes, "In western Europe, there is a rough rule of thumb according to which the closer one gets to the Pope, the fewer children one has."[9]

   Though Catholics share very much the same range of social and cultural influences that affected other denominations, some special factors applied in this instance. As in the United States, part of the decline in Catholic loyalties and solidarity must be attributed to the effects of the second Vatican Council that met between 1963 and 1965, but which did not have its full impact on parochial life until the 1970s. Though the council's effects were complex, they included an elevation of the role of the laity, which made the priesthood a less attractive profession, while the transformation of the mass and the introduction of vernacular languages made the ceremony less mystical and more mundane. The very swift decline of the rite of confession also detracted from priestly power and prestige. Changes in devotional practices, such as the rules for fasting and abstinence, reduced the cultural markers separating Catholics from non-Catholics and eroded a sense of cultural distinctiveness.

To stress the role of "Vatican II" does not necessarily mean subscribing to the traditionalist Catholic argument that the reforms launched by Pope John XXIII were of themselves negative or destructive. Many of the worst effects arose not from any decisions of the Council itself but in how they were implemented in practice, at the local level. The Council was intended to bring the Church more in line with some powerful secular trends, but few could have foreseen just how overwhelmingly powerful these social currents would have been in the post-1965 decade, or how poorly prepared the hierarchy was to deal with them.

The rapid pace of reforms raised expectations of a more thorough accommodation with the secular world, which might for instance include clerical marriage, the approval of contraception, and greater tolerance of homosexuality. When the 1968 encyclical *Humanae Vitae* reasserted traditional teachings against contraception, liberals were shocked, while many ordinary Catholics made the decision to use birth control whatever the church ordained, a dramatic departure from familiar patterns of obedience. Once that precedent was established, it became easier to contemplate disobeying the church in other matters, including political causes, and in tolerating more easygoing sexual practices. Also during the 1970s, the publicity surrounding high-profile Catholic liberals like Hans Küng and Edward Schillebeecx undermined the idea that Catholic leaders spoke with a single voice. And the popularity of liberation theology encouraged young Catholics to challenge hierarchical structures in the church as much as in society at large. The focus of many priests on left-liberal political activism also created the impression that believers might just as well pursue their struggle for justice in secular settings, since the church seemed to offer no distinctive message. Not until the election of John Paul II did the Vatican once more project an air of confidence and assurance, a sense that the church spoke authoritatively on moral and political issues. By that point, though, many Western Catholics were already deeply disaffected with the institutional church.[10]

Particularly worrying for Catholic authorities is the precipitous decline in practice in several nations that in the 1960s would have been regarded as heartlands of the faith. In Italy and Spain, church attendance has been in steep decline since the early 1990s, and each new

survey depicts the situation in grimmer terms than a predecessor from
a year or two previously. The hard core of observant Catholics, long
the bedrock of Catholic power, has contracted steadily, to become an
aged remnant. In France in 1950, perhaps a quarter of the population
was *pratiquant*, compared with under 5 percent today. Cardinal
Joachim Meisner of Cologne has said that "We've never had as much
money as in the last 40 years, and we've never lost the substance of
the faith as much as in the last 40 years. . . . In the Cologne archdiocese, there are 2.8 million Catholics, but in the last 30 years we've lost
300,000. For every one baptism, there are three funerals."[11]

The clearest example of institutional implosion is Ireland, which as
recently as the 1970s enjoyed the highest level of religious practice in
Europe: 85 percent to 90 percent of Catholics regularly attended Sunday mass. When Pope John Paul II visited Dublin in 1979, the million
people who gathered to greet him symbolized the continuing power of
Catholic Ireland, a nation that still at that date prohibited contraceptives
and refused to allow divorce. Even today, Ireland records figures for regular church attendance that are impressive by European standards and
close to American norms: about half of Irish Catholics probably attend
mass weekly. For most nations in Europe or North America, even that
diminished figure would represent a spectacular manifestation of religious devotion; but this is Ireland, where expectations are so much
higher. Moreover, underlying trends among the young reflect those of
the wider Europe. In the words of one Dublin professional, "I don't go
to church, and I don't know one person who does. Fifteen years ago, I
didn't know one person who didn't."[12]

Catholics also suffer from the falling number of vocations to the
priesthood or the religious life, so that surviving clergy today increasingly tend to be old men, commonly in their sixties or seventies. Europe
as a whole had 250,000 priests in 1978, counting both diocesan and religious priests, but that number fell to 200,000 by 2003.[13] Decades of
state repression might explain the shortage of priests in a nation like the
Czech Republic, where the average age of priests is sixty-seven, and only
half the parishes have a priest in residence; but that figure is quite close
to the situation in democratic western Europe. France, typically, had
50,000 priests in 1970, but barely half that number by 2000. Shortages
of priests and contracting numbers of the faithful have led the church to
close or consolidate parishes, making quite outdated the once-familiar
institution of the well-known parish priest faithfully serving a village or
an urban parish. The consequences of decline are evident in any region
of France. In Normandy, "the pastor of the Notre-Dame Cathedral in
Évreux in Normandy, must minister to two other area churches. Two
dozen more under his authority have no priest and remain closed except for a few holidays and special occasions." In the diocese of Cahors,
priests must care for thirty or even forty churches, in which elderly

clergy meet graying parishioners. In many villages, the question is whether a church will even survive in a decade or two. That diocese, like many others, survives on manpower imported from the global South, commonly from Francophone West Africa.[14]

The number of seminarians has plunged. While Europe in 1978 accounted for 37 percent of candidates for the priesthood worldwide, the figure for 2003 was only 22 percent, with a marked decline in numbers setting in around 1995. At the height of postwar enthusiasm in 1966, the Catholic Church in France ordained 566 men, compared to just 90 in 2004. In the 1990s alone, the number entering French seminaries fell from 1,200 to 900. The famous seminary of Saint Sulpice, near Paris, is built to accommodate two hundred pupils if the demand was there, but today it actually houses only fifty. Many are from global South nations such as Vietnam and Rwanda, which outsource to Europe the task of clerical training. Even Ireland's once-booming seminaries have to cope with much smaller enrollments. The nation's great seminary is Maynooth, itself a key monument of the Irish-Catholic tradition. Maynooth, which in earlier eras usually counted on five hundred students at any time, now has sixty, and many of those do not intend to follow the familiar career path that would take them into the priesthood, in Ireland or elsewhere. They are instead lay students interested in the academic study of theology. In 2004, just fifteen men were ordained priests for the whole of Ireland. In a typical year, the archdiocese of Dublin, with around a million faithful, ordains *one* new priest. Time and again, we encounter the rule of ten: in most west European countries, whether we are looking at vocations or seminarians, the present figure is commonly one-tenth of what it was forty years ago.[15]

Across Europe too, orders of monks and nuns have contracted, and surviving members of religious orders are much older than their counterparts would have been in earlier decades. In the 1960s, the world's best-known nun was probably Sister Luc-Gabriel (Jeanine Deckers), the thirty-year-old-Belgian "singing nun" who in 1963 had a worldwide hit with her recording of the song "Dominique." (Though other sisters were making far more significant contributions, none of them—including Mother Teresa—achieved anything like the same degree of public attention in those years.) While Sister Luc-Gabriel's case is in no sense representative, her later career did have some points of resemblance with those of many other younger nuns in that era. She grew disenchanted with the church's failure to follow through on the reforms of Vatican II, and in 1967 recorded a song supporting contraception. She left her order and probably lived in a lesbian relationship until she and her partner committed suicide in 1985.

From the late 1960s, convents and monasteries suffered a continuing exodus. Germany in 1971 had 70,000 nuns; today the figure is 30,000. In 1960, France had thirty nuns for every 10,000 Catholics, but by 2000, the figure was only ten. In the Netherlands, the ratio fell in the same period from seventy-seven to eighteen, in Germany from thirty-two to thirteen. This trend has direct consequences on the public face of Christianity, since religious orders had long been heavily engaged in staffing the schools and hospitals of Catholic Europe. With fewer religious, and specifically nuns, Catholic institutions continued to function, but with ever fewer, and older, sisters.[16]

The consequences can be imagined. The Catholic Church must struggle to present its views to a rising generation commonly suspicious of institutional and traditional authority of any kind, and quite accustomed to ideas of gender equality, sexual freedom, and acceptance of sexual difference. The clergy on whom this burden of argument must fall are not only exclusively male but, in most cases, well above the retirement age common in most of Europe. Even apart from hints of sexual deviance, the age and gender of priests seems to confirm every accusation that the church is hopelessly patriarchal, hidebound, and out of touch with contemporary realities. As an institution, the church becomes indefensible.[17]

The Age of Scandal

As in North America, Catholic loyalties have been severely strained by persistent sex scandals over the past fifteen years, scandals that illustrate the apparent hypocrisy of the Catholic Church in condemning the sins of its flock. While these incidents have contributed to declining Catholic practice, they are symptoms of secularization as much as causes. If the Christian consensus had not been undermined already, stories of clerical abuse probably would not have reached the media and would have had nothing like the effect they did. But coming at a time of softening support for the institutional church, their effects were devastating.

Some of the cases involved adult homosexuality, but the most notorious incidents arose from cases of serial child abuse. Catholic dioceses have repeatedly had to deal with clergy who sexually abused or molested young people, including both small children and older teenagers. Abusive priests continued their misdeeds for many years, as church authorities ignored complaints and transferred wrongdoers to new parishes where their criminal careers continued unabated. Such official misbehavior suggested that the church institution was engaged in a systematic cover-up of sexual crime while failing to protect innocent children.

The abuse stories served as a perfect symbol of church crisis. In France in 2001, the Bishop of Bayeux received a three-month suspended sentence for concealing information about a pedophile priest in his diocese. In 1998, Cardinal Hans Hermann Groer, the head of the powerful Austrian church, was forced to resign following charges that he had molested seminarians many years previously. In 2004, a new Austrian scandal arose when a seminary computer was found to contain child pornography and pictures of priests engaged in sex acts with seminarians. In Great Britain, dozens of Catholic priests have been removed for sexual misconduct since the mid-1990s, and in 2001, the church-sponsored Nolan Report proposed a thorough reform of procedures for reporting and investigating abuse. More recently, extensive abuse charges have hit Ampleforth boarding school, one of the most prestigious institutions of the English Catholic elite. In 2002, a Polish archbishop resigned after he was charged with sexual encounters with young priests.[18]

None of these cases had anything like the impact of their Irish counterparts, which have accumulated steadily since the early 1990s. The sequence began in 1992 with what in retrospect seems a relatively mild story, in which popular bishop Eamonn Casey was exposed for fathering a child by a young American woman, and paying her hush money. Shortly afterward, however, accounts of serial molestation by clergy began to emerge, most notoriously involving Fr. Brendan Smyth. This scandal moved beyond church circles when, in 1994, controversy over attempts to extradite Smyth from Northern Ireland provoked the collapse of the Irish government. By 2006, 250 priests were under investigation for child abuse. A long-term study of priests working in the diocese of Dublin implicated over a hundred in possible abuse, a rate comparable to that in major U.S. dioceses like Boston.[19]

Scandals reached their greatest intensity in the diocese of Ferns, in the southeast of the country. The epicenter was Fr. Sean Fortune, a grasping and tyrannical parish priest who potentially generated quite enough scandal in many ways, even apart from sexual molestation. After his suicide in 1999, pressure mounted for a systematic investigation of the whole diocese, which eventually appeared in 2005. The Ferns Report was devastating, depicting a diocese with an alarmingly high proportion of sexually troubled priests whose activities were tolerated by two successive bishops. And while a case could be made that authorities in earlier years probably did not appreciate the harmful effects of molestation on victims, Ferns authorities continued to treat abuse cases lightly up to the end of the 1990s. The Irish media, which in bygone years had been reluctant to criticize church authorities, now found no words too harsh for the scandal. The Ferns case involved "pure evil," "abominable evil"; it was the "devil's diocese," "the horror of Ferns." Adding to the ongoing disasters was the scandal of the Magdalene Homes, grim semipenal institutions to which young girls were confined for suspected sexual misbehavior. The homes endured for decades but were exposed in the 1990s, and in 2002 were commemorated in the exposé film, *The Magdalene Sisters*. In 2005, Dublin's new archbishop delivered an address with the sobering title, "Will Ireland be Christian in 2030?" Though his conclusions are quite positive, the title is meant to stun: will *Ireland* be Christian?[20]

Christianity Leaves the Picture

The shriveling of church institutions has had complex effects on European societies, most visibly in the form of deteriorating church buildings. When congregations shrink, it makes economic sense to combine parishes, but such a policy can strike a grave blow at religious sensibilities. This is a familiar story in American cities, when closed Catholic churches might represent ethnic and communal loyalty. But imagine the scale of the trauma when the building itself is several centuries old and stands on a site consecrated by Christian worship over a millennium or more. Moreover, the churches contain the monuments, art, and material treasures assembled by that community over the centuries. Great medieval churches were built to assert pride in the community and in the faith, and conversely, the sight of an abandoned or ruined church sends a powerful message about the eclipse of the faith that it symbolized. Across Europe, church authorities agonize over deciding the appropriate fate for disused buildings.[21]

The buildings of England's established church normally stood open and accessible through the 1970s, when concerns about crime and vandalism resulted in their being locked outside service times and thus less available to the curious or pious. Since then, the Church of England has faced constant problems about how to cope with a building stock designed for an utterly different religious landscape. Between 1970 and 2005, the Church closed 1,700 of its structures, over 10 percent of the total. Some have been demolished; developers have transformed others into warehouses and apartments, spas and pubs. The revolution has been just as marked, and as painful, for the nonconformist Protestant churches that coexisted with the Anglicans, the churches of the Methodists, Congregationalists, and Presbyterians. Just since 2001, some five hundred London churches of all denominations have been transformed into private dwellings. In the 1970s too, British cathedrals began charging visitors for admission, a sound economic decision, but one that sent the disastrous message that these buildings were museums rather than living places of worship.[22] Some ancient sites attract visitors uninterested in their orthodox Christian associations, as former abbeys and cathedrals have become centers of a booming New Age tourist trade. Seekers converge on Glastonbury Abbey or Chartres cathedral, or Scotland's Rosslyn Chapel, made famous by Dan Brown. Bowing to the inevitable, some French and German convents and abbeys try to survive by presenting themselves as retreat houses for the New Age-oriented market.

Other tokens of Christian decline are less tangible, but nonetheless significant. Abundant anecdotal evidence, supported by opinion surveys, suggests the depth of ignorance about even the most basic Christian doctrines. One British poll found that over 40 percent of respondents could not say what event was commemorated by Easter. Churches have been forced to respond with remedial measures that would have appalled earlier generations. The standard information leaflet offered to visitors at England's ancient York Minster begins by exploring, "What Do Christians Believe?" A sample:

> York Minster is built in the shape of a *cross* to symbolize the most important Christian belief: that Jesus Christ, the Son of God, died on the cross for our sins. . . . Some [crosses] will show Jesus at his *Crucifixion* to remind us of the terrible death he died. Others will be empty to remind us that death is not the end of the story: Christians also believe in Christ's *Resurrection*. . . . The principal service for Christians is *Holy Communion*. . . .

and so on. Art galleries can assume no knowledge of terms like Ascension and Transfiguration, any more than a casual visitor can be expected to understand the rituals of an Amazonian tribe. One Czech observer complains that her younger compatriots "don't know what Christmas is about. They are lost in art galleries when they see paintings of Jesus Christ. One girl looked at a picture of the Crucifixion and asked, 'Who did that to him?' Her friend responded, 'The Communists.' "[23]

Europe's Jews

While contemporary commentators have often noted the decline of Christian practice, similar trends have also affected the other religion with deep European roots, namely Judaism. The massacres and pogroms of the 1940s massively reduced Europe's Jewish population, and many of the survivors emigrated to Israel. Including Russia and the east, Europe accounted for 80 percent of the world's Jews in 1900, compared to perhaps 11 percent today. The whole of wider Europe today contains only some 1.5 million Jews, with just a million in the European Union proper. Though exact numbers are shaky, Europe is home to more Buddhists than Jews.[24]

Besides the historic factors reducing Jewish populations, we also see powerful secularizing trends. In Britain, Jewish religious leaders are as pessimistic about long-term trends as are their Anglican counterparts. British Jews, of course, escaped the disastrous fate of continental populations, but the communities have since shrunk badly due to the sheer force of assimilation. Fifty years ago, Britain had around half a million Jews, a number that has today shrunk to 266,000. Emigration partly explains this contraction, though counterbalancing this has been a significant countermigration of Israeli Jews to Britain. A more important explanation has been demography, together with a decline in self-identification. With a disproportionately large number of educated and professional members, Jewish communities usually have small families, and between 30 and 50 percent of British Jews marry outside the faith. In France too, Europe's largest Jewish community has also contracted, if not so dramatically. A Jewish population of 535,000 in 1980 has now fallen to around 500,000, a drop of 7 percent in a very few years.[25]

The picture is not entirely negative, and there are some signs of growth, chiefly in Germany, where the Jewish population has now climbed to over 200,000. Given the history of the past century, the thought that Germany might soon have more Jews than Britain sounds like a sick joke. To put this change in proportion, though, the increase in Germany does not reflect natural internal growth but rather a rearrangement of existing populations. Around a million Jews have left the former Soviet Union since the 1980s, and while most chose Israel as their destination, a sizable fraction preferred Germany. Even with this apparent revival, then, long-term trends are gloomy. Jews today constitute a minuscule fraction of Europe's population, some 0.25 percent, and that proportion seems set to fall even further. Not just for Christians, Europe does not provide healthy soil for religious institutions.

Public Faith

For American observers, the transatlantic religious difference is most evident in terms of the public expression of faith. For all the rhetoric of the separation of church and state, Americans are well accustomed to politicians invoking God and religion, even if in merely conventional terms: no member of the U.S. House or Senate publicly admits to atheism. Matters in Europe are generally quite different. When Great Britain joined the 2003 invasion of Iraq, Prime Minister Tony Blair initially planned to end his address to the nation with a remark like "God bless you." His horrified advisers urged him to remove such a phrase, which for them, connoted "American-style" religious fanaticism or hypocrisy. In Germany, the former Chancellor Gerhard Schroeder and several of his cabinet refused to add the anodyne formula "so help me God" when swearing their oath of office.[26]

Other recent events demonstrate a hostility of political elites at least to any acknowledgment of religion, and arguably to the toleration of overt Christian sentiment as such. During the debates over the European Constitution at the start of this decade, framers sought an exalted protocol that would describe the roots of European values and civilization. Though many wished to include at least a passing nod to the Christian heritage, others strenuously resisted even such an acknowledgment. Instead its preamble declared,

> Drawing inspiration from the cultural, religious and humanist inheritance of Europe, which, nourished first by the civilizations of Greece and Rome, characterized by spiritual impulse [sic] always present in its heritage and later by the philosophical currents of the Enlightenment, has embedded within the life of society its perception of the central role of the human person and his inviolable and inalienable rights, and of respect for law.

The 70,000 words of this prolix document thus fail to include a single specific reference to Christianity. This omission was appropriate for those who believed, in the words of former French president Valéry Giscard d'Estaing, that "Europeans live in a purely secular political system, where religion does not play an important role."[27]

For George Weigel, the constitution affair indicates the "self-inflicted amnesia" provoked by Christophobia among Europe's elites, for whom Christianity is at best irrelevant, at worst an obstacle to social progress and the expansion of human rights. Historically, this reactionary image was far from inevitable. On many issues, the churches found no difficulty supporting liberal or even socialist reforms, and both Catholic and Protestant churches have for over a century included powerful components supporting social activism. Labor unions have long been able to ground their operations in the clear statements of Catholic social teachings. From the late 1960s, however, social reform increasingly became identified with issues of personal identity and rights, particularly as these involved gender and sexuality. On some critical issues, especially abortion and gay rights, secular progressives found themselves in stark conflict with traditionally minded Christians, by no means only within the Roman Catholic Church.[28]

One contentious issue has been the spread of forms of gay marriage or civil union, a recognition of homosexual status that goes far beyond the mere removal of legal impediments to personal sexual expression. The idea is so controversial because homosexuality is so explicitly condemned in the Christian scriptures, not to mention in centuries of scholarly tracts and commentaries. As Pope Benedict writes, the mere idea of gay marriage "would fall outside the moral history of humanity." The spread of liberal legislation in this area provides a rough index of secularization. As recently as the 1970s, the gay marriage issue barely existed even as an idea for most Europeans, but it has since become commonplace. In 1989, Denmark became the first nation to approve civil unions, and over the following decade, most Scandinavian countries allowed gay couples adoption rights. By 2001, several European nations including France and Germany had introduced some form of civil union granting same-sex partners rights comparable to those of heterosexuals, and Britain followed by 2005. The

Irish government has promised that some form of civil partnership will soon be introduced in that nation too. Generally, liberal north European nations of Protestant heritage took the lead in liberalization, but Catholic states followed only a little way behind, despite staunch opposition from the Vatican and local church hierarchies. In 2001, the Netherlands became the first country to approve full-scale "gay marriage," followed by Belgium in 2002 and Spain in 2005. In the Spanish case, the legislation was strongly supported by Socialist Prime Minister Luis Rodríguez Zapatero, who on this and many other matters stood out as an aggressive opponent of church influence and doctrine.[29]

Gay issues indicate the mainstreaming of attitudes and policies condemned by most Christian churches, to the point that Christian critics of homosexuality found themselves labeled as politically deviant, and perhaps as too extreme for public office. As the European constitutional debate was in progress, Italian politician Rocco Buttiglione was a candidate for the position of European Commissioner for Justice, Freedom and Security, the kind of appointment that is rarely challenged. Buttiglione, however, had expressed the view that, based on his Catholic faith, homosexual behavior was sinful. However, he continued, "I may think that homosexuality is a sin but this has no effect on politics, unless I say that homosexuality is a crime. . . . The state has no right to stick its nose into these things, and nobody can be discriminated against on the basis of sexual orientation." Yet with all these qualifications—mildly expressed, from an American perspective—he was rejected for the office.[30]

Pursued to its logical outcome, the decision excludes any and all Christians of traditional or orthodox leanings from office within the European Union, and soon, presumably, within member states. In 2006, Catholic politician Ruth Kelly acquired a new position within Britain's Labour government as Minister for Equality: the office's title itself reflects a dramatic statement about the proper scope of government intervention in social arrangements. Kelly, however, was widely attacked because her religion, and especially her affiliation with the rightist group Opus Dei, attracted charges that she would be unable to act sincerely on behalf of gay equality. Critics pressed her to declare forthrightly whether she felt that homosexuality was a sin. In a response that would have startled most earlier generations of Christian politicians, Kelly replied only that "I don't think it's right for politicians to start making moral judgments about people. That's the last thing I would want to do."[31]

Like the Buttiglione affair, the Kelly controversy suggests the subordination of Christian moral imperatives—even the right to "make moral judgments"—to liberal concepts of personal rights. Tony Blair reputedly holds strong Christian beliefs and is said to be on the verge of conversion to Catholicism. Yet when discussing his views in the media, he sounds apologetic. Asked if his faith shaped his politics, he replied, almost nervously, "Well I think if you have a religious belief it does, but it's probably best not to take it too far." Buttiglione himself uses such cases to argue that the European Union is succumbing to "soft totalitarianism," founded upon a state religion that is "an atheistic, nihilistic religion—but it is a religion that is obligatory for all." Former Irish Prime Minister John Bruton sees in the constitution controversy "a form of secular intolerance in Europe that is every bit as strong as religious intolerance was in the past."[32]

How Much of a Change?

In many ways, then, organized Christianity is in dire straits in most European nations, and certainly in comparison with the United States. Of course, before we can talk about "decline," we need to specify the earlier period to which we are comparing, and we cannot simply assume that religion in general or Christianity in particular has always attracted the loyalty of the European masses. Religious indifference and militant unbelief were both commonplace in the nineteenth century, when plebeian religious sentiment was often diverted into secular movements such as socialism, anarchism, and communism, and we can see each of these rivals as religious in their particular ways. Each used its sacred symbols and banners, venerated its martyrs, possessed its own ritual calendar and familiar songs, and all shared a powerful eschatological vision. Across the continent, it was a commonplace that churches of all shades had failed to penetrate the rising cities and industrial centers, and horrified religious activists complained at the staggering religious ignorance expressed by the poor of Paris, London, or Berlin. If modern Europeans are denounced for preferring the occult or mystical to religious orthodoxy, so were their forebears in the seventeenth and eighteenth centuries.[33]

Yet when full allowance is made for the peaks and valleys of religious enthusiasm, Christianity enjoyed a strength and popularity from the mid-nineteenth century through the 1960s that was far more solid and pervasive than anything we see today. To say that is of course to make no necessary claims about the quality of that faith—millions of Christians succumbed to the fascist temptation in the 1930s—but the cultural force of the religion is indisputable. Much of the appeal of Winston Churchill's wartime rhetoric was its explicit appeal to the idea of Christian civilization, which stood in absolute day and night contrast to the Nazi regime. The threats arising from armed conflict helped focus minds on the supernatural and stimulated a revived interest in spirituality. We think of the vast popularity of C. S. Lewis's writings in Great Britain, the work of Henri de Lubac in France, or the postwar surge in vocations by military veterans.[34]

This enthusiasm survived the war. The Taizé monastic community was organized in 1949. Among Catholics, Marian devotion reached new heights with the proclamation in 1950 of the doctrine of the Assumption. Through the 1950s, a series of Marian apparitions excited the faithful in Amsterdam—an amazing thought in a setting that would become synonymous with religious decline. The euphoria surrounding the coronation of Britain's Queen Elizabeth II in 1953 gave a renewed visibility and prestige to the Church of England, and to the link between church and state. The stunning success of Billy Graham's European crusades in 1954–1955 demonstrated the continuing power of evangelicalism: Graham's final meeting in London attracted 200,000, gathered in two massive stadiums.[35]

After 1945, too, the churches were critical to social and moral reconstruction across Europe, and German leaders like Cardinal Josef Frings enjoyed enormous prestige in a devastated society. In several nations, the main counterweight to the communist challenge was the Christian Democratic parties, rooted firmly in the Catholic tradition. The Moral Rearmament movement was at its apogee, and the group organized the conferences at which German and west European leaders gathered to foster reconciliation, and to lay the groundwork for what became the European Community. Through the 1950s, the project of European unification found fertile soil in Catholic political circles. The European flag—twelve stars arranged in a circle—was borrowed from traditional images of the Virgin Mary, the woman crowned with the stars, though with the central figure diplomatically omitted. Catholic labor organizations also remained potent. In noncommunist Europe, both Catholics and Protestants knew a complex world of interrelated Christian schools, organizations, societies, and leagues, a whole civil society linked at least notionally to churches. When communists took power in eastern and southeastern Europe after 1945, they rightly identified the Catholic clergy as the most likely source of determined resistance and they singled out obstreperous priests and bishops for persecution. Thousands suffered violence, death, or imprisonment. Across Europe, then, the churches genuinely were flourishing in the mid-twentieth century, which makes their subsequent decline all the more striking.[36]

Commentators have not been shy in offering explanations for the apparent death of Christian Europe, and some theories are far more convincing than others. Some of the commonsense approaches are actually among the weakest, particularly those that link the decline to the bloody political experiences of the twentieth century, the churches' alleged involvement in wars and totalitarianism. For all their other effects, though, events like the Nazi occupation played little role in modern secularization. In most countries, the churches played a role that was at least creditable, and sometimes heroic, and charges about alleged Vatican complicity with the Nazis have never gained much credibility outside the United States. To the contrary, Pius XII remained for most Catholics an inspiring symbol of anti-Nazi resistance, and the scurrilous fantasy of "Hitler's Pope" had not yet been invented. As we have seen, Catholic and Christian Democratic politics enjoyed enormous success through the 1960s.

Explaining Secularization

Other factors, though, contributed mightily to the decline of religion, apparently making Europe a wonderful model of secularization theory in action. If these explanations are correct, this would have dramatic implications for the fate of other religions in that same environment, and particularly of Islam.

Secularization theory portrays traditional institutional religions as fitting best in a premodern or prescientific setting dependent on agricultural production. Circumstances change when new economic arrangements disrupt older communities and advance urbanization and industrialization. Modernity is characterized by the rise of "empirical science and technology, of industrialization and capitalism, of urbanization and social mobility, of legal bureaucracy, democracy and the nation states." Modernity promotes individualism, privatization, and the dominance of a scientific worldview that makes obsolete religious claims to provide healings or miracles. The modern welfare state provides the social services and education once supplied by religious-based charities or movements, so that citizens know they can comfortably rely on government-provided assistance in time of crisis. Once ordinary believers can assert with confidence that "the state is my shepherd," organized religion declines sharply. This does not mark the end of religion as such, since a notion of higher powers appears to be hard-wired into our consciousness, but now the religious instinct is manifested in a more personal, autonomous, nondogmatic and nonjudgmental spirituality.[37]

At first sight, Europe seems to fit this pattern splendidly, offering an impressive negative correlation between economic development and traditional piety. European churches have felt the full force of secular rivalry usurping their traditional functions, with the growth of social welfare systems from the start of the twentieth century. Secular-minded Europeans are happy to accept this explanation of religious decline, which they use to rebuff pessimistic American accounts about Europe's alleged moral and social collapse. In this view, Europe has suffered neither a loss of faith nor of its will to survive: there is no Europe Problem. To the contrary, the United States should worry that it has not matured socially and economically to the point that it can afford to abandon the crutch of religion.

The best argument in favor of secularization theory is the gradation of religious decline across Europe and how well that correlates with economic development. The deepest-rooted welfare states are those of Scandinavia and northern Europe, where orthodox Protestantism has been in free fall for many years, while Great Britain has long been the most urbanized and industrialized section of the continent. Classic secularization theory would predict the most advanced decline in traditional religion in nations such as Britain, the Netherlands, and Sweden, and that is what we find.

Since the 1950s, industrial growth has been marked in areas that had largely escaped the earlier waves of development, and it spawned mass migrations from rural areas in Spain, Italy, and France. It is not just a coincidence that the areas of western Europe demonstrating the most marked and rapid secularization in the last quarter of the century were exactly those that experienced conspicuous economic growth and modernization in those years. These included Ireland, following its accession to the European Community in 1973; Spain, after the death of dictator Francisco Franco in 1975; and Italy, which boomed during the 1980s. All three were economic laggards in the 1960s: as late as 1975, 43 percent of Italy's economically active population worked in agriculture, and over a quarter of Italians lived in small towns or villages. In 1987, though, Italy triumphantly celebrated its *Sorpasso*, the moment when its GDP (temporarily) overtook that of Great Britain. Irish GNP per capita grew from just 60 percent of the EU average in 1973 to match that average in 2001, while Ireland's per capita GDP actually exceeded the British figure during the 1990s. Ireland became the Celtic Tiger, an Atlantic counterpart to the then-booming economies of the Pacific Rim. And in these very years—roughly, the last quarter of the century—levels of church attendance and vocations were declining rapidly. Conversely, countries like Poland maintained both a strong rural and agricultural sector and high levels of religious practice.[38]

Adding to the crisis of traditional religion and morality was the growing social status of women in an economy founded on the information and service sectors. Women entered increasingly into the world of paid employment, and also into the public sphere. Business and the mass media recognized the importance of women as consumers of both material goods and of popular culture. Soaring divorce statistics indicate both new expectations by women and stresses on traditional concepts of family and gender roles. Britain and Germany have long held the unenviable record for the fragility of marriage, but since the early 1990s, divorce rates have grown sharply in what were once the most solidly Catholic lands of Europe. Between 1995 and 2004, the divorce rate grew by 89 percent in Portugal, 62 percent in Italy, and 59 percent in Spain. While Irish rates are much lower, the country finally legislated the possibility of divorce in 1997, following a contentious referendum in which the Yes side gained a paper-thin margin of 50.28 percent.[39]

Doubts about the chances of lifelong commitment make people more cautious about entering into marriage, especially when no stigma is attached to unmarried couples living together, or to illegitimacy. The word, illegitimacy, is itself fading into disuse because of its judgmental connotations. In Britain and France, around 40 percent of births involve unmarried mothers, and the Norwegian figure is 49 percent. Even in Ireland, the illegitimacy rate is over 30 percent. Across Europe, households are smaller, and people are far more likely to be living by themselves or in transient relationships. Between 1971 and 2004, the number of British households containing just one person grew from 18 percent to 29 percent of the national total.[40]

By the 1980s, family and gender issues increasingly played a central role in national politics, with a growing social focus on themes of enhancing women's rights and protecting women from harassment and sexual violence. Other powerful issues on the social agenda were child protection and the struggle against child sexual abuse, both increasingly defined in much more ambitious ways than hitherto. Meanwhile, working women were more concerned about regulating their fertility, resulting in greater social pressure for easy access to contraceptives and, in many nations, to abortion. The growing separation between sexuality and reproduction made it vastly easier to present a case for gay rights, which advanced alongside political feminism. If the bearing and raising of children was no longer the primary goal of married heterosexual couples, by what right could marriage be denied to homosexual pairs?

Moreover, while European economies have experienced all the same pressures as the U.S.—a move to a postindustrial economy, a huge upsurge in female employment, the growth of feminism—these changes have been still more far-reaching in Europe because of the greater tradition of enforcing social change through law. The European Union has strongly encouraged women's emancipation and equality, using measures that many Americans would find startlingly interventionist, and some individual nations have gone still further. In Spain, long one of Europe's most entrenched social backwaters, the national government proposed in 2006 that women must make up at least 40 percent of the candidates from any political party and provide the same share of the members on corporate boards. Portugal now requires that women must comprise a third of the names on all electoral lists.[41]

The changing role and expectations of European women contributed massively to the decline in family size in west European nations, and the birth dearth commonly cited as a looming potential crisis for the European Union. These social transformations also had religious consequences, especially for the Catholic Church, with its male-dominated character and its staunch opposition to contraception and abortion. In a society marked by women's social emancipation, an institution that appears determined to resist that trend in every possible way is likely to be regarded as outmoded and unacceptably antimodern. When abuse scandals further suggest that that church tramples the interests of children as well as women, it is bound to become the target of pervasive hostility.

The End of the Chain

Declining religious participation coincides neatly with the trend to much smaller families, though we can argue about the exact relationship between empty pews and empty cradles. One recent study stresses the wide-ranging social effects of the decline in vocations, and especially the shrinking cohort of nuns. According to this argument, fewer school and parish activities, fewer social services, and less of a Catholic support network meant that young couples faced much higher "shadow costs" in child-raising, and most decided to limit their families. This approach is broadly convincing, although it is difficult to separate cause from effect in such matters.[42]

While the shrinking number of children reflected social change, it also had its own powerful impact on religious life and thought. Only by taking children out of the picture can we appreciate how much of the institutional life of any religion revolves around the young. At the height of the baby boom in the 1950s and 1960s, churches of all shades devoted immense effort to teaching and socializing the young, whether in Sunday schools or classes for first communion or confirmation. While teenagers and young adults might drift away from religious practice, they were likely to return when they had young families of their own, to whom they hoped to pass on values and a sense of community. When adults returned to church life, they judged religious institutions by the quality of their programs for the young.

But without the children, very different attitudes prevail. Imagine a region like the Italian province of Ferrara, which for most of the past century bustled with children. Since 1986, though, the birth rate has fallen below 0.9 in every year, with the consequence of closing schools and worryingly quiet streets. A priest who in the 1970s might have guided 1,200 children through the confirmation process in a year now deals with perhaps a tenth of that figure, with all the consequences for diminished family interest and involvement in the life of the local church. The linkage between low fertility and secularization is not perfect. Though Catholic loyalties still thrive in Poland and Slovakia (and clergy and nuns are both abundant), these countries are marked by characteristically low European birth rates. Yet in the absence of countervailing cultural and historical trends, religiosity often declines alongside family size.[43]

The absence of children has more subtle long-term consequences. George Weigel remarks on the striking European reluctance to discuss or acknowledge death and thus to explore its spiritual dimensions. Partly, this reflects a growing trend to medicalization, as people die in hospitals rather than at home, but German philosopher Rüdiger Safranski also stresses the role of low birth rates:

> In the past, it wasn't possible to ignore death. Living in large families meant that people learned to deal with death as a matter of course. An atomized society of singles, on the other hand, will suppress thoughts of death, and this will create an underlying sense of panic. All this results in a dramatic lack of maturity in the way people choose to live their lives. . . . for childless singles, thinking in terms of the generations to come loses relevance. Therefore, they behave more and more as if they were the last and see themselves as standing at the end of the chain.

Without a sense of the primary importance of continuity, whether of the family or the individual, people lose the need for a religious perspective.[44]

The Limits of Secularization

For the sake of argument, let us assume that secularization is indeed closely connected with social and economic modernization, and especially with the changes in gender attitudes wrought by those processes. From some perspectives at least, it is a deeply optimistic idea, since it assumes that recent immigrants, especially Muslims, will experience the same collapse of religious fervor when exposed to European culture and society, and that present signs of militancy or extremism represent a last-ditch effort to defend traditional religious systems that are already under siege. This is a critical conclusion for the fate of European Islam and, by implication, for the practice of Islam in the countries from which Europe's Muslims derive, in Pakistan and Turkey, Morocco and Algeria.

But are current theories of secularization correct? Interpretations that seem to work well in Europe perform abominably badly when tested in the United States. Claire Berlinski, for instance, uses a familiar secularization model to explain what she sees as the annihilation of European Christianity in modern times: "The rise of modern science facilitated the death of Christianity . . . by replacing religion as a framework to interpret human experience." But the obvious retort is to ask how the United States experienced the impact of modern science, not to mention very much the same range of social and economic forces, but with quite different outcomes. As conventionally stated, secularization theory provides only a part of a much more complex story.[45]

Following rapid industrialization, the United States experienced an early decline in its rural population, with the 1920 Census the first to show the urban population representing a majority. The United States has continued to thrive and innovate economically, usually far better than its European counterparts. In terms of overall wealth, measured by GDP per capita, Europeans are 25 percent worse off than Americans, and the gap is widening. By the same measure, a leading European nation like France is about as rich as one of the poorer American states, such as Alabama or Mississippi. And although they may fall short of European standards of comprehensive welfare provision, Americans can expect extensive public support in times of poverty, unemployment, or old age. In terms of gender equality, too, and the proportion of women in the workplace, the United States is comparable to the most developed nations of western Europe.

Particularly strange is the demographic divide. The United States experienced its own baby boom, of course, followed by a plunge in birth rates that between 1970 and 1985 actually left the country with lower fertility than western Europe, and with a relative dearth of children. Yet far from that decline being manifested in a collapse of religious loyalties, churches and religious institutions of all kinds flourished in these same years. Subsequently, despite all the factors apparently promoting small families, U.S. birth rates bounced back impressively in the 1990s, and have remained high. Today, the United States is one of the few nations in the world—not just among the advanced countries—to resist the trend to sharply falling fertility.

Whether we are measuring statistics for belief or attendance, religion does survive in the United States. Moreover, its strength is evident throughout the country, and not just in the red states of the South and Midwest, where Republican candidates dominated in the opening years of this century. European visitors are usually amazed not just by the public affirmations of faith in political life but by the evident signs of religious life—the abundance of active churches, the proliferation of new church buildings, and not least, the vast car-parks designed to accommodate legions of congregants. Of course, some American churches have floundered, and some Protestant mainline denominations may be entering terminal crisis. Yet decline in these groupings has been more than offset by the growth of other churches, often of more conservative and evangelical temperament. And many of the most successful new churches and denominations operate in areas of vigorous economic growth and innovation.

Roman Catholics present a surprising component of the story. After years of internal dissension in the church, largely involving debates over gender roles and sexuality, American Catholics were battered by the sexual abuse scandals that reached new heights with the revelations in the Boston Archdiocese in 2002. Yet even in such an atmosphere, the proportion of Catholics who report attending mass at least weekly held steady from 2000 through 2005, at a solid 33 percent. To say the least, the American model poses difficulties for secularization theory.

Free Markets

We have three ways of explaining the situation. Either Europe is following the natural path of secularization, from which the United States has deviated; or the United States represents a normal trajectory, while Europe is different; or else secularization theory itself is flawed. In explaining Europe's Exceptional Case, Grace Davie argues that Europeans have not so much accepted secularism en masse, but rather that their history has led them to see religious institutions almost as public utilities, to provide services as needed, rather than as in the United States, where believers see churches as voluntary associations demanding their support and participation.[46]

Even so, we must wonder why American and European trajectories should be so very different. Why would the United States be so conspicuously more actively religious than other nations, a fact noted by European observers since the earliest years of the Republic? In 1831, Alexis de Tocqueville remarked that "there is no country in the world where the Christian religion retains a greater influence over the souls of men than in America." De Tocqueville found part of the difference in the role of church establishment: Europeans created formal links between church and state, linking religious practice to political loyalty, while Americans separated church and state. "In Europe," he noted, "Christianity has been intimately united to the powers of the earth. Those powers are now in decay, and it is, as it were, buried under their ruins. The living body of religion has been bound down to the dead corpse of superannuated polity; cut but the bonds that restrain it, and it will rise once more."[47]

In modified form, many contemporary observers still see weight in this argument, believing that American religion flourishes in a free market environment that contrasts to the monopolistic character of European churches. According to this view, religious practice is highest in competitive situations, and weakens under the force of monopoly. The larger and more varied the supply available to fickle consumers, the higher is the demand. Some European nations did and do grant particular churches official status and a preferred role in public life, so that even the most liberal nations of northern Europe pursue practices utterly puzzling to Americans, such as collecting a church tax. And in some of these nations, especially in Protestant northern Europe, the decline of the state church seems closely linked to the near-collapse of institutional Christianity.[48]

Denmark offers a classic case study of the dead hand of monopoly: 83 percent of the population are nominally affiliated with the Lutheran state church, the Folkekirke or People's Church, but only 1 percent or 2 percent attend with any regularity. Meanwhile, church resources are overwhelmingly devoted to the upkeep of historic buildings and virtually nothing to education or evangelism. Many argue that the church tax itself discourages religious participation, since payers feel that they have already done enough for their religion and feel no need to attend services. Nor does the church care particularly about the beliefs of its clergy, or at least that was the lesson of a recent scandal in which pastor Thorkild Grosbøll kept his job after proclaiming his rejection of basically every Christian doctrine, including the existence of God and the Resurrection. In this instance at least, the state church monopoly looks like a recipe for the gradual uprooting of religious belief. One study of the church's role in Danish life is aptly titled *The Distant Church*, and the institution seems to recede further into the background with every passing year.[49]

Official monopoly, moreover, sometimes accompanies the active discouragement of rival churches that can provide alternative vehicles for those disenchanted with the official religious regime. Spain's Catholic Church long enforced its religious hegemony and made life difficult for Protestant rivals: under Franco, the official ideology, religious and political, was *Nacionalcatolicismo*. When Catholic practice declines, therefore, no other forms of Christianity are available to believers, who face the choice between official religion and no religion at all. In theory, at least, dissidents find secularism the only viable alternative.[50]

In other cases, though, we see the limitations of the free market argument. For one thing, the fact that a state church long succeeds in suppressing all rivals does not mean that such competitors cannot emerge quite successfully when that stranglehold is removed. Across Latin America, Catholic churches long exercised an official power quite comparable to their counterpart in Spain, yet this history has not prevented Pentecostal and evangelical churches from surging in popularity over the past thirty years. The question is not why Spaniards or Danes were unable to organize new churches beyond the establishment, but why they have not felt the need to do so. When we note that states with monopoly religions have low levels of religious observance, we should not confuse cause and consequence. Perhaps the religious monopoly just means that people have not felt the need to set up rival religious bodies.

In other European countries, too, religious establishment by no means implied monopoly, since granting legal privileges to one particular denomination does not mean that disaffected believers were not free to move to other denominations, or to create their own free market if they chose. In western Europe at least, it is some centuries since most states had the will or the ability to suppress religious dissidence outside the official establishment. In England or Wales, the established character of the Church of England meant that more radical Protestant groups such as Methodists, Presbyterians, and Baptists labored under some legal difficulties, but these Nonconformist sects still managed to flourish. From perhaps 1840 through 1960, the sects substantially out-numbered the official church population in industrial regions of the country, where they probably represented the Christian mainstream. England and Wales long offered an example of a competitive free mar-ket quite as vibrant as that of the United States. During the late twen-tieth century, though, these Nonconformist or Free Churches experi-enced a collapse in numbers at least as dramatic as that of the Anglican establishment.[51]

Ireland offers a still clearer example of the chasm separating the legal fact of establishment from the creation of a working monopoly. From the sixteenth century through the nineteenth, the legally estab-lished church of Ireland was the Protestant Anglican body associated with the British Crown. Only in the 1860s did the government give up the shallow pretence that this body was anything other than an elite minority denomination massively outnumbered by the Catholic pres-ence. In France, the obviously powerful Roman Catholic Church was not established, and at various times in the twentieth century it was in acute conflict with the secular regime.[52]

Elsewhere, we find strong evidence of thriving religious practice in countries where churches enjoy near-monopoly status. Ireland again offers a convincing example of a church near-monopoly on religious life, and as we have seen, for all its recent difficulties, the Catholic Church still maintains a hold over a large section of the population. In Poland too, a nonestablished church holds the loyalty of the over-whelming body of the people, and by any statistical measure, religious life flourishes. Consumers freely exercise their power of choice, but they do so by attending different churches or parishes of the one Catholic entity. Whether legally enforced or not, neither legal estab-lishment nor monopoly status does much to explain the relative weak-ness of organized Christianity in much of modern Europe.

Religion and Mobility

We must then look elsewhere for the dramatic and continuing differ-ences in religious behavior that separate modern Europe and the United States. One distinguishing feature is America's constant history of immigration, and the ethnic diversification that accumulates over time. When people move to a new country, they form institutions that allow them to combine together for mutual support and to help them share and transmit the values of their familiar societies. Commonly, the most important such institutions have been religious, whether churches, synagogues, or mosques. Through American history, succes-sive waves of immigration have produced many new denominations, which at least for the early generations are closely linked to national or ethnic loyalties. As Martin Marty famously remarked, ethnicity is the skeleton of American religion.[53]

Also, involvement in migrant churches produces a much greater degree of active religiosity than was common in the home country. This was true, for instance, of Italian-Catholic migrants to the United States during the early twentieth century, who came from societies with a lively streak of anti-clericalism, and in which religious life was often assumed to be a female preserve. On American soil, however, Catholic practice and identity both grew more intense. Among modern Latino immigrants likewise, the journey from Central America to El Norte produces much greater religious interest and involvement than is customary at home, and the new enthusiasm resonates through both Catholic and Protestant congregations. Of course, international population movements have also occurred in European history, in terms of both labor migration and political exile, but until modern times the continent has known nothing to compare with the constant infusions of new stock that have marked the United States.

Within the United States too, domestic mobility has been much greater than in Europe. Throughout American history, people have moved far and often, to the point that late twentieth-century families were quite likely to uproot and move their homes every few years. Moreover, such movements have occurred over a much larger geographical area than is common in Europe, and this would be the appropriate place to point out the very different geographical scale of the two regions under discussion, a theme to which we will return on several occasions.

As a country, the United States is far larger than any European nation. If we take the eight European nations with the largest land areas (France, Spain, Sweden, Germany, Poland, Norway, Italy, Great Britain), then their combined physical size is still less than a third that of the United States. Britain covers about the same land area as Oregon, Italy as Arizona; Belgium is about the size of Maryland. The United States is a nation; it is also a subcontinent. An American who travels from New York City to Dallas has traversed 1,600 miles but remains entirely within a single nation throughout the trip. A European who travels a like distance has gone from London to Moscow, perhaps, or to Istanbul; or has gone from Stockholm to the far south of Sicily. In the process, our European traveler has passed through or over several different nations, cultures, and language zones. Traveling from New York City to Phoenix covers 2,500 miles of United States territory. A comparable journey within the Old World would take a traveler from London beyond the confines of Europe altogether, into Kazakhstan or Iraq, or to the legendary African city of Timbuktu.

The difference in geographical size has many implications, but let us just consider the consequences for internal migration. A German or a British person who relocates to the far distant end of his or her own country has usually traveled at most a few hundred miles, while a move of comparable distance within the United States might well leave a family within the same state. Even before the advent of modern air travel, a migrating European was thus likely to maintain touch with his or her roots, unlike an American counterpart who moved, say, from the East Coast to the West Coast. In the United States, therefore, frequent movement and internal migration are more likely to leave individuals cut off from their homes and familiar social networks, driving them to seek new networks and forms of instant community. Often, the best and easiest place to find such interaction is within a hospitable church in a well-known denomination, a singularly attractive setting for young families with children. A society marked by constant movement, by frequent uprooting and replanting, by ever-growing cultural diversity is more accustomed to seek the institutional support of religious bodies, and also to accept the spiritual ideas presented in that environment. Attendance at these institutions thrives, even as styles of belief and practice increasingly accommodate to the standards of the wider society and as denominational distinctions fade steadily. Secularization theory does work in general, but other factors can counterbalance it.

While such social factors do not necessarily offer a complete explanation of Euro-American differences, they are suggestive. They also have implications for projecting the likely religious coloring of a Europe that has in recent decades accepted non-European migrants on an unprecedented scale. Powerful social pressures drive migrant communities to conform to European secular norms. The most potent of all concern gender roles and concepts of family, with birth rates and numbers of children as a vital index of assimilation to European societies. At the same time, though, constant infusions of new stock help make mosques, churches, and temples the critical centers for immigrant religious life, promoting a sense of community and ethnic identification. Thus Turks in Germany or Moroccans in Sweden are likely to attend mosques, much more so perhaps than they might have done in their home countries. Continuing immigration and extensive cross-border movement do not defeat the process of secularization but might well slow or modify it. Ethnicity might yet become the skeleton of European religion.

Not even the most optimistic observer could pretend that European Christianity is in a healthy state, whether in comparison with global South societies, or with that great transatlantic anomaly, the

United States. But institutional weakness is not necessarily the same as total religious apathy, and among all the grim statistics, there are some surprising signs of life. European Christians, after all, have the longest experience of living in a secular environment, and some at least attempt quite successfully to evolve religious structures far removed from the older assumptions of Christendom. Contrary to widespread assumptions, then, rising Islam will not be expanding into an ideological or religious vacuum.

3

Faith Among
the Ruins

The mass Church may be something lovely, but it is not necessarily the Church's only way of being.

Pope Benedict XVI

The divine demolition of any Church means that every Church arises as a signpost, threshold, and door of hope. . . . Broken, the Church can bear its message with its head erect, for the Gospel belongs to the Church that is lost.

Karl Barth

To overcome the many restrictions that limit their activities on the Sabbath, observant Jews sometimes construct a symbolic boundary called an eruv, which might cover a few blocks or indeed a whole community. Space within this area is legally defined as equivalent to the home, so that people can travel and undertake tasks that they could not properly do in public space. Historically, the presence of an eruv marks a Jewish community that is both sizable and tradition-minded, which makes it all the remarkable that only as recently as 2002 did London, with its lengthy Jewish history, first acquire such a boundary, stretching over an eleven-mile perimeter. That is, the eruv arrived not in 1902, when tens of thousands of unassimilated Jews had only just arrived from the shtetls of eastern Europe, nor in 1952, when English Judaism was flourishing and self-confident, but at a time when a much-shrunken Jewish community was heavily secularized. Indeed, the most vocal opponents of the eruv scheme were themselves Jews, who denounced the plan as medieval and segregationist: they had no wish to designate a ghetto, still less to live in one. Whatever the merits of the case, though, the eruv debate does symbolize one potent theme in contemporary European religion, namely, the growth of smaller and more traditional-minded groups—in this case, Orthodox Jews—amidst the prevailing secularism.[1]

A similar pattern is evident in Europe's much larger Christian communities. Undeniably, trends in secular society have hit church institutions hard. Far from Christianity having vanished, though, religious belief is still an important force for many old-stock Europeans, though expressed with less public fervor than in the United States. We see many signs of the latent power of faith, of a persistent undercurrent of spirituality, which manifests in surprisingly medieval forms of devotion, including pilgrimage and the veneration of saints.

Some believers actually find the eclipse of comprehensive national churches to be a positive feature. In a minority setting, Christianity can restructure itself to serve the needs of a new society, demanding more commitment and involvement in some areas of life while acknowledging greater flexibility in others. For our present story, this continuing life matters because as European governments try to accommodate the needs of rising Islam, they will also, still, have to consider a Christianity that is now the other component in a multifaith society.

Counting Christians

As we have seen, some commentators come close to suggesting that Europe has already suffered total and sweeping dechristianization, a "death of Christianity." Claire Berlinski claims that "Europe has in the past several centuries seen a complete—*really* complete—loss of belief in any form of religious belief, personal immortality or salvation." This is a gross exaggeration, and however broadly we define the term, Europe is still home to a large number of people described as Christians. As of 2005, the World Christian Database still recorded a European Christian population of 531 million (including Russia). This is down marginally from the 1970 figure, but still constitutes the largest geographical component of the religion. As we have seen, in terms of practice or actual commitment, that is a very optimistic figure, but even if we demand stricter criteria for imposing the Christian label, Europe still has a solid minority of committed believing Christians. Some 60 million to 70 million west European Christians assert that religion plays a very important part of their lives, and many of those attend church regularly. If commentators worry that the presence of some 15 million Muslims in the same nations portends the imminent conquest of Europe, it is curious that more attention is not paid to a Christian phalanx several times larger.[2]

Some countries are far more secular than others, and Greece stands at the opposite end of the spectrum. The Constitution recognizes the special role of the Orthodox Church that nominally holds the allegiance of 98 percent of the population, and the government pays clergy salaries. Eighty-one percent of Greeks acknowledge the existence of God, against only 3 percent atheists. The church has also done an effective job of guarding its interests against potential rivals. Religious proselytism is illegal, and plans to erect a mosque in Athens have been moving slowly since discussions began in 1939. Even Greece's quite radical socialist and leftist parties see little practical chance of separating church and state. In practice, likewise, Portugal pays little attention to official separation, and bishops and clergy regularly participate in public ceremonies.[3]

The New Europe of the former Soviet bloc includes other areas of continuing Christian strength, notably in Poland. Though the Catholic Church here suffered some decline after the fall of communism, it has since rebounded. The number studying for the priesthood grew from 4,500 in 1998 to 7,000 in 2005, and great seminaries like Krakow's are as packed as those of western Europe were before Vatican II. In Poland, the rate of seminarians to ordained priests is 22.5, meaning that the church has an excellent prospect of maintaining priestly numbers into the foreseeable future, and indeed of expanding. The comparable U.S. rate is 10 seminarians per priest; however, Polish seminarians are virtually all of Polish stock, whereas the U.S. figure now includes many foreign born. The rate for Italy is 11.6, for France 5.6, and for Ireland 3.6. Polish monastic life still flourishes, with 1,845 monks and 23,000 nuns. Regular attendance at religious services is reported by 78 percent of Poles, and around a third attend Catholic services weekly. Enduring Polish piety is in evidence during great holidays like All Souls Day, when millions travel to visit the graves of their forebears. Here, at least, individuals show no obvious sense of standing at the end of the biological chain.[4]

As Andrew Greeley remarks, Europe's religious picture is by no means uniform. In recent decades, he suggests, "religion declined abruptly in England and the Netherlands. It is stagnant in West Germany, and it is flourishing in Poland, Slovakia, and Slovenia." Slovakia records 50 percent regular attendance, comparable to the Irish or Austrian figures. Perhaps such nations are on the verge of rapid secularization on the west European model, but they are not there yet. Now, we can dispute the significance of such regional variations. Despite its large population, Poland does not and never will have an influence within Europe or the world comparable to the influence of Germany, Britain, or the Netherlands, which are the lands where the vital cultural and religious conflicts will be decided. Greece, Slovakia, or Slovenia are of course still more marginal. But Greeley's fundamental point is well taken: "Religion is always declining and always reviving."[5]

The continuing health of east European churches has a direct impact on the West because of the westward migration of labor as the

European Union has expanded over the past decade. In theory, united
Europe is pledged to the free movement of labor, but many governments have placed limitations in the way of cheap Eastern labor—the
"Polish plumber" who represents such a nightmare figure for French
labor unions. Some countries however, especially Britain, have been
far more welcoming, and the religious consequences have been dramatic. Including earlier waves of migrants, Britain is now home to at
least 750,000 Poles, possibly a million, so that Poles now outnumber
Britain's Pakistanis. Polish migrants, like Pakistanis, are also disproportionately young, with some 83 percent under thirty-four years of age.
By some estimates, the greater London area has perhaps a million east
Europeans, legals and illegals. Many are Catholic, and Britain now has
a network of Croatian Catholic churches, but the Polish influence is by
far the most marked: 82 of Britain's Catholic churches serve Polish
communities, and the new demand has overwhelmed them. In the
words of one London parishioner, "We used to celebrate mass three
times on a Sunday, and we were never full. Now we have six or eight
services every Sunday and people are standing outside in the street."
Ireland now has more speakers of Polish than Gaelic.[6]

Recognizing the global opportunities, Polish dioceses and seminaries
are exporting priests in large numbers, making a special point of teaching them the English language they will need to evangelize Britain or
Ireland. Poland in the twenty-first century seems poised to fulfill the
role in the global Catholic Church that Ireland did a century ago.[7]

Saving the West

In western Europe too, some incidents suggest that Christianity is less
moribund than the formal statistics might suggest. While a battery of
numbers points to the institutional decline of European Catholicism,
those do not necessarily indicate an uprooting of faith. Among Italians,
88 percent claim to be Catholic, though around two-thirds disagree
with official church positions on assisted fertility and divorce. And
even when people quarrel with the church, and attack the hierarchy
bitterly, it is curious that so many feel the need to retain the Catholic
definition and to struggle to change the church according to their vision. In Spain, where overt participation in church activities has declined so steeply, dissidents are passionately committed to opposition
networks like the libertarian and feminist Somos Iglesia, We Are
Church.[8]

We might draw an American analogy. Vocations to the U.S.
Catholic priesthood have also shriveled in recent decades, as have the
numbers of religious, and the average age of remaining clergy has risen
sharply. Millions of lay Catholics are unwilling to accept the Church's
moral teachings on a host of issues—above all, contraception. But the

shortage of parish priests has not, at least yet, destroyed Catholic loyalties, and millions of Catholics attend mass regularly. In Europe too, parishes have learned to cope with only occasional visits from priests, as they develop a new emphasis on lay leadership and participation, often by women. Declining numbers of priests are offset by an impressive growth among permanent deacons and catechists, who are not bound by vows of celibacy. Services without priests look Protestant in their character, though they conclude with the distribution of hosts consecrated previously. Irish Archbishop Diarmuid Martin has experimented with creating parish councils staffed by the laity, a device viewed suspiciously by traditional-minded priests. While such alternatives may not satisfy everyone, they fall a long way short of the extinction of Christianity.[9]

Within particular countries, we find regions moving at very different paces. In Bavaria, at least a superficial observation suggests that Catholicism is thriving much as it ever has. Priests and nuns are regularly seen in the streets, and the astonishing Rococo churches still contain sizable arrays of photographs of the children about to take first communion. While attendance statistics indicate grave decline even in this once very Catholic land, the remnants of faith are still unavoidable.

Elsewhere too, spectacular public events based on religion, and specifically on papal pageantry, have drawn forth astonishing displays of enthusiasm and (apparently) devotion, especially among those teenagers and young adults who long seemed to have dropped off the religious map. Pope John Paul II's visits to European cities drew vast crowds, while his death and funeral in 2005 evoked enormous interest and grief. While Berlinski sees in such an event an outbreak of atavism, Grace Davie writes more plausibly that the reaction to John Paul's death "exposes the fragility of European secularism."[10]

One might attribute that response to the superstar celebrity image attached to that pope, even as his physical health decayed, but his less charismatic successor also attracted a dedicated following. This was all the more striking since he was so demonized as a bitter foe of radicalism and feminism. Later in 2005,

> a sea of 150,000 people [is] waiting in St. Peter's Square for Pope Benedict XVI to appear at a special celebration for Catholic children who have made their first communion in the past year. Rock bands and kids' choirs entertain the faithful until a roar sweeps through the crowd at the first sighting of the Popemobile, carrying the waving, white-robed Benedict down barricaded lanes through the throng. The crowd goes wild.[11]

In Spain in 2006, a million turned out in Valencia to see Pope Benedict. Arguably, this enthusiasm reflects not the charisma of any one individual but the widespread need that many feel for a visible, tangible symbol of religious feelings. Leadership is a function of followership.

The Golden Age of Pilgrimage

The continuing popularity of pilgrimages also refutes simple claims that European Christianity is dead. Now, critics might question the kind of faith that such pilgrimages demonstrate, and both Protestants and many liberal Catholics are nervous about the theological content of a Marian healing shrine. But if we regard the pilgrimages to Mecca or Varanasi as symbols of the passionate faith of Muslims or Hindus, then we should treat Christian expressions with equal respect.

The world's largest Marian shrine is Guadalupe in Mexico, which attracts 10 million visitors a year, and 6 million visit Brazil's church of Our Lady of Aparecida. But Europe is still home to several thriving centers that draw pilgrims on a near-Latino scale, and over the past half century, those numbers have grown substantially. Partly this reflects greater ease of travel in the modern world, but the demand is also there, sufficiently so in fact to make the early twenty-first century a glorious era for European pilgrimage. Perhaps Catholic believers are seeking here the kind of religious expression that they would previously have found in their parish churches, a sense of mystery and spiritual power that became scarcer after the reforms of the second Vatican Council. Lourdes, for instance, drew about a million each year in the 1950s, before the Council. That number is now closer to 6 million annually, and 50,000 might pass through even on a quiet day.[12]

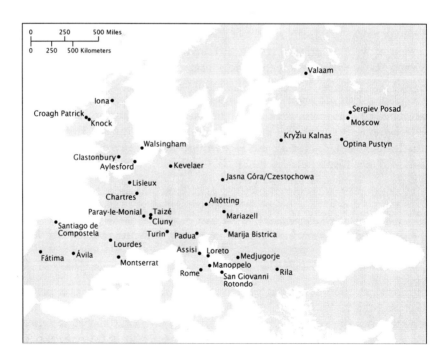

Faith Among the Ruins*61*

While estimates vary, Europe's second most visited shrine is Poland's Jasna Góra, in Czestochowa, which attracts 4 or 5 million, with a heavy youth representation. They come to see a miraculous picture of the Virgin, supposedly drawn from life by St. Luke the Evangelist. Each year, 6 million Poles, or 15 percent of the population, make a pilgrimage to some site. But shrines flourish in every nation of what can still, without irony, be described as Catholic Europe. Though Czestochowa has the most celebrated Black Madonna, Europe as a whole has probably five hundred other images of the black Virgin, and many are venerated at active pilgrimage sites. Among the best-loved of these, Bavaria has Altötting, Croatia boasts Marija Bistrica, and Spain has Montserrat (though separatist-minded Catalans insist it is theirs rather than Spain's). Other popular Marian sites include Portugal's Fátima, with a reported 4 million visitors annually, while a papal visit in 1983 revived Austria's chief Marian center, at Mariazell. John Paul's visit to Croatia in 1998 also helped restore the popularity of Marija Bistrica.

Besides the Virgin Mary, many other saints attract the faithful, at Lisieux in France, or Ávila in Spain. Just since the late 1980s, pilgrimage has enjoyed a breathtaking revival at Santiago de Compostela, which now attracts some half a million pilgrims in a regular year, rising to a million in special holy years. Shrine-rich Italy draws many pilgrims, though in a place like Rome or Assisi, it is difficult to distinguish between pilgrims and tourists. But for whatever reasons, millions each year visit the Holy House of Loreto or the tomb of St. Anthony of Padua. When the Shroud of Turin was exhibited publicly in 2000, all the accumulated scientific doubts about the relic's authenticity did not prevent the attendance exceeding a million.[13]

Ireland too has its sacred landscapes. The most spectacular site is the mountain shrine of Croagh Patrick, which each year draws a million or so people, many dedicated enough to complete the arduous climb to the rocky summit. On Reek Sunday each July, 25,000 pilgrims climb the mountain, many barefoot. Nearby in county Mayo, the Marian shrine of Knock has grown enormously since John Paul II visited in 1979, and now has one and a quarter million pilgrims each year. So common is pilgrimage that few trouble to count the tens of thousands each year that attend healing shrines of merely local significance, like the Italian church of Sarsina where pilgrims seek blessing by having the iron collar of St. Vicinus clamped around their necks.[14]

From a different theological tradition, we also find the monastic center of Taizé in France, famous since the 1950s for its meditative hymns and devotions, and its ecumenical mission. Though founded as a monastery in the Catholic tradition, it appealed at least as strongly to Protestants and Anglicans, who saw in it a revival of the church's ancient contemplative work. After the death of its founder in 2005, Taizé devotees discovered with some embarrassment that since the 1970s, founder

Brother Roger had been in communion with Rome, raising charges that the monastery had served as an ecclesiastical Trojan horse. Whatever the controversies, though, Taizé's retreat center hosts several thousand young people each week, a number that has tripled since the early 1990s, and Eastern Europe contingents account for much of that growth. Every summer, 100,000 people, again overwhelmingly teenagers or young adults, attend for a weeklong sampling of Taizé spirituality.[15]

The Taizé story reminds us how new some of the most popular shrines are, however ready some might be to characterize the mind-set they represent as "medieval." Some east European pilgrimage sites boomed under communist rule, when they offered a form of clandestine resistance to official repression. In the nineteenth century, Lithuanians began the custom of erecting crosses on the Hill of Crosses, *Kryžiu Kalnas*, near Vilnius. These symbols flourished under Soviet rule, and the harder the authorities tried to sweep them away, the more devotedly people set up thousands of new crosses, until eventually, in the 1980s, the government acknowledged failure. By now, the total of crosses large and small runs into the tens of thousands. Under the patronage of John Paul II, the Hill reinforced its position as a shrine of nationhood as well as Catholic devotion, and a center of pilgrimage. Other new shrines have also developed. Just since 1981, the village of Medjugorje in Bosnia-Herzegovina has enjoyed European celebrity for the apparitions of the Virgin and for the words of counsel that she reportedly addresses to the faithful. By some accounts, Medjugorje has attracted 30 million visitors in this relatively short period. Also in response to John Paul's efforts, at least a million people each year, chiefly Europeans, now visit the alleged site of the Virgin's house in Ephesus, in Turkey. (The shrine is also popular with Muslim visitors.)[16]

Among Orthodox churches too, the revival of monasticism since the fall of communism has led to a reestablishment of ancient shrines that once more draw large numbers of pilgrims. Such once great landmarks of Russian Christianity as Sergiev Posad and Valaam are flourishing anew, offering spiritual direction to seekers. So is Optina Pustyn, which in its day welcomed Tolstoy and Dostoevsky. In 2006, many thousands of Russians stood in line to visit the relic of the hand of John the Baptist, which had been removed from the country during the 1917 revolution but was once more on display in Moscow's Cathedral of Christ the Savior. Symbolizing the resurrection of Russian Christianity, the cathedral itself had been demolished in 1931 but was wholly rebuilt in the 1990s. Bulgaria's national shrine is the ancient monastery of Rila, which a million now visit each year to engage in the distinctly unsecular pursuits of venerating relics and seeking healing. Across Russia and eastern Europe too, the end of communism coincided with a renewed interest in painting icons, a devotion that seems set for a potent revival.[17]

The wide geographical spread of these pilgrimage sites is important. If the boom was occurring only at Jasna Góra, say, then it would be easy to dismiss that as "just a Polish thing," an obstinate refusal to march with the times; or the Irish or Italians or Russians could be seen as equally stubborn and antimodern. But we are dealing with a broader phenomenon, which extends into the continent's supposedly secular heart. That at least is the impression we get from the Marian shrine of Kevelaer on the German-Dutch frontier, which draws 800,000 visitors a year. To use a cliché, many Europeans evidently are searching for something, and they are doing so in larger numbers than their American counterparts. Though the United States has great shrines like Chimayo and Emmitsburg, the number of visitors falls far short of what we find at the great European centers.

We cannot simply gauge the popularity of pilgrimage just by adding together the visitors to various shrines, since there would be so much overlap: today, as in the era of the *Canterbury Tales,* some people are serial pilgrims. Also, many visitors to European shrines might well come from elsewhere, from North or South America. But the overall numbers are significant, as we can see if we apply an inter-religious perspective. At some point in coming decades, Muslims will almost certainly develop pilgrimage sites in Europe, probably at the tomb of some famous sage or holy person. Making this very likely, most European Muslims come from north African or south Asian societies in which such veneration of shrines is a standard expression of faith. Such a trend would be very important, in marking the recognition of sacred space on European territory, and it would be decisive evidence that Muslims were now firmly at home on the continent. Conceivably, this site—in Leeds, perhaps, or Lyon—could become popular enough to draw hundreds of thousands each year; and the media will use images of that flourishing pilgrimage to demonstrate the strength of European Islam, and even the Islamization of Europe. Very rarely, though, do the now-regular media reports of the pathetic state of European Christianity use the dramatic footage that they could choose of the vast and still growing crowds at Christian shrines, presumably because it so contradicts the image they want to project of the death of that religion.

Believing and Belonging

Besides the hard core of acknowledged believers, millions more who might not set foot inside a church except for baptisms, weddings, and funerals definitely refer to themselves as Christian (see Table 3.1). Even in England, 72 percent describe themselves to census-takers as Christian, an impressive 35 million people. The European Values Survey shows quite high levels of acceptance of supernatural belief among those who are barely affiliated with any Christian denomination, and

Table 3.1 Religions in England, 2001 Census

Religion	Number	Percentage
Christian	35,251,244	71.7
Muslim	1,524,887	3.1
Hindu	546,982	1.1
Sikh	327,343	0.7
Jewish	257,671	0.5
Buddhist	139,046	0.3
Any other religion	143,811	0.3
No religion	7,171,332	14.6
Religion not stated	3,776,515	7.7
TOTAL	49,138,831	

Note: These figures refer only to England, whereas other statistics cited here describe conditions in Great Britain.

that is true for Protestant as well as Catholic countries. Moreover, these beliefs include not just generic acceptance of the idea of God but also of more specific beliefs such as sin, judgment, and the afterlife: 46 percent of Europeans believe in Heaven, 34 percent in Hell. We might be tempted to dismiss the faith of such nominal Christians as a matter of sentiment, a fossil of traditional faith, but even if that is true, Europe is presently home to several hundred million "cultural Christians."[18]

Grace Davie stresses that falling levels of observance and church attendance cannot simply be equated with pure secularism, suggesting instead that people are "believing without belonging." Presently, strict secularism is very advanced among cultural and political elites, but has not yet made enormous inroads among ordinary people. Davie argues that the Christian presence still survives through social memory. This is all the more potent in cities and small towns that still retain the Christian imprint on every street, every Heiligegeiststrasse (Holy Spirit Street) and Paternoster Row, and in which the whole urban plan is still shaped by parish boundaries. Neither God nor the church is easy to miss. You know when you have arrived in Catholic Bavaria or Austria when people start greeting you with Grüss Gott (Greet God, or originally "God guard you"), rather than the coldly secular Guten Tag, which sounds so *German*. Europe's cultural Christians are "content to let both churches and churchgoers enact a memory on their behalf," secure in the knowledge that Christianity is there if and when they need it. The churches represent accumulated capital that can be drawn on as needed. In this comfortable and nondemanding sense, most do still define themselves, however vestigially, as Christians.[19]

Even in the most apparently secular countries, Christian customs are surprisingly evident. In Norway, typically, confirmation in church is an almost universal rite of passage, which is also followed by 80 percent of Danes—though the amount of preparatory religious instruction is close to nonexistent. In most of Europe too, Christianity also still dominates the round of the year. Catholic countries are famous for their proliferation of saints' days and religious-based public holidays, when work shuts down entirely. Apart from the Christmas and Easter season, Italians observe All Saints and the Marian holidays of the Assumption and the Immaculate Conception. Yet even the holiday calendar of Protestant Denmark includes three weekdays around Easter, three for Christmas, and two for Pentecost, as well as Ascension and Common Prayer Day (*Store Bededag*). Also in Denmark, all forms of print media have suffered a sharp decline in recent years, the only exceptions being the business newspaper, *Borsen*, and the *Christian Daily*, *Kristeligt Dagblad*. Though the *Christian Daily* has only 100,000 readers, that number has grown impressively just since 2000.[20]

However diluted the Protestantism of Scandinavia, thoughtful observers suggest that it means more than simply going through the ecclesiastical motions (and even that on rare occasions). In this view, Christian practice has declined there not because it is irrelevant but precisely because the norms and values of the faith have become so inextricably part of social consciousness. Living in a society that tries to achieve the Christian social vision—through a generous welfare state, care for the poor, and wide-ranging humanitarian ventures overseas—one no longer needs to participate in public rituals. However skeptical other Christians would be of such claims, they do reflect a perception of how thoroughly Christian values have penetrated European thought, and formed cultural identity. Being Danish or Norwegian means defining oneself as Christian in that particular mode, just as Catholicism is intertwined with Italian or Bavarian identity.[21]

The strength of latent Christianity can be seen in the surges of formal religious activity that occur sporadically even in the most notionally secular regions. In Britain, an opinion survey in 2001 found that just 33 percent of adults attended a church service during the Christmas season, admittedly a minimal sign of Christian commitment. Since that point, however, the figure has grown, to reach 43 percent in 2005. Without longer-term comparisons, it is difficult to make too much of this fact, but one possibility is that a vague interest in Christianity has become somewhat more explicit as a result of growing world tensions since 9/11, and the open discussion of religious conflicts and rivalries. In 2005, the German Protestant Convention in Hannover attracted a record crowd of 400,000, under a convention poster that proclaimed, aptly, "It's good to have answers." The Italian church recorded a sudden and quite unexpected surge in the number of young women entering convents, from 350 in 2003 to 550 in 2005.[22]

Reinforcing the power of cultural Christianity is the widespread presence of religious-oriented institutions that in the United States would be purely secular, above all in the educational system. Indeed, if American activists proposed the degree of state/church involvement and overlap that is common in Europe, they would be accused of preaching theocracy. When the Catholic Church recently restored the historic Dom (cathedral) in Freising, the ancient heart of Bavarian Christianity, there was never a moment's doubt that the state of Bavaria would spend lavishly on the project, using taxpayers' money. The lack of separation between church and state is also evident in schools. In Ireland, 95 percent of elementary schools are state-funded, though run by Catholic authorities. That could be regarded as a survival of the long Catholic dominance, which might well perish shortly, but other more secular nations also mix church and state quite happily. In Italy, where the state pays teachers of Catholic catechism in public schools, a recent official commission to draft rules of conduct for teachers was under the honorary chairmanship of a Catholic cardinal.[23]

Britain, too, has a long tradition of state funding of faith-based schools. There are currently 600 such secondary schools and 6,400 primary schools, the vast majority of them Christian (Jews, Muslims, and Sikhs account for just fifty "faith schools" in all). Anglican and Catholic schools, which account for the vast majority of places, currently educate 1.7 million pupils. Often, these schools represent a very desirable alternative to state-run community schools, and middle-class parents make an effort to participate in church activities in order to qualify their children for admission. One recent survey found broad support for the schools operated by the Church of England, with over half of those of no religious faith believing that the schools played a positive role. Over 60 percent of non-Christian respondents agreed, including many Muslims, who liked the schools for their stronger commitment to discipline. The overt religious content of Christian schools might well be slim in comparison with bygone eras, but at least Christianity remains part of the cultural landscape. As in the United States, moreover, religious-based charities still provide a vast range of social services across Europe, and the overwhelming majority are Christian in their orientation.[24]

Now, such evidence for "latent faith" does not necessarily offer comfort for Christians in the longer term, as it is not clear how many decades cultural memories can survive. Residual Christianity may be in reasonable health a generation or so after institutional structures went into free fall, but the situation in thirty or forty years could be very different. We might presently be seeing only a transitional phase in religious decline, on the path from active affiliation to total indifference. Still, the picture of sudden Christian decline is more complex than it initially appears.

Not Dead Yet

In some parts of Europe, Christian and particularly Catholic politics retain their strength. In Poland, not surprisingly, conservative Catholic parties still do well. The winner of the 2006 presidential election was Lech Kaczyński, an opponent of abortion and same-sex marriage, while some influential voices adopt a still harder line. In recent years, issues of church and state have focused on the popular station Radio Maryja (Mary), which was founded by a Redemptorist priest. The station is anti-European, xenophobic, and conspiracy minded, and has supported far-right political parties; it also flirts with anti-Semitism, denouncing the "Holocaust Industry." As it claims to offer a distinctively Catholic voice, the station embarrasses both the Polish hierarchy and the Vatican, which have tried to suppress it, but Radio Maryja has powerful friends in government. The story demonstrates the survival of old-style reactionary church politics at least in corners of Europe.[25]

The strength of orthodox Catholic positions in some European nations poses real problems for the leadership of the European Union, which views abortion and gay rights as unassailable components of fundamental human rights. Neither right, though, has anything like mainstream status in the still Catholic lands, and members of a Polish party created consternation when they mounted a pro-life exhibit at the European Parliament in Strasbourg. Infuriating observers, the display explicitly compared abortion to Nazi war crimes. Legal strains between the Union and its Catholic members threaten to cause serious constitutional tensions. In 2006, a concordat between Slovakia and the Vatican attempted to give Catholic employees a conscience exemption to prevent them participating in abortions and certain fertility treatments that violated Catholic doctrine. The agreement drew down the anger of the European Commission, which warned Slovakia that it was violating its obligations to European concepts of basic rights. Recently too, the European Parliament resolved that all member states should revise their national laws to treat same-sex unions on the same terms as traditional families. The decision drew forth instant condemnation from the Vatican, and that response was echoed in several east European nations. Croatian Catholics, too, resist secularizing trends. Since 2003, church leaders have blocked the introduction of sex education classes in the public schools, where such teaching would promote condom use.[26]

In western Europe too, Christianity retains a surprising influence in public policy even in nations where belief and church attendance are in decline. As we have seen, the steady march of gay marriage laws suggests a near collapse of the political power of the churches, though such changes have not occurred without fervent efforts at resistance. In Ireland as recently as 1995, a referendum on the question of legalizing divorce still showed 49.72 percent opposed to even this reform. In

Spain too, movements to legalize gay marriage have been met by sizable popular demonstrations, organized by a weakened but still combative Catholic Church.[27]

In this instance, religious conservatives have shown themselves very much in the minority, but conservatives have won victories. In 2005, a church-sponsored campaign persuaded enough Italians to stay home to invalidate a referendum permitting greater latitude in embryonic research and artificial insemination. Even in matters of abortion, liberal assumptions have gained rather less than a sweeping victory. Abortion was legalized in the predominantly Protestant nations of northern Europe in the 1960s and has gradually become more easily available in Catholic lands. Italy legalized abortion in 1978, and that law survived challenge in a national referendum in 1981. These two events are commonly taken as marking a decisive defeat for the once invincible power of the Catholic Church in that nation.

Yet Europe's abortion laws have developed rather differently than in the United States, and in many ways are more restrictive. While many nations make abortion available virtually on demand through the end of the first trimester, very few are anything like as liberal as the United States in terms of later-term abortions. Also, attitudes to abortion appear to be becoming more restrictive. While abortion remains strictly forbidden in only a few nations (Poland, Ireland, Portugal), other countries are debating new restrictions or have limited payment for abortion and contraception under national health systems. When Britain legalized abortion in 1967, the limit for termination was set at twenty-eight weeks, which was subsequently trimmed to twenty-four, and may soon be further restricted to twenty or twenty-two.[28]

In themselves, abortion rates do not necessarily reveal much about attitudes, since low abortion figures in a particular society might just indicate that women have excellent access to contraception. But comparisons are interesting. In the United States, abortion terminates about 24 percent of pregnancies, which is somewhat higher than the figures for the United Kingdom (22 percent) or France (21). These are however much higher than the percentages for Germany (15) or the liberal Netherlands (13).

The rather different attitudes to gay marriage and abortion offer a significant commentary on the proper scope of religion in legislation. In the case of gay marriage, few cultural Christians see any obstacle to consenting adults pursuing their own moral decisions in ways that do not harm others. In the realm of abortion, though, there is a greater acceptance of the conservative Christian and specifically Catholic view that abortion does claim a victim in the form of the unborn child, a perception that becomes much stronger in later-term pregnancies. Restrictions are therefore appropriate in such cases.

Monopoly and Minority

In surprising ways, Christianity continues as a ghostly presence even in secular environments. Some intriguing signs also suggest how churches might have learned to accommodate themselves to the world of post-Christendom, with its very different social and moral assumptions. They are coming to appreciate the positive virtues of minority status.

The idea of a state church has always contained within itself a fundamental contradiction. Notionally, such a church tries to serve the needs of everyone within a community, and in practice the church has to accommodate political realities: at its worst, the situation forces churches to offer a faith that appeals to the lowest common denominator. At the same time though, Christianity preaches demanding calls for spirituality and personal morality, and the gospels teach counsels of perfection that seem directed to a rigorous minority.

Throughout European history, state churches have produced dissidents who try to stress the stricter Christian ideals, either by imagining a revolution within the state mechanism, or else by defecting to a new autonomous structure. Either way, it was essential to challenge the link with a stultifying secular authority. The English church of the seventeenth century produced its separatist Puritans and the German Lutherans spawned the Pietist movement. Under Pietist influence, the British Methodist movement created a cell-structure of more committed believers within the established church, groups that met to share and reinforce each other's faith, and ultimately, this alternative movement evolved to become a fully fledged independent church on a global scale. And though he did not create a separate church, the theological insights of Søren Kierkegaard grew from his profound critique of the entrenched hierarchy of the Danish Folkekirke. In different forms, similar conflicts also occurred within the Catholic churches that officially claimed the loyalties of everyone within particular nations.

In modern times, the rapid decline in church attendance has helped resolve the dilemma of trying to operate a comprehensive church framework. If in fact a church stands no realistic chance of incorporating all members of a society, then it can become a smaller and more focused body, more rigorously committed to personal holiness and transformation. Pruning can promote growth, and the sharper the pruning, the stronger the growth.

Perhaps surprisingly, it is within Europe's Roman Catholic churches that such a reorientation has been most intensely discussed. These churches, after all, have for centuries maintained very close alliances with states, and they acted as if all baptized members of a community were sons and daughters of one church, which in practice meant virtually all members of society. Yet however powerful the idealistic vision of an all-embracing Catholic society, some influential thinkers have recognized that it no longer bears much resemblance to political reality. Coming from a Polish background, Pope John Paul II was exasperated by the signs of weakness he saw in the Catholicism of western Europe, which often seemed to be abandoning the faith. This vision was pursued to its logical conclusion by Cardinal Joseph Ratzinger, who would of course succeed him as Pope Benedict XVI.

Under John Paul, then Cardinal Ratzinger frankly asserted that the Christian role in a future Europe would be radically different from earlier times. How, he asked, could one speak of a Christian society if "in a city like Magdeburg, Christians are only eight percent of the total population, including all Christian denominations. Statistical data shows irrefutable tendencies. . . . there is a reduction in the possibility of identification between people and Church." Christians needed to accommodate themselves to the idea of minority status, a staggering idea from the viewpoint of nineteenth- or twentieth-century Catholicism: "The Church of the first three centuries was small, without being, by this fact, a sectarian community. On the contrary, it was not closed in on itself, but felt a great responsibility in regard to the poor, the sick—in regard to all."[29]

At times, Ratzinger seemed to suggest a two-tier approach to church membership, consciously admitting the tenuous ties of many Europeans to Christian belief. He drew a distinction between the core of believers and those who "never enter a church during the year, go to Christmas midnight Mass, or go on the occasion of some other celebration." Yet even these weaker forms of religious expression could constitute "a way of coming close to the light. Therefore, there must be different forms of involvement and participation. . . . The process of numerical reduction, which we are experiencing today, will also have to be addressed precisely by exploring new ways of openness to the outside, of new ways of participation by those who are outside the community of believers." In his view, the future church would be smaller and strong. It "will be reduced in its dimensions, it will be necessary to start again. However, from this test a Church would emerge that will have been strengthened by the process of simplification it experienced, by its renewed capacity to look within itself." Borrowing a phrase from historian Arnold Toynbee, Ratzinger has spoken of the potential of a "creative minority."

Catholic Revival?

For Pope John Paul, the changed position of Catholicism in a secular modern world demanded a New Evangelization, a phrase that became almost the slogan of his papacy. Sobered by the church's numerical decline, Catholics needed to become missionaries not just to what was long seen as the "non-Christian world" in Africa or Asia, but to those notionally Christian territories now falling prey to what Ratzinger called the "dictatorship of relativism." Arguably, Ratzinger's election as pope in 2005 reflected an acceptance of this analysis by the Catholic hierarchy, which realized the urgency of defending the embattled faith in Europe rather than appointing an African or Asian from areas of the world where church growth was still booming.[30]

The idea of a new evangelism helps explain many of the aspects of John Paul's papacy that attracted great public attention, often to the consternation of liberal Catholics. One was the pope's obvious commitment to making saints, to canonizing those figures who might attract popular devotion. John Paul canonized 484 saints, more than all his predecessors combined, not to mention a still larger cohort of blessed, *beati*, a status on the road to full sainthood. He showed a special preference for those whose careers carried a weighty symbolic message, such as the thousands of priests and religious slaughtered by the forces of revolutionary leftist secularism during the Spanish civil war of the 1930s. For John Paul, their martyrdom pointedly demonstrated the violent intolerance that was thinly veiled by the liberal secularist language of all-encompassing benevolence. He also recalled the church's sufferings under communism, canonizing martyrs and confessors from those years, and acknowledging shrines like the Hill of Crosses.[31]

John Paul showed intense devotion to the figure of the Virgin Mary, and to sites associated with reputed visionary encounters. While John Paul had a fascination with the Virgin—his papal motto proclaimed him *Totus Tuus*, "All Yours"—his effort to build up public devotion to her could not have succeeded if it had not struck a chord among European Catholics, as it clearly did. Another of his new saints was the Italian Padre Pio, reputedly a miracle worker who had received the stigmata, showing in his body the wounds of Christ. Though the story of Padre Pio has been criticized as pious fraud since his death in 1968, he was canonized in 2002, and a vast new church was built to receive pilgrims, at a cost of over 40 million dollars. The structure, at San Giovanni Rotondo, in the south Italian region of Puglia, accommodates a throng of 6,500 seated inside, with space for 30,000 more standing outside. Like Knock and Medjugorje, the shrine flourished during the John Paul years, and continues to do so. In 2006, a survey found that 70 percent of Italians regularly invoke the saints, with Padre Pio and St. Anthony of Padua far ahead of other heavenly luminaries, including the Virgin Mary herself.

Benedict too seems to be following in John Paul's tradition. In 2006, he visited the Italian shrine of Manoppello to visit the famous relic of the Holy Face or the Veil of Veronica, supposedly the cloth given to Jesus on his way to the Cross, and which miraculously preserved an image of his face. Some weeks later, he prayed before the Black Madonna of Altötting, one of the most sacred images of Catholic Bavaria.

For any student of church history, the policies of Popes John Paul and Benedict must recall the era of the Catholic Reformation of the sixteenth century, when an earlier generation of prelates had to confront the prospect of a Europe slipping rapidly away from the faith, on that occasion to radical Protestantism. Then too, the church restored its fortunes by a renewed emphasis on sanctity and devotion to saints, and a revived focus on Mary. But not even the most charismatic pope, the greatest saint, could have achieved much unless he had rather more to work with than merely the cooling ashes of a near-extinct faith.

Ecclesial Movements

Another aspect of reform, then as now, was the foundation of new religious orders pledged to the defense and expansion of the faith. In a famous passage, the nineteenth-century Lord Macaulay admired the resilience of the Roman Catholic Church, which "may still exist in undiminished vigor when some traveler from New Zealand shall, in the midst of a vast solitude, take his stand on a broken arch of London Bridge to sketch the ruins of St. Paul's." Explaining this resilience, Macaulay stressed how the church absorbed and coopted the dynamic spiritual experiments that arose among the faithful, experiments that in other churches, would have led to the creation of new breakaway sects. Even when the church was apparently at its weakest and most corrupt—especially when it seemed weakest—saints and reformers launched revival movements, which helped restore its power and confidence. Though their numbers were not huge as an absolute proportion of the overall population, such movements enjoyed a wholly disproportionate influence.

In the sixteenth century, the Catholic Reformation found most conspicuous expression in the Society of Jesus. But in recent times too, as European Catholicism has suffered repeated blows, so a spate of new religious orders and societies have arisen, many just as controversial as the original Jesuits were in their day. Among the most successful have been Opus Dei, the Neocatechumenate, the Focolare, and Communion and Liberation, though smaller examples include the Sant'Egidio Community, L'Arche, the Schönstatt movement, the Emmanuel Community, and Regnum Christi. Whether the new wave of orders will enjoy anything like the same success as the Jesuits remains to be seen, but they have won the faithful support of both Popes John Paul and Benedict. In the mid-1980s, Pope John Paul publicly acknowledged "the great and promising flowering of ecclesial movements and I have singled them out as a cause for a hope in the entire church and for all mankind." In 1998, he welcomed representatives of the orders at a vast convocation that gathered at Pentecost, the day that marks the outpouring of the spirit upon the church. At another Pentecost in 2006, Pope Benedict addressed 300,000 members of the new movements gathered in Rome's St. Peter's Square.[32]

The best known of the new religious orders is Opus Dei, which attracted notoriety when the *Da Vinci Code* depicted it as a super-secret society pulling the strings of power behind the Vatican—arguably the most abundant free publicity that a religious group has obtained in modern times. Like most of the new movements, Opus Dei predates the second Vatican Council, and it bears the authoritarian and triumphalist stamp of the pre-Council world. The group was founded in Spain in 1928 by St. Josemaría Escrivá, who earned the special affection of John Paul II. Through the pope's enthusiasm, Escrivá earned a fast track to canonization, which was eventually granted in 2002: 300,000 attended the ceremony. Despite the *Da Vinci Code*'s claims, Opus Dei is not a large movement, having perhaps 85,000 members around the world, in addition to 164,000 "Co-operators." Nor does it possess inordinate power in the higher reaches of the church: presently, only two cardinals are members, and just forty out of 4,500 bishops. Yet it does exercise influence, due largely to the intense involvement and commitment it requires of its members, and it reaches younger Catholics through universities and schools.[33]

At least as influential is the Neocatechumenal Way, founded in a slum area of Madrid in 1964 by artist Kiko Arguello, and by Carmen Hernandez, a former nun. The title refers to the ancient status of "catechumen" that prospective members of the early Christian church enjoyed before baptism, a period of study and initiation. The suggestion is that modern Christians too need to relearn the basics of faith through intense interaction with fellow members, and through regular retreats. The movement subsequently spread worldwide through enthusiastic proselytizing. By the early 1990s, the Neocatechumenate operated in 3,500 parishes, and claimed 80,000 members in Italian parishes alone. Today it reports activities in 6,000 parishes around the world, and a recent meeting with Pope Benedict involved an impressive roster of members and sympathizers, including five cardinals, thirty bishops, 1,100 priests, and 2,000 seminarians. In terms of its future influence, the seminarians are of course the most important element, but the group feels that overall numbers are unimportant. The image one always hears is that of leaven or yeast, which gives life to the much larger body. The group has a special commitment to parts of the world experiencing dechristianization, particularly in Europe.[34]

Apart from formal orders or societies, Spanish Catholicism is the source of other new structures through which people can interact, often using small group settings. One influential model is the Cursillo movement, which originated in Spain in the 1940s, in the traumatic aftermath of the civil war. Members gathered in small groups for a

three-day weekend of prayer, discussion, and interaction that constituted a short course in Christianity, *Cursillo de Cristianidad*. The course
idea has since spread across denominations, and some 10 million people worldwide have participated.

Italy has also produced its share of new orders, which expanded
mightily during the political and social turmoil of the 1960s and 1970s,
when the country seemed ripe for open revolution. At the same time,
the Catholic Church was experiencing the aftermath of the second
Vatican Council, which opened up new possibilities to lay organizations. From this environment came the Sant'Egidio Community, a lay
movement founded in 1968, which today has 50,000 members organized in small groups. Though mainly concentrated in Italy, the Community also has branches in a hundred other countries. Also influential is Communion and Liberation, which although notionally dating
back to 1954 was effectively restarted in 1969. The group was founded
by Fr. Luigi Giussani, who developed the Catholic presence in schools,
colleges, and universities, and who tried to promote Catholic social
principles in mainstream politics. The group operates today throughout Europe, with branches in seventy countries around the world.[35]

Also active has been the Focolare movement, which traces its origin
to the visions and revelations received by its founder, Chiara Lubich, in
Italy in the 1940s. The movement has influenced millions worldwide,
though its core membership in the 1990s stood at around 80,000. The
Focolare present themselves strictly in New Testament terms, with
heavy use of agricultural symbolism: they plow and reap, and gather
members like a bunch of grapes. The Focolare itself takes its name from
the word for "hearth," where the spiritual fire is cultivated. Members
cultivate prospective disciples, who are brought into ever-deeper levels
of interaction and communion with the group, which they are expected
to serve like faithful children. Characteristic practices include ritualized
public confessions and retreats that serve as a kind of total immersion in
the group and its doctrines.[36]

The Church with All Its Lights On

Other groups trace their origin to the charismatic movement, which
grew in parallel with the Pentecostal and charismatic movements
within Protestantism. Counting Catholics and Protestants together, the
numbers are impressive, especially when we compare them with the
Muslim population that has received so much media attention in recent years: roughly, Europe's evangelicals, charismatics, and pentecostals outnumber Muslims by almost two to one, and will continue to
do so for the foreseeable future (see Table 3.2).

Charismatics became a potent force within the Catholic Church
during the late 1960s, and in 1975 they received the powerful backing
of Pope Paul VI. In the 1970s, the movement developed a significant

Table 3.2 **Some Religious Minorities In Europe**
(in millions)

	1900	1970	2000	2025
Muslims	9 (2.3%)	18 (2.7%)	32 (4.3%)	36 (5.1%)
Evangelicals, Charismatics and Pentecostals	32 (8%)	30 (4.6%)	59 (8.2%)	69 (9.8%)

These groups can belong to any denomination. The figures for charismatics, for instance, include Roman Catholic and Anglican charismatics, and most British "evangelicals" are members of the Church of England. Please also note that the authors include Russia as part of Europe, which accounts for the high number of Muslims given here.

Source: David B. Barrett, George T. Kurian, and Todd M. Johnson, *World Christian Encyclopedia,* 2nd ed. (New York: Oxford University Press, 2001), 12–15.

following in Italy, where the *Rinnovamento nello Spirito* (RnS) became an ecclesial movement in its own right. By 2000, the RnS claimed 250,000 followers organized in 1,300 communities and groupings, with at least some presence in every Italian diocese.[37]

The movement also boomed in France. Initially led by Pierre Goursat and Martine Catta, a French network of charismatic prayer groups spread rapidly, as groups grew and then split to form new cells. Martine Catta reported that "we had the feeling that we were reviving Pentecost." Soon, the network institutionalized in the form of the Emmanuel Community, which was formally recognized by the church in 1992: today, it has some 6,000 members, including 130 priests. Like other Catholic charismatics, they distinguish themselves from their Protestant counterparts by their profound veneration for the Virgin Mary and their use of pilgrimage. Since 1975, the community has based itself at Paray-le-Monial, which in the seventeenth century became famous as the site of the first reported vision of the Sacred Heart of Jesus, and which continues today as a pilgrimage site: it still attracts 300,000 visitors annually. In addition to that total, some 20,000 attend the summer sessions and retreats organized by the Emmanuel Community for priests, families, and young people. Suggesting the wealth of spiritual sites that survive in contemporary Europe, Paray-le-Monial is close to both Taizé and the ancient monastery of Cluny.[38]

Catholic charismatics flourish in other countries, though in more decentralized form. England is home to several dozen charismatic communities and settlements, as well as summer camps and conferences, and regional Days of Renewal. In 1985, English layman Myles Dempsey was visiting the French shrine of Ars when he had a vision that included the words "Walsingham" and "New Dawn." Largely through his efforts, Walsingham, a great medieval Marian shrine, became the center of the annual New Dawn summer conference, which seeks to present "the beauty of the church . . . in all its splendor, the church with all its lights on and all its aspects celebrated—the charismatic, the liturgical, the Marian, the Eucharistic, the Sacramental, the mystical."[39]

Though little known outside their immediate region, other Catholic communities have produced revival movements, often operating within the charismatic framework. In the Czech Republic, which normally represents a malarial swamp for mainstream spirituality of any kind, Fr. Vladimir Mikulica led an influential charismatic revival that also drew on Orthodox and mystical currents. In neighboring Slovakia, Silvo Krčméry was a Catholic physician who was long persecuted by communist authorities but who subsequently helped turn St. Martin's parish, Bratislava, into something like a Catholic megachurch. In the early 1990s, members visited Taizé and Paray-le-Monial, "which is full of the Holy Spirit," and returned to launch a revival. Members practice street evangelization, and the parish's media operation reaches millions.[40]

The Movements and Their Enemies

For all their successes, the various movements have been subject to charges of bizarre and cult-like behavior that press the limits of Catholic orthodoxy. These charges have been thoroughly presented in Gordon Urquhart's exposé titled *The Pope's Armada*. Urquhart, himself a disaffected Focolare member, describes a subculture of "fanatical personality cults surrounding the charismatic leaders; demands of blind obedience on members; a rigid and highly secretive internal hierarchy; the use of mind control techniques and unscrupulous methods of recruitment." Its enemies attack Opus Dei for religious practices that include self-mortification, and a requirement for celibacy among fully committed adherents. As they tried to win over the Italian working class, Communion and Liberation attracted the title "Stalinists of God," and members were criticized for excessive political dabbling. The Czech hierarchy ultimately suspended Fr. Mikulica for his supposedly manipulative tendencies.[41]

The movements are also accused of presenting themselves as churches within the church, and of exalting their structure and founders above the mainstream hierarchy: the charismatic Chiara Lubich claims the stature of a spiritual Mother. The most spectacular scandal has undoubtedly been that of Regnum Christi, founded by the Mexican Fr. Marcial Maciel, and influential among southern European Catholics. Fr. Maciel was, however, the subject for many years of charges of pederasty and sexual abuse. Though the Vatican under John Paul was reluctant to listen to these mounting allegations, his successor Benedict did acknowledge them, disciplining Maciel in 2006.

In many ways, Urquhart and other critics make a plausible case, but as with all anti-cult movements, we have to be careful about accepting the stereotype that followers are slavish or robotic. Usually, people follow such committed and enthusiastic movements because they want to, and for just as long as they find spiritual rewards there. Nor do the charges against Focolare and the rest differ significantly from claims against other Christian movements of bygone eras, including the Methodists on the Protestant side of the equation. What makes today's new movements so noteworthy is their adaptation of Catholic practice and belief to a society in which Christianity as an institution can no longer hope to reach the vast majority of people, and in which churches must reorganize on the basis of voluntary minorities encouraging each other in devotion and the Christian life. While remaining Catholic, they are moving beyond a historic structure of territorial parishes and dioceses, of a Christianity rooted in well-defined communities and hierarchies. The Focolares, for instance, found their voluntary and autonomous pattern very useful in promoting Catholic survival behind the Iron Curtain. Other followers feel that this precedent might soon be valuable in operating within a secularized Europe that is itself deeply hostile to Christian belief.

The Catholic movements also have a special appeal to the groups who are most disaffected from traditional structures and clerical hierarchies. Women founded or co-founded several of the groupings, including the Focolare, the Emmanuel Community, and the Neocatechumenate, and two-thirds of Focolare members are female. Women are also central to the organization of the charismatic movements. In the Italian *RnS*, women make up half the membership of the national coordinating committee, as well as 40 percent of the regional coordinators. The Neocatechumenate also faces charges of exalting lay power above clerical, and lay people play a much more active role in services than they would in a conventional Catholic liturgy.[42]

Repeatedly, we note the resemblances of the new movements to transnational sects within European Islam, an analogy that is guaranteed to offend both sides equally. I do not intend to suggest that groups like the Neocatechumenate serve as fronts for terrorism or subversion. Yet we see similar trends on both sides of the interfaith divide, as religious practice can no longer be assumed to be a familiar part of everyday communal life. In a period of rapid transition and social disruption, new evangelistic orders and groupings appear, usually organized from the grass roots. Both demonstrate a thorough disregard of conventional frontiers and hierarchies that allows them to reach potential believers wherever they may be found, and often to follow paths of migration. Both Christian and Muslim "sects," commonly, are rigidly conservative in tone and speak the language of traditionalism, although both in values and structures, they are in fact much more innovative than they care to admit. And both—whether the Neocatechumenate or the Tablighi Jamaat—tend to regard ordinary moderate believers as virtual infidels: only total commitment to the faith is valued.

At their worst, both types of movement, Christian and Muslim, have the potential to become authoritarian and cultish; more positively, each offers plausible responses to preserving faith in the fluid and dynamic societies of postmodern Europe.

The new Catholic movements sponsored several innovations in church life. In the mid-1970s, the Focolares organized mass youth events called Genfest, which were imitated by the mainstream church a decade later as World Youth Day. These events have subsequently attracted mass followings and have become legendary for their rock concert atmosphere. Critics denounce their "manipulated mass hysteria," and older and staider believers complain of the heated fervor on exhibit. In Germany in 2005, for instance, critics of World Youth Day denounced "a well-nigh feverish and frenetic cult of the personality . . . it has nothing to do with the collected, simple life of Jesus of Nazareth, who would have had nothing to do with this ruckus." While the "cultish" origins of the event can be conceded, it is striking that it can so successfully mobilize many young people who would at best be lukewarm cultural Christians and who have no direct connection whatever with the various new ecclesial movements: a million attended the events in Cologne in 2005. Though the organizers and leaders are indeed connected to the movements, the ordinary followers are there because they find the event fills their spiritual needs, whoever is supplying the opportunities. And after all the denunciations of Europe's spiritual torpor, it is refreshing just once in a while to find young Christians denounced for their religious excesses.[43]

Minority Solutions

Outside the Roman Catholic Church, too, other Christian bodies have offered imaginative responses to the prospect of Christian decline and minority status. In some ways, they are unconsciously following the fashionable management theory proposed by Gary Hamel and C. K. Prahalad, who warned that organizations with a dominant share of the market tended to become smug. In order to compete, companies, and presumably churches, need to focus on their areas of core competence, identifying what they do best rather than trying to please everybody. "At worst, laggards follow the path of greatest familiarity. Challengers, on the other hand, follow the path of greatest opportunity, wherever it leads."[44]

We see several examples of this willingness to experiment. Germany, for instance, now has a substantial revivalist movement that fits poorly with the sober state-oriented traditions of that nation's Protestantism. In the 1990s, former YMCA director Ulrich Parzany formed the movement ProChrist, which modeled itself on the North American Billy Graham Crusade, adapted to the electronic age. (Parzany himself is a Lutheran pastor.) The movement holds revivals at a central location, which are then broadcast to a thousand local centers scattered across twenty European nations, so that over a million can participate remotely.[45]

Finland offers another innovation. The country has a state church on the classic Scandinavian model, the Evangelical Lutheran Church, in which people are assumed to belong, although most devote minimal attention to religious life. Church life is normally confined to births, marriages, and funerals: on average, every Finn attends at least one of these events each year. Over the past twenty years, though, regular church attendance has fallen by a third, and barely 3 percent of members attend weekly. As one pastor observes, "the trouble with the church in Finland is that everybody loves it, and nobody goes there."[46]

Since the late 1980s, though, in exactly this period of contraction, Finland has become home to the so-called Thomas Mass, which has succeeded admirably in attracting substantial numbers of highly motivated urban teenagers and young adults. The service is named for the doubting disciple who makes a splendid patron saint for contemporary seekers. It combines contemporary liturgical innovation (drawing on Taizé) with a revival of the church's ancient liturgical resources, Catholic and Orthodox. The Thomas Mass is also strongly voluntary and participatory in nature, a reversal of the familiar clerical top-down model. In order to draw the largest possible attendance, services are held in the evenings, when students and professionals are most likely to be available. Groups of people undertake different responsibilities, so that, for instance, music students combine to offer lively accompaniment, and a typical liturgy might involve nine or ten priests, as well as perhaps fifty lay people fulfilling some kind of function. At one point in the service, as songs and hymns are sung, individuals can choose the activity they wish to pursue. Some write prayers that will later be read publicly, others go to confession or seek counseling from the pastor. Many go to side-altars to light candles or venerate icons, a practice borrowed from Finland's small Orthodox community. The service culminates with the Eucharist. Today, Thomas Mass services take place in 150 locations across Finland and draw over 100,000 participants annually. The Thomas liturgy is widely imitated throughout Scandinavia, in Germany, and in the Netherlands.[47]

Anglicans

This kind of innovation is not surprising when we consider the substantial intellectual and spiritual resources available to the mainstream churches. Even his most severe critics acknowledge that Pope Benedict XVI possesses as powerful an intellect as any predecessor for centuries past. And however sick the Church of England might be in its attendance levels, its leadership still includes figures as distinguished as any in its history. Since 2002, the Archbishop of Canterbury has been Rowan Williams, a formidable intellectual who is one of the greatest living Protestant theologians. Among other achievements, he is the first holder of that office who knows Russian and is thoroughly at home in the spiritual traditions of Orthodoxy. Among the church's other leaders, the Bishop of Durham is N. T. Wright, one of the world's most respected scholars of the New Testament. The other most prestigious see, besides Canterbury, is York, which is now headed by Ugandan John Sentamu, a creative appointment that recognizes the global role of the Anglican Communion. If this is a church in its dotage, it is doing an excellent job of disguising the fact.

For the Church of England as for other bodies, the fact that uniform belief can no longer be assumed has had a liberating effect, permitting the rise of new movements that almost assume the role of new churches in their own right. The greatest beneficiary has been the evangelical movement within the Anglican Church. Through most of the nineteenth and twentieth centuries, the Church of England was divided between two parties, high and low, respectively, the liturgical Anglo-Catholics and the evangelicals: in popular parlance, they were respectively the high and crazy, and the low and lazy. Since the 1960s, the high party has shrunk into virtual insignificance, and some of its leaders have defected to the Roman Catholics or Orthodox. Evangelicals have flourished, however, and have come to resemble an enthusiastic U.S. denomination, although often worshiping in venerable Gothic churches.[48]

The movement is seen at its strongest in a London parish such as Holy Trinity, Brompton (HTB), which attracts over 3,000 to its Sunday services. Like an American megachurch, the life of Holy Trinity is based on intense small group activities, organized through its fifty pastorates, lay-led groups of twenty-five to thirty each who meet fortnightly in non-church locations. As the church advises members, "The pastorates are not one program amongst many that the church supports; the pastorates are the church." Holy Trinity is committed to church planting and has established seven offshoot churches following its evangelical principles and worship style. Though HTB has acquired worldwide fame, it is by no means the only church of its kind. In Chorleywood in Hertfordshire, we find the charismatic church of St. Andrew's, which is also part of the Anglican church and also offers an impressive range of levels of involvement. Besides full-scale services, the church's Mid-Size Communities "give a fresh and exciting new expression to our life as a church by setting free the creative dynamic of a group of church members that is larger than a small or cell group but considerably smaller than a Sunday service gathering." Some of Britain's most flourishing evangelical congregations are either Anglican, or involve Anglican alliances with other traditions; other examples include All Souls in Langham Place, Holy Trinity Cheltenham, or St. Thomas's Sheffield.[49]

Anglicans within the church cooperate with evangelicals from other bodies, including the remnants of the old non-conformist churches that were once so powerful a force in British politics and culture. British Christianity also has its own version of the new ecclesial movements, groups that originated as ad hoc fellowships and networks but which have since acquired an institutional life of their own. Spring Harvest began as a Christian conference in 1979 and has now become a regular event, attracting up to 100,000 enthusiastic believers in several locations around the United Kingdom. Its sponsors claim it as "the largest Christian conference in Europe."[50]

We also find parallels both to the Thomas Mass and the U.S. emerging church movement, gatherings that try to convey Christian experience without the trappings that some find alienating. British examples include Tribal Generation or London's Grace service:

> The monthly Grace service is experimental and hence rarely the same twice. We don't work to a fixed structure, giving us the opportunity to create a space, atmosphere and service suitable to the theme that we have chosen. Walking through the door you'll probably find soft lighting, candles, TVs and projections showing words and images. . . . Alongside the visuals will be chilled-out music shaping the atmosphere. . . . Beyond the general styling the service is less predictable. There may be things to look at, touch and do, a chance to wander around and explore, write things down or simply sit or lie still. Meditation, discussions, readings and prayers may be said, written or read. Just don't expect a sermon. . . . It's an event which questions what a church service can be, what kind of things it can contain, what kind of issues can be explored and what kind of questions can be asked.[51]

Some movements have grown out of evangelical efforts within the Church of England, though they have subsequently acquired a more independent identity. One creative figure has been David Pytches, former Anglican bishop of Chile and vicar of St. Andrew's, Chorleywood. Pytches's roots are firmly within Anglicanism, "with seven generations of family vicars behind me. . . . I have two brothers ordained and a son-in-law, all clergy." Even so, he drew freely on other Christian traditions. Pytches imported to England the enthusiasm of Latin American charismatic revivalism and was also influenced by John Wimber, founder of the U.S.-based Vineyard church. From the late 1980s, Pytches became involved in two successful parachurch organizations. One is Soul Survivor, which since 1993 operates a charismatic Christian version of a rock festival, where young people gather "to pray, sing, dance and have fun." New Wine operates training events and summer conferences, and has many resemblances to the Vineyard.[52]

Britain's most important national federation remains the old-established Evangelical Alliance, an umbrella that includes congregations both within and outside the established church. It claims "a constituency of 1 million persons and includes about 3,000 local churches, 750 parachurch organizations, 30 denominations and 32,000 individual members." Other informal means of national organization include a network of bookstores, radio shows, and Christian publishers, and occasional meetings and revivals that owe much to the American tent meeting tradition. The movement grew during the 1970s and gained strength from moral and political campaigns of the era, including a celebrated attempt to revive blasphemy legislation against irreverent media, and controversies over skeptical academic accounts of the Christian faith. Meanwhile, interdenominational Christian fellowships popularized ideas of charismatic worship and deliverance. By the end of that decade, the charismatic House Church Movement had some 50,000 members drawn from various denominations, including Catholics.[53]

Evangelicals are well established among Anglican clergy and in the church hierarchy. From 1991 through 2002, the strongly evangelical George Carey was Archbishop of Canterbury. He also indicates the influence of charismatic doctrines and practices in modern evangelicalism, and he himself reported a spirit baptism in which he spoke in tongues. The strength of evangelicals and charismatics in the modern Church of England is illustrated by the persistent struggles within that church over issues of gay rights and gay ordination, which command solid support from liberals, backed enthusiastically by most of the British media. These ideas are of course anathema to conservatives like David Pytches, and the church leadership has to tread warily lest it drive its vital evangelical constituency into schism. A senior official of the Evangelical Alliance recently infuriated many when he compared same-sex unions to "people wanting to marry their horse."[54]

Some practices of charismatic Christians have also attracted controversy. Charismatics have a powerful belief in deliverance and healing, believing that the miraculous powers described in the New Testament are available to modern-day Christians. David Pytches reports, for instance, that "I have seen hundreds of people healed of blindness in one or both eyes. Cysts on ovaries the size of grapefruit have miraculously disappeared, and the surgeon says simply, 'It's gone.' Healings are a sign of the Kingdom of God." The website of his former church at Chorleywood includes abundant testimonies of the mighty deeds of "the H.S." (Holy Spirit), including these in just one week:

> Pain went from cancer patients . . . A girl from a mental hospital overwhelmed by H.S. . . . . Person with perforated ear drum healed . . . Leg lengthened and hip realigned . . . Someone whose husband died 6 weeks ago, and [ministry team] member had a word "Jesus is your bridegroom". Person greatly encouraged.[55]

This charismatic element became controversial during the 1970s and 1980s as clergy and activists became increasingly interested in— some would say, obsessed with—ideas of spiritual warfare, with its quite literal ideas about demonic assaults. As Pytches declared, "People get delivered from demons. I have seen many delivered from demonic possession. Demonization is in your life because it is affected by a demon in some way. . . . Often we need to clean out people's houses. Many owners are into spiritism, Ouija boards and their homes need to be delivered." Publishers like Kingsway did a roaring trade in accounts of deliverance and possession, with American-spawned exposés of the dangers posed by Satanists, witches, and New Age believers.[56]

These matters reached the headlines in the late 1980s when British evangelicals and charismatics, including some wealthy and politically powerful families, accepted theories about the danger of alleged Satanic cults, human sacrifices, and literal demonic conspiracies. In some ways, these stories helped the growth of charismatic churches, whose members found it exhilarating to believe they were engaged in a cosmic struggle for the national soul. Yet the overall effects were disastrous, as some activists became notorious peddlers of outrageous conspiracy theories. For a few years, Britain was rife with tales of Satanic child abuse rings, and several quite literal witch hunts resulted in the destruction of families and the incarceration of many innocent people. Charismatic Christians should not take the full blame for these absurdities, as Satanic stories won equal credence among radical feminists and child protection activists, but spiritual warfare themes were much in evidence. Such charges surfaced elsewhere in Europe, most dramatically in a Dutch case in the village of Oude Pekela. It is remarkable that such ritual abuse stories made their deepest European impact in the two nations generally regarded as among the most secular, namely, Britain and the Netherlands, perhaps suggesting that the decline of formal religious structures had left the popular religious imagination open to excesses. Much like pilgrimage, the willingness to believe in demonic assaults suggests the survival of undercurrents of popular religious belief that are in search of an outlet.[57]

Alpha

The unpleasant publicity accorded to British evangelicals gave a distorted picture of their major interests, religious and social, and made them appear extreme and even fanatical. A more positive contribution is the famous Alpha Course created at Holy Trinity, Brompton, in the early 1980s, and subsequently popularized through the work of the Reverend Nicky Gumbel. Like the new Catholic movements, the Alpha Course is designed for a society in which Christians possess minority status and can assume no wider knowledge whatever of their doctrines or beliefs. With its assumptions of individualism, popular skepticism, and nonhierarchical networking, and its unwillingness to invoke dogmatic authority, it is intended to confront the forces driving toward secularization and to use those forces for evangelistic ends.[58]

The course is an introductory series of lectures and discussions that present Christianity to a society that is seen as a religious blank slate. Curious inquirers are recruited through friends and informal contacts, who invite them to meet for dinner, a lecture, and a discussion, generally using a videotaped presentation by Gumbel himself. In attracting participants, the course relies on precisely none of the means that form and sustain social interaction in a more organic community. Members are not there because of people they meet at church or school settings, or even at the workplace; they almost certainly do not attend church, they might well be childless, and they often work on short-term contracts that do not allow long-standing acquaintance. Nor, critically, does the course assume that members are parts of a family, or have children; it is designed for inquiring adults. In England, the average age of participants is twenty-seven.[59]

The social setting is an important part of the formula, since nonbelievers are expected to progress to faith under the guidance of the more spiritually mature. Alpha represents an acronym:

A—Anyone interested in finding out more about the Christian faith.
L—Learning and laughter.
P—Pasta.
H—Helping one another.
A—Ask anything. No question is seen as too simple or too hostile.

The first session assesses charges that Christianity is "boring, untrue and irrelevant"; later meetings explore the role and nature of Jesus and concepts such as Bible reading, healing, and the church. Three sessions on the role of the Holy Spirit should ideally take the form of a retreat.

Its creators intended the course to be militantly nondenominational, a nonpartisan bare-bones description of the faith. In fact, it leans heavily toward the evangelical and charismatic, while its stern prohibitions of homosexuality or extramarital sex arouse attacks from more liberal believers. One journalistic account in the liberal British newspaper the *Guardian* reported some disaffected inquirers dismissing their experience as part of a "brainwashing cult" staffed by "weirdos," who gradually led their pupils to accept bizarre doctrines like speaking in tongues.[60]

As an introduction, though, the course is powerfully effective, and inquirers often make a declaration of faith in Jesus and affirm the truth of Christianity. Over the past decade, the Alpha Course has enjoyed worldwide popularity and has spanned denominations. The Catholic Archbishop of Paris has described the course as one of the two greatest gifts of Protestants to Catholics in modern times—the other being the charismatic movement itself—and hundreds of French churches now sponsor Alpha. Globally, by 2005, some 7 million people had attended a course, including 1.6 million in Britain.

We have to be careful about seeing such committed and activist movements entirely on their own terms. Listening to charismatics, for instance, or to some of the new Catholic movements, it can sometimes seem as if they are the only Christians, while liberal or mainstream believers scarcely deserve the Christian title at all. That is of course a partisan view, just as much as the liberal assumption that enthusiastic groups like these represent a fanatical cult on the distant fringes of Christianity. In British debates over ordaining gay clergy, for instance, neither side, liberal or conservative, seems to acknowledge the Christian credentials of its rivals. There is always the danger that such an exclusivist picture might emerge from accounts that pay so much attention to the new movements as signs of growth and vigor within the churches. In reality, Christian life is also alive and well in mainstream congregations and hierarchies, however little that impression might emerge from recent descriptions of European religion. If Christian beliefs did not motivate some people so strongly, we could scarcely have the passionate debates that we do have regularly, within churches great and small.

We See Things as We Are

Looking at such signs of life, Americans might be tempted to ask why they had not received more attention in all the jeremiads about the fate of European religion. Doing a search for information about the new movements within the churches, whether on the Internet or in the mass media, will soon produce tales of brainwashing, extremism, and scandal, which are usually the only manifestations of faith that attract the attention of the mainstream media. Of their nature, the news media rarely report quietly successful religious trends, the news that X million people continue to find spiritual sustenance in a particular tradition (Christian or Muslim) or that they have found innovative ways of spreading it. We hear of the Roman Catholic Church for its conflicts over abortion or contraception, of the Church of England for its feuds over gay clergy, not for the continuing daily religious practices of either church. Americans, too, usually report religious affairs only when they ignite controversy. Religion is visible only when it becomes a problem.

But the consistently negative presentations of European religion point to features of the media on that continent that differ substantially from conditions in the United States. While conservative Americans worry about "elite liberal media" trying to enforce their views on a largely conservative or religious population, such a view is far less accurate in their own country than it would be in Europe. Especially in west European nations, the media genuinely are far more secular than their U.S. counterparts and indeed more hostile to any form of organized religion, which is commonly seen in terms of a problem to be solved. In consequence, European accounts of religious life all but ignore significant trends or events, and this lack of attention means that these movements receive little attention elsewhere. It is thus easy for North American commentators to assume that European Christianity is not just near death, but that there are no signs of remission or revival.

Europe has much more homogeneous ruling elites than the United States, elites concentrated in the same metropolitan centers, and sharing similar backgrounds and values. Partly, this is a consequence of the small geographical size of European nations and the intense concentration of wealth and power in a few major cities. For better or worse, those elites are less subject to expressions of public sentiment, and less democratic. To take an example, opinion surveys consistently show European publics at large to be quite conservative on issues of criminal justice and law enforcement, and that conservatism extends to what we think of as the most progressive Scandinavian nations. If decisions were made by referendum or plebiscite, then European policies on criminal justice would look rather more like those of the United States, and most nations would execute murderers. In reality, no European nation has had the death penalty since France renounced the practice in 1981. In most of western Europe, not only is capital punishment not accepted, but even its discussion is rigorously barred, alongside other policies favored by large popular majorities—the restriction of political asylum rights would be another example.

In other words, at least some apparent differences between Europe and the United States reflect not broad social trends but rather the elitist nature of European decision making. To draw a parallel with the official "European" views on religion, we would have to imagine a United States in which all media reflected the socially liberal values of the *New York Times, Washington Post* or *Boston Globe,* and in which most forms of conservative or charismatic religious expression were greeted with puzzlement, if not disdain. The United States has much more active religious practice than does Europe: but with its very diverse media, it also has far better means of seeing the religious life that is actually going on.

This is not to deny that European Christianity is in deep crisis, but matters are considerably more diverse, and in some areas more successful, than we might glean. Further complicating the picture, while immigration into Europe is usually associated with the rise of Islam, a sizable number of migrants are themselves Christians, and they represent a bracing, and often startling, new presence within the continent's religious life.

4

New Christians

The mission of The Church of the Lord (Aladura) in Europe is therefore to win all new, lukewarm and lost souls for Christ. The mission has been reversed because those to whom Christ Jesus was once preached are now back on the territory of the former preachers to preach Christ Jesus to them in all his goodness. What a "mission reversed" indeed!

Primate of the Church of the Lord (Aladura)

Accounts of the collapse of Christianity neglect the growth of immigrant churches among Africans, East Asians, and Latin Americans. Though far less numerous than Muslims, immigrant Christians represent a potent cultural and religious force. Even if we accept the most pessimistic view of the fate of Christianity among Europe's old-stock white populations, these thriving new churches represent an exciting new planting, even potentially a kind of re-evangelization. At the least, their swelling numbers provide an important counterweight to booming Muslim populations. In many ways too, their experience replicates that of Muslim communities, sharing many of the same diasporic issues and conflicts and, perhaps remarkably, in receiving much of the same disdain and suspicion from the mainstream society. As Christianity worldwide acquires an ever-clearer African and Asian cast, the faith attracts many of the primitive stereotypes with which Europeans have often regarded Africa and Asia.

A Black Thing

Not for many years have immigrants and missionaries been so pivotal to European Christianity. In England, for instance, the conversion in the seventh century was largely the work of Mediterranean missionaries.

Though most were Italian, at least one was a north African, the Abbot Hadrian, who did so much to establish Canterbury's tradition of learning. At York in 627, the Italian bishop Paulinus baptized the region's most powerful pagan king.

For the historically inclined, these precedents came forcefully to mind in 2005, with the inauguration of the new Archbishop of York, John Sentamu, a Ugandan. The ceremony featured African dancers, "dressed with colorful red, white and black feathered head plumages and leopard skin print skirts and T-shirts." They were accompanied by drums, and at one memorable moment, the incoming archbishop himself personally took over the role of chief drummer. In his sermon, he recalled the words of a previous Archbishop of Canterbury, Michael Ramsey, speaking in 1960:

> He was speaking of the stupendous missionary century that saw the wonderful spread of Christian faith in Africa and Asia, by missionaries from these islands, and compared it to the spiritual decay in England. He longed for the day in England when the Church would learn the faith afresh from Christians of Africa and Asia. He ended his address by saying, "I should love to think of a black Archbishop of York holding a mission here, and telling a future generation of the scandal and the glory of the Church." Well, here I am.[1]

Others from the global South play a visible role in contemporary European churches. By far the most successful example today is the Kiev-based church founded by Nigerian Sunday Adelaja, the Embassy of the Blessed Kingdom of God for all Nations. Sunday Adelaja was one of many bright African and Asian students brought to the Soviet Union to receive an education and ideally to become a future advocate of pro-Soviet views. Within a couple of years, the Soviet Union itself dissolved, and in 1994 Adelaja founded a Pentecostal congregation in the new Ukrainian republic.

From seven founding members, the church soon claimed 30,000 adherents, overwhelmingly white, and some very powerful indeed. One celebrated adherent is Leonid Chernovetsky, a multimillionaire banker and politician, who in 2006 became mayor of Kiev. The new church spread widely:

> Over twenty services are held every Sunday in various auditoriums of Kiev, Ukraine. Over fifty daughter churches function in the Kiev region. More than a hundred daughter and satellite churches exist in the cities and villages of Ukraine. Over two hundred churches in the countries of the former Soviet Union, the USA, Germany, UAE, Israel, and Holland have been founded. . . . The church's Christian television and radio programs reach approximately eight million people.

Within the Ukraine, the church's main dilemma was in finding facilities large enough to accommodate its numbers, but fortunately the old

Soviet Union had built many grand auditoria for union functions and sports gatherings. Wry observers suggest that perhaps at last Christians can understand the historic role of communism, in that somebody had to build facilities large enough to cope with Pentecostal congregations. Pastor Sunday's Embassy bases its success largely on its promise of healing, and its website offers testimonies from Russians and Ukrainians who report being healed from all manner of complaints, including AIDS and cancer. Boris, a police lieutenant, reports being raised from the dead.[2]

Sunday Adelaja is only one of many successful Third-World evangelists now operating in Europe, though he stands out in his ability to attract white Europeans. While he was setting up shop in Kiev, another Nigerian named Matthew Ashimolowo was founding a church in London. After beginning in 1992 with only 300 members, his Kingsway International Christian Centre (KICC) now seats 5,000 worshipers at its main facility, the Miracle Centre, as well as several satellite churches. The KICC is claimed as the largest new church to be created in Britain since 1861, and the Miracle Centre's auditorium offers double the capacity of Westminster Abbey or St. Paul's Cathedral. The pastor uses cable television and radio to speak to a wider audience in the United Kingdom, and beyond, in Nigeria, Ghana, South Africa, Malawi, Uganda, Sierra Leone, and the Anglophone Caribbean. His programs also reach much of Europe. He attributes his success to bringing the lessons of the flourishing Nigerian revival "into a very—shall I say—atheistic Europe." Though he has suffered scandals arising from personal enrichment and the diversion of church moneys, the church he planted continues to thrive. He has had little success in reaching out to the white population because his message seems so foreign, so ethnic. Summarizing one image of Christianity in Britain today, he complains that "the trouble is we are seen as a Black thing and not a God thing."[3]

Such spectacular success stories may be untypical, but they indicate the powerful boost being supplied by global South communities. Since the 1950s, a significant number of Europe's migrants were Christian, commonly representing the very successful new churches exploding in those regions. The new Christian growth fell into two closely overlapping categories, namely, the churches established on European soil by and for the new immigrants themselves, and deliberate missionary activity directed from the global South.

Missionaries

In terms of deliberate missionary work, Great Britain today plays host to some 1500 missionaries from 50 nations. Many come from African countries, and these are shocked at the spiritual desert they encounter in this "green and pagan land." Often, too, missionaries have a sense of repaying obligations, in recalling the Europeans who originally converted their lands. Korean missionaries return to England in tribute to the land of John Wesley. Matthew Ashimolowo sees London as "a city which sent many missionaries out, and also a city where great pastors have been raised before: Charles Spurgeon and the Spurgeon Tabernacle, G. Campbell Morgan in Westminster Chapel; T. Kendal is still here, and some other great names." In the late nineteenth century, the strict Presbyterian Church of Wales sent missionaries to the people of Mizoram, in the northeast of India. The endeavor succeeded richly, and in 2006 the Mizo people began returning the favor, sending two missionaries to help reconvert Wales. In the words of one Mizo churchman, Wales suffered from "a perceived lack of relevance of Christianity to lives based on materialism."[4]

Some transnational Christian networks operate in literally dozens of nations, churches headquartered in one of the great missionary nations of the modern world, such as Brazil, Nigeria, the Congo, the Philippines, or South Korea. Particularly important are the AICs, the African-Initiated Churches, bodies of African foundation and worship style. In the early twentieth century, for instance, Nigeria produced the Aladura movement, with its emphasis on healing, prophecy, and charismatic worship. During the 1960s, London became the base for several Aladura churches, including the Celestial Church of Christ, Church of the Lord Aladura, the Cherubim and Seraphim, and Christ Apostolic Church. The Aladura tradition is powerfully represented by the Redeemed Christian Church of God (RCCG), founded in 1952, and which has a strong missionary outreach. "At the last count, there are at least about four thousand parishes of the Redeemed Christian Church of God in Nigeria. . . . In Europe the church is spread in England, Germany, and France." In addition to its African presence, the Congolese Kimbanguist church, Église de Jesus Christ sur la Terre par son Envoyé Spécial Simon Kimbangu, is active in Spain, Portugal, France, Germany, Belgium, Switzerland, and England. Brazilian congregations, such as the Universal Church of the Kingdom of God, are widespread. So are Philippine lay charismatic communities like the astonishing El Shaddai, which operates in some thirty countries, or the Brazilian IURD, the aptly titled Igreja Universal, the Universal Church of the Kingdom of God.[5]

Sometimes, movements from the global South benefit from alliances with new groups within Europe's older churches. David Pytches learned from the Chilean charismatic movement, and Filipino movements like Couples for Christ work closely with Europe's charismatic Catholics. Catholic charismatics also provide speaking venues for African priests, who bring to Europe the very different and more enthusiastic traditions of their own countries. One popular guest in

Britain is Ugandan Fr. Anthony Musaala, who among other achievements is a noted figure in Africa's Christian music scene.

Reinforcing the southernization of European Christianity is the changing character of the Catholic priesthood and the influx of global South clergy now found across western Europe, including in once solidly Catholic regions: the image of African priests ministering in Ireland is particularly memorable. One diocese in southern France is host to some thirty priests from former colonies such as Senegal, Gambia, and Ivory Coast, men who view their new home with a powerful evangelistic impulse. Some years ago, conservative writer Michel Gurfinkiel remarked on how immigrant clergy were being used to reverse the precipitous decline of France's Catholic clergy, and the process is still more advanced today:

> Black African priests can be seen today throughout the country, even in rural areas of France; a black Zairian priest held mass for President Jacques Chirac in mid-1996. Female religious communities are, if anything, even more foreign: a substantial number of French nuns under thirty are of African or Asian origin.

As in the Protestant and charismatic churches, the faces of Christian leadership are now Nigerian, Vietnamese, and Filipino.[6]

Immigrant Christians

Some immigrant communities are numerous and influential. The impact is most clearly marked in Great Britain, which from the late 1940s onward drew heavily on Caribbean labor. Readers of Zadie Smith's *White Teeth* will recall the pervasive religiosity and apocalyptic tone that pervades description of London's Jamaican world of the 1970s in a Jehovah's Witness family. Caribbean ethnic groups are prominent in enthusiastic sects like the Witnesses and the Seventh Day Adventists, and Adventist numbers in particular would be slim if not for recent arrivals from the West Indies. In recent years, though, Africans have arrived in growing numbers, so that today, London has 380,000 black Africans as against 344,000 Afro-Caribbeans. Some regions of the city have a strongly African cast.[7]

The religious impact of immigration is unmistakable. Commenting on a successful African church, a correspondent in the British *Guardian* noted that "London, the cynical capital of the unbelieving English, must be one of the least religious places in the world. Of those who chose to answer the census question, 1,130,616 Londoners (15.8% of the total) said they had 'no religion'. Yet, as the city continues to be Africanized, so it is being evangelized," chiefly by charismatic and Pentecostal churches. Though the absolute numbers may be small, the potential for future growth is immense, as second- and third-generation

members of the newer churches move them into the religious mainstream. As in the United States, black churches have a strong political
orientation and a powerful social outreach, and pastors are well-
known community leaders. As one London African was quoted as saying in a recent news story, "From the day we're born till we die, it's the
church."[8]

When black immigrants arrived in Britain in the 1950s, it was not
obvious that they would be initiating a new church network, but
many encountered discrimination and hostility in the mainstream Anglican and other Protestant churches that they tried to join. Nigerians,
for instance, felt rebuffed by the Anglican churches that they initially
sought out. Africans and Caribbean migrants responded by setting up
their own congregations, which flourished. One example is London's
Jesus House, established in 1994 as a new planting by the RCCG. Today, it claims over 2,000 weekly participants, and numbers are growing steadily. Of Britain's ten largest megachurches, four—KICC, Glory
House, Jesus House, and New Wine Ministries—are pastored by Africans
(Table 4.1).

Britain's black churches today claim around 250,000 members,
and an institutional framework is provided by groups like the Afro-
Caribbean Evangelical Alliance. In 2005, the Church Census found that
people of African or Afro-Caribbean stock accounted for 10 percent of
Sunday churchgoers in England, a number rising to 44 percent in London: nonwhite ethnic groups made up another 14 percent of London's

Table 4.1 **British Megachurches**
Churches with average weekly attendance
of two thousand or more

Church	Attendance claimed
Kingsway International Christian Centre	10–12,000
Kensington Temple (Elim Pentecostal Church)	5,500
Hillsong Church	5,000
Ruach Ministries	4,000
Glory House	3,000
Jesus House	2,500
St. Thomas's, Sheffield	2,500
Holy Trinity, Brompton	2,500
New Wine Ministries	2,100

Source: Andy Peck, "What the Mega Church Can Teach You,"
Christianity Magazine, August 2006, at www.christianitymagazine
.co.uk/engine.cfm?i=92&id=742&arch=1.

worshipers. In religious terms, the empire has struck back, decisively. Nor do these remarks about black churches take account of the considerable black presence in mainstream churches, especially among Catholics. Caribbean and African Catholics are a familiar sight at pilgrimages and other communal gatherings, and so increasingly are east Asians. The ancient shrine of Aylesford in Kent now plays host to a sizable annual gathering of Afro-Caribbean believers. Moreover, black churches no longer exist in a segregated universe of their own. As noted earlier, one of the country's main religious interest groups is the mainly white, million-strong Evangelical Alliance, a venerable structure founded in 1846. In 1998, though, this organization elected as its head a (black) Jamaican-born pastor named Joel Edwards.[9]

New Europeans

Given its history of empire and mission, France not surprisingly has an immigrant Christian presence, among Protestants as well as Catholics. The nation has around 1.1 million Protestants, just 2.2 percent of the population, but that figure includes the most active and enthusiastic charismatics, many of global South origins. Two-thirds of the country's Protestants are Reformed or Lutheran, old-stock churches with deep historic roots: John Calvin was himself a Frenchman. In recent years, though, the fastest growing segment of Christianity has been evangelical and charismatic, and since 1950, their numbers have swelled from 50,000 to around 400,000. This is chiefly the result of immigration from Francophone Africa, but newcomers from Asia and the French Caribbean, les Antilles, have also contributed. Christians are especially numerous among the wave of African immigrants who have arrived over the last fifteen years and who have given such an African feel to sections like Château Rouge, in Paris's 18th arrondissement. The fervor of France's black Christians is difficult to miss. In the words of one native French pastor, "I take the train in from the suburbs every day, and I have plenty of stories of Caribbean or African preachers—men and women—getting up to preach or sing or testify to their neighbors."[10]

The earliest African churches were branches of the European Protestant communities that had sent out missions and now found themselves welcoming these distant brethren on their own soil. Such for example were the Cameroonian Presbyterians, Madagascarian Reformed and Lutherans, Ivoirien Methodists, Congolese Evangelicals, and so on. From the 1980s, though, distinctively African churches spread, especially among Congolese migrants. (Though the Congo/Zaire was a Belgian possession until 1960, knowledge of the French language made France an attractive destination for its citizens.) The Congo experienced a charismatic revival during the 1980s and 1990s, and the wars and political catastrophes of these years drove many believers into exile. The first diaspora churches were formed in 1983–1984, and since then, the Congolese have rivaled the Nigerians in their church-building zeal. By 2003, Europe's largest Congolese churches included the Belgian-based New Jerusalem, with 1,300 members, and 900 attend Sunday worship at Paris's AFPC (Assemblée des Fidèles aux Prières Chrétiennes), founded by pastor Félix Simakala. France today has a series of ethnic church federations, representing for instance the Madagascarian and Haitian communities. The Congolese-initiated CEAF (Communauté des Églises d'Expressions Africaines de France) claims thirty-five congregations across France.[11]

Greater Paris has 250 ethnic Protestant churches, chiefly black African. Significantly for present debates about ethnicity and religion, many of these are concentrated in the poor sections, the banlieues, which have recently become so notorious for unrest and social deprivation. Although these communities are usually discussed in the context of Muslim immigration, in fact they have a lively Christian presence. Immigrants are concentrated especially in the "93," the postal code of the département of Seine-Saint-Denis. Sixty evangelical churches operate in the 93, including a dozen affiliated with the CEAF, with names like the Good Seed and Gethsemane. We find CEAF churches in communities like St. Denis (four congregations), Pantin, Montreuil, or Aulnay-sous-Bois. The RCCG has a presence in Seine St. Denis, where we also find a Laotian church and a Portuguese congregation of the Assemblies of God.[12]

Besides the churches appealing chiefly to one ethnic group, many others draw widely on a range of the new communities. One recent journalistic account of a church in an immigrant suburb, the Evangelical Assembly of the Pentecost, found believers chiefly stemming "from French possessions in the Indian Ocean and the Caribbean, from Haiti, and in large numbers from Africa. . . . Most of [the] congregation is black. On my Sunday morning visit, I meet a woman from Gabon whose husband is from Madagascar." Another recent report focused on the Christian and Missionary Alliance church Église Protestante Evangélique, in La Défense, "a progressive business suburb of Paris." When the pastor

> asked how many among those attending are indigenous, Caucasian French, only ten people raised their hands. Forty are African immigrants—some naturalized, some legal, and some illegal. When he asked them to say the names of their motherlands aloud, they mentioned Gabon, Ivory Coast, Congo, South Africa, Togo, Nigeria. Several are from Asia: Indonesia, Vietnam, Cambodia, China, Japan. Several are from Iran. Two are from Canada; a couple from the States. Some are from Colombia, Brazil, England, Spain.[13]

But the immigrant phenomenon is not confined to Britain and France. Rome is home to anywhere from 50,000 to 100,000 Filipinos, most of whom are loyal Catholics, not to mention a further 50,000 Latin Americans. Cut off from their homelands and isolated by culture, language, and poverty, they turn for support to churches that follow the customs of their homelands. Journalist Michael Mewshaw notes the overwhelming presence of these *extracomunitari*:

> Every Sunday evening, Chiesa della Natività di Gesù throbs with the chants and clapping of Congolese Catholics. Two blocks away at Chiesa di San Tommaso Apostolo, Coptic Christians from Ethiopia and Eritrea fill the Via di Parione, with women in flowing robes and the sounds of drums and reed pipes. . . . [I]n recent years the music from St. Andrew's Presbyterian Church has become more melodious, not to mention more professional. This parish of Scotsmen has welcomed a contingent of Korean evangelicals, many of whom are in Rome to study music composition and opera.

Roman Catholic groups have recognized the importance of preventing immigrants slipping away from their Catholic roots and have formed special missions to target migrants. In Rome, the Scalabrinian missionary order reaches out to Latin Americans, offering social service functions, supplying food and clothing, but also providing religious services in the familiar languages of their homelands, and using local customs.[14]

Other host nations have their new Christian stories. Germany has at least 1,100 foreign-language Protestant churches with some 80,000 members. The first AIC appeared in 1974, when the Nigerian Celestial Church of Christ (an Aladura foundation) opened up shop in Munich. By the end of the century, two hundred AICs were recorded: forty in Hamburg, twenty each in Berlin and Frankfurt, perhaps a hundred in the Rhine-Ruhr valley. Germany has its Aladura churches, its Kimbanguists. While African missionaries established some congregations, many grew out of local fellowships and Bible study groups on German soil, such as the All Christian Believers Fellowship founded in Karlsruhe in 1993.[15]

In some cases—globalization in action!—Africans in Germany formed their own churches, which then set up branches in the mother countries in Africa itself. In 1992, Ghanaian Abraham Bediako founded in Hamburg a Christian Church Outreach Mission, which seems on the way to becoming a denomination in its own right. It has a dozen churches in Germany, and more than sixty in Ghana itself. The church describes itself as "an international, non-denominational multi-racial church and a full-gospel, charismatic faith congregation with branches in Germany, Holland, Great Britain, Spain, United States and Ghana." Particularly evocative is the web page on which the church portrays its European pastors. All the faces are black African, though their places of work include such historic German cities as Dortmund, Frankfurt, Lübeck, Bremen, Kassel, Kiel, and Hannover, as well as Amsterdam, Paris, and Madrid.[16]

Among other countries, Aladura churches have been active in Switzerland since the 1960s, and the country has its own Federation of African Churches. Denmark now has 140 immigrant churches, up from virtually nothing just twenty years ago. Roman Catholics have benefited especially, in a country in which Catholicism has for centuries represented only a tiny fringe faith. Today, though, immigrants are filling Denmark's few Catholic churches and driving a need for new congregations. In Aarhus, the Frue Kirke (Church of Our Lady) offers masses in Vietnamese, Polish, English, Tamil, and Chaldean, and all are well attended. Fourteen of Denmark's Catholic parishes offer mass in Tamil, eleven in Vietnamese, ten in Polish.

The United States too has its thriving immigrant churches, but these operate in a very different environment from their west European counterparts. While in the United States new groups have added an extra stratum to the existing range of churches, in Europe, they more commonly offer a replacement. As the difference is sometimes expressed, when a Christian church goes out of use in western Europe, it becomes a warehouse, a condo, or a mosque. In the United States, a church that becomes obsolete generally reopens as another church, for a Brazilian or Korean congregation. The stereotype has some truth, but increasingly, global South Christians are also demanding and finding their own space in European cities.[17]

Diasporic Faith

Apart from their ethnic character, Europe's immigrant Christians are set apart from the old-stock population by many aspects of belief and practice. Whatever the denomination, global South Christian churches usually have a powerful charismatic quality, a belief in miracles, healings, and visions. Christians, like Muslims, are also "fundamentalist" in the generic Western liberal sense, that is, they tend to take religious texts very seriously and believe they should shape and transform everyday lives. Parallels between the faiths owe something to demographics. Christian churches, like Muslim mosques, appeal to a largely young following and are often led by enthusiastic young adults. Both also come from societies with a definite belief in the power of spiritual forces to combat real evils, including illnesses of body and mind. Both are thus readily accused of extremism or fanaticism.[18]

Also, the fact of operating in diaspora societies, freely crossing national boundaries, sets groups apart from older churches, which are rooted in settled communities and are more subject to the desires of particular states. Repeatedly, we see resemblances between the lived experience of European Muslims and Christians of Third-World origins arising from this diasporic quality. For modern observers, studies of religious diasporas tend to concentrate on the most sinister and potentially lethal movements such as the Muslim extremists organized under names such as al-Qaeda or Takfir wal Hijra. Yet the fact of being "rootless cosmopolitans"—to use the famous derogatory jibe once directed against Jews—need not have sinister implications, nor need a multinational movement have any sinister content whatever. The Christian scriptures themselves include a detailed account of a diasporic religious movement, and a substantial portion of the New Testament comprises the letters and injunctions used to regulate and educate this community.[19]

Today as in the ancient Mediterranean world, religious diasporas have certain features in common, whatever their theological differences. Their presence in many nations provides an immediate framework and social network for migrants, who find a reassertion of familiar values from home but also an incentive to keep up demanding standards of faith and piety. This fact has potent implications for chances of assimilation into the social mainstream. For both Muslims and Christians, infusions of new faith introduced by transnational groups tend to be anti-assimilative and to undermine factors that otherwise would contribute powerfully to secularization. If such transnational networks keep on operating and migrating on a semipermanent basis, that fact works against any kind of mainstreaming, any veering toward the secular norm. Transnational groups thus help institutionalize distinctiveness.

Also, the irrelevance of borders to such movements meshes well with the universal teachings of the respective faiths. Early Christians were taught that "here have we no continuing city, but we seek one to come." For Muslims likewise, transnational groups are more likely to preach the significance of the universal Muslim community rather than flawed human-made nations. To be transnational is to be antinational.[20]

Diasporic religion also serves as a conduit between host nations and the lands from which migrants originate, a role that offers great potential for cultural cross-fertilization but also raises the possibility of internal conflict. Immigrant communities bring to the new country the religious traditions of the old, which in the context of global South Christians means a charismatic faith deeply imbued with ideas of spiritual warfare. At the same time, immigrants returning to their homelands take with them at least some of the ideas of the new world— more expansive attitudes, for instance, about the role of women, and much greater awareness of the potential of new technology. Financial connections are also critical. Again, we read the New Testament and find the repeated conflicts that Paul faced concerning the transmission of donations from the diaspora to "the saints in Jerusalem." Today, Muslim communities in Europe are the economic salvation of their home villages in Pakistan or Turkey, and Christians serve a comparable role for their homelands in Africa or the Philippines.

A New Frankenstein Religion

Looking at the often depressing state of older churches, one might think that white Europeans would be overjoyed to see new signs of Christian growth, specially when this is associated with young and active populations. To a remarkable extent, though, recent controversies suggest real suspicion of the immigrant churches, which media and policy makers regard almost as an alien cult.

In European history, the words "New Christian" carry grim implications, referring as it does to those Jews who were forced to convert in early modern Spain but whose religious practices remained under deep suspicion. New Christians were the primary targets of the Spanish Inquisition, and their activities were its chief justification. Today, of course, no official compulsion requires anyone to confess the Christian faith, yet once again we find quite deep tensions between the old and better-established churches, and those newer believers whose faith they view very coolly. African and African-derived churches especially are often portrayed as extremist, superstitious, and subject to the manipulative whims of greedy or cynical preachers. The portrait of global South churches has many parallels to the familiar American stereotypes of destructive cults.

Media reaction to the rising Christianity demonstrates curious parallels to the treatment of Islam. In terms of mainstream responses to the practice of the religion itself, European media and officialdom have demonstrated rather greater tolerance toward Islam than to immigrant Christianity, which is viewed as a peculiarly sinister faith not worthy of legal protections. Of course, Islam receives the vast bulk of news coverage because of society's fears of terrorism or subversion, which nobody has yet applied to southern world Christianity. Yet having said that, both Christians and Muslims receive a chilly reception from a secular media and officialdom.

In Britain, African and Latin American churches hit the headlines only during exposés of exorcism and spiritual warfare episodes in which children have been harmed, sometimes after they were accused of being witches or possessed by demons. The media largely ignored the new churches until the national scandal surrounding a young African girl called Anna Victoria Climbie, who died from extreme physical abuse in 1999. Her family suspected she was bewitched and took her to a wide range of churches offering healing and exorcism services, including the Brazilian-based Igreja Universal.

Recently, African churches have been subjected to astonishing vilification. Following one quite well documented instance of African human sacrifice in London—an act derived from pre-Christian and non-Christian animist traditions—the media began linking such activity to Pentecostal churches. The affair began in 2001, with the discovery in the Thames of the mutilated body of a five-year-old boy nicknamed Adam. Allegedly, the child was

> the victim of a ritualistic killing linked to a West African form of voodoo-like religion. Officers suspect that gangs illegally importing exotic meat, such as chimpanzee and bush rat from West Africa, are involved in trading in substances used in African witchcraft that may include human body parts.

As the classic *Heart of Darkness* script unfolded, media and police attention inexorably focused on misdeeds attributed to black charismatic churches and AICs, some of which had been engaged in harrowing exorcisms of alleged witches and demoniacs, commonly children. One scandal, which genuinely did involve the brutal death of a child, was linked to the practices of Combat Spirituel, a classic Congolese AIC.[21]

Since 2005, media reports have segued from suggesting that exorcisms were undertaken to fight diabolism, to presenting the rituals themselves as a form of primitive black jungle savagery dressed in Christian guise. Rituals designed to *combat* witchcraft were thus presented as a singularly dangerous *manifestation* of witchcraft. The *Guardian* characteristically headlined "Children Abused in Exorcism Rites," and "Police Investigate Religious Links after Witchcraft Abuse of Child"; the *Observer* announced "Churches Blamed for Exorcism Growth." The *Sunday Times* announced, " 'Witch Child' Abuse Spreads in Britain: Fifty Cases Suspected in London Alone." London's sensationalistic *Evening Standard* reported that

> boys from Africa are being murdered as human sacrifices in London churches. They are brought into the capital to be offered up in rituals by fundamentalist Christian sects, according to a shocking report by Scotland Yard. . . . Last month Scotland Yard revealed it had traced just two out of 300 black boys aged four to seven reported missing from London schools in a three-month period. The true figure for missing boys and girls is feared to be several thousand a year.[22]

In 2006, the BBC television documentary *Witch Child* claimed to investigate the "increase of a disturbing recent crime, in which young African children in the UK are being abused, and even murdered, by parents and relatives in the belief that they are possessed by evil spirits." In the program, academic Richard Hoskins told how he had sought the roots of these primitive Christian beliefs: "I traveled to Africa in search of a young London child who had been sent back to the Congo and came face-to-face with the horrifying realities of exorcism in the 21st century." In his view, exorcism churches practiced "a new Frankenstein religion, an unholy marriage of perverted Christianity and an ingrained African belief in the spirit world."[23]

While everyone admits that members of different faith traditions commit crimes or atrocities, it is much more dubious to assert that such acts form part of the religions themselves or that they are required rituals. To take an American example, not even the most forthright critics of child sexual abuse by Catholic priests claimed that such behavior was demanded or justified as part of secret rituals followed by the Catholic Church. Yet that is the kind of leap made in the context of the African churches, where crimes by sadistic or disturbed individuals are used to condemn mainstream beliefs. Putting all this in perspective, belief in exorcism, spiritual healing, possession, and the defeat of witchcraft are indeed integral to most African (and many Asian) churches, and all these practices are well established in regular denominations, including Anglican, Catholic, and "mainline" evangelical churches. The regular conduct of immigrant churches—involving exorcism and healing, not necessarily with any abusive or violent element—was thus seen as deeply problematic, and criminalized.

Now, police and social services were unquestionably dealing with a few instances of truly abusive and violent behavior, and their concern is laudable. If they were investigating the torture of children carried out under the guise of religion, no one could fail to support their efforts, but they went too far in framing their response. The *Guardian* told how

> Richard Hoskins, an expert in African religions and cultural and religious crime, said he knew of several cases of attempted exorcisms in the UK. He told BBC Radio 4's *Today* programme that "faith healers" from African churches were entering the country. "There are clearly exorcisms taking place in this country," said Dr Hoskins. "I am helping the Metropolitan Police and also social services with six or possibly seven cases UK-wide, and people say there are more."[24]

At least as it is stated here, the characterization of exorcism is odd. To place these comments in the context of African or Asian Christianity, we would have to imagine a story in which an expert in religious deviance warned that "there are clearly Eucharistic services taking place in this country" and that the scholar was assisting police in detecting and suppressing them. Of course exorcisms are occurring in churches of African origin, and there are faith healers. How could there not be? And as we have seen, deliverance and exorcism are a major part of the spiritual arsenal of white charismatics. (Technically, too, every Catholic baptism includes a form of exorcism.)[25] Hoskins's earlier research on Congolese traditions like Kimbanguism had certainly made him aware of the critical role of spiritual warfare ideas, which need not be associated with violence or child abuse. Hoskins can scarcely be blamed for how his remarks were quoted, and possibly misunderstood, by the media; but as the newspapers reported the affair, they presented a dismal view of African Christianity.[26]

In retrospect, the ritualistic abuse affair was mainly a media-driven moral panic, a reprise of the Satanic ritual abuse furor from a decade earlier. Even the *Guardian*, which was itself deeply implicated in scare-mongering, drew breath long enough to investigate "How Media Whipped Up a Racist Witch-Hunt." But the official response to the new cases was to adopt far stricter rules for African clergy and ministers entering the UK, a draconian sanction introduced several months before any like restrictions were imposed on Muslim activists or imams preaching hatred and violence. The affair indicates staggering official and media ignorance of charismatic Christianity, of the distinctive religious practices of African and global South believers, and a tendency to dismiss enthusiastic Christian belief as, in effect, a black thing. The controversy has disturbing implications for Europe's growing religious diversity. If the media are so grimly ignorant of and prejudiced against non-Western Christianity, what hope do they have of understanding the more alien faith of Islam?[27]

Colliding Diasporas

As Europe's immigrant communities assume a more significant role in national life, their respective religious views will also become more consequential. On many issues, Christians and Muslims have a great deal in common—churches and mosques can potentially agree on common struggles against moral and sexual decadence, with homosexuality as a uniquely sensitive issue.

In other ways, though, Christian and Muslim diasporas threaten to come into conflict, especially over issues arising from home countries. We often see the importance of churches and church leaders from nations such as Nigeria, Congo, and Uganda, all of which face the real prospect of internecine struggles between the two faiths. Nigeria, above all, is a source of special concern with its current political uncertainty and the likelihood of a transfer of power in the executive branch from a Christian to a Muslim leader. It is not fanciful to imagine such violence spilling over into the streets of London or Rome. Something of the sort has already occurred, though not by design. During the London subway bombings of 2005, Muslim terrorists targeted civilians regardless of their race or religion. Given the city's multi-ethnic character, though, it is not surprising that some were immigrant Christians, from Nigeria and elsewhere. African Christians were murdered by Asian Muslims, in the European religious theater.[28]

Even setting aside the possibility of violence and retaliation, disagreements between immigrant Muslims and Christians also take political and partisan forms. Migrant politics often intersect with exile politics, with the potential for stirring unrest. In the Muslim instance, official repression drives activists and dissidents to seek exile beyond the reach of the state apparatus. Commonly, those driven from their homelands are religious leaders and exiles, and such exile communities can serve many functions. They are notoriously vulnerable to the machinations of rival governments and intelligence services, which might even find in them the nucleus of an alternative government for the persecuting nation. An exile center—be it a cleric's retreat, a place of worship, or a school—can also become a center for conspiracy and intelligence in its own right, not to mention sources of fund-raising. Also, exiles are free of the need to compromise with the practical realities of their homelands and commonly drift to the most radical and extreme positions, violently opposed to the nations that drive them away.[29]

Now, all these themes are familiar in the context of the radical Muslim networks; but to a lesser extent, they also apply in some Christian settings. For Africans especially, London and other European cities become leading centers of political and politico-religious organization, and this role grows as conflicts in home nations define themselves increasingly in interfaith terms. The Nigerian Christian diaspora especially can be expected to play a critical role in that country's politics over the next decade.

But for all the scenarios that might be imagined, the main issue is the presence of not one but several diasporic faith communities in the emerging polychrome Europe. And an exclusive focus on one of these, however significant, threatens to neglect others of critical importance.

5

The Moor's Return

Before, Muslims were guests who would leave. Today Islam is among us.

Riay Tatari Bakri (Madrid)

For all the potential importance of other religious groups, it is Europe's Muslims who attract the greatest attention and concern, all the more so given the historical context. Near Granada, we find the famous site of "the Moor's last sigh," where Spain's last Muslim king wept as he contemplated the ruin of a once-great civilization, overwhelmed by the Christian *Reconquista*. As Fouad Ajami has pointed out, though, we might yet live to hear the Moor's last laugh, as Muslims again hold sway over large portions of Europe. Not only are Muslims a prominent force in all leading cities, but this presence will inevitably grow. For Europeans, the critical question is whether the Muslim presence can be absorbed into societies that were traditionally Christian or secular, and how that interaction will transform both sides.[1]

"All for to Fight"

When Christians and Muslims meet in contemporary Europe, both sides carry a great deal of historical baggage, whether or not they recognize it consciously. A beloved fixture of English rural folk custom is the Mumming play, a semi-pagan ritual drama in which light and darkness struggle. After the appearance of the heroic King George, there enters his sworn enemy, who announces:

> In comes I, turkey snipe,
> Just come from these turkey lands all for to fight.

His introduction recalls a time when the Turkish Knight—now, the snipe—was the universal enemy of Christianity. Italians still use the threatening phrase *fare i salamelecchi*, literally, to make salaam-aleikums. This is the behavior we find in an enemy who appears grovelingly polite and humble, but who is really plotting against you—the person who is always either at your feet or at your throat. Muslim enemies became sufficiently familiar and stereotyped to spawn another Italian phrase used to respond to vague fears and bogeymen: *Mamma, li Turchi!* The Turks are coming! According to legend, the defeat of the Turkish threat to Vienna in 1683 is unwittingly commemorated millions of times daily when Europeans eat their croissants, which bakers designed as triumphant souvenirs of the great victory over the Muslim crescent.[2]

The history of conflict is well known, though apportioning the blame is controversial. Modern Western accounts of the long relationship between Christianity and Islam commonly give little sympathy to the intentions of Christian Europe. In Euro-American popular history, the encounter is generally framed in terms of the Crusades, and a version of these events in which Christians are unabashed aggressors against thoroughly civilized Muslims. In the film *Kingdom of Heaven*, the capture of Jerusalem in 1099 stands as a monument to Christian fanaticism and proto-imperialism. Similarly, in the widely seen PBS documentary *Empire of Faith* (2002), the Muslim-dominated Spain of the Middle Ages is cited as a near-utopian realm of religious tolerance and cultural achievement, in stark contrast to barbaric Christendom. At its medieval height, Córdoba was the greatest Islamic city in the Mediterranean region, followed closely by Palermo; Córdoba allegedly had a thousand mosques, Palermo three hundred. The Arabs made the Mediterranean "our sea" (*Bahruna*), supplanting the old Roman Mare Nostrum.[3]

According to the modern indictment of Christian misdeeds, Christian expansion and intolerance culminated in the destruction of Moorish Spain in 1492. Over the following century, Muslims were subjected to increasing severity, facing forcible conversion and eventually—between 1609 and 1614—expulsion of the remaining crypto-Muslims. That act of massive intolerance is intimately linked to the persecution of the Jews and the work of the Spanish Inquisition, one of the very few institutions of early modern history of which most modern Americans or Europeans think they have some knowledge. Columbus's discovery of the New World in 1492 makes that date doubly significant, and suggests the heritage of intolerance, racial prejudice, and paranoia on which the modern West would be founded.[4]

In modern times, images of Islam have been profoundly affected by the work of Edward Said, who proposed that European views of the Arab and Muslim worlds were deformed by Orientalism, the projection of one's own violent and erotic fantasies upon an imagined and demonized Other. Looking at past accounts of Turks or Moors, modern

Europeans assume that Christian societies were guilty of stereotyping quite as systematic as that directed toward Jews in modern times. Modern Euro-American observers assume that Christian struggles with Islam prefigured modern atrocities such as the Holocaust, and Muslim writers have been happy to reinforce Western guilt.[5]

Yet the picture of incessant European aggression is misleading, not least because it neglects the issue of how Muslims came to establish themselves in the first place in the Near East, in Palestine, Syria, or Spain. From the seventh century through the seventeenth, Islam expanded into the Mediterranean world through military conquest and a series of bloody wars in which Muslims generally held the upper hand. If Europeans held a common image of Muslims as massacring and enslaving infidel populations, that picture had a solid basis in historical fact. The stories that we regard as the tragedies of interfaith intolerance, the Crusades and the Spanish Reconquista, are the two great—and rather isolated—examples in which Christian forces won major military victories.[6]

Contrary to popular myth, neither side has much to be proud of in terms of religious tolerance. If Moorish Spain tended to accept the existence of Christian and Jewish minorities, most Muslim societies permitted subject communities to continue only at the price of accepting total Muslim dominance in every sphere of social and political life, and anti-Christian persecutions or massacres were common. Popular accounts of the pleasant *convivencia* under Spanish Muslims do not dwell on events like the slaughter of Jews during the Granada pogrom of 1066, or the mass deportation of Christians to Morocco during the following century. It was the Muslims who pioneered the close surveillance of Jewish converts to Islam, removing their children for an orthodox Islamic education, exactly the kind of behavior for which later Christians have attracted such opprobrium. Further afield also, when expanding European states encountered Muslim states in India or the East Indies, these were societies dominated by Muslim elites, who ruled harshly over Hindu or animist subjects.[7]

Through most of the early modern period—from 1400 through 1800, say—the Muslim world more than held its own against Christian Europe, and Ottoman Turkey often played an active and aggressive role in international affairs. If modern Westerners remember dates signifying Christian aggression, 1099 and 1492, events in other years shaped the history of modern Europe, and sometimes threatened the survival of European states. For the Orthodox Christians of Eastern Europe and the Near East, May 29, 1453, marked "the last day of the world," the Turkish capture of Constantinople and the final destruction of the vestiges of the Roman empire. In 1480, the Turks destroyed the Italian city of Otranto, perpetrating one of the worst massacres in an age not noted for acknowledging any restraints in warfare: 12,000 were killed, and leading clergymen were executed by sawing. The atrocity spread terror among west Europeans, who dreaded an imminent Turkish onslaught. In 1526, the Turks conquered Hungary, destroying what was then one of the major European powers. Throughout the great years of Ottoman military expansion, the Janissaries stood at the vanguard of their armies. These were originally European Christian boys, forcibly conscripted as a kind of human taxation on subservient *dhimmi* communities, and converted into fanatical Muslim warriors.[8]

Through the sixteenth and seventeenth centuries, the Turks dominated most of the southeastern quadrant of Europe, and in 1683, they came very close to capturing Vienna, the capital of the Holy Roman Empire. As Hilaire Belloc noted, "Less than 100 years before the American War of Independence a Mohammedan army was threatening to overrun and destroy Christian civilization, and would have done so if the Catholic King of Poland had not destroyed that army outside Vienna." Well into the eighteenth century, coastal residents of western and northern Europe lived in dread of the north African corsairs or pirates, who enslaved many thousands of Christians. True, Muslims and Christians sometimes lived in mutual friendship and respect: Shakespeare's portrait of Othello suggests how the two sides could respect each other's humanity, while Cervantes jokingly attributed the whole of *Don Quijote* to the mythical Moorish scholar, Cide Hamete Benengeli.[9]

Even so, the relationship was more commonly characterized by well-grounded fear, with the Muslims usually occupying the role of aggressors and slave-masters. Balkan Christian populations remained under heavy-handed Turkish oppression until modern times, suffering a brutal occupation that can legitimately be compared to later European experiences under the Nazis or communists. Turkish rule resembled Nazi rule in the creation of a master caste, in this case Muslims, before whom all despised lesser breeds were to cower. The great era of anti-Turkish liberation struggles lasted from the 1880s to almost the outbreak of the First World War. Edward Said's writings on Orientalism can be criticized on many fronts, but he was most radically off-target when he suggested that "the West" had dominated "the East" consistently for the past 2,000 years.[10]

Imperial Encounters

Only in the second half of the eighteenth century did the balance of power between Christian Europe and the Muslim world shift. In 1757, British forces in India defeated the most important Muslim warlords on the subcontinent, while Napoleon's invasion of Egypt in 1798 marks the beginning of the Muslim encounter with modernity. In the early nineteenth century too, the Greek revolt became a focus for romantic enthusiasm across western Europe. Between 1800 and 1914, European powers conquered and annexed almost the whole of Dar al-Islam, engaging in repeated wars and suppressing many revolts and risings. In occupying India, the British dominated the largest single concentration of Muslim populations, though the empire also incorporated millions of other Muslim subjects in Africa and southeast Asia. The mainly Muslim regions of the East Indies formed the heart of the Dutch Empire, while the French annexed much of northwest Africa. Russia advanced into central Asia and the Caucasus, and the Italians, latecomers to the imperial game, absorbed Libya and Somalia. After the First World War, the British and French divided the Arab world between them, and Turkey itself came close to partition.[11]

These various struggles rarely defined themselves in neat religious terms, still less a simple clash of Muslim versus Christian. In nineteenth-century culture, Muslim societies acquired a romantic aura, often because of the presumed similarities between modern tribal societies and the ancient worlds of the Old Testament patriarchs. French and British artists regularly depicted Arab warriors as noble savages riding their proud steeds, as in the famous paintings of Delacroix. Europeans acquired respect for the Muslim civil servants and soldiers upon whose loyalty the empires largely depended. British, French, and Spanish empires all employed Muslim soldiers, who were seen as brave and fiercely loyal. When in the 1930s, General Franco sought to retake Spain in the name of a right-wing Catholic cause, many of his most devoted soldiers were *Moros,* Moroccans. Hitler's Germany used Balkan Muslim forces in its quest for a colonial empire within Europe itself, and the SS formed two Muslim divisions.[12]

Yet the imperial encounter also left many negative stereotypes and themes, which endured long after the empires themselves had dissolved. One was the association of Islam with subject peoples and races, from whom obedience and submission were demanded. Also persistent were ideas of Muslim fanaticism and militarism, and Edward Said correctly observed how Europeans used the Muslim world as a foil, as a dark background against which they could project their own superior values. The negative image of Islam bore many resemblances to modern stereotypes of destructive religious cults, with their brutal mindless followers, exploitative leaders, and sexual excess.

Enlightenment thinkers used denunciations of Islamic fanaticism and credulity as oblique ways of attacking aspects of Christianity of which they disapproved. Humphrey Prideaux's *Life of Mahomet* (1697) condemned Deists and anti-Trinitarians, while Voltaire's 1741 play *Fanaticism, or Mahomet the Prophet* was an attack on all forms of religious extremism and enthusiasm. In 1776, Edward Gibbon imagined an Islamic Europe to show how far religious loyalties were a matter of historical accident, however determined ignorant clergy might be to trace the hand of providence. If the Battle of Poitiers (in 732) had turned out differently, he wrote, "the Arabian fleet might have sailed without a naval combat into the mouth of the Thames. Perhaps the interpretation of the Koran would now be taught in the schools of Oxford, and her pulpits might demonstrate to a circumcised people the sanctity and truth of the revelation of Mahomet."

African and Asian attempts to resist colonialism bolstered images of fanaticism. British concepts of Islam owed much to demon-figures like the Mahdi who led a successful revolt in the Sudan of the 1880s, and to the dervishes the British encountered a few years later in the same territory. Already by the end of the nineteenth century, Europe's popular stereotypes of Islam included visions of charismatic bearded prophets driving their brainwashed followers to massacre infidels. When the British encountered anti-colonial resistance in Somaliland a few years later, the movement was symbolized by the religious and military leader Mohammed bin Abdullah Hassan, popularly labeled the "Mad Mullah." The nickname suggests much about European attitudes: why, apart from insanity or religious fanaticism, would a people choose to resist the blessings of imperial rule?

Much of European military history and lore was formed in conflict with Muslim populations—by the British in India, the French in north Africa, the Russians in the Caucasus, the Dutch in the East Indies, the Italians in Libya. What the British remember as the Indian Mutiny of 1857 was to thousands of its participants a jihad against the British infidel. So common and widespread was jihadi resistance against European colonialism around the world during the second half of the nineteenth century that we should be less surprised by what is often seen as the modern revival of Islamist politics and militancy. The theaters of combat were very much the same then as now, with prolonged struggles in the Sudan and the Horn of Africa, in Algeria and Morocco, India and Afghanistan, the East Indies and the Caucasus. Modern jihadis differ from their predecessors chiefly in their access to modern means of travel and mass communication, which permit the formation of international alliances and coalitions. Nor, of course, could nineteenth-century rebels count on sympathetic Muslim populations within the imperial states themselves.

Modern Muslim nations glorify the leaders of anti-colonial resistance movements, who were often motivated by Islam and the rhetoric of jihad. Perhaps the greatest of the Muslim opponents of empire was Imam Shamil, who fought doggedly against Russian expansion in the Caucasus for thirty years. He became the legendary exemplar for Muslims in the Caucasian states, and modern-day Chechen leader Shamil Basayev was named for him. In the 1920s, Omar al-Mokhtar led mujahedin resistance against the Italian occupation of Libya, becoming a hero for Libyans and others. When Palestinian Hamas supporters parade in contemporary Gaza, they commonly march down Omar al-Mokhtar Street. In modern times too, French politics and history owe much to the experience of the brutal Algerian war of 1954–1962, an experience that was arguably as traumatic in French memory as the Nazi occupation itself.[13]

The Empires Come Home

The historical experience also helps explain the Islamic presence in modern Europe. After the destruction of Ottoman power in Europe in the early twentieth century, Muslim populations were small and isolated. Apart from old-established communities in Balkan regions like Albania and Bosnia, Muslims could be found in some larger seaports of west European nations, in cities like London, Cardiff, and Marseille. The Muslim presence remained small until the 1950s, when western Europe was booming economically and in desperate need of manual labor. Southern Europe provided some workers—in France, indeed, the Portuguese continued to be the nation's largest immigrant group through the 1980s. Another obvious source for workers would have been the poorer areas of eastern Europe, but this avenue was blocked by Cold War boundaries and restrictions. Instead, European nations turned to their former colonies, where their presence had spread some knowledge of their languages and customs.[14]

Incidentally, the forces driving Muslim immigration were so overwhelming that there is no reason to imagine the conspiracy theory devised by Bat Ye'or and since popularized by Oriana Fallaci and others, which suggests that European elites collaborated with Arab states to create a Eurabian federation spanning the Mediterranean. Given the economic forces demanding labor and the political factors conditioning supply, it would be difficult to imagine any outcome much different from what actually occurred. In the United States, similarly, any significant relaxation of immigration laws would inevitably have drawn in millions of Mexican workers, regardless of what any government or private cabal planned or desired.[15]

European nations differ enormously among themselves, and so do their histories of colonial exploration and encounter, which did much to shape modern patterns of migration. These nations have admitted very different kinds of Muslims and have treated them in different ways. The British drew on the widely separated regions of their far-flung empire, with their various religious traditions—on the predominantly Christian lands of the West Indies, on Hindu and Sikh regions of India, and on Muslim Pakistan and (later) Bangladesh. (Bangladesh was until 1971 a component of Pakistan, hence the generic term "Pakistanis" in the early years of settlement.) Other countries, however, drew more heavily on Muslim regions, especially the French, with their north African ties, and the Dutch, with their historic connections to Indonesia. Expanding countries that lacked a colonial heritage turned to north Africa or, especially, to Turkey.[16]

In France more than anywhere, the Muslim population represents a legacy of empire. In the nineteenth century, the French empire included the north African territories of Algeria, Morocco, and Tunisia, as well as many black African lands, and France used these possessions as a source for soldiers and labor, especially during times of crisis such as the First World War. These children of empire were so loyal that in 1929 Paris built its Great Mosque as a token of official gratitude. So comfortable did north Africans feel about coming to the French motherland, in fact, that their presence attracted alarm. In the early 1960s, General Charles De Gaulle explicitly warned that France must sever its ties to Algeria or else the Christian nation would be overwhelmed, to the point that his beloved home village of Colombey les Deux Églises ("of the two churches") would soon become Colombey les Deux Mosquées.[17]

The end of the Algerian war, which marked the effective end of the French empire, did indeed signal the beginning of a large-scale immigration. Complicating matters, new populations came from very diverse political origins: white Christian and Jewish settlers fleeing the new radical regime; Muslim *harkis*, those who had taken the French side in the revolution, and who rightly feared retaliation; and the Muslim children of the nationalist revolutionaries themselves. The *harkis* alone, with their families, represented a sudden influx of perhaps 75,000 Muslims. France contained around a million people of north African descent by 1973, rising to perhaps 4 million today. People of Algerian stock now make up around 35 percent of France's 5 million to 6 million Muslims, with another 35 percent drawn from Morocco and Tunisia.[18]

If French Islam is largely north African, then Turkey accounts for the majority of Germany's Muslims. In 1961, Germany recorded only a few thousand Turks, but this figure reached a million in 1976, and 2 million by the mid-1990s. Today, Turks make up two-thirds of Germany's 3.5 million Muslims, and some 350,000 Turkish-language newspapers are sold daily in Germany. Moroccans and Turks make up the majority of the Muslim populations of the Netherlands and Belgium, with people from the Caribbean territory of Surinam representing another 10 percent of Dutch mosques.[19]

British Islam, meanwhile, is derived mainly from the Indian subcontinent, with perhaps half tracing their roots to Pakistan and a further 25 percent to India and Bangladesh. In fact, the migration was even more concentrated in its character than these numbers would suggest. A third of the 2 million people in Britain who originated in the Indian subcontinent came from just one region—Mirpur in the Pakistani part of Kashmir. Generally, people who came from the same home region tended to settle close to each other in their new countries, so that social and cultural patterns from the homeland were reproduced on European soil.[20]

Settlers

New immigrants naturally settled where work was to be found, and that meant either the traditional urban centers or the then-thriving regions dominated by smokestack industries. A map of Muslim Europe today represents a ghost of the industrial scene of fifty years ago. Perhaps 40 percent of French Muslims are concentrated in the greater Paris region, especially the regions to the north and northeast of the city, in "93" ("nine-cubed") the département of Seine-St.-Denis. Though these areas are now notorious for their rundown *banlieue* suburbs, Muslims initially settled there because of the promise of good wages. In the glory days of the French automobile industry, North Africans came to work for Citroën at Aulnay-sous-Bois or Renault at Flins, and employers actively welcomed them as a contrast to strike-happy French workers. Another 13 percent of Muslims live in Provence/Côte d'Azur, chiefly in the cities of Marseille and Nice, the areas that traditionally had the closest ties to French north Africa. Today, perhaps a quarter of Marseille's population is Muslim, and the city has a strong north African feel. Other major communities cluster in and around the once-flourishing urban and industrial centers of Lyon, Strasbourg, and Lille.[21]

British Muslims are equally urbanized. Some 600,000, or 40 percent of the British total, live in London, where Muslims account for one-twelfth of the city's population. The heaviest concentration is in the borough of Tower Hamlets, home to 75,000 Bangladeshis, who occupy the old sweatshop areas that have played host to successive past waves of poor immigrants—originally French Protestant exiles and later east European Jews. This tradition finds a monument in what was originally the French Huguenot church in Brick Lane, which became a synagogue in 1897 and since 1976 has thrived as a Bangladeshi mosque. Outside London, the main Muslim communities are found in and around old northern industrial cities like Leeds and Manchester. Oldham, Bradford, and Burnley are aptly described as "mill and mosque" towns. The West Midlands also have their strong Muslim areas, and in communities like Camp Hill and Moseley, Muslims make up three-quarters of the population.[22]

Across Europe, Muslims gravitated to cities then experiencing the long boom that faltered only in the mid-1970s. Muslims make up almost half the population of Rotterdam, the center of the Dutch economic flowering in the 1960s, and the city is home to one of Europe's largest mosques. Some 30,000 Muslims settled in the old city of

Antwerp, in what would sometimes be troubling proximity to the city's old-established Orthodox Jews. Muslims constitute about 20 percent of the population of Brussels, the capital of the European Union. In Germany likewise, Berlin is home to a substantial Muslim community, particularly in sections like Kreuzberg and Neukölln. Forty percent of Frankfurt's population hold a foreign passport or come from an immigrant background, and about one person in eight is of Turkish Muslim origin. If the country has a stereotypical Muslim ghetto, it is Marxloh, which stands next to the old industrial heartland of Duisburg in the Ruhr, Europe's largest inland port. Turks represent 60,000 out of a population of 520,000 in the Duisburg metropolitan area, and there are forty mosques. Muslims now make up around a fifth of the population of Vienna, a figure that roughly doubled just during the 1990s.[23]

Here to Stay

At least in the early years of immigration, it was not obvious that Muslims would be a permanent part of the European landscape. As recently as 1970, anyone who suggested that European nations would soon be facing Muslim minorities of 5 or 10 percent of the whole would have been regarded as a hysterical alarmist. Facing the great influx of non-European populations from the 1950s onward, European nations could not agree whether in fact they were dealing with immigration. In Great Britain, the imperial ideology of the day initially meant that the new arrivals from Pakistan or Jamaica were fellow-citizens of the British Commonwealth, exercising their right to come to the mother country, and presumably, to set up homes there. Accordingly, they were frankly described as immigrants, however poorly prepared either the government or the older-stock population was to deal with that new reality. But if they were immigrants, then they would need to be absorbed into British society. Accommodation had to be made for their families and children, and for their religious institutions.

Other nations, however, such as Germany and Sweden, lacking a colonial ideology, starkly refused to recognize the reality of immigration. They admitted foreigners as "guest-workers," to be employed only as long as they were needed, and at that point, it was hoped, the migrants—chiefly men—would return uncomplainingly to their countries of origin. Years after it ceased to correspond to facts, the mantra that "Germany is not a land of immigration" ("Deutschland ist kein Einwanderungsland") was still repeated by German politicians. Since Muslims would never be citizens, Europeans would not have to confront issues of religious or cultural diversity, of how to deal with the presence of mosques and hijabs. Of course, this imagined exodus never happened, and by the 1970s it was evident that guest-workers were creating immigrant communities, with families establishing themselves and new generations being born on European soil. From the mid-1970s, some governments began granting guest-workers the right to bring in their relatives in the name of family reunification.[24]

Occasionally, governments tried to reverse the process by repatriating the foreign-born. In the late 1970s, Jacques Chirac noted that France had 2 million immigrants and a million unemployed, and remarked how easily repatriation could cure France's unemployment problem. During the economic downturn of 1983–1984, the German government offered financial incentives to encourage immigrants, mainly Turks, to return to their home countries, and around 250,000 did so. In fact, though, such efforts slowed the growth of ethnic minority communities only briefly.[25]

No less likely to overstay their supposedly temporary status were asylum seekers fleeing the threat of repression or persecution in home countries. In the liberal Scandinavian countries especially, this type of migrant represented a major component of the newly arrived population. By the early 1990s, Sweden was receiving asylum applications at a rate of 84,000 a year, in a land of only 9 million people, and the vast majority of requests were granted. Now, by no means all of these were Muslims, but a significant number were—not surprising, given the brutal chaos then prevailing in Balkan territories like Kosovo and Bosnia, not to mention the Horn of Africa. In the Netherlands, the number of asylum seekers grew from 3,500 in 1985 to over 43,000 in 2000, and that in a country of just 16 million.[26]

Over the past decade, the abuse of asylum has irritated many normally liberal Europeans, who complain of the very wide latitude on which the privilege is granted. By the standards of western Europe, how many countries in Africa and Asia are not repressive, especially if one factors in discrimination on the grounds of gender or sexual orientation? Also, long experience has shown that asylum rarely proves to be a temporary category, which concludes once conditions have eased in the home nations. Like guest-worker status, asylum has proved an open door for migrants to Europe, who tend to become permanent residents.

Since the 1980s also, members of the new ethnic communities were increasingly likely to acquire citizenship. Over half the Muslims in France or Britain are citizens of their respective countries, and in 2000 even Germany made the historic decision to grant citizenship on the basis of birthplace rather than ancestry. This decision sparked a boom in the citizenship rolls and the prospect that in a few years, the country might have 3 million Muslim voters.

Islam's Old Europe

Muslim numbers grew rapidly. Europe as a whole, from Ireland to Russia, had 18 million Muslims in 1970, rising to some 32 million by

2000. And despite the recent concern about "Eurabia," the strongest presence continues to be in regions outside what was traditionally considered the European heartland.

By far the largest Muslim population and the sharpest "Islamic challenge" is in fact to be found in Russia, which many exclude from that European category. Russia is rarely discussed in accounts of contemporary religious conflicts because its Muslim population is largely concentrated in regions far removed from the heartland, chiefly in Tatarstan, and in the north Caucasian territories of Chechnya, Ingushetia, and Dagestan. Yet the numbers are significant and have profound implications for traditionally "white" and non-Muslim parts of the country. Russia today has 15 million to 20 million Muslims out of a national population of 143 million, anywhere from 10 percent to 14 percent of the whole. The country has as many Muslims as the whole of western Europe, and almost as many mosques—5,000 to 6,000. The gap between Muslim and non-Muslim birth rates is more acute than anything found in western Europe, suggesting that people of Muslim stock may gain more influence over time, as the country needs more labor and more internal migration. Already, Muslim central Asians are a common feature in Russian cities, much like Moroccans in Rome or Amsterdam, portending a much greater impact in urban life in coming years.[27]

Even if we exclude Russia, many of Europe's Muslims do not fit the now familiar image of a flood of recent immigrants. The ghosts of the former Ottoman realm survive in the substantial Muslim population in southeastern Europe, overwhelmingly people of European stock. Over 7 million Muslims live in the Balkan states, with another 900,000 in Bulgaria. The vast majority of Balkan Muslims, some 6 million strong, are concentrated in Albania and in the southern territories of former Yugoslavia—in Kosovo, Bosnia-Herzegovina, and Macedonia. Albania, in fact, is Europe's only majority-Muslim nation. The wars in this region during the 1990s actually made the Muslim presence in this region more visible and more coherent, as a result of the mass expulsion of Christians from Kosovo and neighboring territories. In the city of Pristina, for instance, an Orthodox population that once totaled 40,000 has now been reduced to just 120, and hundreds of churches and monasteries have been destroyed. On the other side of the religious divide, the polarization of the war years fostered a more marked (and militant) Islamic identity.[28]

Incidentally, these Muslims of European stock represent a strong if underrated element in immigrant communities in western Europe, where their ethnic background often startles Arab and Asian Muslims. These Balkan migrants need travel only short distances within the continent to find jobs and prosperity. In the 1990s, over a quarter of Italy's Muslims were Albanians, who had crossed just the couple of hundred miles to reach their new homes. In terms of providing virtually open access to immigrants, legal or otherwise, Italy's coasts somewhat resemble the U.S.-Mexican border.[29]

The Balkan states also play a significant if little-noted role in debates over Europe's religious future, since they are all but certain to obtain full membership within the European Union within a decade or so. In the past, opponents of European expansion have been able to exclude candidates like Turkey and Morocco on the grounds that they were only marginally linked to Europe and had slim geographic or historic grounds for claiming European identity. None of these objections apply to Albania or the successor states of the former Yugoslavia. If these nations can maintain democratic institutions for a few years, they can scarcely be denied full admission to the community. That fact will immediately expand the Union's Muslim population by 40 percent or so, and these new citizens will have the right to travel and work where they please within the wider community.

Into the West

For most west Europeans, affairs in Sarajevo or Pristina or even Moscow appear distant and exotic. What has changed in recent years has been the upsurge of obvious Muslim communities on their own soil, and it is in western Europe that the Muslim presence has grown most sharply and attracted most attention. To put the overall numbers in perspective, if western Europe's 15 million Muslims represented a single nation, they would be the sixth largest country of the European Union, more populous than Belgium.[30]

Also, as we have seen, these communities are not spread evenly across the country but are instead heavily concentrated in major cities and metropolitan regions. While overall numbers have risen in the last thirty or forty years, growth has been particularly sharp in areas that come within the consciousness of Western opinion makers, especially in the capital cities. An Italian observer remarks how Muslims have in a very few years moved from the exotic to the everyday, to *quotidianitá*.[31]

Apart from the growing numbers of visibly non-European people, Muslims have over time become more confident about building their own institutions. People of the first generation had little incentive to invest time and effort in building mosques or other facilities, to plant religious roots in unbelieving soil, since they thought they would ultimately return to their homelands. Over time, this resolution faded as families formed and children were born. From the mid-1970s, we see a clear shift toward building communities and religious institutions, and this is the point at which mosques and Muslim schools began to proliferate. Literally as well as figuratively, Muslims now established themselves in the European landscape. In 1966, Britain had just eighteen mosques, but that figure grew by seven a year over the next decade: 338 mosques were registered by 1985, and a thousand by 1997.[32]

Mapping Muslim Europe is a difficult task, since terms like "mosque" are somewhat vague: some writers reserve the term for a specialized institution with a minaret, describing smaller facilities simply as prayer rooms. Taking both categories together, Europe as a whole today has around 9,000 mosques and prayer rooms, of which 1,200 are found in Bulgaria alone. About 7,000 mosques can be identified in the nine west European nations listed earlier, with 80 percent concentrated in just three countries: Germany (2,400), France (2,000), and Great Britain (1,500). Italy, Spain, and the Netherlands combined account for another thousand.[33]

From the 1980s, some Muslim communities signaled their presence by building conspicuous religious facilities to compete with the great cathedrals that traditionally dominated the skylines of Christian Europe. France, for instance, has eight such "cathedral mosques" that can accommodate a thousand worshipers apiece, places like the Great Mosque in Paris. Duisburg-Marxloh now has a three-story mosque complex on this scale, modeled faithfully on Ottoman styles. Other facilities are even grander. The evocative great mosque of Córdoba opened in 2003 and overlooks the Alhambra palace, the heart of the once-great Moorish kingdom of Spain. Its sponsors explicitly want this to serve "as a focal point for the Islamic revival in Europe." Also in 2003, the Ahmadiyya Muslims opened in Morden, England, a facility that holds 10,000 worshipers. Another proposed mosque, the London Markaz, would accommodate at least 40,000, becoming indisputably Europe's largest, and if built, it would provide the backdrop for many events in the London Olympics of 2012. Adding to the controversy surrounding such a dominating structure, the Markaz project is the work of the missionary order Tablighi Jama'at, which many have linked to extremist causes.[34]

Cause for Concern

The growth of visible symbols of Islam helps explain why white Europeans have become so perturbed about the Muslim presence, which is presently not immense when set beside the continuing Christian strength suggested earlier. Some other factors explain why a society should be so concerned about a minority of only 4 percent or 5 percent. One is a matter of perception. Projections of ethnic minorities sometimes conflate nonwhite immigration with the Muslim presence, so that imagining European cities achieving "majority-minority" status late in the present century implies Muslim domination. In fact, many recent immigrants are Hindu, Sikh, or Christian.[35]

But even allowing for just Muslims, we have to recall the novelty of a non-Christian presence in Europe. Until recently, no non-Christian faith was anything like as much in evidence as Islam is today. For centuries, most European conflicts over religious tolerance involved rival Christian denominations rather than non-Christian faiths. Through the nineteenth century, Jews would have made up perhaps 2 percent to 3 percent of the European population, but the great majority of these were found in the eastern parts of the continent, in Poland, Ukraine, or the Baltic states, while the Jewish populations of England, France, Germany, or the Netherlands were numerically tiny. Only from the 1880s onward did migrations create significant Jewish minorities in western Europe, and the hostility they attracted, even in tolerant Britain, closely resembles modern charges against Muslim immigrants. In most Western nations, of course, the high Jewish population was a transient phenomenon and was savagely reduced by the persecutions of the 1940s. To put this earlier non-Christian presence in perspective, between 1880 and 1940, the European continent as a whole had almost as many Muslims as Jews, though their geographical distribution made them virtually invisible to western Europeans.[36]

In race as much as religion, European Muslims represent a real novelty in most countries. While dark skins have been familiar to Europeans for centuries, they were usually confined to major cities and

Table 5.1 **The Expansion of Muslim Populations in Western Europe**

Muslims (thousands) in

	1900	*1970*	*2000*
France	50	1,353	3,850
Germany	0	450	2,850
Britain	0	635	1,050
Italy	1	43	600
Spain	1	5	170
Netherlands	0.2	60	533
Belgium	0	90	335
Sweden	0	2.4	137
Austria	0	18	139
Switzerland	0.4	16	158
Denmark	0	12	55
Total	52.6	2,684	9,877

Source: David B. Barrett, George T. Kurian, and Todd M. Johnson *World Christian Encyclopedia,* 2nd ed. (New York: Oxford University Press, 2001).

seaports and never represented large numbers. In 1930, Sweden recorded a Muslim population of exactly fifteen—not 15,000, but fifteen. Today, the figure exceeds 400,000. The United Kingdom had 23,000 Muslims in 1951, rising to 369,000 in 1971, and topping a million by 1991: the present-day figure is 1.6 million. France in the 1940s had just 100,000 Muslims, compared to perhaps 5 million today. Illustrating this mushroom growth, we might look at a table of Muslim growth offered by the *World Christian Encyclopedia*. We can certainly challenge these figures in detail. The compilers of these data missed some Muslim populations at the start of the century while underestimating figures at the end of the period. Even so, the table does give some idea of the scale of growth and its speed. Realistically, the increase of Muslim populations was even steeper than is suggested here, with the figure perhaps quadrupling between 1970 and 2000 (see Table 5.1).

The Growing Crescent

Europeans concerned about Islam are worried less about the minorities of the present day than their likely growth in the near future. If Muslim numbers quadrupled in that short historical period, could they balloon just as impressively in coming decades? Some demographic evidence suggests that this prospect is not far-fetched. Allowing for illegal immigrants, Muslims already comprise 8 percent or 10 percent of the French people, and that figure could plausibly grow to 20 percent or 25 percent by 2050. Already, Muslims comprise a quarter of the population under twenty-five years old. Germany as a whole might be dealing with a Muslim population of 20 percent by 2050, with heavy Muslim concentrations in all the major cities. The Muslim population of the Netherlands doubled just between 1990 and 2005, growing from perhaps 3 percent to 6 percent of the population. In Sweden—traditionally a land associated with Nordic purity and ethnic homogeneity—around an eighth of the population is foreign-born. To put this in perspective, this figure recalls the proportion of immigrants recorded in the United States at the height of the great influx of eastern and southern Europeans at the start of the twentieth century.

Immigration continues to reinforce Muslim strength. Western Europe as a whole receives about half a million new migrants a year, and that number could rise significantly. United Nations projections suggest that to maintain the 1995 level of working to nonworking population, Europe would need to take in 1.4 million migrants each year from now until 2050. The figures are all open to further expansion if we assume a European Union with essentially uncontrolled borders, open to barely restricted mass immigration from north Africa and the

Levant. Drawing together various estimates, the U.S. National Intelligence Council suggests that a European Union Muslim population that stood at 5 million in 1985 has now reached 15 million. The number would probably rise to about 28 million by 2025, but the council also offered alternative low- and high-end projections, respectively, of 24 million and 38 million.[37] These numbers are all the more impressive when we recall that the total European population will fall in coming decades, so that Muslims will represent an ever-larger proportion of the smaller whole.

At first sight, such figures do indeed seem to comprise the opening chapter of the history of Eurabia, but matters are not quite as straightforward as they appear. Undoubtedly, some leading European nations—France, Germany, and the Netherlands—will have significant Muslim minorities of 10 percent to 15 percent by 2025, and these communities might account for 20 percent or 25 percent of the respective populations by 2050. That is a historic and cultural fact of vast importance. But if we consider Europe as a whole—everything west of the former Soviet Union and including the Balkans—the picture is a little less overwhelming. By 2025, the continent would have perhaps 40 million Muslims out of a total population of 500 million, about 8 percent. That figure might well rise higher in subsequent decades, to a probable 15 percent or so by 2050. The Council on Foreign Relations veers a little on the high side when it suggests that by 2050 one-fifth of Europeans will be Muslim by cultural background, if not in religious practice.

But that is a crucial difference. As we have seen, modern European society does not seem hospitable to institutional or dogmatic religion of any kind, and by 2050, European Muslims will have been exposed to this ambience for several generations. At the least, we can expect that ethnic birth rates will have fallen to something like mainstream norms. Nobody can deny that European nations in coming decades will have to take account of aspects of Muslim culture, or rather of the north African and Asian cultures brought by Muslim immigrants; but that is quite different from envisioning wholesale Islamization.

While acknowledging the new ethnic diversity, then, Europeans inevitably ask what kind of Islam the new communities would practice. Although old-stock Europeans hope for the emergence of a moderate Euro-Islam in line with their own traditions, the kind of Islam they more commonly see in daily media reports is fanatical, politicized, and intolerant, with a marked penchant for violence. If in fact that was to be the faith and ideology of 15 or 20 percent of the population of leading nations, then Europe's prospects would be bleak indeed, and the far-sighted would need to consider how to escape the coming wreck, how to obtain U.S. or Canadian passports for themselves and their families. Muslims really would have returned "all for to fight."

Yet matters are not so terrifying. While sections of European Islam in recent years have acquired a strongly militant and politicized character, we have to understand this as a response to temporary circumstances; moreover, hard-line approaches still command only minority support. In the longer term, the underlying pressures making for accommodation and tolerance will prove hard to resist.

6

Making Muslims

Brother, our society needs to be reformed, and reform cannot emerge out of wretchedness, fear, and conservatism. What are we conserving? This backwardness? The Westerners ride our backs with their armies, with their economy, their media, and their science, and we just sit there being conservative? . . . By Allah, our faith will become stronger if we go to the countries of the West. Our faith will only grow. My faith grew stronger in Europe, in France, in Britain. My faith grew stronger, and so did my knowledge, Allah be praised.

Hassan al-Turabi

Over the centuries, Islam has adapted successfully to the various societies in which it has found itself. A critical question for policy makers today is whether the same process can occur within a European setting, so that Islam in Italy becomes Italian Islam, Islam in Britain acquires the distinctive coloring of a British Islam, and so on. If Catholicism in the Netherlands has become so thoroughly acclimatized to the Dutch polder landscape, to become polder Catholicism, might we before too long imagine a polder Islam? Could Swedish Islam acquire a "blue-yellow" patriotic tinge, as many hope? In fact, powerful forces favor such assimilation. Islam historically has few international or global institutions, so there is no equivalent of the Vatican to regulate religious interactions in a particular society. Also, many European Muslims follow styles of belief and practice that would not flourish under strict or puritanical clerical regimes, which would make them the first targets of a hypothetical Euro-Taliban. They have a vested interest in preserving religious tolerance and diversity.

So strong in fact are the forces working against orthodoxy or militancy that the recent trend to hard-line positions demands some explanation. Partly, this was a matter of historical accident, that the great age of immigration coincided exactly with the global resurgence of aggressively political forms of Islam, which became engaged in several emotive battlefields around the world. But we also see a pattern reminiscent of changes within Christianity in the same period. In both cases, a faith that had flourished successfully in small and deeply rooted local communities suddenly found itself facing much greater social complexities that proved hostile to traditional religious structures. While many believers slipped away from the faith, others turned to smaller and more activist groups that demanded more commitment and dedication. Some younger Muslims turned to transnational forms of the faith that preached strict orthodoxy and heavy political involvement. People responded to the painful encounter with modernity by returning to ancient purity, or at least, to what they imagined it to be. Heavy-handed intervention by Muslim nations has encouraged this turn to orthodoxy and clericalism, making it difficult for Europe's migrant communities to develop their own kind of accommodation with the mainstream societies they encountered.

Yet we must keep this kind of militant neo-orthodoxy in perspective. It does not represent the beliefs of most religiously active Muslims, still less of the large populations who identify little with religion in any form, who are anything but religious in any approved or institutional sense. The nonobservant "cultural Muslim" is a familiar type. In France presently, just 5 percent of Muslims attend mosques with any degree of regularity, and a third of Muslims reported praying every day, figures that suggest almost Anglican detachment from formal religious commitment. Of course the mosques always look full and bustling, since worshipers are trying to squeeze into a relatively small number of facilities. As Olivier Roy comments, "You have many millions of square meters of churches in France, but only a few thousand square meters of mosques." Popular impressions of mass Muslim devotion, he argues, are in fact no more than a trompe l'oeil, an optical illusion. Muslim populations in contemporary Europe already contradict the familiar stereotypes of Muslims as strict and monolithic in their piety, still less as fanatics. Moreover, life in a secular state forces a fundamental rethinking of the relationship between the secular and religious spheres, especially when Muslims are conscious of their minority status.[1]

Also, it is too easy to characterize any religious or political view by quoting its most extreme advocates. Imagine the picture we would form of American Christianity if we heard only the views expressed by Pat Robertson or Jerry Falwell. Among Muslims similarly, the voices quoted in the media are often far removed from the sentiments one hears in ordinary conversation. Commentators find it easy to condemn Islam by citing the words of rabid extremists like Omar Bakri Muhammad or Abu Hamza: easygoing and tolerant people simply are not newsworthy. Asked about the political coloring of his British mosque, boxer Amir Khan replied "Yeah, but in Bolton they're all so normal. They do the prayers and maybe talk about the Koran and that's about it." And that statement characterizes a large proportion of apolitical and unexceptional mosques across Europe. Without suggesting the speaker is typical, we might turn to the poor Moroccan man in France, as quoted by scholar Farhad Khosrokhavar. He complains of the repressive state, noting that

> with Islam, you don't need the state any more to do right, you seek what is right in yourself. Islam means speaking without shame, it means not being disturbed, speaking gently and considerately [*avec douceur et delicatesse*], speaking from your heart and also speaking from your head. It is peace and tranquility. . . . It means you have to educate your children, respecting family and neighbors, doing the five prayers, giving alms without stinting, being generous. Religion means peace toward yourself and your neighbor. *Al Rasul* [the prophet Muhammad] prayed with Christians as brothers, while Muslims reject them today. A neighbor is also a brother. You mustn't do to others what you don't want for yourself. It's God who judges.[2]

The more European states can limit the influence of militants, the more likely it is that this kind of observant Islam will become the norm. The best sign that such an accommodation is in progress will be when Muslims form their own sacred space in Europe, their own shrines and pilgrimage sites, which the puritanical hard-liners will denounce with holy passion.

When we contemplate the disturbing face of Islamist extremism, we should recall that this represents a desperate reaction to these broadly progressive directions rather than its natural expression. Islam in modern Europe owes much of its extremist qualities to the consequences of globalization and migration, but those same factors are also promoting more expansive and broad-minded forms of the faith. The Islam proposed by reformers need not be "moderate" in the sense of apathetic, but it rejects violence and extremism: its advocates are comfortable with social and religious diversity and find active advantages in living in an atmosphere of official secularism. If indeed this is the emerging Islam of multifaith Europe, the future is anything but doom-laden.[3]

Shades of Islam

We cannot speak without qualification of a European Muslim, as if such a generic individual was easy to find. After all, when we speak of Europe's Christians, we are including Dutch Calvinists and Sicilian Catholics, Romanian Orthodox and English Quakers. Muslims worldwide are almost as diverse in their styles of belief and practice. Islam, similarly, has over the past 1,400 years acquired quite different characters in different lands, and there are Moroccan Muslims, Turkish Muslims, Nigerian Muslims, and so on, representing very different forms of the faith, and varying degrees of commitment.

Too often, Western concepts of Islam are drawn from the characteristic models of the Arab Gulf states, and especially of Saudi patterns, with their ferocious intolerance of any customs or practices that deviate from what they perceive as the historic faith. In fact, the dominant form of the faith in Saudi Arabia, known as Wahhabism, is itself a fairly modern development, arising from reform movements of the eighteenth century, and it owes its contemporary power to the vast wealth acquired by the Gulf states in the twentieth century. Oil gave these nations the resources to build mosques and schools around the world, to train and pay imams and teachers, and to publish literature.

If in fact Wahhabis are correct, then a great many Muslims around the world are not truly Muslim, and European communities often draw on traditions that are anathema to the Saudi establishment. Around the Mediterranean, established religious forms, whether Catholic or Muslim, merge with popular religious beliefs that a strict observer might call superstitious. In Algeria, the lived religion of ordinary believers usually focused on holy men, wandering marabouts, who were channels of divine blessing, *baraka*. After death, their power survived at the sites of their tombs, which became venerated shrines and pilgrimage centers, around which annual fairs are held. Festivals are celebrated with ritual dramas. Nothing in this picture would have surprised the medieval Christian devotee of his or her own saints. Ordinary north African Muslims, moreover, often have a lively belief in spirits or *djinn*, and a powerful belief in fate or destiny is indicated by the regular use of the word *mektoub* ("It is written"). Morocco has a rich subculture of fortune-tellers and diviners (*shawafat*), who diagnose curses and hostile spells, and helpfully dispense amulets and talismans. Alternatively, one can frequent a *fkih*, a spiritual healer. Saudi Muslims view these customs with all the nausea of a seventeenth-century English Puritan observing the folk-customs of Neapolitan Catholicism, and they are just as likely to use terms such as devil-worship and witchcraft. Yet despite all the criticisms, all these ideas survive and flourish in migrant communities in Europe.[4]

Western media and policy makers sometimes imagine a more moderate form of Islam that would serve as a counterweight to Wahhabism, which is seen as strict, intolerant, and puritanical. Somewhere, they feel, they can identify a more authentic Islam, more broad-minded and tolerant, a "religion of peace." Generally, such hopes are quite plausible, but with the caveat that strictness is not a Wahhabi prerogative. For one thing, the term "Wahhabi" is sometimes applied over broadly, to cover fundamentalist movements with origins distinct from the Arabian-based sect of that name: the Indian Deobandi school is particularly influential. More important, throughout its history, schools of thought and belief of enormous variety have indeed proliferated within Islam, and many have spawned enduring institutions in the form of brotherhoods or informal networks, and these differ radically from the stark simplicity affected by Wahhabism. The problem for Western interpreters is that many, in their various ways, possess their own elements of strictness, intolerance, and puritanism, and some confound religion and politics to a degree that unsettles secular Euro-Americans.

Some of these other traditions within Islam are well known, especially the Shi'a version dominant in Iran, and strong in Iraq and Afghanistan. Though Wahhabi believers question its claims to authentic Muslim status, Shi'ism is no less radical in its assertions of God's supremacy, no less theocratic, and has powerful apocalyptic and millenarian currents. The Shi'a are a minority among European Muslims, but they do represent a real force in Germany especially. Twenty percent of Germany's 3.1 million Muslims are non-Sunnis. This includes 400,000 of the Turkish-based Alevi sect, a form of Shi'ism that rejects many of the basic tenets of orthodox Islam: they do not even recognize prohibitions against pork or alcohol. Fifty thousand more are Ahmadiyyas, a tradition that many Muslims regard not just as heretical but as simply non-Muslim.[5]

Sufis

By far the most significant such movement within Islam is the Sufis, who are not a sect but rather a tradition of belief and devotion that is absolutely critical to the development of the majority Sunnis. Trying to understand Islamic realities, past or present, without taking account of the Sufi is like trying to comprehend Catholic Christianity without understanding the religious orders, or Protestantism without hymns.

Though in the West the Sufis are most commonly known for gentle speculative mysticism—we think of the New Age fascination with the poet Rumi—the Sufi orders (*tariqat*) represented the spearhead of Islamic expansion through north Africa, through south and central Asia. The Sufis were at once elite knights who led military campaigns, and evangelists and teachers who preached the faith in new lands, winning converts by both their mystical achievements and intellectual daring. The Sufis created institutional networks in the forms of brotherhoods claiming loyalty to particular founders, from whom later leaders claimed spiritual descent: such are the Naqshbandi, Chishti, and the Mevlevi. Settlements of the Sufi warrior mystics were known as *murabitun*, and in European history, this name gave rise to the Almoravids, the mortal enemies of legendary Christian warlord, El Cid. A generation of Westerners encountered this movement through the 1961 film of that name, in which the Almoravids are the martial desert fundamentalists who despise the tolerant faith of the easygoing Spanish Moors.[6]

Still, today, we cannot hope to understand political realities in much of the Muslim world without grasping the critical significance of the Sufi orders, the tariqat. This is certainly the case with the post-Soviet successor states in Central Asia, the "Stans." Nor do Western media recognize the Sufi roots of the militant anti-Russian resistance in the Caucasus, especially among the Chechens. Islam survived decades of communist persecution in this region only through the resilience of the Sufi orders. Soviet authorities tried in vain to eliminate the *zikristi*, the Sufis who performed the ecstatic mystical exercise of the *dhikr*. Though loathed by the Wahhabis (and long banned in Saudi Arabia itself), the Sufis yield nothing to them in their stringent piety or, on occasion, in their political activism.[7]

Because of their role in Islamic expansion, the Sufis are central to religious practice in the historic frontier territories of the faith, beyond the ancient Arabic- and Persian-speaking heartlands stretching between Egypt and Iran. This is a critical fact for European Islam, which draws its numbers so heavily from exactly the greatest areas of Sufi loyalty—from Turkey and from the North African maghreb, from Pakistan and India. Sufism also has deep roots in the Islamic borderland of the Balkans, where the city of Skopje is a center for several different orders. Where Sufi traditions flourish, we find customs and practices such as pilgrimages to the tombs of saints and sheikhs, who are venerated with song and ritual dance. This devotional Sufi tradition is represented by the Brelwi movement that emerged in nineteenth-century India. The Brelwis are influential in Dutch Islam, but in Britain too, mosques have endured long conflicts between fundamentalist Deobandis and the more inclusive Brelwis. Today, Sufi societies still dominate the practice of Islam in many parts of west Africa, and Senegalese societies like the Tijaniyya and the Muridiyya are represented among African migrants to Europe. Sufi orders are widespread in Europe: Italy has three separate branches of the Naqshbandiyya order.[8]

Toward Orthodoxy

For many reasons, then, we might expect European Islam to be wildly diverse in practice and often heterodox and quite resistant to pleas for uniformity of any kind, least of all for anything partaking of Saudi norms. In theory, one of the first results of Wahhabi dominance in a community would be the prohibition or exclusion of Sufi activities and the introduction of stern sanctions against Alevis, Ahmadiyyas, and other deviants. Russian scholars note the open struggle in their country between Wahhabism and Tariqatism, that is, Sufism.[9]

Yet while Islamic practice has grown in Europe since the 1970s, it has actually become more orthodox, more conscious of pan-Islamic identities and causes. We also see a renewed movement toward Islamic enthusiasm, not just to the conventional forms of the religion practiced by the elders but also to fiery and committed versions, often with a potent political dimension. At its most extreme, puritanical and evangelistic forms of Islam reject cooperation with the mainstream society and even reject the legitimacy of the nation-state. This movement to a more stringent Islam is critical for the future of Muslim societies in Europe and indeed for the wider society, since this kind of demanding religion is competing for the loyalty of young Muslims, the second and third generation descendants of Asian and African immigrants.

This shift demands explanation. Olivier Roy stresses how deeply integrated Islam was in its countries of origin, with its ties to particular communities and clan structures, to shrines, saints, and sacred landscapes, all of which were severed with the move to Europe, so that Islam was deterritorialized. While early immigrants kept their personal memories alive, none of these traditions were available to younger generations born in Europe, who were cut off from their roots. "The religion of their parents is linked to a culture that is no longer theirs."[10] The young respond by turning to a new universalized or globalized Islam, which in practice offers the sternest and most demanding standards of the Wahhabis or Deobandis. But in return, believers receive a vision of themselves as the heroes of a glorious historical narrative, in which faith defeats the temporary and illusory triumph of disbelief and paganism.

In a European context too, the ideals of the Umma, the Muslim community, become sharply more evident in societies in which Muslims are not the majority and where the practices of the faith cannot be taken for granted in the same way that they can in an overwhelmingly Muslim nation. In some cases, Muslims found that familiar customs were now prohibited in their new countries, which demanded that the dead be buried with coffins and tried to limit the mass slaughter of sheep during the festival of Eid ul-Adha. This latter practice proved extremely sensitive for urban white Europeans who were so far removed from their farming roots that they had no contact with the realities of animal slaughter. As Brigitte Bardot complains, non-Muslims were appalled by "unacceptable behavior which left homes covered in blood, and filled rubbish chutes with skin, bone and oozing brains." As concepts of animal rights and vegetarianism grew in Europe, white residents were increasingly likely to label Muslims as cruel and barbarous, and to limit their ritual life. Other practices, though not banned, became much more difficult. As Roy writes,

> Fasting during Ramadan in Afghanistan, Pakistan or Egypt is very easy, even if one is not very religious, because social pressures push one in that

direction. But Muslims living in Europe are forced to make choices: they have to decide whether the prescriptions of religion are at the centre of their lives, which ones are essential and how to carry them out in practice. . . . Such believers have no recourse to ulemas (religious scholars) and are obliged to seek out criteria for religious observance which no longer have any connection to a given culture.[11]

Europe's Muslim communities are in daily contact with secular societies that pose constant challenges to familiar beliefs and moral codes. Without struggle, one cannot assume that employers will grant time off for prayer, that appropriate foods will be available, that a social consensus will enforce moral rules. Asserting and defending these practices creates a sense of unity against the mainstream culture.[12]

In addition, Muslims in Europe are subject to the same trends as populations in their countries of origin, and thus to the upsurge of the more fundamentalist and politicized Islam that has been such a fact of global affairs since at least the 1970s. Transnational networks have been crucial to spreading these views, especially pious orders undertaking Islamic *da'wa* (Call), which means the proclamation of the faith to non-Muslims, but also stirring nominal Muslims to greater devotion. In modern times, da'wa was often a response by faithful Muslims to the spread of Western ideas and Christian evangelism. One key activist was the early twentieth-century Indian thinker, Maulana Muhammad Ilyas, who founded the influential religious mission known as the Tablighi Jama'at, dedicated to preaching (Tabligh). Though he was himself a Sufi shaykh of the Chishti order, he adopted some aspects of Sufism, while rejecting others that he regarded as superstitious, aligning him to the conservative Deobandis.[13]

Tablighi believers join in a society or *jama'at*, and agree to go on journeys in which they strengthen each other's faith while promoting Islam among others. Though little known in American media, the Tablighi order has played a major role among European Muslims. From the 1980s, Muslim communities across Europe were intensely evangelized by the Tablighis, while Middle Eastern and Pakistani tariqat became increasingly powerful in immigrant mosques. Today, the Tablighis claim tens of millions of members and sympathizers worldwide, and since 1978 they have had a European headquarters in the northern British town of Dewsbury. Birmingham is the European home of another evangelistic movement with roots in south Asia, the Ahl-i Hadith, which resembles the radical Wahhabis or Salafists.[14]

Islamic Politics and Political Islam

Traditionalist religious attitudes did not necessarily have political consequences. Well into the 1980s, European Muslim leaderships were politically quietist. Most Muslims accepted their status as immigrants or transients who could reasonably expect to return some day to their home countries. Significantly, the Arab-Israeli wars of 1967 and 1973 evoked little activism among Europe's immigrant populations. Meanwhile, ordinary immigrants were generally to the left, inevitably, since it was the left-wing parties who supported them against racist and nativist attacks. Africans and Asians found their warmest advocates in parties such as the Communists in France and Italy, Socialists in Britain and Germany, and everywhere the small radical sects to the left of the communists. Immigrants' religious views were often secularist or anti-clerical. In retrospect, it is difficult to recall the strongly conservative nature of Islamic politics before the late 1970s. In this earlier era, Islamism was associated with the reactionary royalism of states like Saudi Arabia, which was starkly opposed to the modernizing nationalism of Nasserism, Ba'athism, or revolutionary socialism, the fashionable and exciting Middle Eastern ideologies of the day.[15]

But distinctively Islamic political thought revived when corruption and economic failure discredited secular regimes and politics across the Muslim world. Repeated oil crises gave much greater visibility and prestige to Islamic states, especially in the Gulf, while Marxism and secular nationalism entered a period of terminal crisis. In north Africa and the near East, the Islamic revival was associated with the Egyptian-based Muslim Brotherhood, al-Ikhwan al-Muslimin, founded in 1928. Pakistani thinkers like Maulana Maududi (Syed Abul Ala Mawdudi) were also vital. Maududi preached the doctrine of *iqamat-i-deen*, "the establishment of religion," the theocratic idea that society and the state should be subjected entirely to Islamic law: he was especially hostile to new concepts of women's rights. In 1941, he founded the Jamaat-i-Islami (JI), which became a leading force in the religious politics of Pakistan when that nation emerged from British rule. (This organization is not to be confused with the Indonesian JI, the extremist Jemaah Islamiyah.)[16]

These two movements, the Muslim Brotherhood and the JI, have provided the essential background for modern Islamist organization within the Muslim world and in Europe itself. Hamas, for instance, is the Palestinian offshoot of the Ikhwan. Egyptian radical Sayyid Qutb—a massive influence on modern-day Islamist extremism—drew on both the Muslim Brotherhood and on the thought of Maududi himself. The strong presence of JI supporters in Pakistan's military and security apparatus goes far toward explaining the tight Saudi-Pakistani alliance that has done so much to support fundamentalist Islam in south Asia, including, for several years, the Taliban regime in Afghanistan.[17]

Maududi died in 1979, the very year that the Iranian revolution brought revolutionary Islamism to the center of global affairs. Also during this pivotal year, a coup attempt by Islamist radicals in the holy city of Mecca terrified Saudi authorities and encouraged them to find ways of exporting dissent outside the limits of the kingdom. During the 1980s, accordingly, Saudi money sponsored hard-line mosques and schools around the world, encouraging the growth of more militant and confrontational varieties of Islam. Meanwhile, international conflicts aroused young Muslim activists worldwide. The war in Afghanistan mobilized radicals from around the Muslim world, who often traveled to join the struggle against Soviet imperialism. In most nations too, the U.S.-led attack on Iraq in 1991 raised qualms about Western imperialism in the Middle East. By the early 1990s, other political and religious struggles included the Chechen revolt against Russia.[18]

Other detonators had a special effect in particular countries. For Britain, which in recent years has produced some of the deadliest Islamist plots, by far the most significant conflict was the religious/political struggle in Kashmir, the area from which so many Pakistani immigrants came. Though Americans are familiar with the broad outlines of the Israel/Palestine conflict, the no less emotive Kashmir crisis remains unfamiliar. Like Palestine, Kashmir represents another hangover from a messy colonial partition of the late 1940s—in this case the breakup of Britain's old Indian empire. Depending on religion, territories affiliated either with the mainly Hindu nation of India, or with Muslim Pakistan. However, the Hindu prince of Kashmir led his domain into India, contrary to the wishes of the substantial Muslim majority. Irregular Muslim forces seized part of the area for Pakistan, but the remainder continues under Indian rule. Since 1947, Muslim activists have fought to win the whole of Kashmir, and in recent years, the separatist movement has become increasingly dominated by Islamist radicals. After the Soviets left Afghanistan, extremists moved their attention to Kashmir, and the presence of Qaeda forces in neighboring Pakistan reinforced the hardliners. Kashmir's neighbors to the west are the unruly tribal peoples of the North-West frontier, who still, probably, play host to Osama bin Laden. Pakistan's secret services and military have also dabbled extensively in the Kashmir conflict, provoking fears of full-scale war between India and Pakistan, both of which are now nuclear powers.

Militant Islamist movements also grew steadily in Algeria, from which so many French Muslims derived. Radicals followed the Salafist movement that aspired to return to the strictest interpretation of Islam as practiced by the Prophet Muhammad and his earliest disciples, abhorring any later developments or accommodations. In 1990, the Islamic Salvation Front, FIS, did so well in national elections that the military was forced to cancel the election process to avoid the establishment of an Islamist regime. Through the 1990s, the nation endured a destructive war that left 100,000 dead, as the government tried to suppress the Armed Islamic Group, the GIA (Groupe Islamique Armé). This movement in turn spawned an even more hard-core grouping, the GSPC (Salafist Group for Preaching and Combat). By the end of the decade, the Algerian government won the struggle, driving many extremists into exile, chiefly in Europe.[19]

Egypt suffered its own Islamist insurgency, the leaders of which pioneered some influential ideas. Building on the thought of Sayyid Qutb, radicals evolved a system in which believers claimed a revolutionary duty to struggle against regimes that claimed to be Muslim. Radicals should respond with an act of *takfir*, proclaiming the traitors as kaffirs, unbelievers, in effect reading them out of the faith. Members of the purified true-Muslim remnant should then make hijra, undertaking a self-exile that would remove them from that false society, usually withdrawing inward, to an alternative Islamic culture. In 1971, extremist members of the Muslim Brotherhood founded the movement Takfir wal Hijra. As Egyptian radicals came under mounting official repression during the 1990s, many fled to Europe, taking the movement with them, and it has proved a fertile recruiting ground for militants.

Meanwhile, the complex wars that swept the former Yugoslav federation had a special impact for Europeans. Some of the refugees from the Balkan war zone carried radical ideas with them: Germany alone has around 170,000 Muslims of Bosnian origin. While the conflicts drew international jihadist forces into the Muslim-Christian struggles in Bosnia, these events also deeply affected ordinary and hitherto nonpolitical Muslims. As Melanie Phillips remarks,

> What made this carnage so much worse was that it was taking place in the middle of secular, multicultural Europe. The Muslims being wiped out were pale skinned and clothed in jeans and track shoes. They looked and behaved like any other Europeans. And yet Britain and Europe were dragging their heels about doing anything to stop the slaughter.[20]

As interest in Islam grew, the appeal of secular leftism was diminishing. For the European left, the 1980s began with enormous promise, with popular revulsion against the Reagan regime and a deepening economic crisis. The U.S. decision to base missiles in western Europe in 1983–1984 galvanized a mass antinuclear movement that drew on environmentalism and feminism as much as traditional leftist opinion. After 1984, though, it was clear that aggressive U.S. policies had not only failed to ignite a nuclear war, but they appeared to be bringing the Soviets to the bargaining table. By the end of the decade, the fall of communism across eastern Europe created an ideological crisis for the Western left, which moved rapidly away from familiar socialist doctrines. In the process, these parties lost many of their most active and idealistic supporters, those most likely to reach the urban young. As Olivier Roy remarks, "When the left collapsed, the Islamists stepped in. . . . Islam has replaced Marxism as the ideology of contestation." Or to quote Farhad

Khosrokhavar, "Islam is becoming in Europe, especially France, the religion of the repressed, what Marxism was in Europe at one time."[21]

In their purest and most extreme form, theories like those of Qutb and Maududi influenced only a small minority of European Muslims, but the new wave of Islamic political thought and activism enjoyed wider influence. From the late 1980s, Islamic activists, and especially clerical leaders, demonstrated a much greater sense of confidence in their dealings with the mainstream society, while the campaign against Salman Rushdie's *Satanic Verses* in 1989 galvanized militancy across Europe. Rushdie himself describes this as "a pivotal moment in the forging of a British Muslim identity and political agenda. I did not fail to note the ironies: a secular work of art energized powerful communalist, antisecularist forces, 'Muslim' instead of 'Asian.'" The younger generation growing up in the 1980s and 1990s found such assertiveness both natural and attractive, and in some cases, they criticized the political passivity of their parents.[22]

Reinforcing these trends was the arrival of exiles from the Muslim world, radical and fundamentalist activists who faced prison or execution at home but who could speak and publish freely in Europe. London, above all, came to occupy a pivotal role in Middle Eastern life comparable to that of Beirut prior to the outbreak of the Lebanese civil war in 1975. It was here, not in Algiers or Cairo or Damascus, that one could readily find Takfiris and Salafists, Wahhabis and Deobandis, apart from the many representatives of moderate and democratic Muslim traditions, feminists, and secularizers. Far from being a distant fringe of the Muslim world and occasionally receiving the latest cultural and intellectual trends, European cities played a leading role in shaping those movements.

We must stress the novelty of this situation for Muslims. Intense intellectual debate was anything but new for the Islamic world, but for some centuries, clergy and religious thinkers were limited by the demands of the states in which they worked. They had somewhat more freedom in European colonial settings, such as the British Raj in India, when European rulers cared little about Muslim theological debate, provided it did not venture into open sedition. In modern Europe, however, even that degree of restraint rarely applied. Radical imams need no longer look over their shoulders at their respective ministries of religious affairs, nor could moderates reliably count on police intervention against even the most hare-brained extremists.

Foreign Hands

European Muslims have always been subject to competing pressures, with domestic forces pushing toward conformity with the established society, while international factors encouraged commitment to global and pan-Islamic causes. Clergy and religious institutions were particularly subject to globalizing forces, because of their greater awareness of trends in home countries, but also because certain Middle Eastern states have been so proactive in funding mosques and ministries. Across Europe, the expansion of Islamic institutions has been led and controlled throughout by foreign governments and transnational institutions, which compete freely for influence in Muslim communities. It is impossible to understand the shades of Muslim religious thought and political activism in Europe except in the context of these rival interests: Saudi, Algerian, Moroccan, Turkish, and Pakistani.

Foreigners look with some puzzlement at the operation of Middle Eastern religious-political empires on European soil: at the least, the tolerance of activities by overseas governments looks like a dereliction of national security. In fact, European attitudes do have a rational basis, although it is rooted in a now-bygone political order. From the 1950s through the 1980s, west European political attitudes were shaped absolutely by the Cold War confrontation, and the Middle East featured chiefly as a theater of East-West ideological rivalry. The ultimate nightmare was that communists would establish themselves throughout the region, probably using secular socialist and nationalist parties as fronts, and that would place the region's oil resources in the hands of the Soviet bloc. To combat this threat, Western governments and intelligence agencies actively cooperated with the enemies of secular governments like Nasser's Egypt or Ba'athist Syria and Iraq, and that meant tolerating and allying with Islamists like the Muslim Brotherhood. As Islamist exiles fled to Europe in the 1950s, Western governments made no objection to them establishing mosques and institutional networks, which would serve as valuable foundations for later organization. Internationally, the West saw conservative monarchies like Saudi Arabia as its principal allies in the region and welcomed Saudi efforts to spread its conservative varieties of Islam, as a bastion against leftism. In 1962, for instance, the Saudi government founded the World Muslim League as a means of financing mosques, preachers, and propaganda that reflected its particular form of Wahhabi Islam, and at the time, the move seemed unexceptional. Not until the 1990s did fundamentalist Islam seem vaguely as threatening to western Europe as Soviet communism had in its day.[23]

In itself, foreign support of fellow Muslims seems only laudable. What better way of showing charity than helping poor believers build a mosque that will help them develop a faithful community in a non-Muslim land? Recipients, too, find such a gesture hard to criticize. For a largely poor community, it is wonderful news when a wealthy government like Saudi Arabia offers to finance the building of a sumptuous mosque, which acts as a symbolic proclamation of the Islamic presence. Manchester lawyer Mohammed Afzal Khan, one of Britain's most respected Muslims, makes no apology for seeking Saudi funding for an Islamic Cultural Center in his city: "My attitude is, if it's a good cause, everyone has a right to contribute." In practice, though, such support makes it difficult for local communities to become autonomous, to develop a wholly European Islam, and even the best-intentioned donors impose their ideological preferences. The Saudis in particular have a strong theological agenda in encouraging one particularly rigorous and exclusive form of Islam, to the exclusion of what might be the traditions of many in the community concerned. In the words of a Muslim leader at Villeurbanne, near Lyon, "When Saudi Arabia gives you a million euros with one hand, with the other they give you a list of things you must or must not say." Accepting such benevolence means, in practice, acknowledging the charge that Islam on European soil is a foreign importation, even an arm of the imperialist ambitions of wealthy oil states.[24]

The Saudis have been among the most enthusiastic sponsors of mosques, including the ostentatious monumental structures. Around the world, the Saudis have funded the construction of over 1,300 mosques, including many in Europe. The King of Saudi Arabia personally sponsored the new Oxford Center for Islamic Studies that is intended visually and culturally to rival the medieval Christian foundations: the building has a showy minaret a hundred feet high. (Niall Ferguson sees this as a "fulfilment of Gibbon's unintended prophecy" of an Islamicized Oxford). Saudi money funded the Great Mosque of Lyon and the imposing Islamic Centers in London, Geneva, Edinburgh, Rome, and elsewhere, besides supporting countless smaller facilities. Other monuments to Saudi generosity include Madrid's vast Islamic Center, commonly known as the M30 because of the major freeway that it overlooks. This "comprises a very capacious mosque, a prayer hall for women, a library, a lecture hall and a medical clinic." The Saudis provided a million pounds toward the cost of the sumptuous new East London mosque. Even in Russia, Saudi money supported the vast new mosque built in the kremlin of the Tatar city of Kazan. In addition, Saudi money directly or indirectly supports 8 percent of the funding of France's mosques and Islamic centers. The splendid new mosque at Granada was built with support from the governments of Morocco and the United Arab Emirates (UAE). A wealthy sheik from the UAE paid for Stockholm's Great Mosque.[25]

While building activity is important, it does not necessarily determine the form of Islam that takes place inside the new structures. Across Europe, faithful congregations ingeniously shop around between the various charitable organizations to find donors who will attach the fewest strings to their benevolence: Moroccans are least interventionist, Saudis the most intrusive. But once a mosque is built, many believers find it difficult to escape from the interfering hands of

Muslim governments who want to shepherd their former citizens now living overseas.[26]

While the Saudis are famous for projecting their militant agenda, other governments like those of Algeria and Turkey have a vested interest in reducing extremist influences among their communities abroad. As we have seen, Western governments were happy to promote such foreign dabbling as a means of preventing the upsurge of radicalism among immigrant communities. To accomplish their goal, states and their ministries for religious affairs become closely involved in choosing the imams who will teach in such mosques and prepare teaching material for children in religious schools. Algeria and Morocco serve this function for their former citizens in France, as does the Turkish DITIB, the foreign branches of the Religious Affairs Directorate (Diyanet Isleri Baskanligi), in Germany and elsewhere. (The DITIB was the primary sponsor of the new Duisburg-Marxloh mosque.) The Diyanet controls about half the Turkish mosques in Europe. The organization appoints imams for the 140 Turkish mosques in the Netherlands, while the Moroccan government tries to control the hundred or so Dutch mosques of that ethnic group through a network of friendly associations.[27] In consequence, clergy are conspicuously the least assimilated members of many Muslim communities, and the most likely to have close foreign ties. In the 1990s, only 4 percent of France's paid professional imams held French citizenship.

Sometimes, states compete for influence using only the slimmest pretence of a religious motive. Across western Europe, we find Algerian- and Moroccan-supported factions in constant conflict, sometimes reaching the point of physical violence. At Evry, near Paris, in 1996, a battle for control of the mosque led to a Moroccan victory over the Algerians, but only after both sides had wielded iron bars. The hostility is not surprising when we recall that the two nations fought a virtual proxy war in the western Sahara from 1975 through 1991. What such foreign-controlled networks have in common is a shared desire to prevent migrants from assimilating too easily into European societies, so that they commonly oppose attempts to integrate Muslim children fully into public schools.[28]

The War of the Mosques

Over the past quarter century, European Islam has witnessed freewheeling debates over the nature of Islam and particularly its political role, controversies in which radicals made quite outrageous demands, often using bloodthirsty and apocalyptic rhetoric. Usually, too, such fiery words have come from mosques and from religious leaders, who present warfare and religious intolerance as integral parts of faith. Often, the most extreme views are heard from foreign-born imams who do not hold citizenship in the countries in which they operate, and who are based in mosques supported by overseas governments and charities. For most European observers, moreover, such extremism has come to represent the normal picture of Islam, which appears in the most severe and intolerant guise. More disturbing, these ideas also came to epitomize Islam for many European-born Muslims.

It is difficult to know whether outside observers are more shocked by some recent outbursts than are the older and more moderate leaders of the mosques that have found themselves in turmoil. Conflicts usually revolve around the same issues: radicals condemn secular Europe for its vice and immorality, they urge support for jihad in various countries around the world, they condemn Jews and Israel, and even, in some instances, call for armed violence and jihad in Europe itself. What is striking in such exposés is less that such outrageous words are used, but that dissidents within the congregation are willing to report or record them, suggesting the vigor of partisan divisions. Hellfire sermons continued unchecked in one Berlin mosque until the media were induced to use hidden cameras, whereupon they broadcast an imam telling the congregations that "Germans can only expect to rot in the fires of hell because they are nonbelievers."[29]

Across Europe, ideological battles have raged in many mosques, from the largest to the smallest. Italy has produced some notorious examples. In Naples, the Corso Lucci mosque has long been the setting for militant sermons, including one notorious example in 2001 that justified the slaughter of September 11. An (Egyptian) deputy imam here proved to be a leading militant of the Algerian GIA, who faced a lengthy prison term in his home country. Another Egyptian imam at Rome's prestigious Great Mosque called on God to give victory to jihad fighters around the world, especially in Palestine and Chechnya. Turin's Muslim community was for several years divided between a charismatic imam named Bouriqui Bouchta, who controlled three mosques, and a more established moderate leader, Ahmed Cherkaoui, who supported assimilation and accommodation. Cherkaoui was ultimately forced to leave Turin after being denounced as an apostate to Islam and receiving a series of threats to himself and his family. Bouchta, meanwhile, went on to defend Osama bin Laden, and his mosques recruited militants to fight in Bosnia, Chechnya, and Afghanistan. (The Italian government eventually deported him).[30]

Spain has produced many such cases. One well-recorded controversy occurred in the territory of Melilla, a small Spanish enclave bordering Morocco. In recent years, rival factions have struggled for control of the mosque, with moderates denouncing a new imam for sermons justifying participation in jihad and urging violence against Jews. Reportedly, he took control of the mosque with the aid of young radicals, who threatened his predecessor with death. In 2001, following the U.S.

invasion of Afghanistan, the extremist preacher urged that "any Muslim who does not take part in the Afghani jihad, whatever country he or she may be from, is a sinner, because in this moment the jihad is more important than prayer or fasting." In Germany, the official Islam favored by the Turkish government competes with the fiery Islamism of the Millî Görüş (National Vision) movement, organized in "Islamic Associations" (IGMG, or Die Islamische Gemeinschaft Milli Görüş).[31]

National Voices

Clashing overseas interests bedevil the social and political organizations that have developed since the 1970s and which should in theory become the expressions of increasingly self-confident autonomous Muslim communities. Also, they become much more activist, politicized, and religiously conservative than the people they claim to represent.

Earlier observers of the new immigration imagined that social problems would be defined in terms of race rather than religion. In Britain, migrants from the Indian subcontinent were conventionally grouped together as "Asians," whether Muslim, Sikh, or Hindu. Only gradually did Muslim migrants define themselves more clearly in religious terms and begin to perceive themselves as a united interest group. By the end of the 1980s, some were beginning to think of Europe as Islam's newest frontier territory and the migrants as the pioneers of a glorious future. In Britain, as elsewhere, the great leap toward self-identification came when the Rushdie affair provoked the formation of a national federation, the UK Action Committee on Islamic Affairs. Other more radical networks emerged at the same time, including the Muslim Parliament that was intended to exercise separate political and legal authority over Muslims. The effort died with its radical founder, Kalim Siddiqui, but in 1996, the various movements came together in the Muslim Council of Britain (MCB). In other nations too, we see the emergence of national Muslim federations, such as Italy's UCOII, the Unione delle Comunità e Organizzazioni Islamiche in Italia, founded in 1990.[32]

Despite their unifying goals, such organizations reflect deep divisions within the Muslim communities of the respective nations, and their activities enhance these splits. Commonly, these coalitions involved different kinds of pressure groups, each oriented to international perspectives, and each in its way pledged to oppose the assimilation of Muslim communities. Some Muslim organizations are dominated by foreign governments, whether overtly or as thinly disguised front groups; others are controlled by hard-line traditionalist movements, whether the Muslim Brotherhood or the JI.

The Muslim Brotherhood is a more complex organization than it appears from some recent Western exposés, where it is often presented as a simple manifestation of Islamic terrorism and confrontational extremism, engaged in a single-minded quest for global domination. The Brotherhood is a large grouping with diverse currents, and its Egyptian leadership recently startled observers by asserting that it would have no objection to seeing a Christian president of that country, were he (or even she) to be elected democratically. Both the Egyptian Ikhwan and Hamas field women electoral candidates. While no one pretends the Ikhwan are closet liberals, an association with the group should not of itself condemn any organization as a terrorist ally. But undeniably, the Brotherhood does represent a strict current of Islamic politics, which leaves a strong mark on the organizations it dominates. While UCOII includes mosques with diverse views, the organization itself is closely connected to the Brotherhood, and the most militant and obstreperous mosques are usually affiliated with UCOII.[33]

France, meanwhile, has three major national organizations. The Muslim Brotherhood has close and continuing ties to the Union of the Islamic Organizations of France, which includes a range of thinly disguised front groups, including the women's section, LFFM, Ligue Française de la Femme Musulmane, and the student organization, EMF, Étudiants Musulmans de France. The Union itself admits that a quarter of its budget comes from overseas sources, in Saudi Arabia, Kuwait, and the UAE. Another French network, headed by the Paris Great Mosque, is "openly bankrolled by the Algerian government" while Morocco favors the National Federation of French Muslims (FNMF). In 2003, the three combined to form the Conseil Français du Culte Musulman, CFCM, but individual groups maintained their rivalries. Ironically, the French government contributed mightily to expanding the influence of the more conservative and reactionary elements by the formula it chose for elections to the new body. Lacking a religious census, votes were apportioned according to the ground area covered by individual mosques, which gave a huge advantage to the spacious buildings financed by the Saudis or other Gulf states. In the first national election to the CFCM, the UOIF won fourteen out of forty-one seats, leaving sixteen to the pro-Moroccan FNMF. The UOIF dominated the vote in the Paris area, and in the cities of the southern coast, and initially took control of twelve of twenty-five regional councils.[34]

In Britain too, the main national structure has a hard-line quality, in this instance reflecting conservative Pakistani interests. The organizations that merged to form the MCB include the extremist Ahl-e-Hadith, while the Islamic Foundation is connected to JI, and promotes Maududi's books. Another component is the Muslim Association of Britain, which is ideologically close to the Muslim Brotherhood. Illustrating its conservatism, the MCB follows a strict line when it comes to accepting the Muslim credentials of sectarian groups. In 2003, the council dismissed news of the huge new Ahmadiyya mosque at Morden on the grounds that the building was not really a mosque.

While the Ahmadiyyas were welcome to practice their own religion, said the MCB, "it is clearly misleading to describe them as Muslims. They are not." The MCB also looks dimly on the Sufi traditions that have such deep roots in Pakistan and India. So rigid, in fact, did the MCB become that in 2005, other, broader-minded mosques formed a new rival organization, the British Muslim Forum (BMF). Among other innovations, the BMF has issued a stern fatwa against terrorism and suicide bombings, and cultivates a warmer relationship with Jewish organizations.[35]

Spain's best-established Muslim organization is FEERI, La Federación Española de Entidades Religiosas Islámicas, largely led by converts of European origin. FEERI has repeatedly promoted a distinctive Spanish Islam, in which only imams with Spanish citizenship would preach in the nation's mosques. The group also favors sending children to public schools and is open to women's leadership. Its secretary, Mansur Escudero, became the first Muslim leader to issue a fatwa condemning Osama bin Laden as an apostate. He argues that

> [Bin Laden's] association with the Taliban movement shows that he advocates an Islam which has lost all its richness and its open character. They pick up a few phrases and convert them into legal precepts stripped of all nuance. This loss of context robs Islam of all its human dimension and in fact bypasses the greater part of the Quranic message.

Besides this moderate organization, however, and representing very different stances, we find the mainly immigrant UCIDE, Unión de Comunidades Islámicas de España, and a Moroccan-dominated federation, Consejo Islámico Cultural de Cataluña.[36]

Conflicts between national interests and the governments behind them undermine efforts at creating any kind of Muslim unity, with the result that Muslim political endeavors remain scattered and much less effective than population numbers would suggest. These conflicts scandalize many of the faithful, who often refuse to take part in the national organizations for just these reasons. In Versailles, near Paris, local Muslims refuse to participate in the affairs of the CFCM, asserting that foreign interventions "feed divisions" among Muslims. According to the local imam, "there should be no nationalism. We are all French here." In practice, though, Europe's Muslim institutions are far less European—far less French or German or Dutch—than are many such ordinary believers.[37]

Reforming Islam

Extremism in European Islam owes much to globalization, in the sense of new media, wider access to news and information, and much greater opportunities to travel and communicate, to explore alternative ideas.

Yet exactly the same forces have inspired Muslim reformers, who see heady prospects in Europe's intellectual freedom and whose ideas are transmitted back to the Muslim nations.

Europe serves for the Muslim world the same role that the Netherlands did for Europe's Christian societies during the Enlightenment. In the century after 1660, the Netherlands represented liberated space where exiles could take refuge, where truly radical ideas could be explored, and books of virtually any intellectual content could be safely published before being exported across the continent. It was the sort of society in which a radical Jewish skeptic like Baruch Spinoza could write without being executed.

Today, Europe provides territory in which scholars, Islamic and others, can perform on the Quran the same task of scholarly criticism and analysis that their predecessors did on Jewish and Christian scriptures. Many scholars accept that the Quran, like the Christian Bible, is a text formed over a long historical period and drawing on diverse sources and influences: variant readings competed for authority until one final text achieved canonized form. Such an approach directly challenges the common view of a perfect Quran directly dictated to the prophet in the seventh century A.D. One scholarly pioneer is Nasr Hamid Abu Zaid, whose innovative Quranic studies led to his life being threatened in Egypt. He fled to the Netherlands, where he teaches at Utrecht and Leiden. France is the base for Syrian-born scholar Bassam Tahhan, who seeks a progressive and individualistic "Protestant Islam." He argues that

> to read the Koran rationally is to accept that the Koran is open [to inter-
> pretation] and has many meanings. The tradition regards the Koran as
> one-dimensional and fixed. This approach is not rationalist. To be a ratio-
> nalist is to accept that each era, with its [particular] methods and discov-
> eries, presents its own reading of the Koran, and this is the way it will be
> until the end of days. . . . In the year 901—an unfortunate year for
> Muslims—a Muslim *qadi* named Ibn Mujahid canonized [one version of] the
> Koran. Before that, there were many different versions of the Koran, and
> this did not upset the good Muslims!

Radical scholarly findings about the early history of Islam are popularized in books such as *The Rock*, a novel written in his London exile by Iraqi Kanan Makiya. The book reconstructs a time in the seventh century when Islam, Judaism, and Christianity were virtually branches of one common faith. In this view, "Islam" as known by scholars through the centuries was invented long after Muhammad's time, and Muhammad's life and work were constructed retroactively. In the words of a British observer, the book is

> an attempt to smuggle the latest research on the Prophet Mohammed to
> an Arab audience. Censorship and the appeasing of Islamic fundamental-

ism means that historians tend to hide their work in obscure academic journals for fear of receiving the Rushdie treatment. Makiya believes their conclusions deserve a wider readership.

And that goal can best be achieved from a European base. Though it might take decades for the results of such scholarship to have their full impact upon ordinary believers, work of this kind should in the long run have an enormous impact on Muslim belief, and particularly the nature of scriptural authority.[38]

Another central question is that of citizenship and national loyalty. Since earliest times, Muslim thinkers have assumed that the normal state of affairs for Muslims involves living in a society dominated by Islamic government and law, and radicals dream of returning to such conditions. Egyptian Sheikh Yusuf al-Qaradawi, an important if controversial thinker, wrote a book with the loaded title *On Law and the Jurisprudence of Muslim Minorities: The Life of Muslims in Other Societies*. By implication, one either lives as a Muslim in a Muslim society or as a transient resident in an Other and presumably hostile community. From their experience in Europe, though, other thinkers ask what it means to live in a pluralist multifaith society in which the government shows preference to no religion, treating all equally. In that case, Muslims must accept a secular notion of citizenship, and in fact, must learn to separate religious and secular loyalties, to recognize a firm distinction between mosque and state.[39]

Europe now provides a base for several leading reformers who are exploring the implications for Islam in living in an advanced Western society. Bassam Tibi, for instance, urges Muslims to accept what he terms the *Leitkultur* (the leading or guiding culture), which in the European context means the Enlightenment-derived idea of the dignity and freedom of the individual. For Tibi, this idea is

> based on the foundation of a democratic community whose members are bound together through a collective identity as citizens of that community. Such a collective identity—in the sense of the French *citoyenité* (citizenship)—stands above religious identity. Religion may, of course, be practiced privately, but in public only citizenship counts. Such a concept would unite Muslims with non-Muslims.

Once European Muslims accept this core value, he suggests, other conflicts—for instance over free speech issues—can be resolved through debate and compromise.[40]

Similar ideas are explored by Tariq Ramadan, who in recent years has been widely seen as the prophet of a new Euro-Islam. *Time* magazine has named him one of the "hundred most important intellectuals of the 21st century," while the *Washington Post* calls him a "Muslim Martin Luther." Ramadan is a controversial figure. His critics portray him as a sinister ally of the hard-line extremists, who has nevertheless succeeded in winning the favor of gullible Westerners. The hard-line connections can in fact be traced quite easily, though it is an open question whether they detract from the content of his message.[41]

Tariq Ramadan's family origins give him immense prestige among traditional and conservative Muslims. His grandfather, Hassan al-Banna, actually founded the Muslim Brotherhood, and his father, Said Ramadan, carried the organization's activities into Europe, establishing the Munich mosque that would become a center of Islamist radicalism in Germany. (Much has been written about the circumstances surrounding the creation of this mosque in the early 1960s. Among the bewildering network of clandestine forces involved, we find the intelligence agencies of several Western countries as well as the Muslim Brotherhood and cliques of ex-Nazi Muslims.) Said Ramadan founded the Islamic Society of Germany (Islamische Gemeinschaft Deutschland), and was associated with the Saudi-funded World Muslim League. Tariq himself was born in Switzerland in 1962, and he came to prominence in the mid-1990s. According to critics like terrorism expert Antoine Sfeir, he personified the Muslim Brotherhood strategy to gain influence in Europe. Within France, the militant and anti-assimilationist tone of his preaching won him an enthusiastic following among radical young Muslims in the banlieues. Sfeir directly linked his influence in Lyon to the radicalization of young men from the region, many of whom pursued careers in jihad.[42]

For Sfeir and other critics, Tariq Ramadan's writings and public pronouncements almost have to be decoded, since he uses such different approaches for different audiences. To Westerners, he sounds like a breath of liberalizing fresh air; to Muslim audiences, though, he presents a more familiar Brotherhood message. Critics accuse him of adopting the strategy of *taqiya*, dissembling, or double-talk for infidels. Ramadan remains close to the extreme and confrontational al-Qaradawi and has written favorable introductions for his books. His reputation in France suffered in 2002 during a controversy that began when his brother publicly supported the stoning of adulterous women. When asked about this in a televised debate with political leader Nicolas Sarkozy, Ramadan himself refused to denounce the penalty outright, suggesting only a moratorium on the practice.

Having said this, Ramadan has in recent years called explicitly for fundamental revisions of Muslim political and social assumptions, putting forth ideas that will find a large audience precisely because of his traditionalist credentials, and he describes his own ideological stance as Salafist reformism. This initially sounds as if he is aligning himself with the most committed extremists and fundamentalists but rather implies a stripping away of the doctrines that have surrounded Islamic teaching since the time of Muhammad. A Christian equivalent might be the social progressive who claims to be a fundamentalist in the sense of returning to the pure words of Jesus, minus later accretions.[43]

Whatever the label, Ramadan, like Tibi, explores questions of identity and loyalty in a quite innovative way, arguing that Western Muslims "are at home, and should not only say so but feel so." Muslims should feel comfortable being citizens of their particular nations: "Muslim identity is a response to the question 'Why' while national identity is a response to the question 'How?' and it would be absurd and stupid to expect geographical attachment to resolve the question of being." Ramadan himself has written that "In my memories, I'm Egyptian; in my citizenship, I'm Swiss; in my belief, I'm Muslim." Critically, he feels that Muslims must abandon the ancient division between *dar al-Islam* and *dar al-harb*, the world of Islam and the world of war. Instead, the non-Muslim world should be seen as the *dar al-da'wa*, the world of proclamation or of calling to God, in which Muslims should seek to spread their teachings by example. And once they do spread their views, the results would by no means involve a denial of Europe's Enlightenment tradition. After all, "in medieval Europe, Islam contributed significantly to the formation of rationalist, secular and modern thought." Taken together, this looks like a recipe for a new pluralistic European Islam that fully acknowledges the realities of living in the contemporary multifaith West.[44]

Though Ramadan's thought is nuanced, he offers consistent responses to the catechism he regularly receives in interviews:

> *Does a Muslim have to heed the constitution?*
> Yes.
> *No exceptions?*
> No, because the right to practice a religion is guaranteed in all European constitutions.
> *And if the headscarf is forbidden in schools, as is the case in France?*
> The law must be respected, even if it is bad.
> *Does a Muslim woman have the right not to wear a headscarf?*
> Yes, she has the right to a free choice.
> *Do Muslim women have the same rights as their husbands?*
> Yes, there can be no discrimination against women.
> *What would you do if your son were homosexual?*
> He would still be my son and I would still respect him.
> *Can a Muslim change his or her belief?*
> Yes.
> *Can a Muslim woman marry a man of another religion?*
> Yes.[45]

Ramadan argues further that this quest for a reconstructed identity represents a powerful new movement in the Muslim world:

> More and more young people and intellectuals are actively looking for a way to live in harmony with their faith while participating in the societies that are their societies, whether they like it or not. . . . Far from media

attention, going through the risks of a process of maturation that is necessarily slow, they are drawing the shape of European and American Islam: faithful to the principles of Islam, dressed in European and American cultures, and definitively rooted in Western societies. This grassroots movement will soon exert considerable influence over worldwide Islam: in view of globalization and the Westernization of the world, these are the same questions as those already being raised from Morocco to Indonesia.[46]

Even if we hold the darkest views of Ramadan's secret intentions, the mass circulation of his ideas cannot fail to generate debate about how the children of immigrants can live authentically Muslim lives in a secular West.

Other thinkers are more aggressively reformist or secular minded, while remaining within the fold of Islam. Turkish-German writer Zafer Senocak complains about how much Islam has lost over the centuries, not least in the twentieth century. Turkey's last caliph was

> a caliph that painted extremely beautiful pictures, including nudes; a caliph that was further along in the debate at the start of the last century than we are today. And he was more liberal. . . . Naturally, I have no sympathy with people who want to reduce this fantastic culture to dogmas.

Senocak publicly defended Salman Rushdie's right to blaspheme, and he denounces honor killings and gender inequality.[47] Such thinkers have not historically organized into political movements, precisely because they are uncomfortable accepting the religious label as their primary identifier. They have rather affiliated to mainstream secular parties, generally on the left, which means that most self-identified Muslim organizations are conservative, and often extremist. To counter the idea that Islam necessarily implies Islamism, some liberals have now organized into avowedly reformist movements, like Denmark's Democratic Muslims, founded by a Syrian-born member of that country's parliament. Though such movements are presently sparse, they have a substantial potential for future growth.

Far from remaining in the world of academic theory, liberal ideas have been popularized by leading clergy, who have a potent influence over the Muslim community. One of France's best-known Muslim leaders is Soheib Bencheikh of Marseille, who praises secularism as a means of defending the rights of all minorities, including his own faith: "Due to secularism, Islam can stand equally with Catholics in rights and duties. . . . We can interact with the French culture that has a background of Catholicism, while holding on to our own spirituality and Islamic values." But far from being simply defensive in character, he believes, secularism actually benefits Muslims:

> The separation between religion and politics will clarify Islam as a divine spiritual doctrine, not as an instrument which (can) be misused to gain power. Moreover, due to that, Islam can return its original formulation,

meaning it will return as the *promoted* teaching not as a forced teaching—
as the Koran affirms—"Anyone who will believe may believe, and anyone
who will be an infidel may be an infidel!"

For Muslims to accept these principles in France would mark a mile-
stone; applying them to many Muslim nations would constitute a
revolution.[48]

The same media that allow the propagation of extremist doctrines
also spread more innovative ideas. One vital figure in contemporary
Islam is Amr Khaled, an Egyptian preacher whose whole style and presentation powerfully recall Christian televangelists, and who has an
enormous following among Muslims in Europe as well as the Middle
East. His image is thoroughly modern and progressive, and he makes
quite as much use of contemporary media and technology—the Internet, as well as satellite television—as does a Christian like Matthew
Ashimolowo. Khaled's website is the third most popular Arabic website in the world (Al Jazeera's is the top). Wherever he travels, his avid
followers fill stadiums to hear him. He encourages his listeners to accept Islamic principles not on the basis of traditional authority, but on
the principles they discover through their own inward journeys: in the
words of Samantha Shapiro, he "blends Islam with the feel-good opti-
mism of Western management literature." Like Ramadan, Amr Khaled
has been accused of clandestine ties to the Muslim Brotherhood and
other hard-line organizations, while his glitzy presentation often accompanies a conservative theological message. But he too proclaims
the need for a thorough renaissance, a *nahda*, which would free the
Muslim world of its backwardness: "It wasn't my principal plan to
make the people become religious. My plan was the *nahda*. This was
my plan all along." Increasing his potential impact in Europe itself,
Khaled has relocated his main base of operations to Birmingham, in
England.[49]

The case of Amr Khaled prevents us from drawing too sharp a contrast between Islam in Europe, supposedly progressive and modern,
and the hidebound societies of north Africa or south Asia. However
many radicals despise the *jahili* (pagan) West and dream of its apocalyptic fall, at least some theological conservatives have grasped the idea
that an agonizingly poor Islamic world might learn much from Western
ways. At the start of this chapter, I quoted the remarks of Hassan al-
Turabi of the Sudan, long notorious as a violent Islamist radical, who in
the early 1990s gave refuge to Osama bin Laden. In 2006, however, he
gave an interview that was breathtaking in its willingness to contemplate reform, especially in matters of gender and sex roles. Forcing his
new perception was an awareness of the economic and social gulf that
separated the Islamic world from the West and the crying need to nar-
row the gap. Also in 2006, a glittering array of the world's leading

Sunni clergy and theologians meeting in Istanbul issued a statement of principles that was sensational in its condemnation of violence and terrorism ("a cancer"), and specifically denounced suicide bombings. Among the most daring presenters was Tariq Ramadan, who used this venue to criticize domestic violence, forced marriages, gender inequality, and brutal legal punishments. If Muslims did not act on such matters, he said, then Europeans would be right to fear their influence.[50]

Globalization can contribute to the spread of extremism—we recall the very rapid spread of protests against the Danish cartoons of Muhammad—but it also promotes awareness of progressive alternatives. When Libya decided to make its peace with the international community in 2003, one powerful factor was the growing awareness among ordinary Libyans of just how badly they had fallen behind the Western world, a knowledge spread by the Internet and satellite television. Across north Africa, satellite dishes, *paraboliques,* are everywhere, and so potent is their influence on traditional mores and beliefs that conservatives denounce them as *paradiaboliques.* Middle Eastern migrants in London or Amsterdam watch al-Jazeera or the still more radical al-Manar, but their relatives at home might be tuning to CNN or the BBC. Add to that the influence of migrants returning home from Europe, who are appalled by the poverty and restraint they see all around them, and the pressures for social and cultural change become overwhelming.

Muslim governments, too, have a vested interest in promoting quite radical reforms within their religious structures in order to combat the rival appeal of Islamism. When radicals take refuge in London or Rome in order to mount propaganda against their home countries, they cannot be killed or imprisoned, but must rather be confronted ideologically. We see this process in Morocco, which for a decade has faced a terrorist challenge from the extremist GICM (Groupe Islamique Combattant Marocain, or Moroccan Islamic Combat Group). In 2003 a dozen suicide bombers attacked five Casablanca sites chosen for their Jewish associations, leaving forty dead.

Recognizing the extent of the religious and ideological crisis, the Moroccan government made a systematic attempt to promote moderate forms of Islam. A new *mudawana* (family code) issued in 2003 expanded women's legal rights. In 2006, the authorities commissioned fifty women as religious teachers, granting them diplomas of *murshid* (religious guides). While these women would not have the full status of imams, community leaders, this is still a major step in incorporating female participation. And the close link between Morocco and Europe's Muslim communities means that this decision will assuredly have international implications. In Paris, the Algerian-sponsored Great Mosque now operates a theological school that trains young women as spiritual counselors for hospitals and prisons. The fact of having women clergy or chaplains in itself says nothing about the content of the message they present, but in the context of changing women's roles in Europe, it poses a real challenge to ultraconservatives.[51]

No one can underestimate the severity of the struggle currently in progress for control of the religious structures of European Islam, the "battle for the soul of Islam" that has become a journalistic cliché. Undeniably, the public voices of Europe's Muslim communities are often shrill, and some leaders assuredly are extremist, militant, and in some cases, actively subversive. In many countries too, Muslim populations seem deeply alienated from mainstream society, and some ordinary Muslims appear willing to follow the extremists. Yet the religious situation is much more complex than it might appear. While radicals and militants flourish, their opponents are numerous and significant, and so are the historical forces working against extremism.

7

Young and Old

Amid these lukewarm partisans and ardent antagonists a small number
of believers exists who are ready to brave all obstacles and to scorn all
dangers in defense of their faith. They have done violence to human
weakness in order to rise superior to public opinion. Excited by the effort
they have made, they scarcely know where to stop . . . they look upon
their contemporaries with dread, and recoil in alarm from the liberty
which their fellow citizens are seeking to obtain. As unbelief appears to
them to be a novelty, they comprise all that is new in one indiscriminate
animosity. They are at war with their age and country, and they look
upon every opinion that is put forth there as the necessary enemy of faith.

Alexis de Tocqueville, 1835, commenting on European Catholics

If a single individual personifies Europe's current Muslim nightmare, it
is Mohammad Sidique Khan. Mohammad's father was one of many
thousands of Pakistanis who moved to the west Yorkshire industrial
complex based on the cities of Leeds, Bradford, and Wakefield, a classic
rust-belt landscape. Born in 1974, Mohammad grew up in Dewsbury,
near Leeds. He attended college, married (not an arranged match), and
settled down; and he found a respectable and fulfilling job as a youth
worker. In every sense, he seemed like a model of integration. Like
most British Muslims, "Sid Khan's" patterns of speech and behavior
were thoroughly English and more specifically Yorkshire—proud residents insist on the regional distinction. All of which made it seem
incredible that he, together with three others, would undertake the
suicide bombings on the London subway in July 2005.[1]

At least from a commonsense viewpoint, one would expect the first
generation of immigrants to retain the customs and beliefs of the old
country while their children would become ever more closely integrated

into the lives of the new countries in which they grew up. The Khan case suggests the exact opposite process, that a largely docile and nonassertive immigrant generation was succeeded by children who were far more politicized, indeed fanatical. As Salman Rushdie remarks, in the Leeds area, "many traditional Muslims lead inward-turned lives of near-segregation from the wider population. From such defensive, separated worlds some youngsters have indefensibly stepped across a moral line and taken up their lethal rucksacks." Their actions puzzle and horrify their elders as much as they do members of the mainstream society.[2]

We should not exaggerate the wider significance of this story. Though Khan represents one possible trajectory for young European Muslims, his case is extraordinarily rare. But the radicalization of a few does highlight the strongly generational nature of social and ethnic tensions and conflicts in modern Europe. In any era, the young and energetic are the most likely to participate in a mass migration, and such people also tend to have young families. In a few decades, immigrant communities themselves age and their birth rates fall to something closer to the norms of their host societies. Until this occurs though, there is for a generation or so a conspicuous gap between the age profiles of immigrant and host communities, and that is the situation in which Europe presently finds itself. Muslims make up a far higher proportion of young European communities than they do of the society at large, and they are a conspicuous presence in schools. While people aged sixteen or younger make up 20 percent of the British population, the figure for people of Asian origin is 29 percent, for people of Pakistani descent, it is 38 percent. In Denmark, Muslims represent 200,000 out of a total population of 5.4 million, a mere 3.7 percent of the total. Even so, non-Danish mothers now account for 10 percent of all children born in that country and a quarter of those born in Copenhagen, and a substantial portion of those foreign born are Muslims. In Amsterdam, Rotterdam, and the Hague, immigrants outnumber the native Dutch among those younger than twenty. In Brussels, the most popular name for baby boys is now Mohammad. The *Economist* noted that in the local paper of the French town of Evry, "death announcements speak of 'Pierre' and 'Charles'; the births are of 'Moussa' and 'Fatih.'"[3]

Increasingly, young urban and suburban Muslims confront the middle-aged and elderly white population, a divide with strong overtones of class and relative wealth. The confrontation is a recipe for mutual grievance and the source of much street crime. Urban politics, which have long been bedeviled by racial tension, have acquired a powerful theme of generational resentment. As traditional white populations become relatively older and richer, nonwhite communities, with their roots in Asia and Africa, are younger and poorer. While dangerous in themselves, such conflicts do not necessarily take on a religious coloring. In fact, one could almost write the story of Europe's angry Muslims—to use the phrase coined by Robert Leiken—without mentioning religion at all, except insofar as Muslim provides a convenient ethnic label. In recent years though, specifically religious grievances have become more apparent, and that pattern could become still more marked, particularly if Europe suffered a sharp economic downturn. At that point, the careers of jihadis like Mohammad Sidique Khan would become of more than academic interest.[4]

To consider such a future does not mean accepting the inevitability of continuing religious conflicts, still less an apocalyptic scenario of urban jihad. Young Muslims have to deal with sharply different cultural messages, some pressing toward religious conservatism and fundamentalism, but others pushing inexorably toward assimilation and secularization. Moreover, societies can and do survive with severe underlying tensions: how many Americans would have believed in 1968 that the dreadful wave of urban race riots would soon pass, and that similar events would not become an enduring feature of American life? In the European context too, we must remember how very recently the current social and religious situation has been created. Arguably, the unrest and disaffection we see in contemporary Europe marks only a temporary phase in the process of absorption into a sustainable multicultural society, and religion will never become a dominant theme in social conflict. European nations may indeed face a threat from religiously motivated violence, but they are still a long way from open crisis. What governments have learned from recent events, especially the French riots of 2005, is that any successful attempt at integrating Muslims into European societies must depend above all on easing generational tensions and grievances.[5]

Invisible Cities

Accounts of contemporary Muslim Europe resemble journalistic explorations of black America thirty years ago, in the sense that it is easy to dwell on poverty, crime, and the world of the underclass as if that were the only reality. Not long since, European visitors to the United States were shocked to discover prosperous middle- and upper-class African-Americans, as professionals, businesspeople, and corporate leaders. In modern Europe too, some Muslim communities have done very well socially, and Britain in particular has a thriving middle class of Pakistani origins. A recent lord mayor of Manchester was Pakistani-born Mohammed Afzal Khan, while the country has corporate tycoons like Sir Anwar Pervez. A rising star in London's Metropolitan Police is Assistant Commissioner Tariq Ghaffur, a Muslim of Pakistani descent. Even in France, where segregation seems best established, some Muslims do very well. In recent political feuds over regulating illegal music downloads, the most visible advocate of a free Internet has been teenaged student Aziz Ridouan, founder of the Audionautes and a hero to technologically sophisticated youth. Of such backgrounds are high-tech careers made.[6]

Even so, large sections of Europe's Muslim population do find themselves confined to underclass conditions, living in poverty and having little opportunity of improving their lives. Muslim immigration historically focused on the areas of traditional heavy industry where work was easy to come by. Often, idealistic governments had tried to construct special communities for workers in these industries, apartments, and housing projects that followed the urban planning ideas of the time. From the 1970s, however, these areas were the hardest hit by a sharp economic downturn and a major reorientation away from older manufacturing industries. Some countries were able to absorb these changes: Britain, especially, coped relatively well because of the radical free market traditions established under Margaret Thatcher, who curbed the power of the labor unions. France and Germany, however, kept their labor markets tightly regulated, and unemployment soared. Immigrant and low-skilled labor were the primary victims. What had been intended as model towns and suburbs swiftly slid into poverty, while old-stock white residents left if they possibly could. The late 1980s proved another difficult period, and Europe recovered slowly from the global recession of 1990–1992. Repeatedly, we will find the years around 1989–1990 marking a major rise in urban disaffection and protest, and at the same time a new rise in self-consciousness and militancy among new ethnic populations.[7]

By the 1990s, Muslims were likely to be living in classic ghettos surrounding the shuttered shells of traditional factories, and it was in this setting that the new generation of European-born Muslims grew up. Though it is tempting to speak of ghettos, that word is misleading if it implies separated areas within the larger city, since in reality many of the most troubled sections stand outside the older city boundaries. But whatever their exact geographical location, these communities have acquired a very strong foreign identity, which marks them off radically from the urban mainstream.

Sweden offers a model example of the failed hopes of the 1960s and the making of what Stefano Allievi has aptly called "invisible cities." Nationally, the Swedish economy is doing exceptionally well, but some of the communities built during that earlier industrial boom have been left far behind. Around Malmö, with a population that is almost 40-percent foreign or foreign stock, the once-vaunted working-class housing projects have declined badly, leaving the newer immigrant residents as the chief victims. As Christopher Caldwell remarks, the Rosengård project "appears to be all-immigrant. The public schools have virtually no ethnically Swedish children." In another area some miles from the port of Gothenburg, "70 percent of the residents were either born abroad or have parents who were. The same goes for 93 percent of the schoolchildren." And in this context, immigrants are very likely to be of Muslim origin. "Forty percent of the families are on outright welfare, and many of the rest are on various equivalents of welfare that bear different names. Far below half the population is employed." As in other European cities, the concentration of immigrants in the schools need not in itself create problems, but when coupled with poverty, high crime, and deep alienation, the gulf between teachers and pupils becomes dangerously wide, and immigrant communities become notorious for failed or problem schools.[8]

Europe's Muslims are disproportionately young and undereducated, and in the context of largely stagnant European economies, they suffer acutely from social ills and dysfunctions. Apart from having the largest Muslim population, France has probably done the worst job of integrating it and has most successfully created an urban underclass. The worst social deprivation is found in the immigrant communities surrounding Paris, the suburbs or banlieues, where work had been so easy to come by in the 1960s. By the end of the century, though, employment had shrunk and the residential areas were declining fast. In the words of the *Economist*, they were "home to rain-streaked concrete high-rise estates; multiple faiths, tongues and colors; and the usual cocktail of joblessness, broken families, truancy and drug-dealing." Clichy-sous-Bois had become "Clichy-sur-Jungle." Adding to the irony of the situation, these areas bear names hallowed in the most ancient days of France, when they were the estates and monasteries of the Merovingian and Carolingian kings. The ancient royal church of St. Denis is now surrounded by sprawling housing estates, mainly populated by people of north African stock.[9]

Making the similarities to Third-World societies even stronger, the areas that Gilles Kepel calls *les banlieues de l'Islam* also have a very young age profile. In Aulnay, over 40 percent of the population is under twenty-five. And as in contemporary north Africa, Muslim communities across Europe have very high levels of unemployment and underemployment. At the time of the riots by Arab and African youth in 2005, France's national unemployment rate was 10 percent, but the youth rate was 23 percent, and in the banlieues, usually over 40 percent.[10]

Other European countries fare little better. Among Berlin's 180,000 Turks, the unemployment rate is presently over 40 percent, compared with a citywide average of 17 percent. Some immigrant communities in Sweden commonly report unemployment rates of around 50 percent. In Britain, a government report in 2004 found that "Muslims are more likely than other faith groups to have no qualifications (over two-fifths have none) and to be unemployed and economically inactive, and are over-represented in deprived areas." British men of Muslim origin have an unemployment rate three-and-a-half-times higher than old-stock residents. British children of Pakistani or Bangladeshi ethnicity are more than twice as likely to be poor as the national average—far higher than the white population but also greatly exceeding the rates for other nonwhite immigrant communities such as Hindus, Sikhs, or Parsis.[11]

Aggravating a sense of grievance against the wider society is a common perception of the strength of racism and of pervasive discrimination. Such charges need to be sifted carefully, since as we have seen, some European Muslims have prospered, and the success of many Asians of non-Muslim origins means that we cannot be dealing with a simple color line. The Chinese in particular have flourished. Britain's south Asians have produced an impressive number of tycoons and entrepreneurs, and Asian-owned businesses contribute mightily to the British economy, particularly in London. Even so, the annually published "Asian Rich List" is heavy on Hindu and Sikh names, on Patels and Singhs rather than on Muslim Khans or Mohammeds. Europe's wealthiest Muslims are more likely to have made their fortunes elsewhere, usually in the Arab world, and to have brought their wealth with them rather than struggling up from humble beginnings.[12]

In contrast, ordinary Muslims trying to enter the system face multiple obstacles, not least in the language used to describe them. Even thirty-year-old men born in Germany or the Netherlands still face the terminology of "immigrants" or "foreigners," and there seems little prospect that this practice is changing even for the third European generation. Time and again, conversations with urban Muslims produce the same despairing phrases: with a name like mine, I couldn't even get an interview; they would take one look at my name and I'd have no chance; with my name, I could never get a sales job. As journalist Henri Astier observes, in modern France, Ali and Rachid are much less likely to get ahead than Alain or Richard. In consequence, it is much more difficult to create a professional or entrepreneurial class. The overall unemployment rate for France's university graduates is 5 percent; for graduates of north African origin, it is over 26 percent, and very few north Africans hold senior ranks in the French corporate world. And while French people of Muslim origin find it hard to enter the mainstream society, hostile stereotyping prevents them from developing businesses within their own communities, which could serve as a base for later progress. Entrepreneurs who set up stores specifically targeted at Muslims—for instance, marketing *halal* foods—run the risk that banks and suppliers will stigmatize those areas as ghettos, as candidates for urban renewal, and withhold credit. The French situation recalls the plight of America's struggling black entrepreneurs in the mid-twentieth century.[13]

As in the United States, urban communities suffering multiple social deprivation tend to develop a strong sense of neighborhood in which outsiders are clearly identifiable and readily identified as enemies. Also, a sense of exclusion or rejection promotes a sense of solidarity among the young, who find few obvious role models in the mainstream. The only universal heroes are stars of sport or popular culture. In contemporary France, one of the few popular idols whose appeal crosses boundaries of race and religion would be a football megastar like Zinedine Zidane, born in Marseille of a Maghrebin family. In Britain, even Asian Muslims who are thoroughly disaffected with most forms of Britishness remain committed to cricket, a game long acclimatized in the Indian subcontinent.

Crime and Injustice

Across Europe, youth grievances focus on the police and the criminal justice system. From the 1980s onward, poverty and desperation led to rapidly rising crime against persons and property, which in turn encouraged white hostility against ethnic communities, Muslims and others. In turn, hard-nosed policing turned young city dwellers against authority, bolstering a sense of street solidarity. Encouraging a perception of official racism, Muslim officers are seriously underrepresented in most of the forces policing cities with large immigrant communities: although London's population is perhaps 9 percent Muslim, the Metropolitan Police has only three hundred Muslim officers, about 1 percent of the whole. As legitimate social structures declined in many suburbs and projects, so gangs and criminal organizations became powerful. With legal means to advancement closed, many young people aspired to rise through crime or drug activity, seeing as role models the characters in iconic American films like *Scarface* and the *Godfather* trilogy.

Organized crime and narcotics activity in Europe is incomprehensible except in the context of Muslim-dominated syndicates, often with terrorist connections—Albanian, Kurdish, Turkish, Pakistani, and Moroccan. Obviously, this activity implies nothing about the nature of Islam or its adherents but rather illustrates the well-known phenomenon of ethnic succession, in which crime represents the usual stepping-stone for the newest arrivals in any given society. For creditable reasons, scholars wishing to avoid negative stereotyping are reluctant to work on Muslim criminal underworlds, yet such activity is critical to understanding these communities, and as we shall see, for the potential for political radicalization. Muslims today represent the main component of criminal underworlds and prison populations in Germany, France, Sweden, or the Netherlands. Within the French banlieues, local gang leaders or *caids* wield an influence strongly reminiscent of the north African village chieftains from whom they borrow their titles. So powerful are such structures in some areas that state representatives—social workers, firefighters, even police—think twice before venturing in. In the phrase devised to describe areas of Irish Republican Army (IRA) control in the Northern Ireland of the 1970s, they have virtually become no-go areas.[14]

As Muslims are heavily overrepresented among petty thieves and robbers, among gangs and drug dealers, then naturally they contribute heavily to the prison populations of their respective countries. Exact numbers are hard to come by, since France especially, with its traditions of strict secularism, resolutely refuses to identify inmates by faith or ethnicity. Even so, scholar Farhad Khosrokhavar has no hesitation in describing Islam as "France's main prison religion." He suggests that Muslims comprise over half of inmates nationwide, the proportion rising to 80 percent or more in prisons near the banlieues. The overall prison population has grown steeply in recent years, as various administrations have adopted get-tough policies in response to public outcries over street crime. Usually, such waves of draconian sentencing chiefly affect low-level nuisance offenders, particularly petty drug dealers, which in practice means that Muslims are far more likely to be incarcerated. Muslims comprise around 2 percent of the Italian population but 30 percent of the country's prison inmates, with even higher shares in urban prisons such as Milan's Bollate. Nations vary in how far they accommodate Muslim needs, especially in providing appropriate halal food. British prisons do supply halal, but France requires inmates to buy it specially in the commissary, meaning in practice that poorer prisoners are systematically forced to eat forbidden food.[15]

As for urban black Americans, the prison experience has become a distressingly normal expectation of life for the poor. The result is to foster already strong forces alienating Muslims, and especially the young, from the mainstream society, and to foster new forms of solidarity. Increasingly too, those exposed to criminal and prison subcultures make those values and expectations a normal component of youth culture and of street society. Invisible cities develop their own laws, their own ethics, their own governments.

Defining Muslims

Like other writers on contemporary Europe, I have repeatedly used the word "Muslim," but in this context more than most, the term demands greater precision. Normally, when discussing the social problems facing modern France or Italy, the word Muslim is actually shorthand for "a member of ethnic communities established in Europe in the second half of the twentieth century, and drawn from African or Asian nations where Islam represents the default religion." To say that

Muslims in this broad sense face unemployment or poor housing conditions, or that they resent maltreatment at the hands of police, says nothing necessarily about the religious attitudes or beliefs of the individuals concerned, or whether that religious identity has anything to do with their social or economic situation. In accounts of conflict and deprivation in France, we would not be going far wrong if we replaced the word "Muslim" with "Arab and African"; in Germany we could use the word "Turkish," and in Britain, "Pakistanis and Bengalis."

Over the past twenty years, though, social grievances have increasingly expressed themselves in religious terms, so that a minority of young Muslims—by no means all—have come to stress their religious identity and also to view their situation in religious terms. Given the depths of the social problems many face, this new religious self-identification does raise the threat of conflict with the wider society, which some see not just as white or European but as Christian.

That young city dwellers would protest against the established order needs little explanation, but it would be a long time before dissent took religious forms. As we have seen, early migrants tended to be politically passive, but their children saw European countries as their homes, from which they had higher expectations. From the early 1980s, ethnic youth became active in street protests in France, Britain, and other countries and also in frequent nonpolitical confrontations with police. Asian youths rioted in Britain in 1981, and young people of north African origin made both 1983 and 1990 long hot summers in France. French youths pioneered so-called rodeo riots, in which gangs stole and burned cars, luring police into areas where they could be engaged in wild street battles. In Britain, politicized young Asians adopted the rhetoric of race and blackness, accepting a shared political cause with Afro-Caribbean people in the face of white racism and discrimination. This sense of black identity was a startling development for anyone accustomed to the harshly offensive connotations of the term "black" in a south Asian context. The main organization for young British Pakistanis and Bangladeshis took the name Asian Youth Movement rather than any religious label. As in France, these were racial or ethnic outbreaks, not religious.

In France too, Arabs and Muslims allied with white leftists in opposition to the electoral power of the right-wing Front National. In 1983, French and Arabs (*Beurs*) joined in a vast national Marche des Beurs, under the slogan "black-blanc-beur." The goals of the march were strongly integrationist, and its prime movers included both a radical Catholic priest and immigrant leader Harlem Désir, a black Catholic of Caribbean origin. In 1984, SOS-Racisme became an effective national network, while the slogan *Touche pas à mon pote!*, "Don't touch my buddy," promoted white/Arab solidarity in the face of racist attacks.[16]

Observers praised the Marche des Beurs as an equivalent to Martin Luther King's great 1963 March on Washington, yet as in the American context, dreams of integration and harmonious antiracism soon confronted new claims of ethnic nationalism. Both the level and character of militancy changed from about 1989–1990, with the emergence of a stronger cultural-religious consciousness among Muslims. This trend owed much to evangelistic organizations that deliberately targeted disaffected youth. The Association of Islamic Students in France disseminated Islamist writings in French, and this group was soon reinforced by the Tablighi Jamaat. Some have seen in this upsurge an ambitious and deliberate strategy. Gilles Kepel argues that in 1989, inspired by the anticommunist revolutions in Europe, the Muslim Brotherhood made an explicit decision to advance into Europe by means of front groups and associated organizations, a Trojan Horse strategy. Brotherhood-related groups were now strongly in evidence, and the Union of Islamic Organizations of France (UOIF) recruited heavily among students. Radical ideas spread through mosques little connected to any religious establishment, forming instead part of an amorphous *Islam des caves*, the Islam of the cellars.[17]

The growth of immigrant communities in an age of economic decline led to the formation of more sharply defined ethnic/religious neighborhoods. Peter Schneider, whose novels explored the divided consciousness of Berlin in the era of East-West division, writes that "there is a new wall rising in the city of Berlin. To cross this wall you have to go to the city's central and northern districts—to Kreuzberg, Neukölln, and Wedding—and you will find yourself in a world unknown to the majority of Berliners." Turks and Kurds predominate here, followed by Arabs and other Muslim groups. Every country has similar areas. Brussels has its Little Morocco in the section called Sint-Jans-Molenbeek, where, in the words of Moroccan-Belgian journalist Hind Fraihi "a separate Muslim state is grown and where Belgium feels sometimes so far away." Bruce Bawer argues that Muslim residents "already view [Molenbeek] not as part of Belgium but as an area under Islamic jurisdiction in which Belgians are not welcome." Some French banlieues acquired the cast of an Arab suburb, a *dahiya*.[18]

For some new-stock Europeans, racial rhetoric and grievances transformed into religious ones. Just to illustrate the shifting allegiances of the time through one notorious career, we might look at Zacarias Moussaoui, convicted in a U.S. court as a conspirator in the 9–11 attacks. Through the 1980s, his African appearance led to him being called *négre* (nigger), and his black identity became steadily more pronounced after the Gulf War. It was at this point that he began dismissing white people with the crude racial epithet *toubab*. By the mid-1990s, though, he had aligned himself with extreme Islamist militancy and began military training.[19]

Islam as Counterculture

Once Islam was on the agenda, the main issue was to determine which form of the religion was likely to gain most support. For Muslims, as for immigrant Christians, authoritarian, charismatic, and demanding styles appeal to a particular market, namely, adolescents and young adults, commonly suffering from multiple social deprivation and moreover observing gender roles in the process of rapid transition. At a time of social upheaval and chaos, rigid forms of Islam offer an island of stability and certainty, especially for young men. These developments echo Antonio Gramsci's remark: "The crisis consists precisely in the fact that the old is dying, and the new cannot be born; in this interregnum a great variety of morbid symptoms appear."[20]

For some young Muslims, Islam refers to a cultural identity much more than to strict adherence to particular beliefs or practices. In France in 2001, some 85 percent of young Muslims followed very few of the five pillars, the practices formally prescribed by Islam. Islamic identity mainly took the form of avoiding pork and ham and hostility toward alcohol. Yet in some countries, this latter belief marked quite a radical step in itself, since by the 1990s mainstream youth culture was associated with heavy drinking and, in England, with a disturbing tendency to binge drinking and the associated violence. Just by staying aloof from this world, young Muslims are making a powerful statement of faith.[21]

Professions of sexual purity also serve as sharp cultural markers separating Muslims from young white Europeans. In the 1997 British film *My Son the Fanatic*, based on a story by Hanif Kureishi, a convert to radical Islamism explains his new beliefs as part of a quest for "belief, purity and belonging to the past." He condemns white members of a society who "live in pornography and filth and they tell us how backward we are—their society is soaked in sex." In the Pew Global Attitudes Survey, attitudes toward gender and sexuality go far to explaining the noticeable disaffection of British Muslims. When asked whether Westerners were disrespectful of women, just 13 percent of Spanish Muslims and 23 percent of French thought they were. The figure for British Muslims was however 44 percent, which was in a similar range to the results from Turkey, Egypt, and Indonesia.[22]

Across Europe, radical ideas were making headway by the 1990s, urging young Muslims to separate themselves from a corrupt mainstream society. In Britain, radical Wahhabi and Salafist recruiters spread their views among students and young professionals, urging them to separate themselves from British society, condemning voting as *haram*, forbidden. In a recruitment video for the militant Hizb ut-Tahrir (Liberation Party), a young man with a working class British accent asserts,

Muslims in this country need to answer some very serious questions. Where does their allegiance lie? . . . I think Muslims in this country need to take a long, hard look at themselves and decide what is their identity. Are they British or are they Muslim? I am a Muslim. Where I live, is irrelevant.[23]

Some take the Muslim identification further, to reject much of Western culture as irredeemably corrupt.[24]

The Old-New Religion

For its young followers, the new Islam is anything but new: it is the purest and most pristine old-time religion as preached in the deserts of Arabia 1,300 years ago. Yet although radicals presented themselves as returning to the authentic spirit of Islam, the message they offered was in fact modern and globalized both in form and content. In Europe, radicals gained influence because they spoke, literally, in the same language as their young hearers, which was usually the local vernacular, French in France, English in Britain. The first generation of migrants had existed in a complex linguistic world, drifting between four or five languages. In Britain, Pakistanis were taught in English at school, heard classical Arabic at the mosque, watched videos and television in Hindi or Punjabi, while using Urdu for most matters. The second and third generations, however, were mainly comfortable in English, which was also the lingua franca of radical Islam. As a conservative older Muslim protested,

> It doesn't matter what the imam says inside the mosque because the young people don't understand. The real education goes on outside. In mosques our religious leaders are speaking in Urdu. The only people speaking in English are extremists like Abu Hamza and [Omar] Bakri Mohammed. Youngsters do not get the real message of Islam.[25]

Also strictly contemporary were the means of recruiting and training militant followers, whether or not groups planned to use violence. In recent years, academics and intelligence agencies have tried to formulate a profile of the kind of young person most likely to be drawn into extremist Muslim activities, but no simple answer emerges. Many are well-qualified students and recent graduates, particularly those with degrees in engineering or information technology; at the other extreme, we find "underachievers with few or no qualifications, and often a criminal background."[26]

What most have in common, though, is the classic dilemma of the second-generation resident who finds himself caught between cultures, who feels utterly separated from the country of family origin and yet cannot identify with his own country of birth and upbringing. As one observer notes, "People recruiting for Islamic Jihad know exactly who to be on the lookout for in the Netherlands: second-generation Moroccan youths suffering from an identity crisis with few prospects and plagued by the thought that the Islamic world is being suppressed." Such prospective recruits can readily be persuaded to identify their own sense of oppression with that of fellow Muslims throughout the world. Older mores are rejected as staid and irrelevant, newer values as callous and materialistic. As Olivier Roy notes, "Adrift from both, they are attracted by a simple, electronically disseminated version of the faith which can readily be propagated among people of all cultures." The result is an individualized kind of religion that sets the believer not just against secular society but against any forms of religious authority that preach moderation or restraint. One conservative Muslim complains that when the young reach this stage, "all doors close for them. 'Everything else is black,' they think, 'but I'm white and I'm going to paradise.' Those who see black and white think they are angels, they think they are flying. If a Dutchman speaks to them on the street, they think 'he's a Zionist' or 'he's a Satan.' "[27]

Recruits who reject their European homelands are instead offered visual images of the spirit of true Islam, as expressed in the self-sacrificing purity of jihad in Chechnya, Algeria, or Iraq. Commonly, recruiters use videos, usually via the cell phones that were the ubiquitous tools of the European young some years before they became so common in the United States. Interested candidates for the movements would attend meetings, conferences, and special summer camps, all the while participating in Internet chatrooms focused heavily on themes of jihad and martyrdom. And constantly, members and prospects would watch and discuss videos of suicide missions and of the ritualistic murder or beheading of infidels—American captives in Iraq, Russian soldiers in Chechnya. A classic story of such a recruit would be Mohammed Bouyeri, the young man of Moroccan origins who in 2004 earned notoriety as the assassin of Theo van Gogh. Born in 1978, Bouyeri had a solid college career but was imprisoned for a violent attack. "He emerged from jail an Islamist, angry over Palestine and sympathetic to Hamas." He joined what became a particularly extreme cell, the Hofstad Group, which devoted itself to watching violent video clips, with a special interest in beheading. As one Dutch security expert observes, "The breeding grounds [for extremism] are websites, prisons and the mosques."[28]

This process of radicalization is a very modern confection. Throughout the long history of Islam, images of jihad and martyrdom have existed but have seldom played a significant role in encouraging conversion. More commonly, missionaries have won followers by stressing the mystical aspects of the faith, or else its superior morality and social organization. The whole cult of suicide martyrdom that is so central today is a recent innovation. Islamists did not invent the modern fashion for suicide bombing, which was developed by Hindu Tamil extremists, and the Muslim association with the tactic dates only to the early 1980s. In the past two decades, though, the suicide cult has become a major selling point in some circles.[29]

Moreover, the means of spreading the word make wonderful sense for many young Westerners. Islamist recruiters urge followers to spend long hours on the Internet, where they encounter gory snuff films and exchange fantasies of death and dismemberment. Enthusiasts collect and trade particularly gruesome items portraying torture or decapitation, which are studied to produce a thorough desensitization to bloodshed. And as in such circles, we find a kind of comedy of errors. Watching gruesome videos, discussing bloody plans, an individual might find such themes sick or upsetting but is afraid to admit the fact lest he lose status; therefore he compensates by contributing his own ever-more extravagant flourishes of machismo. Through this process of escalation, a group of quite normal boys and young adults drive each other into an upward spiral of bloodthirsty fantasy. Admittedly in extreme form, the whole phenomenon sounds very much like the thought world of disturbed teenagers in North America, the sort who, in a few cases, actually carry out their fantasies of gunning down rivals in the corridors of their high schools. If only the Islamists packaged their message to the young through raucous heavy metal music, the resemblance would be perfect.

We can understand how such a glorification of religious militarism might arise in conditions of terminal political stress, in war-ravaged societies in Palestine or Iraq, though even there, the stress on armed resistance is never more than one facet of the complex faith. Yet in prosperous Europe, we find a cultish perversion of religion in which the bombings and beheadings almost become the central tenets of practice. In Europe too, unlike north Africa or south Asia, young enthusiasts are not subject to the very powerful constraints of traditional values and social structures, the iron laws of village and clan that mandate strict customary limits to the use of violence and disorder. Older Muslims complain of losing their children to militant recruiters. Following the London bombings of 2005, one father declared,

> This is another tragedy: the generation gap between young and old in the ethnic minorities is much greater than in the indigenous population. Our elder generation were law-abiding and hardworking. Where they failed was they put all their God-given hours into work and didn't spend time with their children. When these people are brainwashed, they are brainwashed to an extent that they don't talk to their parents.[30]

Similar complaints are heard across Europe. The teenage son of prominent Danish imam Ahmed Abu Laban was expelled from a largely Muslim public school after he used Friday prayers as an opportunity to call for the annihilation of Israel and to denounce Danish democracy. His father complained that the Hizb ut-Tahrir "sell a simple package by giving young Muslims martyrdom in fifteen minutes. If they were good Muslims, they would have told my son to listen to his father." The desperate need to compete with the Hizb and like-minded groups goes far to explaining the seemingly hysterical reaction of mainstream Muslim leaders to apparently petty slights, since they must not be seen to be too accommodating. Abu Laban himself later attracted worldwide fame as the leader of protests against the cartoons of the prophet Muhammad.[31]

Severed from both past and present ties, young men find themselves open to the formulation of a new religious synthesis, potentially an emerging new Islam that might be truly pan-European, neither south Asian nor Maghrebi, Balkan nor Turkish. The prospect might be encouraging in the long term; but at least in its early stages, the Islam of Young Europe has some terrifying elements.

Alienation

Radicals also established at least a rhetorical presence in poor and working-class areas. Even if young Muslims did not accept or debate their ideas in any detail, Islamic guerrillas and terrorists became a powerful symbol of resistance to the mainstream society. In the immediate aftermath of the September 11 attacks, Berliners were appalled to see residents of the immigrant neighborhoods of Neukölln and Kreuzberg firing bottle rockets in celebration. Some weeks afterward, France and Algeria met in a soccer match, and when the Algerians were obviously losing, a mob of French-born north African youths invaded the pitch, chanting "Bin Laden! Bin Laden!" Surveys of Dutch Muslims showed just 62 percent disapproving of the 9–11 attacks.[32]

Several notorious cases suggest the appeal of Islamic militancy to young adults with lengthy criminal backgrounds. In 2006, Muslims across Europe protested the Danish cartoons of Muhammad, and some instances, demonstrations involved overt threats of violence. One young British protester, Omar Khayam, paraded dressed as a suicide bomber, complete with fake explosives. The photograph infuriated many, and police questioned him with a view to possible criminal charges. Significantly, the charge to which he was most vulnerable was a parole violation, since this advocate of ultra-puritan rigorous Islam had a record for dealing crack cocaine and had served half of a five-and-a-half year sentence. Omar Khayam's conversion draws attention to one aspect of the appeal of radicalism, which offers solutions to young people with little chance of achieving success through approved means. Encountering stern varieties of Islam at critical moments in their lives, some come to identify secular Western capitalist society as the source of their difficulties.[33]

Many individual case studies suggest the appeal of Islamic militancy within Europe, though we have to make some allowance for media reporting that focuses on the sensational. When Italian journalists want to illustrate the depths of Islamist fanaticism, they can readily find an incendiary quote from Adel Smith, leader of the Unione Musulmani d'Italia which claims some 50,000 members. Yet a more recent examination raises doubts about whether his organization really contains more than two full-time members, plus a dozen or so hangers-on. In an important study of French news coverage of Muslim affairs, Thomas Deltombe found evidence not only of a focus on unrepresentative extremists but in a few cases, the deliberate manufacture of news about fanatics preaching and recruiting in "hidden mosques." As remarked earlier, the media rarely feel the need to quote the views of the peaceful or contented.[34]

But some survey evidence does suggest the disaffection prevailing among teenagers and young adults. Muslim communities as a whole are largely prepared to accept the fact of living in modern societies, which in the European context implies a multifaith situation not dominated politically by Islam. In 2006, the Pew Global Attitudes Survey found that 71 percent of Spanish Muslims and 72 percent of French saw no conflict between being a devout Muslim and living in a modern society; the figure for German Muslims was 57 percent, though just 49 percent for British. (Strikingly, non-Muslim Europeans thought that such an accommodation was far more difficult than did Muslims themselves.) Consistently though, the figures for young respondents suggest more radical views.[35]

In the mid-1990s, one major study of Turkish youth in Germany found a remarkable affinity for religious extremism, all the more remarkable given the long-standing dominance of secularism in Turkish culture. Almost a third believed that Islam should come to power in every country, and around 40 percent agreed that Zionism, the European Union, and the United States threaten Islam. Over half of the Turkish youth felt that they should not adapt too much to Western ways but should live by Islam. Nor have conditions improved in subsequent years. A survey of German Muslims in 2004 found that over 20 percent denied that the German constitution was compatible with the Quran. Following the Van Gogh assassination, television news programs across Europe undertook street interviews to gauge the reaction of European Muslims. In Germany and France, many of those questioned reacted with little surprise to what they saw as justified retaliation for van Gogh's crude attacks on their religion; "If you insult Islam, you have to pay" was a typical response.[36]

British Muslims have produced the most troubling signs of disaffection, with a minority regularly agreeing to quite extreme political statements. By 2004, 13 percent of British Muslims thought the 9–11

attacks were justified. Immediately following the 2005 subway bombings in London itself, a survey of British Muslims found that 6 percent
thought the attacks justified, with 11 percent more seeing them as "on
balance not justified," a pale condemnation. Polls of young Muslims,
aged eighteen to twenty-four, showed still more sympathy for radicalism: 21 percent believed that suicide bombings were justified in Israel,
and 12 percent thought that this tactic was justified within Britain
itself. "A fifth of all Muslims, and a quarter of men, say suicide attacks against the military can be justified, though only 7 percent say
this about civilians." Another poll taken some months later found 7
percent of the whole Muslim community (all ages) supporting suicide
attacks within the United Kingdom, 16 percent in Israel. New polls in
2006 showed that 13 percent of British Muslims regarded Mohammad
Sidique Khan and the other bombers as martyrs; over and above that
number, "a further sixteen percent believed that although the attacks
were wrong, the cause behind the bombings was right." These figures
indicate (minority) support for positions that have been repeatedly denounced by virtually all mainstream Muslim organizations, again suggesting an insurgency of sons against fathers. Also indicating disaffection are the surveys in which young Muslims in many countries assert
their nationality as "Muslim" rather than that of the European nation
in which they notionally hold citizenship. In several recent polls, between 20 percent and 25 percent of Muslims in Britain claim not to
identify with the nation in any way.[37]

Now, we can read these polls in different ways. One Muslim organization takes an optimistic line, reporting accurately that "a sweeping
majority of British Muslims said there were no circumstances that
would justify suicide bombings in Britain and that they would feel
shame to learn that a close family member had joined al-Qaeda, . . . an
overwhelming 93 percent think that suicide attacks on civilians in the
UK cannot be justified and 86 percent rejected targeting military establishments." Yet the dissident minorities are substantial, and we have to
ask how representative these figures are of wider European conditions.
Britain has an unusually long and sophisticated tradition of social and
political polling, and events like the 7/7 bombings have inspired the media to take repeated surveys more frequently and in more detail than in
most other nations. It might be that a comparable set of surveys would
find other youth communities just as unhappy as those in Britain, but
more likely, the British case really is unusual and reflects conditions pe-
culiar to that nation. One factor is the south Asian origin of the majority
of British Muslims. Islamist politics of a quite intolerant variety have
surged in Pakistan in the past twenty years and enjoy a mainstream status that they do not in Algeria, Morocco, or Turkey, while the war in
Kashmir has done much to stir radical passions. (And that burning
grievance would remain even if the crises in Iraq and Palestine were

resolved tomorrow.) Accordingly, young British Muslims seeking to get in touch with their roots might well identify with those causes. Many have also been exposed over the past decade to the intense propaganda of radical groups like Hizb ut-Tahrir at a time when British authorities were allowing such groups amazing latitude to operate on their territory. Official attitudes to radical agitation are now much stricter, and we can hope that the disaffected minority will shrink in coming years.[38]

Having said this, recent developments in media, especially the growth of satellite television, mean that literally Muslims can if they choose inhabit a different world of news and information. Looking at the British community as a whole,

> more Muslims trust what they hear about what is going on in the Middle East from English-language Muslim channels (68 percent) than from the BBC (58 percent). As many people are likely to listen to the clerics at their local mosque to find out about the Middle East as tune in to the BBC. More are likely to turn to the English-language Muslim press (49 percent) as to national newspapers (42 percent).[39]

Reading these comments, we should recall that the BBC is anything but a mouthpiece of government, to the extent that the corporation refuses to apply the judgmental word "terrorism" even to the most blatant attacks against civilians. If Muslims find even the BBC too unfriendly a source, that is a troubling fact.

Middle Eastern media are popular throughout Muslim Europe. One working-class area of Amsterdam bears the nickname Satellite City because so many residents have minisatellite dishes on their balconies in order to receive al-Jazeera and Moroccan television. In Belgium, journalist Hind Fraihi remarks similarly that

> with the satellite dishes, the connection with the Arab world stays so strong that many immigrants don't even try to build up connections with Belgium. And those Arab broadcasters fill most of the days with news reports about Iraq, Afghanistan, Palestine. Sensational pictures and stories, with the main goal to make sure that people don't concern themselves with the enormous internal problems in the Arab countries.

Another long-popular channel was the Lebanese based al-Manar, which is affiliated to the radical Hizbollah. Adding to its appeal and its credibility, Hizbollah was one of the very rare Muslim organizations that could claim military success against Israeli occupation, and that was true long before the hard-fought battles of 2006. In this instance, though, European governments have acted to suppress the channel because of its openly anti-Jewish content. Following France's lead, several nations have since 2004 prohibited networks from carrying the station.[40]

This suspicion of domestic media helps explain the openness to conspiracy theory, even among those who would not necessarily support violent attacks themselves. In 2006, just 17 percent of British Muslims believed that Arabs carried out the 9–11 attacks, compared with 35 percent of Germans and 48 percent of French Muslims. Many British Muslims have no hesitation in attributing the September 11 attacks to the Israeli Mossad and believe that Britain's own security service, MI5, sponsored the subway bombings. In the immediate aftermath of the London bombings, 34 percent of Muslim respondents denied that these attacks were the work of Muslims, while 26 percent were unsure.[41]

Jews and Zionists

Across Europe too, Jewish issues emerge consistently as a basis for Muslim grievances and also for a critical dividing marker between old- and new-stock populations. After Europe's own horrendous experiences with anti-Semitism, few Europeans apart from the most extreme ultra-rightists have any sympathy whatever for anti-Jewish views or conspiracy theories. In most countries, such expressions would be designated as hate speech and thus subject to severe penal sanctions.[42]

Europe's Muslims usually have quite different approaches, not because of any deep-dyed anti-Jewish sentiment. Indeed, Turkey and Morocco, two major sources of migration to Europe, have long been among the Muslim nations most consistently sympathetic to Israel. Still today, Muslims in Europe have a more generally positive feeling toward Jews than do those in home countries. The Pew Global Attitudes Project survey found that attitudes in most Muslim nations were extremely hostile: only 2 percent of Egyptians had favorable attitudes toward Jews. Matters were quite different in Europe, where 71 percent of French Muslims reported favorable attitudes, as did 38 percent of German Muslims.[43]

However, as European Muslims in the 1980s developed a more intense global consciousness and a wider awareness of Muslim conflicts and grievances, the plight of the Palestinians became increasingly central to political rhetoric. The formation of Hamas in 1987 brought the specifically Muslim political aspects of the crisis to the foreground, while the continuing violence since 2000 has meant that Palestinian complaints have never been far from the headlines. Extremist groups like Hizb ut-Tahrir make much use of anti-Jewish as well as anti-Zionist rhetoric, drawing on conspiracy materials that are in common circulation in the Middle East. In a leaflet available on its website, Hizb ut-Tahrir alleges that Islam commands Muslims to "kill them wherever you find them, and turn them out from where they have been turned out. . . . The Jews are a people of slander . . . a treacherous people . . . they fabricate lies and twist words from their right context." We do not have to go far to find similar venom from extremist Muslim preachers and media.[44]

Such views do not necessarily have a wider impact, but many Muslims who would be conservative or moderate on other issues often show themselves open to militant rhetoric. Partly, this is a matter of frustration at the policies of their respective countries. Muslims are told repeatedly that they should participate in the constitutional process within their countries of residence, but their views seem to have little impact on Middle Eastern matters. Perhaps the closest European Muslims have ever been to unanimity was in their opposition to the Iraq war in 2003, and hundreds of thousands protested in Britain and elsewhere. Yet European nations joined the "coalition of the willing" supporting the U.S. invasion, leading Muslims to conclude that their countries were serving the will only of the United States and of the Israeli interests that supposedly dominated American policy. When the Pew survey asked European Muslims about relations between Muslims and "the West," quite solid numbers felt that things were generally good—41 percent in France, 49 percent in Spain. The outlier was Britain, where only 23 percent agreed that things were generally good, a much more pessimistic number than was recorded even in Egypt. Several explanations are possible for this feeling, including the continuing aftershocks from the subway bombings; but another obvious fact is that Britain, unlike France or Spain, still had a major military commitment in Iraq. British Muslims also recorded quite low rates of favorable attitudes toward Jews, of just 32 percent.[45]

Issues of equity between the faiths have proved thorny. At least from a common perspective, European nations repeatedly commemorate bygone Jewish sufferings in the Holocaust but are reluctant to mark gross abuse of Muslim populations in Palestine and elsewhere. Recently, British Muslims have attacked the focus of the Holocaust Memorial day introduced in that country in 2001. In the words of British Muslim leader Sir Iqbal Sacranie, "Muslims feel hurt and excluded that their lives are not equally valuable to those lives lost in the Holocaust time." Muslim activists have instead proposed a Genocide Day that would also acknowledge Muslim deaths in Palestine, Chechnya, and Bosnia. Activist Ibrahim Hewitt complains that "there are five hundred Palestinian towns and villages that have been wiped out over the years. That's pretty genocidal to me." In the Netherlands and elsewhere, schoolteachers report real difficulty in teaching the events of the Holocaust to predominantly Muslim classes, who resent the single-minded focus on Jewish events, particularly when these are so often used to justify the existence of Israel.[46]

The sense of double standards to Israeli and Palestinian interests, together with perceptions of Israeli dominance of Western foreign policy, easily leads Muslims to be vulnerable to anti-Zionist conspiracy theories. In a recent poll of British Muslims commissioned by alarmed Jewish organizations, more than half the respondents supported boycotting

Holocaust Memorial Day while agreeing that the Jewish community has too much influence over British foreign policy. Only half accepted that Israel had a right to exist, with 37 percent of those questioned agreeing that the Jewish community in Britain is a legitimate target "as part of the ongoing struggle for justice in the Middle East." On all these issues, young adult Muslims emerge as by far the strongest opponents of Zionism and Jewish interests.[47]

The Halimi Murder

Few observers of contemporary Europe would doubt that many young people of Muslim origin are deeply alienated and often angry, and that a sizable number show themselves sympathetic to radical agitation. Western Europe may indeed have a social and political crisis on its hands. But we need to be cautious about making a further leap, in assuming that violent actions by the Muslim young necessarily have religious or extremist motivations. In some cases, young Muslims do adopt the hard-line Islamist positions offered by groups like Hizb ut-Tahrir; yet in others, religion provides a convenient label for more generalized disaffection that in slightly different circumstances could easily have been expressed in terms of class or race.

Many examples illustrate the difficulties in deciding the motivation of an act. One of the most wrenching instances of violent crime in modern France involved the 2005 murder of a young Israeli named Ilan Halimi, who was kidnapped by a gang who themselves claimed the apt title of the Barbarians. The gang held him in the suburb of Bagneux, south of Paris, while attempting to win ransom money from his family or the local Jewish community—and many neighbors were aware of his presence. Halimi was tortured, repeatedly stabbed, burned, and attacked with acid, so that he ultimately died of his wounds. The Barbarians were led by Youssouf Fofana, from a Muslim family derived from the Ivory Coast, and Islamist literature was found in the home of one gang member. In one telephone call to the family, a kidnapper "recited verses from the Koran while Ilan was heard screaming in agony in the background."[48]

The murder attracted international outrage, as a symbol of brutal anti-Semitic violence, orchestrated by fanatical young Muslims. This was the interpretation offered by Jewish and Israeli media and also by the American conservative press. The *Jerusalem Post* spoke of "a terrorist gang of French Muslims," while the *Wall Street Journal* commented that in his death, Halimi became "a symbol of this Continent's failures in dealing with its poor and maladjusted Muslims." Yet other observers read less ideological significance into the murder. Fofana's confederates included "the children of blacks from sub-Saharan Africa and the

Caribbean, of Arabs from North Africa, of at least one Persian from Iran, and of whites from Portugal and France." And while Fofana had definitely decided to target Jews for abduction or extortion, that was because he had decided that French Jews were likely to be richer than non-Jewish whites. In his confession, he declared simply, "It was done for financial ends."[49]

Whether stressing or underplaying the role of religious bigotry in the attack, a number of ideological agendas were at work. For American conservatives as for Jewish observers, such an outbreak of vicious anti-Semitism demonstrated the hypocrisy of French or European claims to moral superiority and any right to criticize the United States position in Iraq or elsewhere in the Middle East. The crime, and its official neglect, recalled European hostility or negligence toward Jews in bygone years, most notoriously during the 1940s. To quote the *Jerusalem Post* again, "today, as seventy years ago, the Jews are disserved by poor and weak leaders who refuse to see the dangers." The *Jewish World Review* headed a story about the case, "From 1933–1945, The Enemy Was Nazi Germany. Today, It's Political Islam." Such commentators had a vested interest in making the murder seem as religiously motivated as possible, while French officials had just as strong a motive in depoliticizing it, in making it seem a regular crime. Both approaches had obvious policy consequences. If French Jews lived under the pervasive threat of racist violence, that would of itself demand a response by police and government, possibly extending to adjusting official policies to the Israeli-Palestinian conflict. If, on the other hand, the crime was "mere murder," then it remained a limited matter for the criminal justice system.[50]

Ultimately, it is all but impossible to tell the real origins of the crime. To think of an analogy, imagine an American Jew robbed and murdered by a gang of African-American youths. One might interpret this as a manifestation of antiwhite prejudice, or of black anti-Semitism, or perhaps of class resentment; but it would also be quite plausible to understand it as a straightforward crime. Barring detailed insight into the minds of the perpetrators, we will not know which of these interpretations is most plausible.

Understanding Violence

Issues of interpretation arise more centrally in other recent instances of crime and violence in France and other European nations. While Muslims are the main component of the immigrant poor across Europe, and especially in the legendary French banlieues, they are by no means the only group, nor are the poor defined exclusively by religion. In recent rioting in France, we find activity by black Africans of Christian origin as well as by poor whites, chiefly of southern European origin. Moreover, a young man from a Muslim family may have virtually no sense of religious identification. In all societies, people have multiple identities from which to choose, and religion may or may not occupy a primary place.

The racial angle should be stressed much more than it customarily is. Most observers note a change in the consciousness of European ethnic groups in the late 1980s, and unquestionably, some people did turn vigorously to Islamic loyalties, but racial identification continued to be powerful for many. This was true in France, which, given its colonial past, inevitably has a substantial population of African descent, drawn either from Africa itself or from the Caribbean. While the French refuse to count the membership of their ethnic or religious groups, estimates of the country's black population run anywhere from 2 to 4 million. Many of those would also be counted among the nation's Muslims, but religion is not necessarily the major factor in deciding their self-identification. Blacks, like Muslims, also suffer from racism, they feel an enormous sense of exclusion from mainstream society, and they have often been involved in urban unrest. The black French population has virtually no political representation, nor do they have any presence in the corporate world.

Violence against French white residents might thus be incited by racist sentiment as much as by religious fervor. In one incident in 2005, white students demonstrated in Paris against proposed education reforms. The march was disrupted by hundreds of black and Arab youths who beat and robbed many demonstrators, not through any concern about the political issues involved but explicitly from antiwhite prejudice, to take revenge against privileged white people. In response, leading thinkers issued a petition denouncing antiwhite violence and pogroms of a kind that has become quite common. On New Year's Day, 2006, "a gang of some forty young, mostly Arab men terrorized a Nice-Lyon train, sexually assaulting and robbing passengers, car by car." Similarly, while U.S. media accurately report the grave dangers facing Jews traveling in or near immigrant areas of France, Jews may be in no greater peril than are white French people of any religious persuasion.[51]

French conditions are not unique. In Muslim areas of Britain, people of Pakistani descent define themselves not against Christians or infidels but against whites, and the term need not have hostile intent. British boxer Amir Khan happily recalls attending a mixed school where he had lots of white friends. But it also becomes a hostile racial epithet, as when a young British woman whose dress fails to meet local community standards encounters shouts of "white bitch" or "white slag." Riots erupt between Asians and whites, or (more frequently in recent years) between Asians and blacks.[52]

In Sweden too, we observe conflicts of race, culture, and ethnicity rather than religion. The country has now become accustomed to frequent violent crimes by immigrants of Muslim origin, usually directed against white old-stock Swedes. As Christopher Caldwell remarks, this represents a conscious choice by gang members: "White Swedes in the center of Stockholm are easier marks—identifiably middle class and unlikely to have developed the habit of defending themselves aggressively." In no way should any of these comments be seen as trivializing or underestimating the violence or criminal activity, but they do raise questions about the origins of minority unrest, and specifically its religious character.[53]

Gangsters

Contemporary forms of youth culture illustrate the strength of racial and ethnic grievances, more than religious ones. During the 1980s, new forms of youth culture spread among Europe's ethnic communities, including Muslims but also African and Asian ethnic groups from other traditions. As with Muslims, disaffection was particularly strong among the second generation, who had been born in European nations but who felt alienated from the host societies. These cultures were not necessarily political, still less oppositional, but they increasingly served to differentiate the young both from the mainstream society and their elders. In music, styles and subcultures merged with one another to create innovative fusions. Among the most influential was the Algerian-based Raï culture, which attracted a mass youth following in France and which popularized the image of the *hittiste*, the unemployed street youth. In England, Indian and Pakistani teenagers horrified their elders by their enthusiasm for Punjabi-based Bhangra music, which became the mainstream pop culture of Asian youth in the 1980s. (Though the music itself was quite inoffensive, it encouraged social and gender mixing.) One of Germany's best-known artists today is the Turkish-descended Muhabbet, who comes from the rough Cologne neighborhood of Bocklemünd but whose image is clean-cut, socially and politically moderate. His music integrates Turkish and Balkan themes into a rhythm and blues framework to create a style called R'n'B-esk.[54]

Also influential, though less appealing to conservatives, was American-derived rap and its attendant hip-hop culture, which now has acquired deep roots in France and Germany. American rap was reinforced by African and Caribbean influences and attracted a generation of stars, usually African born, like France's MC Solaar or Ménélik, or Britain's Fun^Da^Mental. Germany produced Turkish stars like Eko Fresh and Kool Savas. These artists varied enormously in their degree of politicization, and some, like MC Solaar, fit into the category of best-selling pop.[55]

Some others, though, explored radical themes, and in a few cases, Islam became a motif, or rather, a symbol of protest. In his 1996 song "Je Suis l'Arabe," French artist Yazid sang:

> I'm the Arab, stopping oppression is my mission.
> The country of secularism doesn't tolerate Islam
> Unemployment ravages, they talk of immigration
> And when the banlieue burns, they talk of integration.[56]

Muslim themes also surfaced in the 1990s in the work of IAM, Imperial Asiatic Men, one of the best known groups, whose adoption of Egyptian names like Akhenaton lays claim to an African-Mediterranean heritage. Their songs often use phrases like *Allahu Akbar* and Muslim terms like *ulema*, though the Islam referred to is mystical rather than political. In contrast, in songs like "Mera Mazab," the British-Pakistani Fun^Da^Mental offered abundant references to Islamic warriors, injustice in Palestine, Nubians with jihad on their mind. Lead singer Propa-Gandhi sings,

> I was born a Muslim, and I'm still livin' as a Muslim
> My spirituality determines reality
> You're running after false gods
> Forgettin' the true one . . .
> There is no other way brother, Allah uh akbar . . .

The song's lyrics incorporate the Arabic text of a whole Quranic sura, number 112, *al-Ikhlaas*. Using scriptural verses in such a profane context alienated older Muslim community leaders as much as did the religious radicalism and contributed to the ongoing generational struggle in Britain's Pakistani community.[57]

Even so, such militant religious sentiments stand out because of their relative rarity, in a culture that complained primarily of social and racial injustice. Overwhelmingly, most of Europe's contemporary hip-hop music addresses issues of alienation, deprivation, and frustration. And although people of Arab and north African origin make up a large proportion of the audience for such music, little of the content is overtly Muslim.

At the most extreme was an authentic strand of gangster rap that fantasized openly about violence against symbols of authority. Ironically, the boom in this music was the direct result of a decision by the French government, which in 1994 ordered radio stations to maintain a 40 percent quota of French-language music. This drove record companies to scour the country for local acts, and they found them—though these artists were not what the authorities wanted to hear. Among the starkest, and most obscene was the very popular group NTM, which stands for Nique Ta Mere, roughly "Fuck Your Momma." The group sang, "Screw the police, I sodomize and piss on the law! Our enemies are the men in blue." In 1995, the song "Qu'est-ce qu'on attend" included this warning:

For years everything should have already exploded . . .
But you know it's all going to end up badly
The war of the worlds, you wanted it, here it is . . .
From now on the street will not forgive
We've nothing to lose for we've never had anything to begin with
(Nous n'avons rien à perdre car nous n'avons jamais rien eu)[58]

NTM's artistic efforts led to prosecutions for obscenity and incitements to violence, a tactic also used against other groups like La Rumeur. In 2004, the rap group Sniper won a law case in which they were accused of inciting hatred and violence. In their song "La France," they sang

La France est une garce, on s'est fait trahir . . .
On se fou de la république et de la liberté d'expression
Faudrait changer les lois et pouvoir voir
Bientôt à l'Élysée des arabes et des noirs au pouvoir
Faut que ça pète!

Roughly: "France is a bitch and we've been betrayed. . . . Screw France, we don't care about the Republic and freedom of speech. We should change the laws so we can see Arabs and Blacks in power in the Elysée Palace. Things have to explode."[59]

Other French gangster rappers included 113, who warned "There better not be a police blunder, or the town will go up / The city's a time-bomb / From the police chief to the guy on the street—they're all hated." On Mr. R's album "PolitiKment IncorreKt," his song FranSSe denounced official repression by comparing France to the German SS. He sang, "France is a bitch. . . . Don't forget to fuck her to exhaustion. You have to treat her like a whore, man! . . . My niggers and my Arabs, our playground is the street with the most guns!" In words that sounded prophetic after the rioting of 2005, Alpha 5.20 boasted "Clichy-sous-Bois, it's gangsta gangsta / and Aulnay-sous-Bois, it's gangsta gangsta."[60]

The November Riots

Issues of causation were much debated during the French riots of November 2005, which attracted worldwide attention. The riots represented an explosive intensification of what was already a high level of ongoing violence in the French banlieues, where parked cars were likely to be burned. On average, somewhere in France, around ninety cars burned every night in the first ten months of 2005. Normally, the news media paid little attention to such outbreaks, but this situation changed dramatically in late October, when two teenagers of Muslim origin were killed fleeing police in the town of Clichy-sous-Bois in the "93." The two men—one with roots in Tunisia, the other in Mauritania—were electrocuted while trying to evade a police search. Adding to the tension, Interior Minister Nicolas Sarkozy made provocative remarks denouncing gang control of poor towns and authorizing a police crackdown. He also promised to get rid of *racaille*, "scum," a loaded word recalling popular racist rhetoric against Arabs and Africans: parodying the pressure group SOS-Racisme, a right-wing website used the title SOS-Racaille. Sarkozy threatened to clean up the areas with a *Kärcher*, an industrial-strength pressure washer, which some took to mean that the police would literally clean up the streets using water cannon.

Protests spread across the crescent of banlieues to the north and northeast of Paris, as young residents attacked police and public buildings, using arson, rock throwing, and Molotov cocktails, sometimes ramming stolen cars into banks and restaurants: in a few instances, bullets and buckshot were also used. By mid-November, riots had struck perhaps twenty of the largely immigrant communities around Paris. One flashpoint was Antony, close to Bagneux, where Ilan Halimi spent his tragic last days. Adding to generalized antipolice and antigovernment sentiment, particular grievances stirred unrest in certain areas in which communities had recently undertaken sweeping drug raids. Local imitators struck in thirty or so provincial cities, so that virtually every large or middle-size French city was affected to some degree. Night by night, the authorities tallied the severity of the violence by the number of cars set ablaze—420 in the Paris region on November 3 alone, with the national total reaching 1,300 on November 6, 1,400 on November 7. Reducing that figure to just fifty or sixty a night was regarded as a successful return to normalcy. Together, the riots constituted the nation's worst public order crisis since the popular revolts of 1968. The French police union spoke of "a civil war that spreads a little more every day."[61]

As in the Halimi case, American media outlets prominently stressed the religious angle, seeing the riots as reflecting Europe's failure to absorb its Muslim immigrants. Conservative magazines stressed the Muslim activism supposedly underlying the outbreaks, with Fox television news regularly headlining "Muslim Riots." Commentators drew far-reaching political lessons, with the British *Spectator* asking "Will London burn too?" and asserting, "It's the demography, stupid." Typical headlines from other newspapers and magazines included "The intifada comes to France," and the intifada concept was cited in French papers such as *Le Figaro*. Reporting from the hard-hit community of Aulnay-sous-Bois, the British *Independent* termed the area Baghdad-sur-Seine. Conservative journalist Mark Steyn saw the riots as a warning of a future religious apocalypse. Contemplating such an event, white Europeans might console themselves into thinking, "Fortunately I won't live to see it." However, Steyn remarks, "As France this past fortnight reminds us, the changes in Europe are happening far faster than most people thought. That's the problem: unless you're planning on croaking imminently, you will live to see it." For outspoken pro-Israel media, the riots reflected the failure of French "appeasement" in the face of radical Islam.[62]

Conversely, liberal and left politicians underplayed the riots, specifically the Muslim elements. The director general of France's news service TCI decided early on not to show footage of burning cars, partly in order to avoid encouraging further violence but also to prevent right-wing politicians drawing rhetorical ammunition from the conflicts. In the United States too, the Associated Press made very limited use of the word "Muslim" in its account of the riots, preferring, like the BBC, to stress themes such as immigration, unemployment, poverty, and deprivation. Conservatives mocked such discretion, seeing it as a sign of journalistic cowardice in the face of Muslim threats, of dhimmitude in action.[63]

But were these really Muslim riots? Undoubtedly, a sizable majority of the participants came from Muslim stock, from families who had immigrated from predominantly Muslim regions. Generally, too, rioters tended to avoid harming stores or businesses owned by local Muslims. Yet we see little evidence of the kind of political or religious consciousness that would allow us to speak of a specifically Muslim upsurge. We do not find, for instance, a widespread use of religious slogans or rhetoric, or an attempt to exclude non-Muslim protesters. If a few war cries of *Allahu akbar!* were reported, the question arises why thousands more were not uttered. No one reported or claimed central direction or manipulation by an avowedly Islamic political party or paramilitary grouping, no attempts were made to create "liberated zones," enforcing Islamic rule or moral regulations. It is difficult to contest the logic of the radical International Crisis Group, which declared that the unrest

> took place without any religious actors and confirmed that Islamists do not control those neighborhoods. Even though they had every interest in restoring calm and thereby demonstrating their authority, and despite several attempts to halt the violence, they largely failed: there were no bearded provocateurs behind the riots, and no bearded "older brothers" to end them.[64]

In fact, the riots of 2005 looked very much like the rodeo riots of the 1980s, though on a much larger scale, and nobody had seriously suggested a religious context for those earlier events.

French Muslim authorities sought to distance themselves from the riots, with the Union of French Islamic Organizations (UOIF) condemning violence; and the UOIF represents a strongly conservative variety of Islam. The director of the Paris Great Mosque, Dalil Boubakeur, issued a fatwa forbidding "any Muslim seeking divine grace and satisfaction to participate in any action that blindly hits private or public property or could constitute an attack on someone's life." Such condemnations had little noticeable effect, insofar as the rioters even noticed them. One remarked, contemptuously, "We don't feel represented by those people. We didn't vote for them. They're just filling their pockets."[65]

Race and Class

Instead of invoking the language of intifada and jihad, we might more accurately place the French riots in the context of many other outbreaks that have occurred in the past thirty years and in which religious grievances are obviously far less significant than issues of race and class. Contemplating the French violence, many commentators drew parallels with the 1995 film *La Haine* (*Hate*), about comparable antipolice outbreaks. The analogy is even closer than some think since in that fictional work, the three main characters who epitomized urban youth disaffection included an Arab, an African, and a Jew. Commenting on recent struggles in the French banlieues, novelist Faïza Guène suggests, "I think they've identified the wrong war. They think it's a war between the whites and the blacks and the Arabs. They think it's a war between the secularists and the Muslims. But it's above all a war between the rich and the poor." Some French radicals look longingly at the prospects for an interreligious alliance of the underclass against the elites, a renewal of black-blanc-beur solidarity. Jean-Eric Boulin's recent novel *Supplément au Roman National* imagines how suicide bombings and youth riots in the banlieues might spark a general anti-capitalist mobilization, a new French Revolution.[66]

The best historical analogy for the French unrest can be found in the riots that overtook British cities during the summer of 1981, when black, Asian, and white youths engaged in savage battles with police. In that case too, the motives were chiefly antipolice and anti-authority, aggravated by persistent economic deprivation, and no evidence came to light of central organization or of ideological motivation, still less religious. The rioters had the ethnic composition they did because those groups happened to predominate in poor sections of inner cities. When rioting struck northern British cities in the summer of 2001, many of the participants were south Asians, chiefly Pakistanis and Bangladeshis. Even so, religious labels or grievances made very little appearance in the unrest, which was mainly driven by issues of race—particularly conflicts with white gangs—and by resentment against authority. In the words of the official report, these were "the worst racially motivated riots in the UK for fifteen years."[67]

Religious interpretations are just as inapplicable in other nations. Belgium, for instance, is home to the obstreperous Arab European

League (AEL), founded in 2000 by Dyab Abou Jahjah, a Shi'ite veteran of the Lebanese Hizbollah. His appeal is to Arab and Muslim youth in western Europe, and he rejects assimilation as "cultural rape." League representatives have openly praised terrorist attacks and warned that something like the Madrid bombings could (and probably should) be reproduced in the Netherlands or Belgium. His followers have repeatedly clashed with police, whom they accuse of systematic racism: one conflict in Antwerp in 2002 led to serious rioting. Yet despite his background, his radicalism, and the heavily Muslim nature of his constituency, the AEL's appeal has little to do with Islamism. Abou Jahjah declares, "We're not folkloristic clowns who want to force Islamic law on other people," and he personally supports Belgium's legalization of gay marriage, as clear a repudiation as one could wish of Islamist orthodoxies. In its 1,100 word statement of principles, the League never once refers to Islamic teachings and throughout focuses on the racial and ethnic category of Arabs. In place of Islamism, Abou Jahjah draws heavily on the rhetoric and symbolism of the U.S. Black Panthers and the Nation of Islam; he presents himself as the Arab Malcolm X, a leader of the Arab poor.[68]

Several official investigations explored the causes of the various British riots, and their conclusions read uncannily like the classic Kerner report that studied the U.S. urban rioting of the 1960s. The chief causes were found in issues of class and race, flaws in education and housing, perceptions of official racism and police brutality. If one common strand runs through the different uprisings, American and European, it is the sense that protesters see themselves as acting defensively, responding to perceived attacks on their community, with one particular incident, which might seem minor in itself, symbolizing years of accumulated assaults and injustices by the authorities. Riots thus erupt over a single controversial arrest, the killing of a member of an ethnic minority, or even the rumor of such an incident. Baffled by the apparent overreaction, the media tend to seek clandestine organization where none exists and speculate about the spread of extremist ideologies, leftist or Islamist.

To push this U.S. parallel further, the vast majority of the black Americans who rioted in the nation's cities during the 1960s were Christians, but nobody referred to them as "Christian riots." That may seem natural enough, since nobody suggested that they were motivated by religion rather than grievances based on race or class; but why should the opposite assumption be made of protesters in France, Britain, or other nations in contemporary western Europe? The chief difference between Britain in 2001 and France in 2005 was that in the interim, the media had picked up the terminology of Eurabia and intifada, and sought opportunities to apply it.

Concepts of intifada also seem improbable when current conditions are placed in the context of European history. Viewed over the time span of the past fifty years or so, seemingly anarchistic riots like those in modern-day Paris may seem shockingly unusual, demanding to be understood as the intrusion of some alien force or ideology. In the longer term though—over the past 200 years, say—such events actually seem quite typical. So does the sense that cities or particular sections have become foreign territory, or have fallen under the rule of whole alternative societies who are christened with a title such as the "dangerous classes." Commonly, the underclass express their frustration by striking at material symbols of wealth and power: a hundred years ago, the French invented the tactic and the word of sabotage; today they burn cars. Historically, rioting by the underclass has been so common a fact of European urban life that instead of trying to decode uprisings like that of 2005, we should rather seek to understand the exceptional tranquility of the late twentieth century.

The situation suggested by the French riots and other recent violent outbreaks may be at once better and worse than it initially appears. It is better, since crime and protest are not predominantly driven by Islamist extremism and thus are not likely to become components of a violent resistance that also involves bombings or armed violence. It is also worse because the social tensions exposed at such times respond only slowly to official intervention and can best be dealt with by a general economic improvement that scarcely seems likely at present. Today, then, France and other European countries face a grave problem from a disaffected underclass, a menace that does not presently take explicitly religious forms, but could yet do so.

8

Revolutions at Home

The whore lived like a German.

Comment on the victim
of an honor killing

Stereotypes apart, a great many European Muslims are neither young nor discontented; yet having said this, we must acknowledge that some issues are very sensitive, with the potential to stir deep grievances. Most fall into the general category of "family" and expectations about gender roles. As the experience of Christian churches indicates, powerful secularizing currents in European society work strongly against the survival of institutional religion, as opposed to personal spirituality, and against traditional cultural orthodoxies of any kind. One current, obviously, is the sexual libertarianism that arouses opposition to any form of religious-based regulation of moral conduct, in matters such as premarital sex or homosexuality. The other mighty force for change among Muslims is the changing role of women, as emerging feminist ideologies challenge religious assumptions concerning domestic violence, arranged marriages, or sexual freedom. Also divisive are controversies about the education of children within the bounds of acceptable Muslim standards, especially for girls. Not only is the personal political, to use the well-known feminist maxim, but the key political struggles within Europe's contemporary Muslim communities concern intimate issues of home and family.[1]

In the short run, fears about secularization serve as a powerful incentive to Islamist extremism, as changing ideas about gender and family subvert the most cherished social values. But a historical perspective is useful here. Given the vast gulf that separates western Europe from the Muslim home countries of its immigrants—a chasm at once social, economic, and cultural—it would be fantastic to expect much less conflict after only a few decades of close interaction on European soil. In future, the growth of individualism and feminism assuredly will promote much greater assimilation into European societies, changing demographic projections, with all that implies for cultural and religious orthodoxies.

Moving Cultures

Whatever the religious context, issues of gender and family often prove divisive during eras of mass migration. When migrants move from traditional societies to urban or industrial communities, they find it difficult to cope with the new social and sexual worlds in which they live, and many are slow to realize that they can no longer enforce the standards of the village or farm. When the new community accepts or expects a more independent role for women, this arouses fears about the destruction of family ties and honor. Often, traditional families interpret greater women's autonomy in terms of the betrayal of sexual decency. A crisis of control follows, with all that implies for challenges to parental authority and the transformation of male roles no less than female. The ensuing generational conflicts are familiar in American history, particularly during the mass immigration of east and south Europeans in the early twentieth century. Girls and women faced daily dilemmas blending into the new society, tensions that grew all the more acute among second-generation residents. Then as now, fathers disapproved of the new ways adopted by their sons and, more acutely, their daughters, and in extreme cases, families were sundered.[2]

Most of the overseas migrants to contemporary Europe came from societies with strictly traditional values about family and gender. Such communities strongly preserved the mores of the village or small town, with a powerful emphasis on concepts of family honor, as male relatives defended at all costs the reputation of women and girls. Contemporary ethnic communities derived from Muslim Algeria or Turkey have much in common with earlier waves of migrants from Christian Sicily or Greece. What makes the current situation more difficult is that traditional values are often founded in claims of religious authority.[3]

On many issues, much of the conflict between Islam and "the West" arises from the definition of what constitutes religion, with its particularly weighty sanctions. At least since the Enlightenment, many Western Christians have designated a special realm for religious thought and activity, which is easily distinguished from the cultural or political, while Islam rarely observes such a difference. For Muslims, politics are a subset of religion, and the Euro-American attempt to segregate the two is inconceivable. In matters of gender, likewise, all societies preach certain norms, but in Muslim societies, these roles are generally seen as divinely ordained and not to be changed at the risk of violating God's explicit commandments. In some cases, rules about gender and family do have scriptural basis, in the Quran or the Hadith, while in others, they reflect customs and cultural taboos that over time have come to be seen as essentially Islamic. The Quran indeed commands that women dress modestly, but does not ordain the total covering mandated in strict nations like Saudi Arabia.

The way people are expected to behave in Muslim societies in north Africa or south Asia is largely assumed to represent an Islamic way of life. In modern times, though, Muslims find themselves occupying the status of minorities in heavily non-Muslim nations, with radically different cultural assumptions. In historical terms, European Muslims have had only a very short time to absorb the implications of this cultural disjuncture and to ask searching questions about the nature of religious as opposed to social norms. Over time, religious thinkers undoubtedly will try to redefine the social codes of Islam to mesh more closely with the experience of democratic Western societies. For the present, however, Muslim communities in Europe preserve older notions of the inextricable linkage between religious and cultural values, so that a crisis of control within the family, the problem of rebellious daughters, becomes a matter of religious insurgency, as much as social breakdown.

Transitions

Such family conflicts have become more rather than less vigorous over the past half-century. Partly, this was a matter of conditions in migrants' home countries, as the nations from which they came in the 1960s or 1970s were themselves making efforts to liberalize gender roles, to break down oppressive clerical structures. In this era at least, nations like Pakistan, Algeria, and Turkey were themselves undermining Islamic traditions as part of a general effort to Westernize and modernize. In some European nations, meanwhile, the guest-worker scheme meant that initially, immigrant women were relatively scarce, so that gender problems did not arise with anything like the vigor that they have in recent years. In Germany in 1974, women comprised just over a third of the Turkish population. Not until the 1990s did the gender balance approach parity for Turks and for German Muslims as a whole. In Britain, Bangladeshi males outnumbered females by two to one in 1981, but numerical parity was within sight by the end of the 1990s. It was the late 1980s especially that marked the establishment of nuclear families as the normal domestic structure for west European Muslims, with the simultaneous expansion of mosques and the demand for appropriate schools.[4]

The late 1980s mark a new phase of the European Muslim experience, as a new generation grew up knowing only the conditions prevailing in Western societies. Here, powerful pressures drew them to share the contemporary culture, with its messages of sexual freedom and gender equality. At the same time, though, Islamic religious influences were growing across Europe and in the countries of origin. And social conditions were making assimilation particularly difficult in most nations. In France particularly, the collapse of older heavy industries devastated the high-rise working-class suburbs. The immediate consequence was a growth of crime and gang cultures from about 1989–1990, with poor immigrant areas increasingly turning in on themselves. In such areas, tensions between young men and women grew, as men tried to act as the traditional defenders of the honor of family and community. Women faced new pressures over their freedom of movement and over their association with young men, especially those from outside the community. Conservatives tried to impose the values of the traditional village within the French urban setting and to enforce these by the threat of physical or sexual violence. Facing such challenges, lower-class women in the 1990s found their opportunities limited. The more violence and abuse they faced on the streets, the greater the temptation to hide behind the headscarf or veil; and the more women adopted Islamic dress, the easier it was to enforce traditional standards on holdouts. Meanwhile, imams and religious figures, inspired by fundamentalist ideas in their homelands, enjoyed growing significance as community leaders.[5]

New concerns about threats to gender roles contributed mightily to the Islamist militancy that became more evident during the 1990s. French scholar Antoine Sfeir points out that girls and women were all too able to adapt to the new social arrangements, to the horror of their male relatives. Boys consistently fell behind their sisters and other girls in schools, while the jobs that did become available in the new service and information economies were at least as open to women as men, especially if women had better educational qualifications. In response to over-rapid change at home and in the family, Islamist preachers presented an idealized vision of an older, stable society that was under threat from Western modernity and immorality.[6]

Multicultural Dilemmas

Over the past decade, discussions about multiculturalism and Muslim identity have commonly focused on women's issues. As we have seen, liberal states strongly affirm their belief in women's equality, to the point that many have ministries devoted to enforcing and advancing gender equality. At the same time, both Europe and its constituent states support the principles of multiculturalism, of recognizing and supporting cultural difference without seeking to impose any one set of values as necessarily superior or more correct. Such an approach is all the more vital in matters of religion and faith: how dare a predominantly Christian society seek to impose its values upon Muslims? Yet these equally fundamental values, of equality and multiculturalism, come into conflict on a daily basis, as the situation of Muslim women, especially among the poorest sections of that society, violates deeply held European notions abut gender and family. The right-wing *FrontPage Magazine* complains often of "the Muslims bringing their anti-Semitism, misogyny and homophobia with them [to Europe]" and mocks the reluctance of the multicultural left in condemning these abuses. The basic multicultural assumption is necessary and desirable, in the sense that governments undoubtedly should grant wide latitude to the different societies coexisting on their territory, but conflicts over gender and morality suggest what a delicate balance this approach can involve.[7]

At many points, the change in women's roles and expectations creates issues and conflicts that threaten to draw in state intervention, however much this arouses fears of imposing non-Muslim morality upon minority communities. One persistent issue is the custom of arranged marriages, which is especially common among British Pakistanis. In most cases, both the young people involved consent to the arrangement, so that no problems are caused for outsiders. Sometimes, though, parents intervene to force girls into a match. In some cases, teenage girls who are ostensibly sent to their home countries to visit family find themselves facing marriages to relatives whom they hardly know. In this situation, the individual rights of girls and young women run absolutely contrary to the laissez-faire principles of multiculturalism.

No less controversial is the import trade in wives, as conservative Muslim communities bring in women from their home countries who will be docile and unquestioning, in marked contrast to assertive Muslim women raised in immoral Europe. So powerful though are the forces in the outside society that such wives can be kept pure only by a system of rigid segregation. One German newspaper describes a typical case:

> Zeynep is 28, mother of three children, and has lived in Hamburg for twelve years. She takes care of her family and speaks not a word of German. . . . She is an imported bride, a modern-day slave-woman. Thousands of young Turkish women are brought to Germany each year through arranged marriages. Democratic principles do nothing to help her, and nobody takes the slightest interest in her fate.

Making the plight of imported brides so much worse in European eyes, these women are usually drawn from societies in which the age at marriage is much younger than in the contemporary West, with girls often as young as fifteen or sixteen.[8]

Polygamy provokes other clashes. The practice is permitted in the Quran, though with strict qualifications, and it is particularly common in some nations where it represents a survival from pre-Islamic custom. Muslims of south Asian origin preserve a lively clandestine tradition of polygamy, widely acknowledged by British authorities yet rarely subject to official action. And though France officially prohibited polygamy in 1993, current estimates suggest that anywhere from 150,000 to 400,000 residents, many from Mali and neighboring north African countries, still live in polygamous households.[9]

For many reasons, authorities are reluctant to intervene in such settings, which flagrantly violate the law of the land. No prosecutor wants to be seen tearing apart a loving family, however complex its intimate arrangements. Complicating the matter further has been the near breakdown of traditional ideas about marriage in the mainstream society, which has effectively opened the institution of marriage to many different kinds of consenting adults beyond the familiar concept of one man and one woman. If two men or two women can get married, the logical grounds for prohibiting heterosexual polygamy are eroded. An attempt to enforce the letter of the law would draw charges of ethnic and religious discrimination, to say nothing of hypocrisy. In practice, then, if laws are unenforced, polygamy in Muslim communities will survive indefinitely, however outrageously that conflicts with mainstream European standards.

Across Europe too, the suppression of domestic violence raises issues of interference in patriarchal authority. In many traditional societies—by no means only Muslim—patriarchal authority can in the last resort be enforced through physical sanctions, exercised against wives as well as children. This practice is justified in the Quran, which in the much-debated Sura 4.34 ordains,

> Men are in charge of women, because Allah hath made the one of them to excel the other, and because they spend of their property (for the support of women). So good women are the obedient, guarding in secret that which Allah hath guarded. As for those from whom ye fear rebellion, admonish them and banish them to beds apart, and scourge them.

Muslim commentators treat the line about scourging (or beating) with caution, stressing rival traditions that severely limited any right to domestic violence: it is "just barely permissible, and should preferably be avoided."[10]

In modern European states, though, so heinously is domestic violence viewed that harsh condemnation awaits any group that seems to justify it, whether on religious grounds or not. In Spain, the imam of Fuengirola created a national scandal when he published the book *Women in Islam*, which was circulated by major Muslim institutions in Madrid and Barcelona. Not only did the book favor the practice of beating, but it also proposed ingenious ways of beating without leaving telltale marks. The imam faced prosecution, and the case was widely quoted to illustrate the caveman quality of Muslim gender attitudes.[11]

In other ways too, traditional concepts of gender roles incite conflicts with mainstream European attitudes and legal systems, especially in concepts of female modesty and appropriate behavior. As young women of Maghrebi or south Asian origin tried to adopt the dress and customs of the mainstream, so this behavior was increasingly likely to be defined as immoral. In some tight-knit conservative communities, women who defied community standards—who acted as French or Dutch or German—could be labeled as whores, and even on occasion subjected to mass rape. In 2003, Samira Bellil published a sensational account of the life of a young woman in the French banlieues, *In the Hell of the Tournantes*, tournante being the local vernacular for gang rape. In these communities, "any neighborhood girl who smokes, uses makeup or wears attractive clothes is a whore."[12]

Worse still, responsible Muslim leaders appeared to justify the prevalence of rape by citing the immoral and provocative behavior of young women as a causal factor. One Danish Islamic scholar suggested that a woman who failed to wear a headscarf was virtually asking to be raped. Sheik Yusuf al-Qaradawi, a respected voice among European Muslims, claimed that female rape victims should be punished if they were dressed immodestly when they were raped. He added, "For her to be absolved from guilt, a raped woman must have shown good conduct." Under the *Hudood* law still enforced in Pakistan, any woman alleging rape must prove the charge by producing absurdly high standards of evidence (four male witnesses to the act). Should she fail to validate the charge, she herself faces charges of sexual immorality, *zina*. Even when living under very different Western codes, the attitudes that such laws reflect naturally discourage the reporting of rape.[13]

The most egregious cultural clash, and the one that leads to most forceful calls for intervention, involves "crimes of honor" and the killing of women who violate family codes. In some Middle Eastern countries, such as Iraq, this penalty extends even to women who have spent time unaccompanied with a nonrelated man because this behavior raises the possibility that her chastity might have been compromised. Such stringent enforcement would be impossible in most European settings, but honor killings definitely do occur. Reexamining recent domestic homicides, British police believe that such crimes occur at the rate of at least ten a year in that country, a figure that must be seen as an absolute minimum. Though no case is typical, one London case in 2006 illustrates many common themes. Samaira Nazir was a twenty-five-year-old university graduate aspiring to a career. However, rather than agreeing to an arranged match, she insisted on marrying an acquaintance, an Afghan asylum seeker, whom her Pakistani family despised. When she tried to leave home, she was dragged back and murdered by her brother and a cousin, who stabbed her repeatedly and cut her throat. Her father, also implicated, escaped to Pakistan. Another recent victim was Hina Saleem, a twenty-one-year-old Pakistani woman living in Brescia, Italy. In the eyes of her family, she had committed multiple crimes, including living with an Italian man, wearing fashionably sexy Italian clothes, and working in a pizza restaurant where alcohol was served. As a last resort, her family ordered her to return to Pakistan, where she was to marry a cousin. After refusing the order, she was murdered by her father, brother-in-law, and possibly other male relatives. They cut her throat, and buried her body in the back yard.[14]

Honor killings have emerged as a leading issue in Germany, where in Berlin alone, six examples occurred over a recent four-month period. The Turkish women's organization Papatya reports forty documented instances in Germany between 1996 and 2004. Although the absolute numbers are not large, such crimes exercise a powerful deterrent effect on other women tempted to challenge their families, and as such, they can be seen as a kind of gender terrorism. This is all the more true when German courts treat the crimes as manslaughter rather than murder, in effect accepting the honor defense. In a widely reported case, Hatun Sürücü, a young Turkish woman raised in Berlin "divorced the Turkish cousin she was forced to marry at age sixteen. She also discarded her Islamic head scarf, enrolled in a technical school where she was training to become an electrician and began dating German men." Her three brothers murdered her. Far from such crimes being universally condemned, they find much support in the local community. Activist Necla Kelek records a conversation with one young man who killed another man who had failed to respect his sister's honor. Neither Kelek nor the young man stood any chance of understanding the other's point of view. When asked why he had carried out the murder, he did not grasp that she was condemning the shooting but rather thought she was asking why he, rather than his father, had actually pulled the trigger.[15]

Using the words of a neighbor who supported the perpetrators, a journalistic study of Hatun Sürücü's death was entitled "The Whore Lived like a German!" The phrase neatly epitomizes the multicultural dilemma, which sets the rights of individuals against respect for culture and community. Should a state assist or encourage members of minority communities who want to break free from those groups, in order to achieve full assimilation? One irony in such cases is that European freedoms permit Muslims to enforce traditional rules in ways they cannot legally do in their homelands. Although Turkey has long prohibited parents from forcing their children to marry, Germany has only recently passed such a law, largely in response to demands from Turkish women's groups. Multiculturalism makes it much easier to practice Islamic fundamentalism in Europe than in most Muslim lands.

One of the few areas in which European authorities have been able to move against an immigrant cultural practice is that of female circumcision or genital mutilation; though even here, results have been mixed. The practice is widespread in north and east Africa, especially in Egypt, the Sudan, and the Horn of Africa, and in these regions, some 90 percent of women have been circumcised, allegedly in accordance with Islamic law and custom. In fact, this too represents an honor issue, since families believe that circumcised girls are much more likely to remain chaste than promiscuous Christians or Westerners. Some reputable jurists support the practice, including Sheikh al-Qaradawi. On the basis of a hadith questionably assigned to Muhammad, al-Qaradawi suggests that circumcision should involve cutting only the prepuce, not the clitoris: although "it is not obligatory, whoever finds it serving the interest of his daughters should do it, and I personally support this under the current circumstances in the modern world." However, the practice is widely condemned by other Islamic authorities, including the prestigious leaders of Cairo's al-Azhar mosque, which makes it possible for states to intervene without raising charges of religious discrimination. Even so, suppression has proven difficult. In a decision that arouses complex ethical concerns, one Italian Muslim surgeon despaired of trying to fight the practice and began offering patients the least interventionist form of the operation, carried out in proper medical conditions with anesthesia and due concern for preventing infection. Granting the family's wishes does indeed prevent the worst consequences of the operation, in terms of infection and early death, but it also ensures that the custom will survive.[16]

Gay Rights

Issues of women's rights illustrate the dilemma of how far European societies should, in effect, tolerate the intolerant. The same problem emerges starkly in the area of homosexuality, which we have already seen as marking a critical division between the values of a secular, liberal society and most traditional concepts of Christianity. In such controversies, mainstream media and political figures are generally prepared to make few concessions to Christian opinions, but attitudes are somewhat different where Islam is concerned. Generally, Muslims and especially Muslim religious thinkers are implacably opposed to homosexuality and to legal systems that tolerate it, or that treat the practice as equally acceptable to heterosexuality.

During the 1990s, most west European nations radically liberalized their laws on homosexuality, eliminating legal disabilities and granting various forms of civil union or full-scale gay marriage. Muslims, however, largely retained older attitudes, framing their objections in religious terms. The more homosexuality became associated with Western secularism and sexual libertarianism, the more harshly it was treated in Muslim nations. The Taliban regime in Afghanistan was notorious for its savage anti-gay persecutions and its brutal public executions of offenders. In Western countries, some Islamist militants openly praised these draconian solutions and wished to see them implemented in Europe.

One aggressive voice in the liberal Netherlands is Khalil el-Moumni, a Rotterdam-based imam whose views caused the government of his native Morocco to order him silenced. In the Netherlands, however, he was under no such restraint, and he denounced the immorality he found there. In 1998, he declared, "The Western civilization is a civilization without morals. In the Netherlands it's permitted for homosexuals to marry each other. The Europeans stand lower than dogs and pigs." In an incendiary television interview in 2001, he justified gay-bashing by Moroccan youths, warning that "if the sickness of homosexuality spreads itself, everyone can become infected." A controversial Spanish imam told his congregation that

> our duty is to prepare the men of Islam to fight the spirit of homosexuality that is rising in the West. . . . History teaches us that societies where men have lost their courage and their virility and women govern and walk undressed on the streets, who encourage decreasing birth-rates, sterilizing men and women, end up disappearing. Muslims must struggle with any means whatsoever and must not let themselves be subjugated by pagan Europe.

Sir Iqbal Sacranie, former leader of the Muslim Council of Britain, has warned that homosexuality "damages the very foundation of society."[17]

Of course, Europe's Muslim communities have their share of gays and lesbians, and the societies of north Africa and south Asia both have powerful traditions of same-sex relationships and pederasty. Surprisingly for many Westerners, homosexuality in these societies is often tolerated provided that it is discreet, and countries like Tunisia have lively gay subcultures. At least some gay Muslims try as hard as their Christian counterparts to reconcile their sexual orientation with the practice of the religion. In Britain, the support group Imaan ("Faith") was founded in 1998. Yet gay rights have made strikingly little progress within the Muslim community, surprisingly so given the powerful pressures from the surrounding society and its media. Granted that Khalil el-Moumni is a firebrand, far more moderate Muslims hold quite conservative views on homosexuality, views that would fit well into the American mainstream but which stand well to the right on the European moral spectrum. One representative of moderate, socially activist Islam is Jadicha Candela, a prominent woman leader of the Spanish Muslim community. While standing far from the open incitement of the Islamists, she also asserts her view that "according to doctrine, you are not allowed to provoke the established order—which is heterosexual—by public homosexual activities. But in your private life, you can do what you like."[18]

Gay activists offer pungent criticism of multicultural ideals when the rhetoric of religious freedom supports views that are deeply critical of homosexuality and that justify repression or violence. The conflict found sharp expression in the Netherlands, where leftist Pim Fortuyn became an outspoken opponent of immigration and specifically Muslim immigration, a position hitherto associated with the political ultra-right. For Fortuyn, however, Islam represented a backward repressive culture, and tolerating its reactionary moral views made no more sense than permitting fascists or Nazis to operate openly. In a memorable television debate, he goaded el-Moumni until the latter exploded in anti-gay invective, leaving Fortuyn to draw the conclusion he had sought from the beginning: if Muslims utterly reject "our values," why should we Dutch tolerate their presence? (Fortuyn himself was assassinated shortly afterward, but by a white leftist rather than a Muslim militant). British activists have been equally willing to let their views on sexuality overrule concerns about religious toleration. In 2005, the magazine of the Gay and Lesbian Humanist Association complained that British Islam was growing "like a canker" through "unrestrained and irresponsible breeding" by "ill educated and culturally estranged Third Worlders." The magazine asked, "What does a moderate Muslim do, other than excuse the real nutters by adhering to this barmy doctrine?"[19]

Rebels

The most forthright critic of multiculturalism in these contexts is Somali-born Dutch legislator Ayaan Hirsi Ali, whose experiences caused ever-greater disaffection from Muslim "community values." Born in the Somali capital of Mogadishu, Ali had a conservative Muslim upbringing, which included experiencing circumcision. Coming to the Netherlands as a refugee, she became increasingly visible as a political activist and was elected to the Dutch parliament. Observing the Netherlands, she came to believe that "treating immigrants as groups, rather than individuals, led to isolation rather than integration. . . . Multiculturalism helped keep many immigrant women mired in illiteracy and servitude." Specifically, she demanded the closure of Islamic schools that promoted separatism and female subjection, and urged the authorities to move proactively against domestic violence, honor killings, female circumcision, and other abuses. The social integration of Muslims, she argued, could grow only out of expanding freedom, and above all, women's freedom.[20]

Hirsi Ali was dealing with explosive issues, with enormous potential to cause offense, particularly as a woman criticizing aspects of Islamic culture. In 2004, she cooperated with Dutch director Theo Van Gogh who was making the film *Submission*, a devastating attack on the position of women under Islam. Van Gogh himself was virulently antireligious, with a special animus against Islam, attacking followers of the faith as *geitenneukers*, goat-fuckers. The most provocative scenes of his film illustrated the religious underpinnings of domestic abuse by showing relevant Quranic texts on the body of a woman, a juxtaposition that Muslims denounced as both pornographic and blasphemous. Against this background, a woman narrator tells, "When I was sixteen my father broke the news to me in the kitchen. You are going to marry Aziz, he said. He is from a virtuous family and will take care of you." The marriage is a disaster. She finds him sexually repulsive, partly because of his smell. "Yet O Allah, I obey his commands, sanctioned by your words, and I let him take me because each time I push him away he quoted you." As the film shows the face of a severely bruised young woman, the narrator continues, in the form of an address to God, "O Allah Most High, you say that men are the protectors of women because you have given them more strength than the other. I feel at least once a week the strength of my husband's fist on my face." Throughout, what caused the greatest offense was not the exposé of ethnic customs or even the description of immigrants according to every noxious stereotype (violent, superstitious, hypocritical, smelly), but the specifically religious and scriptural context.[21]

Not just in hindsight, we can say that the filmmakers were asking for trouble, and if they did not realize that very serious consequences would follow, they were incredibly naïve. So controversial was the film that in 2004 Van Gogh himself was assassinated in an Amsterdam street. The assassin, Mohammed Bouyeri, pinned to Van Gogh's bloodstained shirt a letter explaining his deed, and warning that the life of Ayaan Hirsi Ali was also forfeit. She has lived under police protection ever since.[22]

The Van Gogh murder focused concerns about multiculturalism, and the whole issue of integration as a social goal. Presumably feeling that she has little to lose, Hirsi Ali herself has become even more aggressive in her criticisms of Islam, noting that the "despicable" Prophet Mohammed had married "the nine-year-old daughter of his best friend." "Mohammed is, by our Western standards, a perverse man. A tyrant. He is against free speech. If you do not do what he says, then you will have an unhappy ending. It makes me think of all those megalomaniac rulers in the Middle East: bin Laden, Khomeini, Saddam." She describes multiculturalism as an excuse for preserving primitivism:

They are afraid that if you say . . . you must reform Islam, those millions of quiet Muslims who are not up to anything will all fall into the arms of the fundamentalists. . . . I think it's the wrong approach. Because let's go back in time to when Christianity was bloody and barbaric and oppressive. . . . It only changed after the premises upon which that belief rested were challenged by freethinkers.[23]

For many reasons, the Van Gogh murder inspired outrage, not least because political violence had historically been so rare in the Netherlands. But the crime also pointed to the maltreatment of women as a besetting sin of the radical Islamists who reacted so barbarically to any criticism of their customs and conduct. One German Muslim activist has responded angrily to the furor over the murder: " 'It not only took the death of a white man' for people to prick up their ears, she said, but of a 'white European' man (van Gogh). 'A European was killed because he defended us—and the world press stood up to listen. But how many women died before him?' "[24]

Progressives

It would be easy to describe the situation of Muslim women in contemporary Europe entirely in terms of oppression and injustice. We should remember, though, just how many women from Muslim families, whatever their individual faith commitment, live successfully in the mainstream European world. Any exposure to a Muslim ethnic community, whether Turkish, Moroccan, or Pakistani, soon points out the limitations of the stereotype. Some girls and women might be shy and retiring, some are brash and outspoken, and most operate between those two extremes, coping quite adequately with the demands of job and family.

Paradoxically, some have argued that reports of honor killings and domestic violence actually illustrate women's social progress. While no respectable voice defends such conduct, the fact that these crimes occur shows that immigrant women are trying to advance and succeed, and they are succeeding at a rate that deeply discomforts their male relatives. German-Turkish activist Seyran Ateş remarks that

my brothers didn't beat me in Turkey. We knew poverty, but not violence. My father was raised with the idea that you don't hit women or children, and he passed that on to us. In a situation where he himself was humiliated as a gastarbeiter, he was all the more keen to protect his family in evil Germany. In Turkey the problem of domestic violence is often discussed.

For Ateş, domestic violence occurs when immigrant men have learned to accept failure—"never to look up"—but they see their daughters successfully violating this rule. The more intense the domestic insurgency, the sharper the repression.[25]

Furthermore, the fact that we know about violence and honor crimes suggests that activists are bringing these stories to light in a way that would scarcely be possible in Morocco or Pakistan. Though Ayaan Hirsi Ali is the best known, she is not necessarily representative, and her extremism alienates many. To take a minor but suggestive incident, she tried to introduce a law requiring that all immigrant girls be examined annually to ensure that they have not been circumcised. Practicalities apart, the proposal immediately suggests that similar dangers and backwardness affect all Muslims, including those from Pakistan, Turkey, or the Maghreb who make up a large proportion of European Muslims and who know nothing of this practice. One Dutch-Moroccan feminist complains that Ali "lost herself in the falseness of fame and the arena of the media. Her admirers are white people from the upper class." Worse, her words have been counterproductive: "her attacks have raised anger among women, and they are retreating into Islamic identity."[26]

In recent years, a lively and quite militant feminist culture has developed in the best-established Muslim communities, seeking to defend women's rights while rejecting sensationalist rhetoric. Germany's Turkish community has produced some articulate feminist leaders who had themselves come close to suffering serious violence of the kind they subsequently exposed. Of the three best-known contemporary activists,

> Necla Kelek was threatened by her father with a hatchet when she refused to greet him in a respectful manner when he came home. Seyran Ateş was lucky to survive a shooting attack on the women's shelter that she founded in Kreuzberg. And Serap Çileli, when she was 13 years old, tried to kill herself to escape her first forced marriage; later she was taken to Turkey and married against her will, then she returned to Germany with two children from this marriage and took refuge in a women's shelter to escape her father's violence.[27]

All three have attracted national attention. Kelek is the author of *The Foreign Bride*, an exposé of arranged marriages and honor killings, while Serap Çileli's best-known book bears the title *We're Your Daughters, not Your Honor*. Seyran Ateş's autobiographical *The Great Journey into the Fire* describes the enormous difficulties involved in trying to live between two such utterly different worlds, the Turkish and the German, divided from each other by only a few city blocks. All are bitterly opposed to multiculturalism if and when it defends the barbarities of traditional society, and Ateş condemns the "crazy tolerance of [German] society." Suggesting the depth of controversy they face, Ateş was attacked yet again in 2006, this time by the husband of one of her clients. The severity of the threat led her to renounce her legal career and (at least temporarily) to suspend public activism. As she had learned from the case of Theo van Gogh—not to mention the victims of honor crimes—an individual simply could not be permanently protected from determined enemies. Another campaigner for integration is Emel Algan, daughter of the German founder of the Islamist Millî Görüş movement: recently, she took the historic step of publicly abandoning her headscarf, a move she describes as liberating.[28]

Across Europe too, the French book *Ni Putes Ni Soumises* (Neither Whores nor Doormats) has given rise to a burgeoning movement. The phrase's meaning is obvious: just because a woman refuses to accept the submissive role idealized by traditional Islam does not mean she has abandoned all loyalty to faith, family, and common decency. The movement began in 2003 when two young men of north African origin in the town of Vitry-sur-Seine burned alive a woman named Sohanne, who had refused them sexually. The crime, wearyingly unexceptional in itself, attracted attention because of its horrific circumstances. In response, Fadela Amara led protest marches that evolved into a national movement, aimed primarily at breaking the code of silence that permits violence against women. Amara herself, a town councillor from Clermond-Ferrand, now advocates the creation of a distinctively French Islam. France is also home to the Nana Beurs, a term that combines two slang phrases, *nana* for women, and *beur* for second generation French-Arab populations—roughly, the Arab Chicks. The group defines itself against two foes, demanding civil rights and gender equality from mainstream society while resisting attempts to impose sharia principles within the Muslim community. In 2005, a Barcelona conference examined the state of the Gender Jihad, a term that participants preferred to the unpopular and Western connotations of "feminism." The "jihad" was defined as "the struggle against male chauvinistic, homophobic or sexist readings of the Islamic sacred texts."[29]

Other groups provide shelters for women trying to break free from oppressive social and family settings, recalling the U.S. women's shelters of the 1970s but operating in a still more dangerous social environment. Often the shelters are protecting women from imminent death at the hands of their families. The Berlin-based Papatya again offers its facilities to a wide variety of risk categories, including:

Girls under family pressure (e.g., they are prevented from going out or from going to school)
Girls faced by an arranged marriage
Girls who fear being sent back to Turkey
Girls suffering from abuse or sexual violence
Pregnant girls
Girls in need of shelter, a safe refuge.

Also as in the Western nations during the early stages of the modern feminist movement, these specific campaigns against violence or abuse provide a foundation for more ambitious social organization, which will almost certainly have political consequences.[30]

Faithful Women

Of course, there is no simplistic divide between radical secular-minded feminists and faithful Muslim women; the former are not whores nor are the latter doormats. Indeed, some of the most impressive representatives for Islamic organizations across the continent are themselves women, who sometimes hold senior rank in these groupings. In Spain, where white European converts are prominent in Muslim groups, we find leaders like Jadicha Candela, founder of the women's network al-Nisa, who retains the leftist ardor of her preconversion days. The Spanish case might be unusual given the potent role of converts, but other Muslim women of immigrant origins succeed in maintaining public careers while remaining firmly within the faith. When France established its network of Islamic councils to provide ethnic communities with a public voice, the region of Limousin elected as its head Hanife Karakus, a prominent lawyer of a Turkish family. Nighat Awan is a well-known woman entrepreneur in Britain, founder of the popular Shere Khan restaurant chain. London Bangladeshi politician Manzila Pola Uddin, Lady Uddin, became the first Muslim woman to serve in the British House of Lords. (Taking up her office, she swore "by Almighty Allah that I will be faithful and bear true allegiance to Her Majesty Queen Elizabeth, Her heirs and successors.") Women also now hold high office in Britain's two main Muslim national federations, the rigorist MCB and the more liberal BMF.[31]

Popular culture depictions have also undermined stereotypes about submissive Muslim women. In the 2005 television season of the British version of *The Apprentice*, aspirants tried to secure jobs with a corporate tycoon. The winner was Saira Khan, daughter of Pakistani immigrants, who won more than fifteen minutes of fame by an aggressive manner that earned her the nicknames "the Mouth of the South" and "the Foghorn." Though a Muslim, she became a popular favorite by denouncing the religion's lunatic fringe. Asked about Islamist Abu Hamza, she replied, "I want to say to people like him, 'Why are you living in the West? Why don't you go and live in Saudi Arabia? . . . If you live in this country there are democratic ways to behave. If you don't like it, then go and live in a Muslim country." Like Ayaan Hirsi Ali, she condemns all forms of Muslim separatism, and preaches "integration, integration, integration." Her television triumph made her one of the best-known faces of British Islam, and she was soon announcing her aspirations to be prime minister. Obviously, such a celebrity may not represent a mass trend among European Muslims, but her career does achieve much by trampling popular clichés while offering an alternative role model for other young women in the public sphere. One brash young British comedian opens her act with the line: "My name's Shazia Mirza, or at least that what it says on my pilot's licence."[32]

Europe's Muslim communities have also produced some distinguished women writers, most notably perhaps Monica Ali, a British author of Bangladeshi roots. She makes great use of the characteristic problems of immigrant communities, such as the plight of women in arranged marriages. In her book *Brick Lane*, the heroine Nazneen is imported to England at eighteen to marry forty-year-old Chanu. However strange such a match may appear, her mother declares, "If God wanted us to ask questions, he would have made us men." Yet for all the initial passivity and the overwhelming social pressures within a Bangladeshi enclave in London, the book is ultimately the story of Nazneen's liberation. This seditious quality helps explain the fierce conservative protests against attempts to film the novel in the actual area, even though London's secluded Muslim women reportedly bought and circulated thousands of copies of the Bengali translation.

Faiza Guène's bestselling novel *Kiffe Kiffe Tomorrow* similarly describes the lives of Moroccan immigrants trapped in a French banlieue, Seine-St.-Denis, where women are expected to submit to the iron rules of fate, *mektoub*. But as with Nazneen, Guène's characters demonstrate a striking toughness and a hunger to escape their bonds. Suggesting that such stories resonate far beyond fiction is the dramatic growth of divorce in Muslim families in recent years, apparently as a result of women seeking far more autonomy than their husbands will concede. In the Netherlands, the boom in divorce among families of Moroccan and Turkish origin can be traced just to the start of the present decade, with a substantial majority instigated by wives.[33]

Western views of Muslim cultures often assume that women excluded from public life were in effect socially dead, confined to home and family. As anthropologists have found so often throughout the years in encountering many diverse societies around the world, just because men cannot see something does not mean that it does not exist. The view of women's exclusion in Islam was never fully accurate; women always formed their own cultures and social settings, marked by distinctive patterns of celebration and socializing, and that was particularly true of Maghrebi societies. In Europe also, women have found many ways to interact with the mainstream world while respecting traditional constraints. Computers and the Internet have had an enormous impact in permitting extensive socializing online without the physical proximity that raised the hackles of conservative observers. Male-female contacts online even have their own description, as *halal* dating.[34]

Covering

Accumulating signs of assertion and autonomy by Muslim women might seem puzzling in light of recent controversies about campaigns demanding the right to wear veils or headscarves. For some Western observers, women appear to be pressing for the right to wear signs of their exclusion or inferiority, in contrast to their mothers, who had renounced any religious garb. Yet the drift to these visible tokens of Islam can be interpreted in more benevolent and indeed optimistic ways, and devout Muslim women make a plausible case in favor of the various forms of veiling found in different traditions of their religion.

Westerners often confuse the different kinds of Muslim women's dress, and we even hear Europeans complaining of women going veiled when they are actually referring to headscarves. The distinctions are important, however, and we need to be more precise about terms. Generally, Islam offers women varying degrees of covering, the simplest of which is the *hijab,* or scarf, that conceals the hair but not the face, and which is worn with Western clothing. More concealing is the *niqab* or *burqa,* a veil that covers the entire face except the eyes. Head covering can be combined with Western dress or with a floor-length dress, the *jilbab.* In the most extreme form of Islamic dress, women reveal nothing except their eyes and look radically different from their Western counterparts. The different forms reflect very different notions of modesty, and Wahhabi authorities regard wearers of the simple hijab as little better than Westerners, already well along the path to scarlet womanhood.[35]

For many Europeans, the covered woman in full burqa/jilbab represents one of the most controversial symbols of the new Muslim presence, an aggressive proclamation of the arrival of a radically foreign culture, even an assertion of colonization. In one widely publicized instance, so many residents of the small Belgian town of Maaseik responded with anger and fear to the presence of burqas that the mayor secured a local bylaw outlawing full-face concealment in public places, on pain of a substantial fine. Similar bans have been proposed at the national level in Italy and the Netherlands.[36]

Apart from its exoticism, liberal Europeans see the burqa as an assertion of women's inferiority, in which women are blotted out from the public sphere, denied the right to individuality. From this perspective, it seems like a survival of feudalism. Supporting a national prohibition on the burqa, Dutch politicians Geert Wilders complains "that women should walk the streets in a totally unrecognizable manner is an insult to everyone who believes in equal rights." Some Muslim women agree: French-based writer Chahadortt Djavann has compared the veil to the yellow star forced upon Jews under the Nazi regime. Fadela Amara describes the veil as "an instrument of oppression that is imposed by the green fascists," that is, the Islamists. Liberal Muslims usually reject the veil, at least for themselves: Jadicha Candela does not wear the veil, which she sees as a personal choice rather than an obligation ("The most powerful weapon facing women isn't the veil, it's ignorance").[37]

Other women, however, who are anything but doormats, find much of value in the veil, which accounts for its rapid spread in European cities since the late 1990s. Some praise the very elements of the garb that appall white Europeans, namely, its aggressive quality and the implied demand for the recognition of the Islamic presence in public space. Women find it a symbol of cultural and religious identity but also a refuge from an aggressively sexualized culture. In the words of one British Muslim woman, "Since wearing the niqab, I've become a lot more confident. Once you're covered up, people are forced to judge you not as you look as a woman but on your character."[38]

Scarf Wars

The symbolic meanings attached to women's dress help explain the critical importance of the headscarf, which in recent years has become a key marker of religious and cultural difference. Once again, we see the importance of the year 1989 in symbolizing a new upsurge of Islamic militancy, a new self-confidence and willingness to engage in confrontational protests. Apart from the Rushdie protests in several nations, this was also the time when the principal of a secondary school at Creil, near Paris, decided to enforce official secularism by prohibiting ostentatious tokens of faith. Though he also targeted Jewish students observing the Sabbath, most of the public attention focused on his ban on Muslim girls, mainly Algerian, wearing the headscarf. This detonated a national controversy about assimilation and separatism, in which the UOIF first attracted national publicity and now became a major player on the French political scene. The 1989 debate also launched the subsequent Scarf Wars that have proved so divisive in French political life ever since. In 2004, the French government banned all religious symbols from French schools, a policy that was supported by some 80 percent of the French public but which attracted fierce opposition from Muslims in Europe and beyond.[39]

The rancor obvious from *l'affaire des foulards* (headscarves) must be understood in the broader context of French history, which was so long characterized by struggles between church and secularism, conflicts that on occasion came close to civil war. A century ago, France determined that its public life would be totally secular so that all citizens—regardless of religion or ethnicity—would become integrated into a secular and republican vision of Frenchness. The principle of *laicité* excludes all religious displays or manifestations in public life, especially in education. Christians cannot wear ostentatious crucifixes or other symbols of faith,

and Muslim schoolgirls are forbidden to wear the hijab. French governments are anxious to avoid the curse of *communautarisme,* communalism,
the creation of entities that attract the loyalty of citizens who should be
wholly devoted to the state—though, as we will see, French policies toward Muslim organizations have sometimes veered in this direction.[40]

Over the past decade, official secularism has been repeatedly challenged by the seemingly unstoppable growth of Muslim self-assertion.
In 2004, the French National Assembly overwhelmingly passed a law
prohibiting the display of ostentatious religious symbols in public
schools, a law that chiefly affected wearers of the headscarf. The law
attracted protests across Europe and in many Muslim nations, though
French Muslims were far from united in opposition, and demonstrations here were in the thousands, not the hundreds of thousands. The
Muslim community opposed the measure by a strong but not crushing
53–42 margin, although French Muslim women actually supported it
by 49 to 43 percent. The controversy dominated French politics for
several months, frustrating Muslim political leaders who often wished
that public debate would turn to matters of more immediate concern
to largely poor ethnic communities.[41]

Though France stands out in the ferocity of its public controversies
over the foulard, the issue has arisen in every west European country.
Across Europe, the use of headscarves spread rapidly in the opening
years of the new century and reached ever-younger girls. In Malmö, a
center of the Swedish Muslim community, very few girls aged six to
ten wore a scarf in 2003; by 2005, a heavy majority had adopted the
fashion. In Russia's Muslim-majority regions too, women have insisted
on the right to wear scarves in public and to be photographed wearing
them on identity cards, a demand that generates French-style conflicts
with the authorities. Germany has also moved in more repressive directions, and five of the nation's sixteen states now ban teachers and
other public officials from wearing headscarves to work. Unlike France,
most specifically forbid the Muslim symbol while permitting Christian
or Jewish tokens. Bavaria, for instance, prohibits the scarf as "a symbol
of fundamentalism and extremism." Though the German Constitution
prohibits religious discrimination, the courts have justified such policies because their intent is primarily political in nature.[42]

Different countries have responded differently to the upsurge of
Muslim identity, though few have treated the headscarf quite as severely as overwhelmingly Muslim Turkey, with its rigid tradition of
state secularism. Some British schools originally tried to forbid the use
of headscarves, generating media sympathy for the pupils and their religious rights, not to mention their right to individual self-expression.
Schools subsequently found a pragmatic solution, permitting scarves
that used the colors of school uniforms. Most nations, however, draw
the line at the burqa or full face-covering. In 2006, British politician

Jack Straw created a lively controversy when he announced that he requested women constituents to remove their niqabs when visiting his offices. (His Blackburn constituency has a large Muslim minority). Though Straw was attacked for insensitivity and Islamophobia, Tony Blair supported his position, agreeing that the full-face veil "is a mark of separation and that is why it makes other people from outside the community feel uncomfortable."[43]

European critics of the hijab have some powerful arguments on their side. Conservatives condemn the custom because it is so conspicuously foreign and demonstrates a refusal to assimilate, making each scarf a symbol of colonization by an alien culture. In this view, it becomes a badge of tribal loyalties. Liberals or leftists see the scarf as a sign that women are accepting their ordained and thus inferior role in Islam, as well as a concession to a community's hypersensitivity about female modesty. And while the decision to wear any kind of Islamic dress is a personal decision, it also has wider consequences for other girls in a school or institution, who now find themselves marked out as less pious, less willing to conform to religious norms, and in some eyes, more open to lax Western morality. Peer pressure becomes insidious and even raises the prospect of violence against the nonwearers.

All these arguments have some validity. But even without accepting distinctively religious positions about women's role, we can find a more benevolent interpretation of the scarf affair. As we have seen, a faithful following of Islam offers women roles much more complex than mere subjection. But most important, the hijab represents the most powerful statement yet about the arrival of Islam in Europe, a way of asserting the Muslim presence in Europe and on one's own terms. That does not of itself constitute a rejection of assimilation, except in the crudest sense of that term. Assimilation would after all be a pallid concept if it just meant that people of another faith were allowed to live in a society, were permitted to worship and pray quietly, but only provided that they did nothing to attract attention to themselves and did not live, eat, or dress differently. That description could almost apply to the condition of Christians or other unbelievers in some repressive Muslim states. Challenging reports that Muslims refused to integrate, one Austrian journalist asked,

> What's that supposed to mean? . . . That the Muslims in question don't want to eat pork schnitzel under any circumstances? That they wear a head scarf? Or perhaps that they force their daughters into arranged marriages? Or do they still want to say their prayers facing Mecca and refuse to convert to Christianity?[44]

In a multifaith society, different communities should indeed have the right to express their beliefs publicly, whether on their buildings or about their persons. The predominantly Protestant society of the nineteenth century U.S. faced quite similar dilemmas about conspicuous displays of religious symbolism by Catholics, particularly clergy and nuns. In a modern European context, the popularity of the hijab means that families are expressing pride in Muslim identity, but there is no reason why that should not be part of a European Muslim culture.

Time Travelers

What initially appear as some of the most extreme cultural conflicts in gender matters should not be read so pessimistically as tokens of an irreconcilable clash of civilizations. Even under the most liberal interpretation of multiculturalism, nobody can defend some of the recent manifestations of abuse and violence committed by some Muslims in the West or the underlying attitudes to women's inferiority that they imply. Still, these offenses—rape, honor killing, or domestic brutality—are not necessarily linked to religious thought and practice and could well be curbed without insisting on any significant change within Islam.

Admittedly, the Quran includes some hard sayings on moral issues and passages that can lend themselves to promoting the hatred of Jews or unbelievers. Yet these texts are no more fearsome than the Jewish or Christian scriptures, which a determined reader could take as ordering genocide or prohibiting racial intermarriage on pain of inciting the wrath of God. The Hebrew Bible, which is also the Christian Old Testament, includes the appalling story of Phinehas, who averts a plague threatening Israel by slaughtering a mixed-race couple, a Hebrew man who had found a wife among the people of Midian. Far from condemning the act, God blesses Phinehas and his descendants. Some New Testament texts condemn homosexuals or rigidly exclude women's participation in large sections of religious life. Although most modern Christians ignore the passages, the New Testament also demands that women cover their hair, at least in church settings, and Paul's epistles include more detailed rules on the subject than anything written in the Quran.[45]

The exact wording of any scripture matters less than the spirit in which it is read in a particular community of belief: interpretation is all. In fact, many sayings in the Hadith portray a Muhammad who was firmly part of his time but whose personal feelings were marked by a wide-ranging humane concern for the underdog (sometimes literally: he is one of the few thinkers of his time who actually recommended the decent treatment of animals as well as people). To say that Muslim imams express certain views in a given social setting does not indicate that any vice—misogyny or homophobia, racial or religious bigotry—is hard-wired into Islam, any more than tolerance and democracy are coded into the DNA of European Christendom, or indeed of Judaism.

On several key issues, the seemingly vast differences between Muslim and Western values and cultures are not nearly so essential to the respective societies as they appear, nor are the fundamental differences so profound. Do Muslim societies restrict women's rights? Britain granted women suffrage rights equal to those of men in 1928, France in 1944, Italy in 1945, and Switzerland only in 1971. In 1962, France showed itself sufficiently liberal and progressive to grant women the right to sign checks. In terms of women's position under law, medieval Islamic jurists gave women more detailed property rights than their English Christian counterparts would possess until a statute passed as late as 1882.

On the question of rape, again we might initially see an almost unbridgeable gulf between mainstream Europe and its Muslim subcultures. Ever since modern Western feminism emerged in the 1960s, activists have regarded rape as an ultimate violation of women's rights and autonomy, a crime that amounts to sexual terrorism against women in general. Since the 1970s, European nations have adopted legal codes very similar to those of U.S. jurisdictions, which reflect certain assumptions about the crime of rape: that rape is a grave offense demanding serious punishment; that the victim never provokes or asks to be raped; that rape is never justified or defensible. These ideas have also been repeatedly reinforced by their presentation in popular culture. Old-stock Europeans are appalled to see Muslim spokesmen and even clergy asserting that women provoke their own violation or that a rape victim needs to prove that she was wholly innocent in the encounter.

Yet the difference in values and gender attitudes is not quite as absolute as it might appear, and we should always ask what is our point of comparison for supposed Muslim misogyny or homophobia? Though Muslim attitudes are often described as "medieval" (at best), such a description betrays ignorance of recent Western cultural developments. On many moral issues, modern Euro-Americans differ fundamentally not just from many contemporary Africans or Asians but from their own forebears only a few decades ago. In the Europe or the United States of the 1950s, rape was severely punished, but widespread public attitudes suggested that women might easily provoke the offense by immoral behavior or dress, and that many allegations of rape were made maliciously and falsely. Though Americans rightly cherish the generous liberalism of Harper Lee's *To Kill a Mockingbird*, the plot revolves around a bogus and malicious rape charge, and such a theme would attract controversy if the book were to be published today. Rape trials in the 1960s commonly turned into dueling prosecutions, as defense attorneys tried to prove that the victim was an immoral slut who had incited the whole event. However alien the ideas may seem, some of the actions and remarks of contemporary Muslim thinkers indicate less a clash of civilizations than a time lag in attitudes of a generation or two. Moreover, since popular Muslim attitudes to rape are not founded in scripture or overwhelming juristic tradition, they could be altered without calling for any religious transformation.[46]

In the area of domestic violence likewise, Muslim immigrants happened to arrive in Europe at a time of a massive expansion of liberal values and the enforcement of these newer norms through law. European states have long tried to enforce prohibitions against battering, but only in the very recent past have courts and criminal justice systems tried seriously to abolish all violence within the family or school, whether directed against women or children. Not many years ago, the idea that a book advocating battering should be prosecuted as a form of hate speech directed against women as a protected category—as occurred in Spain—would have startled legal scholars of quite liberal disposition. Right up to 1981, Italian law offered the possibility of clemency for those convicted in honor crimes, of very much the same sort that now surface so scandalously in Muslim contexts: such exceptional treatment was felt necessary for the more traditional cultures of Sicily and the *Mezzogiorno*. Severe corporal punishment (birching) was still a legal punishment for young British offenders as recently as 1948, and only in 1986 did a fiercely controversial law outlaw physical punishments in British schools: the principle was extended to private schools in 1998. If Muslim immigrants were amazed by the values and social policies they found in modern Europe, they were scarcely less astonished than European time-travelers from a century or so ago would have been.

Similar comments apply to Muslim attitudes toward homosexuality. Certainly, European or North American societies have not in modern times inflicted on homosexuals such penalties as stoning or crushing, but we do not have to travel too far back in history to find a time when official and popular views of sexual deviance were utterly different from those prevailing today. How many citizens of most Western nations in the 1950s or 1960s could have dreamed of a time in which public figures would speak openly of their homosexuality, when the courts would regard gay rights as worthy of strenuous defense, and when gay marriage would be seriously debated? In the early 1950s, the United States and Britain were in the throes of a sex-offender panic founded on the theory that homosexuality commonly led to far worse forms of perversion, including child molestation and sexual homicide. Even a suspicion of homosexuality could ruin careers. Just twenty years ago, opinion surveys in the United States regularly showed between 40 percent and 50 percent of respondents opposing the legalization of homosexual acts between consenting adults. We have no surveys from the 1980s on the subject of gay marriage because at that point no reputable American authority dared even suggest such a radical departure from tradition. On many issues that today represent critical cultural markers between Europe's majority and minority communities, European Christians from 1960 would have less in common with their contemporary descendants than they would with the Muslim newcomers.

Women in European Islam

The longer Muslims live in Europe and experience its powerful cultural trends, the more they are likely to acquire the common attitudes toward gender and sexuality. This cultural ambience will promote demands for statements of religious doctrine that will accommodate new sensibilities.

One major trend profoundly affecting Europe is the expansion of religious education among women. In traditional Muslim societies, conservatives like India's Deobandis were deeply suspicious of women's involvement in religious life because they saw women as overly sympathetic to superstitious practices and even to syncretism. In some measure, the conservatives were correct: an Islam with women leaders is likely to change its emphases, if not always in directions that Westerners would approve. While remaining firmly within the boundaries of orthodoxy, Muslim women in Europe have made much use of the rich educational opportunities open to them. Women have become the mainstays of the Islamic Studies courses that proliferate in many colleges and in which they often constitute a majority of students. Though the courses teach orthodox mainstream Islam, the fact that women are conspicuously gaining expertise in Islamic thought is bound to have long-term consequences. We think, for example, of the sweeping changes in American Christianity and Judaism that followed the first ordinations of women into the clergy and the huge influx of women into seminaries.

It would in theory be quite possible for progressive religious thinkers to call for a thorough reformation of attitudes, to differentiate between those values based on the teachings of Islam and others based on particular cultures—to point out, for example, just how many customs popularly seen as Islamic in fact derive from the traditions of Egypt or Pakistan. Affirming that such a move might be possible, even some very prominent conservative scholars have made startling gestures toward promoting women's equality within Islam, by reexamining the scriptures and trying to purge beliefs that are "merely cultural." In 2006, Sudanese Islamist Hassan al-Turabi argued that nothing in Islam prohibited women from becoming imams or clergy, and he suggested that rules about female modesty demanded covering the chest, not the face or head. ("You keep hearing hijab, hijab, hijab . . . When these words are distorted, they mislead people.") He also favored permitting Muslims to marry Christians or Jews without insisting on the spouse's conversion. If an al-Turabi could make such an astonishing statement, then it would not take much effort to imagine some future Islamic council in Europe being at least as broad-minded.[47]

In the last forty years, some millions of Africans and Asians have moved from traditional-minded societies dominated by Islam to European nations that differ from them in virtually every basic assumption about social arrangements and political structures, and that were themselves making an epochal transition in their own sexual mores. Against such a background, it is inconceivable that conflicts should not have erupted. Rather than despairing or seeing culture clashes as irreconcilable, we might rather be impressed at just how much convergence of values and beliefs has occurred.

9

Ultras

Our words are dead until we give them life with our blood. . . . Your democratically elected governments continually perpetrate atrocities against my people all over the world. Your support makes you directly responsible. We are at war and I am a soldier. Now you too will taste the reality of this situation.

Mohammad Sidique Khan

We know of New York, we know of Madrid, we know of London and the widespread slaughter of innocent people. There have been streams of tears, rivers of blood, innocent blood. Death in the morning, of people going to find their livelihood, death in the noontime on the highways and skyways, death by faceless people who said they are warriors.

Marie Fatayi-Williams

The modern European encounter with Islam is not as ominous as is often alleged, and perceptions of a naked clash of civilizations are wide of the mark. Yet this is slim consolation given the obvious and potent threat from contemporary terrorist movements. Extreme Islamist politics may appeal to only a small minority, and may be just a transient phenomenon; but committed minorities have destroyed nations and societies, and often in a short space of time. To be optimistic about the general prospects for ethnic and religious assimilation does not mean trivializing the real dangers posed by terrorist violence. The threat must always remind governments of the high stakes they are playing with in debates over integration and assimilation.

Especially since September 11, 2001, Europeans have worried about their societies being torn apart by radical violence. Massive bombing attacks in Madrid, London, and elsewhere, together with several thwarted attempts, raise the prospect of one or many European versions of 9/11, mega-terror attacks launched by Islamic extremists. A report from the normally restrained British intelligence services warned of a possible domestic "insurgency," noting that 100,000 British Muslims came from "completely militarized" regions of the world, such as Somalia or Afghanistan. "Every one of them knows how to use an AK-47. About ten per cent can strip and reassemble such a weapon blindfolded, and probably a similar proportion have some knowledge of how to use military explosives." Fears about terrorism found a convenient face in Dhiren Barot, a Qaeda organizer convicted in 2006 of planning a series of terrorist spectaculars in Great Britain. Among other schemes, he wanted to blow up a subway train in a tunnel under the Thames, in order to cause catastrophic flooding; he fantasized about detonating a radioactive dirty bomb; and plotted to explode limousines filled with gas canisters in parking garages under major buildings.[1]

Though the threat is clear, solutions are by no means obvious. Most important, Europe's problems did not arise simply through weakness or dhimmitude, through a deluded liberal commitment to multiculturalism, and they will not be solved merely by get-tough crackdowns on activists. This point should be stressed because European states have so often been criticized for tolerating extremist groups on their territory, for permitting some mosques to become centers of blatant propaganda and recruitment. In some cases, such tolerance undoubtedly went too far—witness the spread of extremist propaganda among British Muslims—but the official approach was founded on sensible assumptions, not least that keeping extremists aboveground meant that they were easy to watch and to infiltrate.

Much also depends on our analysis of the danger. If European states face one common revolutionary threat, associated with a formidable organization like al-Qaeda, then it is sensible to move forcefully against it and any of its potential allies. In practice, though, Europe's extensive array of militant groups is kaleidoscopic in its goals and ideologies and in the degree of danger such movements pose to European states themselves, as opposed to regimes elsewhere in the world. Western governments have long found it convenient to tolerate such groups operating on their soil, on the understanding that they respect the security of the host state.

States must judge the relative importance of domestic and external threats. If in fact most of the violence is organized and directed by outside groups, then European nations face a classic anti-terrorist struggle, which might well involve external interventions against the groups or governments giving the orders. If, on the other hand, they are chiefly confronting a domestic counterinsurgency, then the answers will lie chiefly in internal political and economic arrangements, in finding means to reduce the discontent of potential jihadis. And many of the worst recent attacks on European soil probably do fit this profile of the domestic, autonomous upsurge, linked only tenuously to any global structures.

Governments must make a difficult judgment call when dealing with European-based Islamic political parties or religious organizations. Failure to treat a subversive danger with the seriousness it deserves permits the growth of an authentic internal menace; yet at the same time, overreaction runs the risk of inciting just the kind of mass radicalization that governments desperately seek to prevent. If an organization uses hard-core Islamist rhetoric, is it an authentic voice of popular sentiment or a cover for terrorism? Handled properly, an Islamist party might provide an excellent means for drawing disaffected Muslims into the political mainstream, while suppressing the same party would incite violence. If, on the other hand, the party is only a façade for clandestine organization, then permitting it to operate aboveground could be a disastrous mistake. European countries probably have erred too much on the side of tolerance and are now correcting their mistakes, but that does not mean that their strategy was wholly wrong.

Generation of Terror

Watching the sudden upsurge of religious-motivated terrorism in Europe in 2004–2005, American media in particular often suggested that outbreaks of this sort represented a radical departure from previous tranquility, that European governments were facing a wholly new reality. A worldwide jihad movement seemed to have arrived on Europe's shores more or less overnight, presumably imported by the continent's new migrants. In reality, Islamist attacks—admittedly on a smaller scale—had been in progress over the previous twenty years, particularly in France. Making this point is not just to plead for a more comprehensive accounting of terrorist violence but to suggest a rather different view of its causation. If in fact the violence was a post–9/11 phenomenon, then we could plausibly associate it with al-Qaeda and its ideology. In reality, though, Middle Eastern-related terrorism in Europe has far more complex origins, which cannot be readily associated with any one ideology, or necessarily, with Islam itself.

However horrifying the Madrid and London attacks, they are not surprising for anyone who recalls the prolonged wave of Palestinian-related terrorism that swept European nations between 1970 and 1976, and that reached its high-water mark with the Munich Olympic massacre of 1972. Some of the European police officers attempting today to detect and suppress Middle Eastern terrorism on their territory are literally the sons and daughters of that earlier generation who pursued almost identical tasks in the early 1970s. In those days too, Europeans

lived in fear of a mega-terror attack that would likely be orchestrated
by the Palestinian followers of Abu Nidal. At first sight, connections
between this wave and the recent attacks are not obvious, not least because the Palestinian campaigns were clearly not Islamist in motivation. The leaders were leftist or socialist, and the most active groupings, like the Popular Front for the Liberation of Palestine and its
offshoots, were founded and largely led by Arab Christians. The Abu
Nidal group was one of several adhering to the militantly secular
Ba'athist regimes of Syria and Iraq.[2]

But continuities do exist. After the main Palestinian campaigns
subsided, extensive terrorist networks still remained in place across
Europe, with sleeper agents and expert bomb makers, and arms supplies. During the 1980s, these groups remained active as agents or subsidiaries for several Middle Eastern governments and secret services,
who waged clandestine war across Europe, partly to advance their diplomatic objectives, partly to enhance their standing within the world of
Palestinian politics. Iran, Iraq, Syria, Algeria, and Libya all cultivated
and used their European networks. One powerful engine driving militancy was the Gulf War of 1980–1988, which set Iraq against Iran and
Syria, leading both sides to put pressure on European governments to
ensure a steady supply of military hardware. In 1986, a series of bombing
attacks against civilian targets in Paris generated a sense of national crisis
in France. The campaign was eventually traced to agents of the Iranian
secret service, who sought to put diplomatic pressure on the French government. Making the investigation of such attacks all the more difficult
was the use of subcontractors, groups or individuals who were hired by
intelligence agencies to transport weapons or to carry out the actual attacks. Such subsidiaries, who would have little knowledge of the actual
motives behind a given attack, were commonly drawn from Middle Eastern immigrant populations, often from underworld subcultures. Otherwise, though, these earlier waves of terror had only minimal connections
with Muslim populations in Europe, which were then far smaller than
they are today.

Terrorism was an imported phenomenon, and this fact is significant for any hopes of reducing or eliminating such attacks in future.
The prevalence of terrorism on European soil is a function of both ge-
ography and history, factors that would still apply even if—to take an
outrageous hypothetical—the continent expelled all its Muslim residents tomorrow. Europeans live in immediate proximity to some deeply
troubled and violent parts of the world, from which they could be separated only by erecting unimaginably high physical barriers. Europe
also provides a lax security environment, which was easily exploited
by the Palestinians in the 1970s, much as it is by Islamist militants today. After decades of progress to unification, Europe still comprises
some thirty nations, each of which plays host to numerous embassies,

consulates, and diplomatic missions, and many of these serve nations sympathetic to radical causes. The principle of diplomatic immunity makes it easy to smuggle weapons, information, or even individuals between nations, and allows intelligence agencies to offer clandestine support for terrorist movements. Also, Europe is an easy place in which to hide. So many states are crowded into such a relatively small region that militants find no difficulty in fleeing from one jurisdiction to another. Different governments have different priorities and outlooks, so that a militant might be seen in one country as a lethal danger and in another as a mere dissident. Such factors made Europe a happy hunting ground for (white, non-Muslim) terrorists, bombers, and assassins in the 1890s and the 1930s, and continue to do so today.

Regardless of the motivating ideology, then, Europe becomes the theater for Middle Eastern terrorism because it is an open society in which militants can move easily, and in which rival states and causes can pursue their conflicts through proxies and surrogates. Moreover, European nations are inextricably connected with Middle Eastern affairs through their dependence on oil from that region, from their economic contacts with Middle Eastern states, and by their long traditions of military support for various regimes, manifested above all in sales of armaments. Another factor is European political and diplomatic weight, which currently makes it a plausible alternative to the United States in global affairs; it makes excellent sense for Palestinians and other minorities to win European support for their causes, whether by reason or intimidation. Terrorism goes with the neighborhood, regardless of the composition of Europe's own populations.

Making Militants

From the 1980s, Islamist ideas became ever more prominent among Middle Eastern radicals. The ascendancy of Islamist radicalism can be dated precisely to the year 1979, with the revolution in Iran and the war in Afghanistan. Iranian events inspired Muslim and particularly Shi'ite groups across the region. Under this impetus, the Shi'ite Lebanese Hizbollah became one of the most determined and effective international terror movements, which carried out devastating bomb attacks in Spain and elsewhere.

The new sense of global jihad also inspired other revolutionary movements that would have a still more direct and more acute effect on Europe, and who often formed tactical alliances with each other. One was the Egyptian-derived Takfir wal Hijra, which is commonly a missing link in discussions of European terrorism and subversion, and the group's members surface repeatedly in militant networks. Part of their appeal lies in their antinomian ideology, their sense that normal moral restrictions can be abandoned for the sake of achieving the

greater good of pursuing jihad. This allows Takfiris to work closely
with criminal gangs and drug dealers, and to recruit freely among the
criminal milieu. The conspirators who carried out the Madrid bombings of 2004 included many with lengthy records of petty crime and
drug dealing, to the point that the network used hashish to purchase
the explosives used in the attack. Over-using the Qaeda label often
prevents us from seeing the activities of distinct Takfiri groups, who
would for instance have included Zacarias Moussaoui and several of
the September 11 hijackers.

The Algerian war of the 1990s also inspired revolutionary ideas
across the Islamic world in Europe and elsewhere while fleeing militants carried the war outside Algeria itself. By the mid-decade, Algerian militants were launching attacks in France, activities that, if not actually undertaken in the name of al-Qaeda, differed little from the
post–9-/11 campaigns. In 1995, the Algerian GIA undertook a ferocious
series of bombings on French soil, mainly targeting public transporta-
tion, railways, and subways, prefiguring the 2004–2005 outrages in
Madrid and London. In 1994, hijackers plotted to crash a fully fueled
airliner into the Eiffel Tower, as much a symbol of national pride for
France as the World Trade Center was for Americans. Critically for
later events, the bombings were organized and largely undertaken by
French-born Muslims of Algerian stock, including Khaled Khelkal of
Lyon, who graduated from a life of crime to open terrorism. When police shot him dead in a 1995 street battle, he became a folk hero in
French banlieues. Algerian exiles pooled their expertise and resources
into the larger network known as al-Qaeda, which drew together Egyptian, Algerian, and Saudi extremists. In 1998, Qaeda issued its formal
declaration of jihad against Jews and Crusaders.[3]

Other battles raged on the fringes of Europe's immediate neighborhood, and the Bosnian struggle had its wider impact. Sarajevo, after
all, is only 250 miles from Vienna or Venice. One Italian Islamist claims
that of the volunteers who traveled from his country to Bosnia, "60
percent returned to Italy. The other 40 percent carried on their jihads
in Afghanistan or in Chechnya, some others went to Algeria or Palestine." Another predominantly Muslim militant group with Balkan
roots is the Kosovo Liberation Army, the KLA, which now represents a
potent force in organized crime and drug dealing across western Europe. In recent years too, one of Europe's most active terrorist movements has been the GICM, which was founded in 1997 by Moroccan
veterans of the jihad training camps in Afghanistan. The group has a
solid infrastructure among the millions of Moroccan migrants scattered across western Europe; and like Bosnia or Kosovo, Morocco is on
western Europe's doorstep.[4]

In earlier eras, different causes would have remained distinct and
mutually independent, but globalization encourages activists to see

linkages between their particular issues. The anti-Soviet resistance in Afghanistan encouraged militants from widely separated parts of the globe to merge their separate organizations into the new al-Qaeda. More recently, the presence of multiple ethnic constituencies on European soil permits still more intense cross-fertilization, as forms of extremism intersect, as Egyptian and Maghrebi militants cooperate with Saudis and Pakistanis, and often with Muslims born in western Europe itself.

Paths to Terror

Combating terrorism would be much easier if the menace came from one unified network with a single cause, allowing authorities to infiltrate networks, to hunt down militants, and to stem sources of arms and money. In fact, for all we have heard in recent years about the threat from al-Qaeda, many of the most notorious attacks have been the work of autonomous or independent local groups only marginally connected with any central organization.

Perhaps surprisingly, the Madrid train bombings of 2004 offer an excellent example of such decentralized organization. At first sight, this attacks looks as if it should have been a manifestation of global strategy, presumably by Qaeda. The attack had a global impact in helping to swing a forthcoming election to the party opposed to Spanish intervention in Iraq. In fact, the new government wasted little time before withdrawing Spanish troops, presenting Islamist radicals worldwide with a stunning victory. But the immediate context of the attack was strictly local, as the perpetrators were Spanish-based Maghrebis linked to the GICM but working largely under their own initiative. They adopted the name Ansar al Qaeda in Europe, meaning "partisans of al-Qaeda," indicating that they were identifying with the larger movement, though without necessarily taking direct orders. While we can link the Madrid terror group to radical imams, contact does not necessarily imply control or direction.[5]

A similar pattern emerges from the London subway bombings of July 2005, carried out by four British-born Muslims. As in Madrid, the attack had global implications, with its goal of punishing the British government for its loyal support of U.S. policies in Iraq, but subsequent investigations do not certainly indicate direction from an international center. This may mean either that no such direction existed or that it was organized subtly enough to escape official detection. Opinions on the matter differ, though the group made martyrdom videos that look like others made by Qaeda supporters, and some of them had access to surprising amounts of money. Whatever the wider links, we know that the group became progressively more radical under the influence of Islamist mosques and propaganda, and made some contact with international Islamist forces. Two of the four had visited a camp of the Pakistan-based Kashmiri extremist group Jaish-e-Mohammed, which operated under the cover of a religious school, a madrassa. But the final attack seems spontaneous and autonomous, the kind of event that could not have been prevented by disrupting the organizational networks of any of the well-known terrorist movements.[6]

Incidentally, looking at these self-organized groups, we are repeatedly shocked less by their bloody plans than by the absolute normality of the participants, the seemingly total assimilation into European society suggested by their appearance and speech. At the trial of some other British plotters, surveillance tapes portrayed a group speaking not in the caricatured Middle Eastern accents of Hollywood villains but in deepest British vernacular. Planning a bombing at a major nightclub, one member asked,

> What about easy stuff where you don't need no experience and nothing, and you could get a job, yeah, like for example the biggest nightclub in central London where no one can even turn round and say "oh they were innocent" those slags [whores] dancing around? . . . Trust me, then you will get the public talking, yeah, yeah . . . if you went for the social structure where every Tom, Dick and Harry goes on a Saturday night, yeah, that would be crazy, crazy thing man.

Like any good Londoner, he pronounces "nothing" as "nuffink," while members addressed each other as "bruv," short for "brother."[7]

Another autonomous operation was the Dutch Hofstad Group, which never accomplished an attack as potent as that of its Spanish or British counterparts but not for lack of ambition. The case grew out of the investigation of the 2004 murder of Theo van Gogh by Mohammed Bouyeri. Bouyeri spoke proudly of his staunch radicalism, modestly dismissing any comparison between himself and Osama bin Laden, but nevertheless, "the fact that you see me as the black standard-bearer of Islam in Europe fills me with honor, pride and happiness." Bouyeri belonged to a wider circle drawn mainly from first- or second-generation Moroccan immigrants. The group's leadership had connections with Takfir wal Hijra and the GICM, but may well have had other international dimensions. One member of the group, Jason Walters, boasted of his connection to the founder and leader of the Pakistani Jaishe Mohammed; another had tried to join Chechen rebel forces. They aspired to be polder-mujahideen, holy warriors within the Dutch polder landscape.[8]

But as in the London case, the Hofstad Group appears to have been mainly self-motivated, spontaneously organized, and even self-propagandized. Members spent their time obsessively watching web materials and videos of the most harrowing kind, with a constant diet of warfare, brutality, and beheadings. They discussed possible targets for terror attacks, including assassinations of Dutch politicians and an attack on a nuclear reactor, and sought means of obtaining weapons and explosives. One man of Moroccan origins was in possession of plans of the Dutch parliament building and Schiphol Airport, as well as night-vision spectacles and bomb-making equipment. When the group was eventually rounded up, one member threw a grenade at police trying to arrest him. Though the ensuing conspiracy trial was a sensation in the Netherlands, matters could easily have been far worse.[9]

Elsewhere in Europe, the celebrated terror attacks give only a limited idea of the potential scale of the subversive danger posed by groups like these, since law enforcement and intelligence agencies usually manage to thwart the great majority of plots. But just in the single year following September 11, planned schemes averted by law enforcement included attacks on the U.S. embassies in Rome and Paris, using lethal chemicals like cyanide; poisoning the water supply of an Italian city; the bombing of French and German synagogues; a bomb attack on a Christmas market in Strasbourg; and attempts to sink British or U.S. warships in the Straits of Gibraltar. In 2004, Moroccan and Algerian extremists were planning a series of attacks that would have destroyed Madrid's National Court and Barcelona's World Trade Center complex. The high-speed train from Madrid to Seville was also targeted. One group in Italy planned a ship-borne attack on an Italian city, using "a ship as big as the *Titanic*, packed with explosives," with the goal of killing 10,000. A raid in London in 2003 discovered "castor oil beans—the raw material for ricin—along with equipment needed to produce it and recipes for ricin, cyanide, botulinum and other poisons, along with instructions for explosives." In the subsequent manhunt, an Algerian suspect stabbed to death a police officer. This list of attempts is in addition to foiled schemes to hijack or bring down airliners, especially Israeli targets. In 2006, British authorities announced that they were investigating at least thirty serious conspiracies on their territory, involving hundreds of suspects. British intelligence services believe there is "no doubt at all" that al-Qaeda aspires to launch a nuclear attack against the United Kingdom.[10]

One significant point to emerge from this list is that many of the most active elements identified in these planned attacks were militants of north African origin—Algerian, Moroccan or Tunisian. That must be stressed in light of recent analyses portraying Britain's Pakistani minority as a uniquely radical and disaffected population. British Muslims might provide fertile soil for extremism, but they are certainly not alone. The reason that so few of the Maghrebi-rooted plots have actually come to fruition might be that the governments and secret services of Algeria and Morocco have been sincerely committed to allying with European states in the struggle against subversion—more enthusiastic, perhaps, than their Pakistani counterparts.

In the aftermath of the British ricin plot, British police made the conventional, and accurate, declaration that "the police service knows that [the terrorists] are not representative of the overwhelming majority of the law-abiding Muslim community who have stated their total rejection of violence and terrorism." But even if violent extremism attracts only a small minority of European Muslims, the potential scale of terrorist violence is still impressive. After all, mounting a serious terrorist campaign need not involve many committed activists. Through its thirty-year campaign against the British government, the Provisional IRA never had more than five hundred or so actual fighters at any given time, with this hard core of shooters and bombers supported by perhaps ten times that number of active sympathizers. For almost forty years, the Basque ETA carried on a war against the Spanish government with a military core of around a hundred; again, with a penumbra perhaps ten times as large. The German Red Army Fraction of the 1970s and 1980s relied on only twenty to thirty actual paramilitary fighters.[11]

These figures clearly demonstrate the danger posed by radical ideas among European Muslims. Let us assume for the sake of argument that 10 percent of adult male Muslims are regularly hearing incitements to jihad, and 10 percent of that audience might in some circumstances be driven to act on those ideas. The British government has recently suggested that some 10,000 British Muslims have attended conferences and gatherings organized by extremist movements, while the British security services report having under surveillance around 1,600 militants whom they believe to pose a serious danger of violence. This would mean that Britain alone has a core of at least a thousand potential jihad fighters, quite enough to levy a potent guerrilla war against that society. The mystery is not so much why Europe has been the setting for repeated terrorist violence but why so little of it has occurred to date.

Identifying Extremists

Depending then on how we define the radical movement, Europe today faces a serious danger from violent extremism rooted in radical Islamism. But terrorism is a broad-brush term covering quite different types of activity that demand quite distinct responses. Some movements—like the IRA or ETA—are deeply rooted in the community and command a degree of popular support. Other groups, in contrast, like those that undertook the Madrid or London bombings, need not necessarily have had any connections whatever in the broader world of Spanish or British Islam.

While a small isolated movement can be defeated and uprooted by conventional law enforcement responses or counterinsurgency initiatives, authorities must be much more careful when a violent organization is affiliated to an authentically popular cause, if repression is not to create steady supplies of new militants. The most dangerous situation of all is when a mass popular party presses radical demands through electoral campaigns and other conventional means, but these are backed up by the operations of a clandestine paramilitary force linked to the aboveground political movement. In order to avoid even greater polarization, governments and police agencies must target their operations against those plotting or undertaking violence while largely tolerating those merely expressing radical sentiments.

To use a historical analogy, in the 1920s or 1930s, a large number of Europeans sympathized with communist or radical socialist parties who at least spoke the language of radical revolution, and fantasized openly about what they might do on The Day when the final conflict erupted. Yet for all the wild rhetoric, democratic nations, at least, responded judiciously. They drew a careful distinction between truly dangerous militants and democratically oriented moderates, and those moderates formed the backbone of the socialist parties that would be the most effective bastion against red revolution or Soviet-inspired subversion. As long as Islam exists in Europe, it will inevitably have an extreme fringe; but it is far from obvious when militant Islamism shades into active terrorism or conspiracy.

If only because of practical constraints, European governments cannot suppress all Islamist movements, and they recognize that they should concentrate their efforts on real terrorists. But how does one distinguish between radical activism and potential armed violence? In an ideal world, terrorist militants would wear uniforms or other distinguishing signs revealing their identity and affiliations. In reality, of course, they usually conceal their identities and commonly operate behind the cover of legitimate—or at least, non-proscribed—organizations. While most mainstream observers would agree that al-Qaeda represents a deadly threat, many militants who sympathize with the movement maintain their overt membership in other organizations, which do not have such an awful reputation. European media that would rejoice at the exposure of a Qaeda plot scarcely know what to make of official claims against less notorious groups such as Salafists or Takfir wal Hijra.

Some movements in particular pose real dilemmas for European police agencies, especially the revivalist groups practicing *da'wa*—the Islamic "Call" to conversion and piety. One is the Tablighi Jama'at, which, depending on one's point of view, is an admirably effective movement for religious revival and moral reconstruction, or a global support network for armed terror. In some ways, it seems odd that the Tablighis should be connected in any way with the strictly puritanical Islam of the Wahhabis or Salafists. Though the movement grew out of

India's stern Deobandi traditions, its activists always refused to lay down over-precise rules about which forms of Islam were correct, and ultra-puritans condemned this liberalism. Although the Saudi regime supports Tablighi activities internationally, the movement is banned in Saudi Arabia itself. In theory, the group is also apolitical and quietist, but some enthusiasts were very attracted by Islamist radicalism, especially as practiced by the Taliban in Afghanistan. Though it would be unfair to taint the Tablighi movement by the misdeeds of a few members, it has on several occasions been linked to Islamist extremism. After all, the fact of undertaking a Tablighi pilgrimage provides a wonderful cover for activists to travel from Pakistan, say, to several Western nations, visiting mosques and madrassas. Some of the terrorist suspects imprisoned by U.S. authorities at Guantánamo Bay are Tablighi activists, and the group has been implicated in recruiting men who subsequently joined armed groups. It was through the Tablighis that John Walker Lindh began the trajectory that made him the "American Taliban." Mohammed Sidique Khan attended the main Tablighi mosque in Dewsbury, together with another of the July 7 plotters; and in 2006, investigators traced Tablighi connections for several of the British group who plotted to blow up transatlantic airliners. By this stage, the media were portraying the movement as a recruitment front for al-Qaeda.[12]

Hizb ut-Tahrir

Another controversial da'waist movement active across Europe is the Hizb ut-Tahrir al-Islami (Islamic Party of Liberation), HT. Some view HT as an outlet for radical Islamist sentiments but nevertheless a legitimate political party that gives voice to popular feelings that would otherwise be channeled into openly subversive activities. Critics see the Hizb itself as a thin cover for radical recruitment and organization.[13]

Hizb ut-Tahrir was founded in Jerusalem in 1953 with the avowed goal of restoring the Islamic Caliphate, the Khilafah. Intense repression sharply curbed the group's activities in the Arab Middle East, and it is banned in most of the Muslim world. This caused it to relocate elsewhere—to western Europe, to Russia, and to the nations of post-Soviet central Asia, where it has often been associated with violent activism. Russian authorities ban the group as a dangerous manifestation of Islamist subversion. It is in western Europe, though, that it has attracted the liveliest media attention. The group first came to public attention in England in the mid-1990s with a national conference and a major rally in Trafalgar Square, and it recruited heavily on college campuses, among students of Middle Eastern and south Asian origins.[14]

That the group is radical is beyond question, and it praises suicide attacks in Israel. But is it a direct threat to European nations? Its ideological statements claim not. The party is pledged to "struggle against the rulers in the Arab and Muslim countries . . . and acting also to remove their regimes so as to establish the Islamic rule in its place," which is avowedly revolutionary. But for the "*Kufr* [infidel] colonialist states," the Hizb aspires only to fight "colonialism in all its intellectual, political, economic and military forms, [and this] involves exposing its plans, and revealing its conspiracies in order to deliver the Ummah from its control and to liberate it from any effect of its influence." Read literally, that implies no plan to overthrow Western regimes.[15]

Some critics are less sanguine about the group. U.S. analyst Tony Corn suggests that Hizb and like groups "are in fact in symbiosis with jihadist networks (al-Qaeda), each playing its part in the Islamist version of the 'good cop, bad cop' routine." Some European nations have come to share this view. In 2005, Germany proscribed Hizb ut-Tahrir and deported some leading militants. The group's legal status elsewhere remains fragile. In Denmark, Hizb activists earned notoriety during the cartoon controversy, and some members were publicly quoted espousing violent extremism. The group's Danish leader is a Palestinian, Abdul Latif, who in 2002 was charged with distributing hate literature that praised suicide bombers as martyrs. In 2004, he urged Muslims to "go help your brothers in Falluja [Iraq] and exterminate your rulers if they block your way"—though, as he stressed, his message was intended to inspire fighters in the Middle East rather than in Europe itself. By 2006, even tolerant Britain was debating a formal ban on Hizb operations.[16]

Al-Muhajiroun

The British section of Hizb ut-Tahrir was founded by Omar Bakri Mohammed, who personifies contemporary European dilemmas about the limits of free speech and the boundaries between militant politics and outright sedition. Originally of Syrian birth, Bakri arrived in Britain in the late 1980s and soon acquired a reputation for sensational statements. Through the 1990s, "the Tottenham Ayatollah" called for stoning to death those guilty of homosexuality, adultery, fornication, and bestiality; and for the abolition of public mixing between members of the opposite sex. He is close to Sheikh Omar Abdul Rahman, whose mosque was the base of organization for the first World Trade Center attack in 1993. More recently, Bakri offered an extended justification of the Madrid bombings:

> What happened in Madrid is all revenge. Eye for eye, tooth for tooth, life for life. Anybody (that) commits a crime should be punished—that's exactly what happened in relation to Spain. Objective number one—break the psychology of the occupier by hitting back in their homeland. To be

worried about their own wives and loved ones. . . . Somebody he fly aeroplane [sic] and he decide to land the aeroplane over 10 Downing Street, for
example, or over the White House. This is a form of self-sacrifice operation.

Bakri described the London subway bombers as the "fantastic four."[17]

In 1996, Bakri became the spiritual mentor of a breakaway group
still more extreme than the Hizb, namely, al-Muhajiroun, the Pilgrims,
a name commemorating Muhammad's earliest companions. (The word
is based on the root hijra, used in the same sense as by Takfir wal Hijra.)
This movement may be the most overt European example to date of
an organized aboveground Islamic party that supports terrorist activities and that actively recruits for armed actions. Muhajiroun gatherings rejoiced at videos of the "magnificent" September 11 attacks and
of subsequent attacks on U.S. forces in Iraq.

Al-Muhajiroun has on several occasions been linked to terrorism
around the world, using young Muslims recruited in Britain for armed
operations in various theaters of Islamist struggle. The movement,
which was about a thousand strong at its height, has close ties with
Pakistan-based extremists. The Muhajiroun dispatched a young
Birmingham-born man who in 2000 drove a truckload of explosives
into an Indian barracks in Kashmir. According to Israeli sources, al-
Muhajiroun brought two British activists into contact with the Palestinian Hamas, and one actually carried out a suicide bombing mission
in Tel Aviv. Another London member was arrested while working for
Sunni insurgents in Iraq.[18]

The group's global contacts became a matter for pressing concern
after the fall of the Taliban regime. The former commissioner of London's Metropolitan Police states that up to 3,000 "British-born or British-
based people had passed through Osama bin Laden's training camps in
Afghanistan and, of these, there were now about 200 committed
home-grown terrorists." According to Manchester-born activist Hassan
Butt, who claimed to represent the Muhajiroun in Pakistan, the movement recruited 200 British Muslims to fight for the Taliban.[19]

According to the group's official stance, Muslims operated under a
covenant of security, which prohibited them from engaging in warfare
against a state in which they were allowed to live peacefully, such as
Britain. Butt, however, rejected that position and called for revolutionary violence within Britain and other Western states. Of the British recruits for the Taliban, he warned, "If they do return, I do believe they
will take military action within Britain, [against] British military and government institutions, as well as British military and government individuals." Responding to the Madrid bombings, Butt expressed his "envy" of
those responsible. He said, "It is my hope that by the age of forty I am a
martyr—and if I hadn't I would probably be a bit dejected in not being

among the martyrs of Islam." (He was twenty-four at this point.) Though not associated with the London subway attacks, Butt lived in the same section of Leeds as Shehzad Tanweer, one of the actual bombers.[20]

Nor was Butt unique. In a 2004 interview, the Muhajiroun leader in Luton pledged his support for suicide bombings within Great Britain: "When a bomb attack happens here, I won't be against it, even if it kills my own children. Islam is clear: Muslims living in lands that are occupied have the right to attack their invaders. Britain became a legitimate target when it sent troops to Iraq." The journalist recorded a bizarre conversation among Luton followers:

> "As far as I'm concerned, when they bomb London, the bigger the better," says Abdul Haq, the social worker. "I know it's going to happen because Sheikh bin Laden said so. Like Bali, like Turkey, like Madrid—I pray for it, I look forward to the day." "Pass the brown sauce, brother," says Abu Malaahim, the IT specialist, devouring his chicken and chips. "I agree with you, brother," says Abu Yusuf, the earnest-looking financial adviser sitting opposite. "I would like to see the Mujahideen coming into London and killing thousands, whether with nuclear weapons or germ warfare. And if they need a safehouse, they can stay in mine—and if they need some fertilizer [for a bomb], I'll tell them where to get it."

While foreign Muslims should not strike an infidel nation that had treated them considerately, they felt that a covenant of security did not apply to Muslims born in those countries. "Most of our people, especially the youth, are British citizens. They owe nothing to the Government. They did not ask to be born here; neither did they ask to be protected by Britain."[21]

Such pronouncements persuaded even the British government that the group had passed beyond the limits of acceptable speech, but in a democratic state, merely banning a movement seldom silences it totally. Though the Muhajiroun were officially dissolved in 2004, the group went underground and was reactivated the following year, with an official declaration of armed support for "the global Islamic camp against the global crusade camp." The Muhajiroun continued to operate through a number of successors and front groups, including al-Ghurabaa', the Strangers. One leader of this group is Abu Izzadeen, who has called suicide bombing "martyrdom operations" and who terms the London subway attacks "completely praiseworthy." (Al-Ghurabaa' has also now been banned.) Another successor is the Savior Sect, the leader of which has proclaimed on television that "the banner has been risen for jihad inside the U.K."[22]

Other groups also manage, tenuously, to maintain footholds in both mainstream and extremist worlds. In Spain, one visible group is al-Murabitun, which was originally formed by New Age–oriented white

Europeans fascinated by Sufi mysticism, and European converts still
provide most of its leaders. Murabitun representatives have appeared
at major Islamic gatherings in Spain, including the 2003 conference
held in Granada to celebrate the opening of the new mosque, an
evocative return of the Muslim presence to one of its ancient capitals.
But despite its apparent respectability, the group has a fanatical streak.
The president of the mosque foundation calls himself the Emir of
Spain and speaks of Granada returning to its "natural origin," that is Islam, after a five-hundred-year hiatus. The Murabitun organization is
also obsessively anti-Jewish. Public policy statements concentrate on
breaking Jewish control of the world financial system, and the Granada
conference was dominated by bizarre calls for Muslims to restore the
gold dinar as a global currency and thus to generate a Western economic crisis that would dwarf that of 1929.[23]

The Mosque Militarist

European governments find it understandably hard to distinguish between windy rhetoric and serious subversion, but in some notorious
examples, radicalism has gone beyond the acceptable bounds of free
political speech, even according to the most permissive definition. Banning a group like the Hizb ut-Tahrir places some strains on Western
traditions of tolerance, but at least the group presents itself as a political organization, a hizb or party. The Muhajiroun, similarly, can easily
be classified as a paramilitary movement rather than a religious sect,
however much distinctions between the two concepts shade into each
other in some traditions of Islam.

More troubling, though, are the numerous cases in which clergy
and religious institutions emerge as centers of violent radicalism. Indeed, it is impossible to describe Islamist extremism in contemporary
Europe except in terms of imams and mosques. We have already seen
the repeated struggles between moderates and militants for control of
mosques, but in some cases, institutions have fallen into the hands of
real fanatics. At least two hundred mosques across western Europe follow militant and extremist positions: admittedly, this is a tiny proportion of the whole, perhaps 3 percent, but they pose an authentic danger of subversion. Responding to this presence demands an official
response, yet at the same time, governments are very cautious about
any action that could be taken as an assault on religious freedom: they
must tread lightly if they are not to detonate an open conflict between
Islam and the respective states. European police agencies look wist-
fully at their counterparts in Egypt or Algeria, who have no hesitation
about closing or purging a mosque suspected of preaching sedition.

Any number of examples illustrate the use of mosques as centers
of revolutionary organization. One of the most notorious is Hamburg's

al-Quds mosque, which was a central meeting place for the Qaeda cell in which the September 11 conspiracy was nurtured. A frequent preacher at al-Quds was Moroccan imam Mohammed Fizazi, whose sermons were openly incendiary. In early 2001, he advocated killing all non-Muslims, all Christians and Jews, "no matter if it's a man, a woman or a child." Contemplating the massacre of unbelievers, Fizazi acknowledged the ethical difficulties but only to the extent that the actual killers might suffer mental qualms or hardship. Still, as he told his listeners, "You have not understood the words of God or the Koran if you believe that the nonbelievers want to do good." Fizazi himself had a long and convoluted career in the terrorist underworld. In the 1990s, he served as imam of a Saudi-funded mosque in Tangier until the Moroccan government barred him from preaching. Subsequently, Fizazi was linked to the 2003 bombings in Casablanca and was also associated with the group that carried out the 2004 train bombings in Madrid.[24]

Worshipers at the Hamburg mosque included Mohamed Atta, Ziad Jarrah, and others who participated in the September 11 attacks, as well as operatives involved in logistics and support. One of these supporters was Mounir el-Motassadeq, a Moroccan, who among other tasks supplied the Hamburg group with money. As investigators tried to follow the money, they found close links between the Hamburg group and another radical mosque in the Dutch city of Eindhoven, which el-Motassadeq visited, probably in the company of some of the eventual hijackers. From Eindhoven, they drew money that had been diverted from funds supplied by Saudi financiers.[25]

Members of the Hamburg group also visited Amsterdam's Saudi-connected al-Tawhid mosque, which was popular with the Hofstad circle: this was the favored mosque of Mohammed Bouyeri. Asked about these activities, mosque authorities replied, reasonably enough, that they could not keep track of every individual passing through the community, and that simply because extremists visited the institution does not mean that these individuals had the institution's official support. Mosque authorities freely condemned the murder of Theo van Gogh and stated their theological stance as "We're strict, but not more than that." But regardless of the degree of knowledge and support offered by clergy or officials, a number of mosques—in Hamburg, Eindhoven, Amsterdam, and elsewhere—clearly did and do shelter extremist networks and active terrorist cells.[26]

Making Londonistan

London has a number of such overtly radical institutions. Most notorious is the North London Central Mosque in Finsbury Park, which was for several years a favorite destination for Islamic extremists worldwide.

Among the firebrand preachers here was the Egyptian Abu Hamza al-Masri, who fought with the mujaheddin in Afghanistan and in Britain worked as a nightclub bouncer. Within Britain, he founded in 1994 the extremist Supporters of Shariah (SOS), which organized military training for young British Muslims, with former members of the British armed forces as instructors. A police raid at the mosque in 2003 found paramilitary equipment. Some SOS supporters, including members of Abu Hamza's family, were arrested in Yemen on charges that they had been sent to that country to destroy Western and Christian targets. Finsbury Park mosque—the "Suicide Factory"—became a center for the Muhajiroun.[27]

The mosque stands in a heavily Muslim quarter called Little Algeria, and it has often been associated with members of the GIA. Visitors to Finsbury Park included Ahmed Ressam, a GIA fighter who was arrested on the Canadian border at the end of 1999 while en route to bomb Los Angeles International Airport, LAX. Another regular attendee was the French-Algerian Djamel Beghal, a member of Takfir wal Hijra, who was radicalized during the 1990s by the combined impact of the struggles in Bosnia, Chechnya, and Palestine. In London in 1997, he became close to Zacarias Moussaoui, and the two men visited Afghanistan together. Beghal was arrested several weeks before September 11 for plotting a series of European terrorist spectaculars. One ambitious scheme reputedly involved flying a helicopter full of explosives into the U.S. embassy in Paris.[28]

The radical activities at the Finsbury Park mosque can scarcely be described as underground or clandestine. Within hours of the September 11 attacks, graffiti near the mosque proclaimed "New York Taliban Triumph." Abu Hamza himself looks like a cartoon villain, bearing as he does a hook in place of a hand that he claims to have lost in Afghanistan (others claim it was severed as a punishment for theft). British media delighted to cover the ultra-radical fulminations of "Old Hooky." In 2006, Abu Hamza was convicted of several offenses including incitement to murder and stirring racial hatred, specifically calling for the killing of non-Muslims.

Abu Hamza was not an isolated figure. Another Islamist leader is Abu Qatada, Omar Mahmoud Abu Omar, a Palestinian by birth. He is connected to both the GIA and Takfir wal Hijra, and has been called "Bin Laden's ambassador to Europe." A Spanish indictment described him as "spiritual head of the mujaheddin in Europe." Allegedly, he was involved in a scheme to attack Western targets in Jordan during the millennium celebrations at the end of 1999, in what would have been the other half of the planned atrocity at LAX. Tapes of Abu Qatada sermons were found in the Hamburg apartment used by some of the September 11 hijackers. According to one journalistic account,

Before the Sept. 11 attacks, militants in Europe followed a well-worn route. They made pilgrimages to radical mosques in Britain, where clerics such as Abu Qatada and Abu Hamza were revered by holy warriors. British-based extremists screened recruits and organized their trips to the camps in Afghanistan, supplying plane tickets and fake papers if necessary.[29]

Mohammed Sifaoui notes that

the most sought-after terrorists in the world have found shelter in the UK. . . . They propagate their ideology there. They distribute booklets on their philosophy—giving them out freely outside mosques. . . . [T]he majority of the young guys who were living in the west and who left to go to training camps in Afghanistan had a tightly outlined itinerary—they went through London to Pakistan. And then from Pakistan to Afghanistan.[30]

Italy too has its extremist mosques. In 2002, intelligence agencies taped a conversation between a member of the deadly Iraqi network that followed Abu Musab al-Zarqawi, and a prominent Egyptian-born imam named Abu Umar, who headed a mosque on Milan's Via Quaranta. The tape linked Abu Umar to the terrorist movement Ansar al-Islam. The imam speaks frankly of the existence of twenty-five or so terrorist cells able to carry out jihad in Europe and assures his friend, "Don't ever worry about money, because Saudi Arabia's money is your money." He also spoke of the widespread international network. Although "the nerve centre is still London," other nations provided rich opportunities:

The country from which everything takes off is Austria. . . . [I]t has become the country of international communications. . . . Now Europe is controlled via air and land, but in Poland and Bulgaria and countries that aren't part of the European Community everything is easy.

Based on such evidence, the U.S. State Department called the mosque "the main al-Qaida station house in Europe." Abu Umar subsequently became the center of an international crisis when, in 2003, CIA agents kidnapped him off the street and rendered him to Egypt where he was tortured. The affair generated a direct U.S. confrontation with the Italian state and court system, not to mention with EU authorities. At the time of writing, Milanese prosecutors are building a case against those said to be involved in the seizure, including several CIA agents.[31]

Every European country has extremist imams and mosques, though few have the seemingly limitless tolerance of Britain in permitting their operations. The French intelligence agency, Renseignements Généraux, suggests that perhaps fifty of the nation's mosques, including thirty in and around Paris, are strongly militant. Belgian intelligence agencies believe that thirty mosques in their country serve as recruiting centers for movements that posed "an immediate, grave and specific risk to the survival of our democratic and constitutional order."

Reportedly, European dependence on Saudi oil made authorities reluctant to investigate radical activities at many mosques in Spain and elsewhere until recent terror attacks forced a wider investigation intervention.[32]

Apart from mosques, some Islamist charities have emerged as important contact points in militant organization and especially the transmission of funds. Most often mentioned are the Saudi-based charities that supply funds to European mosques and religious causes, like the Al-Haramain Foundation. Also under regular investigation is the European network of charities that supports Palestinian causes, groups like the British Interpal, which the U.S. government accuses of funding Hamas. When in 2006 British police investigated the conspiracy to destroy airliners, they alleged that participants were linked through Crescent Relief London, a charity formed to assist earthquake victims in Pakistan.[33]

Terror in the Community

The real problem, though, lies not in a few high-profile individuals or national institutions but in the spread of extreme ideas into ordinary mosques and community centers. These institutions provide recruiting grounds in which enthusiastic young people—usually men—can be identified and tested before being directed to serious training for actions abroad or at home. Dewsbury, Beeston, and other Pakistani communities in West Yorkshire fill such a role for British Islam: the July 7 plot had its origins in a Youth Access Project run by Mohammad Sidique Khan. But similar communities exist across Europe. In Belgium, for instance, the small town of Maaseik was home to several hundred Moroccans. Maaseik proved to be an organizational center for the GICM, and local radicals sheltered suspects associated with the Madrid bombings.

Since the early 1990s, many European mosques have witnessed fierce struggles as younger militant Islamists challenged the apolitical regimes of older community leaders or of other moderates who saw extremism as a path to ruin. One celebrated case concerned British ex-convict Richard Reid who attempted to blow up a transatlantic airliner, using explosives stashed in his shoe. Reid had worshiped at London's Brixton mosque, alongside Zacarias Moussaoui. The Brixton mosque was headed by one Abdul Haqq Baker, who complained that police never paid enough attention to his earnest warnings about terrorist talent scouts preying on mosques like his in search of the young and unstable. As he warned his congregation, "The recruiting has got out of control. Beware. It's your sons, your teenagers who are being plucked into these extreme groups." In 2003, a British Muslim leader warned that if Hizb ut Tahrir are not stopped at this stage, and we continue to let them politicize and pollute the youngsters' minds and other gullible [people's] minds, then what will happen in effect is that these terrorism acts and these suicide bombings that we hear going on around in foreign countries, we will actually start seeing these incidents happening outside our doorsteps.

In his undercover exploration of radical Islamic underworlds on European soil, Mohamed Sifaoui warns of the "warrior-gurus who turn aimless souls into human weapons."[34]

In a number of cases, Islamist radicalism has established a foothold in a particular community, which then becomes a base for wider organization. In such a setting, radical-sounding views become so commonplace that police and intelligence services find it difficult to distinguish between empty rhetoric and threats of actual violence. Outside the formal religious world of the mosques, radicalism also exercises an appeal to criminal subcultures, which have already shown themselves willing to use violence. In principle, conversion to Islam could be a positive development, a turning away from crime and illegality. In some cases, though, criminal gangs have formed street-level alliances with militant Islamic groups. In 2005, France's Interior Minister Nicholas Sarkozy was criticized for remarks about minority communities that were widely taken as racist or insensitive, but many would echo one part of his analysis. Responding to demands that the police, *les keufs*, withdraw their heavy-handed presence in ethnic areas, he urged, "The police presence in the suburbs is vital. The police are the republic's police. They keep order in the republic. If they don't do it, who will replace them? Mafias or intégristes [fundamentalists]." On occasion, though, Mafias and intégristes have allied. According to one official observer, "Although hoodlums of North African descent smoke marijuana, wear Nikes and drive BMWs, many of them also admire Bin Laden. . . . They share turf and services with extremists: documents, weapons, vehicles. And they are susceptible to the extremists' message of discipline and respect."[35]

The extremist appeal gains added force in a prison setting where recruiters can be assured of finding an audience thoroughly hostile to the status quo. Even where prison authorities appoint or supervise imams or chaplains, most have no idea of the contents of sermons given in Arabic or other non-Western languages. Clergy might indeed be urging their listeners to be respectful and law-abiding but would also be free to insert much stronger fare.

Converts

Other aspects of Islamist organization and recruiting raise controversial questions about civil and religious liberties. All European states accept that individuals have a right to adopt or change religions, and they deny that religious adherence should cause people to be treated as likely criminals, except in the case of a few notorious cults. Over the past decade, though, the increasing presence of converts to Islam in the ranks of radical extremists has led to the prospect of special surveillance.

Some of the most notorious Islamist terrorists of recent years have been converts to the faith, including Richard Reid, or the London suicide bomber Jermaine Lindsay. Both men, from Afro-Caribbean cultures, were drawn by extremist evangelism in prisons and criminal milieux. Also from Caribbean roots is Abu Izzadeen, formerly Trevor Brooks, a spokesman for al-Ghurabaa'. Even by the standards of Londonistan, one of the most vociferous Islamist preachers is the Jamaican-born Sheikh Abdullah el-Faisal, formerly Trevor Forest. His threats of mass murder against Jews, Christians, and Hindus led to his imprisonment for soliciting murder and inciting racial hatred. ("How wonderful it is to kill the *Kuffar* [unbeliever]!") No less than three of those accused in the airliner plots of August 2006 were British-born converts. Jason Walters, one of the most vociferous militants of the Hofstad group, was also a convert, and had an American father. Dhiren Barot, who plotted mega-terror attacks in London, converted from Hinduism to Islam at the age of twenty.[36]

French intelligence agencies see the recruitment of converts as an explicit strategy by al-Qaeda and related organizations. One example was Pierre Richard Robert, who was imprisoned for trying to form a terrorist network in Morocco and who had plotted major attacks on French soil. Police surveillance of another French convert led to the arrest of one of his associates, the organizer of the Madrid train bombings. About a third of the members of Djamel Beghal's French network in France were converts, and a large-scale study of French converts to Islam found that almost a quarter identified themselves as Salafists. Radical converts have been active in other countries. Christian Ganczarski, a German citizen of Polish birth, converted to Islam in the strongly Muslim environment of Duisburg. As "Ibrahim the German," Ganczarski was accused of holding senior rank in Qaeda, and he was accused of organizing the 2002 bombing of a Tunisian synagogue that killed twenty-one people. In 2005, a white Belgian woman carried out a suicide bomb attack against U.S. forces in Iraq. Belgian converts have also provided logistics and support facilities for jihadi extremists around the world, including Afghanistan.[37]

Converts do not represent a vast proportion of European Muslims. (Technically, one does not convert to Islam, but rather reverts, accepting the faith as a natural birthright.) The German Muslim population might include 100,000 ethnic Germans, while France reports a like number of native converts, and Italy has anywhere from 20,000 to

50,000. People convert for many reasons, usually laudable: they are drawn to Islam by its intellectual or spiritual appeal, by the glamour of its history, or by close association with Muslim communities. The commonest single factor in conversion is marriage, with European women converting to marry Muslim men.[38]

Conversion to Islam need not imply any adherence to extremist politics, and some of the most prominent advocates of Euro-Islam are themselves European converts. The German Central Council of Muslims (*Zentralrat der Muslime*) elected as its president a moderate and liberal chairman of German origin, named Ayyub Axel Köhler. In many cases, though, people convert to Islam as a way of rejecting mainstream European society: these are "protest conversions." In Spain, converts of native origin constitute an important part of the leadership of the local Muslim community. Many are veterans of the radical left of the 1960s and 1970s who were attracted by Islam's mystical tradition. They grew up under the repressive Franco regime, which boasted of its links to the nation's glorious Catholic past, making the acceptance of Islam a peculiarly subversive act. A close analogy would be the African-American drift to Islam as a conscious rejection of the nation's Christian credentials, and a clutching for a radically alternative ideal. One Spaniard prominent in the restored Muslim community of Granada declares simply that "we've come to offer society the only alternative that exists to lead it out of chaos."[39]

Recent converts to radical Islam fit a long-established pattern in European radicalism in which young people, often of good families, drift to extremist causes, often pursuing a seductive vision of utopian society. In the words of Olivier Roy,

> The young people in working-class urban areas are against the system, and converting to Islam is the ultimate way to challenge the system. They convert to stick it to their parents, to their principal. . . . They convert in the same way people in the 1970s went to Bolivia or Vietnam. I see a very European tradition of identifying with a Third World cause.[40]

Modern Muslim converts include white youth in their teens and twenties who in earlier eras might have given their loyalty to radical secular ideologies, to anarchism or nihilism, communism or fascism. Since the 1980s, though, all those causes have been discredited. Islam, in contrast, offers certainty and assurance in a world with few ideological alternatives. In the words of a British convert to the Muhajiroun, "Look to capitalism, it has only existed for 75 years and it's crumbling already. Communism is finished. The only other ideological belief around now, not a religion, Islam is not a religion. Let's make it clear. It's a political ideological belief."[41]

Especially since 2001, Islam of the fiercest and most radical kind also stands out as a principal challenger to forces of capitalism and globalization. It presents successful practical models of resistance, both political and cultural, and it gives adherents a whole alternative history and set of heroes, immensely more attractive than the often vilified icons of Western Christendom. At least some disaffected youth—white and black—find Islam of the severest kind attractive for its promise of community, fraternity, and strict sexual standards, in contrast to the atomized society of urban Europe. In the words of a young British man named Wayne, who joined the Muhajroun under the name "Osama,"

> Going back before I decided to convert to Islam, my life wasn't any sort of life. I was drinking alcohol, lack of work, lack of family around me, didn't have no family. Now I've got one billion point, so many brothers around me. I couldn't ask for a bigger family in my life now.[42]

Though European converts to radical Islamist politics might not be numerous, their importance is out of proportion to their numbers since they are less likely to attract official suspicion. While security officers might be alert to threats from people of Middle Eastern appearance, they would be less likely to pay close attention to a clearly European individual, especially a woman. Black people would likewise attract little concern if their speech and manner proclaimed them local residents rather than recent immigrants.

Responding

Given the scale of the extremist danger, it is remarkable that many European states have not responded more forcefully to militant recruitment and organization. Tolerance has been particularly marked in Great Britain, which has become a global center of Islamist activism. Not until the Finsbury Park mosque operated for some years as a reasonable facsimile of an Afghan jihadi training camp did British police finally intervene.

Britain has also been extremely hospitable to leading activists who are wanted in their home countries on very serious charges. Some of the perpetrators of the 1995 GIA campaign in France found refuge here, to the horror of French law enforcement. It was in these years that the British capital acquired its unsavory reputation of Londonistan. Abu Qatada was twice convicted in Jordan on terrorist charges, and many other British Islamist leaders stand high on the most-wanted lists of countries like Egypt, Tunisia, and the Gulf states. Yemen has a long-standing request to extradite Abu Hamza on charges of plotting terrorism in that country. Omar Bakri is a British resident only because he claimed asylum there in the mid-1980s while in flight from the Saudi Arabian police. One Islamist militant wanted in the attempted assassination of a former Egyptian prime minister lived freely in Britain for several years despite repeated Egyptian demands to have him delivered for trial. In the words of Egyptian Islamist, Yasser Sirri, "The whole Arab world was dangerous for me. I went to London." Britain was agonizingly slow in responding to Russian threats to extradite Chechen leader Akhmed Zakayev on charges of armed rebellion, murder, and kidnapping. In every case, suspects are allowed to stay in Britain because they allege that their home countries are persecuting them only on religious or political grounds. Other countries also accommodate some remarkable guests. Belgium played host for several years to Abdelkader Hakimi, who was sentenced to death in absentia in Morocco for attempting to overthrow the monarchy and who is believed to be the European head of the GICM.[43]

Beyond supposing a national death-wish, many critics have been baffled by European, and specifically British, tolerance of Islamist dissidence. Partly, it grows from long traditions of ignoring radical exiles, provided that their activities do not directly challenge British interests. There is also a real concern about principles of due process and an awareness that militants wanted in foreign countries might well have been convicted on trumped-up charges, backed up by the pervasive use of torture. Neither Egyptian, Moroccan, nor Saudi police are celebrated for their respect for suspects' rights. European justice systems, in contrast, have tried to preserve due process rights even in some outrageous cases. Members of the Dutch Hofstad Group had for years evaded prison through a series of infuriating technicalities. Though one member had indeed plotted bombings in the Netherlands, he was acquitted on the grounds that his use of the wrong fertilizer meant that the devices were unlikely actually to work as designed.

Also, tolerance of foreign extremists *might* represent a sound intelligence strategy. When a mosque like Finsbury Park operates openly, it is easy for authorities to keep track of the people who frequent it, to keep them under surveillance, and to record what is said and written in that radical ambience. Police can easily identify extremist leaders, chart their networks and connections, and persuade some to become informants. When police arrested the suspects in the airliner plots in August 2006, that action represented the culmination of over a year of observation and infiltration: the worst thing that could have happened in this process would have been any attempt to silence the extremists, to restrict their movements and organizing efforts, or to purge the radical mosques. According to rumors and media reports in 2002, even Abu Qatada may have served as a double agent for British intelligence. In contrast, suppressing overt centers of radicalism drives such activity underground, where its activities are harder to track. Better they should plot in plain sight.

Ultra-liberalism actually involves a degree of self-interest. Even very radical groups have usually respected the covenant of security, under which Muslims should refrain from attacking a nation that has protected them or treated them hospitably, especially when they are forced into exile. In the 1970s, Europe quelled the wave of Middle Eastern violence on its territory by negotiating a series of pacts with the radicals, under which militants could move freely, while not attacking European targets. Even Mullah Krekar, the Norwegian-based Islamist leader, refuses to support armed actions in Europe itself, though "Muslims who go to Afghanistan and Iraq to fight, that is an honor." In an interview published shortly before the 2005 London attacks, Muhajiroun militant Hassan Butt acknowledged that "a bomb in London would be strategically damaging to Muslims here. Immigration is lax in Britain. . . . London has more radical Muslims than anywhere in the Muslim world. A bomb would jeopardize everyone's position. There has to be a place we can come."[44]

Liberal asylum laws also reflect difficult judgments about the nature of political dissidents and the governments against whom they are rebelling, and it is not obvious which exiles or asylum seekers pose a truly dangerous threat to European states. Just as European Muslims come in many nationalities and religious styles, so do its Islamist militants, who might be Sunni or Shi'ite, pro-Iran or pro-Qaeda. Algerian Muslims naturally take a special interest in conflicts in their homeland and might be drawn into activities connected with the GIA or the Salafists; the completely separate struggles in Kashmir or Afghanistan prove critical in radicalizing Pakistanis. And while Europe is home to many veterans of international Islamist campaigns—in Afghanistan, Bosnia, Kashmir, Algeria, or Chechnya—by no means all necessarily want or plan to bring the war home, to undertake their future fighting in the streets of European cities. Since 2003, Islamist groups like the Algerian GSPC and Moroccan GICM have been involved in recruiting jihad fighters to travel to Iraq. That activity poses a real threat to Europe's allies, but not directly to European nations themselves.[45]

Governments often wink at revolutionary activities that are directed against overseas regimes. For an American parallel, we might think of the close relationship between Irish-American communities and the IRA, which to varying degrees has persisted for close to a century. Technically, supporting the IRA violates several U.S. neutrality laws, but the movement long drew its primary funding and material support from American donors, usually channeled through thinly disguised front groups and charities. In this instance too, the militant group was targeting a close ally of the host nation.

European governments must decide how far to wink at such use of their territory for overseas campaigns that do not directly affect them, especially when such activity provides a safety valve for militant sentiment that might otherwise be directed in the homeland. This issue arises in acute form over the struggle in Israel/Palestine. In the United

States, a group pledged to support armed Palestinian resistance against the state of Israel would be regarded as extremist and probably as pro-terrorist, though without too precise a definition of what separates terrorism from legitimate guerrilla warfare. Most European countries, however, would have greater tolerance for anti-Israel militants, especially when pro-Palestinian sentiment runs so high among local Muslim populations. Extremism is a relative concept. At the same time, radical exiles might prove useful intelligence assets, and today's refugee might someday become the leader of a government, who would be grateful for aid received in time of need. Assisting a Chechen guerrilla on the run might offend today's Russian government, but it could win rich rewards for a European government hoping to establish relations with a future Chechen state.

European tolerance of Islamism is based on much more than self-deluding liberalism. Even so, the violence of 2004–2005 created a much chillier environment for the militants and raised serious questions about Hassan Butt's belief that "there has to be a place we can come." If Islamists must indeed be granted a safe haven somewhere on the planet—which is dubious—European legislators and media have increasingly been asking why this should be found on their soil. Some of the most liberal European states have now adopted much harder-line policies toward militants, with a much greater use of deportation, even to repressive countries like Egypt. Italy has deported radical imams and others who reputedly incited terrorism, sending suspects to Senegal, Algeria, Morocco, and Tunisia. Spain, meanwhile, now keeps a close watch on the views expressed in sermons in mosques. Matters have changed decisively.[46]

From long experience, European states know that while terrorist activities can be kept to a minimum, they can never be eliminated altogether. However, even a full-scale terrorist campaign can be fought and overcome. In the 1970s, several west European nations faced a terrorist situation quite comparable to the worst scenarios imagined today in the Islamist context. Apart from the Palestinian and Middle Eastern groups, thousands of active militants fought for the domestic extreme left or the extreme right, and for ethnic nationalist causes. Groups were well armed, and some at least relied on bases and arms supplies in the former Eastern bloc. In some nations, especially Italy, terrorism came close to provoking outright civil war. A horror like the Bologna train bombing of 1980 killed more people than the London subway attacks, while the Birmingham pub bombings of 1974 represented the mega-terror of their day. And yet the terrorists were comprehensively defeated, and governments did not destroy democratic values in the process, or move indiscriminately against the communities among whom the terrorists found sympathy and refuge. If

terrorists have become more lethal since that time, then counterter-
rorist agencies have also acquired far more sophisticated tactics and
technologies. The authorities would assuredly win a renewed war,
though many innocent people would be killed or maimed in the
process.

Obviously, preventing a widespread resort to armed action is critically important. Europe today possesses significant networks of deeply
disaffected activists, who at least potentially could reach out to the
wider constituency of young Muslims. To some extent, responding to
violence and terrorism is a matter of familiar political solutions, of intelligence, diplomacy, and counterinsurgency. Diplomatic means would
also contribute to resolving that threat—for instance by resolving
crises in Palestine, Kashmir, Iraq, or Iran, But any long-term solution
must come within European nations themselves, by reducing tensions
between ethnic communities and Europe's mainstream societies. This
means removing festering grievances that potentially drive people to
militancy, but it also demands serious thought about the best means of
integrating newer ethnic groups into European nations, of accommodating religious needs and interests that until very recently would have
seemed very strange to European policy makers. And these solutions
might demand policies that depart significantly from the political assumptions of late twentieth-century European societies.

10

Transforming Europe

Freedom Go to Hell.

Placard displayed by
Muslim protester in
London, 2006

While most agree that Europe's newer ethnic communities should be harmonized into a new society, the means of achieving this are by no means obvious. Americans can sympathize with contemporary European dilemmas, given their own long debates over minority populations and controversies over assimilation, integration, and multiculturalism. Prior to the 1960s, many American liberals assumed that ending racial discrimination would mean admitting all people of whatever race to the rights and privileges of white Americans, whose values they would accept wholeheartedly. They soon found, of course, that blacks and Latinos had no wish to accept integration if that meant absorption. In Europe too, assimilation may not be a desirable goal if it means the renunciation of distinctive cultural patterns and religious beliefs. Europeans also must decide how far cultural and religious identities should be prized and preserved, and the social costs of doing so.

Domestically, the rise of religious diversity forces European nations to confront issues of tolerance and minority rights that most had thought long settled. How can societies balance the right to religious freedom with the need for balance and secularism in public life? Resolving the competing pressures toward conflict and assimilation challenges European values of tolerance and pluralism. The dilemma can be phrased simply. European states, and the European Union, preach certain core values, including secularism, tolerance, individualism, and progressive views on gender, family, and sexuality. At the same time, they must deal with communities who differ radically from these values at many key points. We are only beginning to see the legal and constitutional battles arising from these struggles.

In fairness to European states, we must acknowledge the very short historical time period in which the present situation has existed: realistically, it would be amazing if cultural conflicts were not developing. Even so, the continuing scale of divisions raises serious questions, all the more so when the European Union seems on the verge of admitting significant new Muslim populations, from Turkey and perhaps someday Morocco. While such admissions make sense in the long run, it is amazing that they are being debated with so little attention to the cultural and religious consequences for a Europe still trying to define its basic values. The prospect of Turkish entry in particular indicates once more that European elites are not only thoroughly secular in their own ideology but they are reluctant to credit the power and authenticity of religious motivations among others. If Europe does succeed in accommodating its Muslim minorities, this happy outcome will occur despite its political and cultural leaders, rather than because of them.

Religion and Race

Historian Sir John Seeley once complained that the British won their global empire "in a fit of absence of mind," and that phrase offers a fair description of the process by which contemporary Europe acquired its multifaith character. Few European states gave much thought to the religious diversity they were creating through immigration. Some countries agonized over the racial dilemmas they might be facing, particularly when immigration debates coincided with the fierce race rioting in U.S. cities during the 1960s. It was in 1968, immediately after the assassination of Martin Luther King, Jr., that British conservative politician Enoch Powell contemplated the prospect of future racial conflict in his own land. He warned, "As I look ahead, I am filled with foreboding. Like the Roman, I seem to see the River Tiber foaming with much blood."

Yet even in such jeremiads, religion featured little, amazingly so given Europe's long tradition of Muslim nightmares: though who could take such a prospect seriously in modern times? As late as 1973, when Jean Raspail wrote *The Camp of the Saints*, his sensational account of a white Europe overthrown by mass Third-World immigration, Islam features little in the work. The nonwhite masses of impoverished invaders are primarily Hindus from the Ganges. In liberal productions too, many authors and filmmakers dealt with the encounter between white Europeans and African or Asian immigrants who were Muslims, but the religious elements were subsumed in the racial. David Edgar's classic political play *Destiny* explores the conflict between Asian immigrants in Britain and a surging fascist movement, but it is never clear whether the migrants are Hindu or Sikh. Nor does religion enter much into a film like *Fear Eats the Soul* (1974), the story of a German woman who marries a Moroccan migrant. The racial themes are weighty and shocking enough in their own right.[1]

There were many reasons for this neglect of religious distinctions. Chiefly, Muslim numbers were still relatively small in 1970, and white Europeans saw little reason to worry about their own population growth. They were not many years removed from their own baby boom and were more likely to be concerned about the dangers of population explosion rather than decline. In the 1960s and early 1970s, too, most observers assumed that religion was declining worldwide in the face of secularization, or at least evolving into privatized forms, and few thought that religious motives might once again incite political conflict. (Although the troubles in Northern Ireland then appeared wildly exceptional, such a religious conflict appears much less startling in retrospect.) European politics through the 1970s and 1980s were dominated by issues of East-West confrontation and by the threat that the continent would become a militarized European theater in a U.S.-Soviet confrontation. And even at this late date, internal subversion still implied the risk of Marxist or leftist activism. Realistically, no rational western European intellectual or policy maker worried about the presence of (then) perhaps 3 million largely poor immigrants in their countries. Even in the 1990s, with the Cold War over, concern about Islam remained a fringe issue, largely the preserve of the nonrespectable Right. Only as recently as September 11 did the notion of a Muslim Challenge decisively enter European public discourse.

Through the 1980s, most leftist or liberal Europeans saw the new ethnic presence in racial terms, a local parallel to the long U.S. dilemma over dealing with its own African-Americans. Problems could thus be solved by a recognition of difference, but above all, a refusal to succumb to prejudice or bigotry. If the United States could, after so many centuries, accomplish its civil rights revolution, then Europe should be able to solve its own newer color problem with much less difficulty.

The more the European far right denounced immigrants in racial terms, the stronger the analogies became to American conditions. When British skinheads adopted the loathsome pastime of "paki-bashing," they were attacking Asians indiscriminately, regardless of their religious identity. In the early 1980s, German neo-Nazis were still writing graffiti warning, "Yesterday the Jews, tomorrow the Turks"—Turks, not Muslims. The National Front flourished on the British far right in the 1970s, while the French Front National was founded in 1972. Both parties, like other counterparts across the continent, preached that the presence of African and Asian migrants would spawn violence and civil unrest, regardless of their religious character. Only recently have such

organizations turned to attacking Islam as such, presenting it as a revolutionary antiwhite ideology (and thus harking back to earlier ultra-
right thinkers, such as Lothrop Stoddard). The modern British National
Party (BNP) denounces "islands of Islam in our communities," portending "the imminent extinction of the white man." Against such enemies, it is natural for moderate Europeans to see hostility to Islam as
a simple form of racism.[2]

Muslim organizations themselves have appropriated this racism
theme effectively, presenting any criticisms of Islam under the blanket
term Islamophobia. The term literally implies that criticism reflects an
irrational fear of Islam, on the model of homophobia, and the analogy
demands that such behavior be properly stigmatized alongside other
forms of racism and anti-Semitism. Undeniably, criticisms of Islam do
sometimes shade into flagrant attacks on Muslims as a community, as
well as ethnic slurs against the African and Asian adherents of the religion in contemporary Europe. Yet the term Islamophobia must be
treated with caution, since it is often applied in a more sweeping sense,
as a means of disarming reasonable criticism not just of the religion but
of any actions taken in its name, even by its most extreme and militant
followers. Labeling such critiques a *–phobia* by definition means that they
are irrational and, presumably, are a matter for the psychologist rather
than the political scientist.[3]

Tolerating Intolerance

Viewing Europe's Muslim communities in ethnic or racial terms was
certainly not foolish in its own right, especially since it avoided applying the blanket religious label to such very diverse communities. And
as we have seen, an ethnic approach works well in explaining recent
riots and disorders. In practice, though, the American analogy encouraged a multicultural model, in which the state acknowledges group
identities, and recognizes and celebrates diversity, allowing a generous
latitude in interpreting differences. The problem with this approach, of
course, is that it assumes a broad consensus between minority and majority communities about core beliefs and cultural values, which is the
basis of any effective pluralism. As we have already seen in matters of
gender and family, though, that assumption is not always correct. Multiculturalism is also challenged when minority groups hold views or
pursue activities that are anathema to the mainstream society, which
reject its most deeply cherished beliefs.[4]

The bitterest conflicts have arisen over words or images that offend religious believers and that are seen as an attack on the religious
system itself. Many European countries provide some protection for
religious sensibilities, and blasphemy laws at least exist on the books
in some. With a few exceptions, though, such laws have not been

enforced in recent years. Muslim societies, however, have never given up their religious sanctions against blasphemy, and these laws returned with new force during the Islamic revival of the 1980s, in Pakistan and elsewhere. The clash of cultures emerged with full force in 1989 with the Rushdie affair. Fierce protests in European countries regularly involved book burning, an action with horrible connotations of the Nazi past, while protesters openly demanded Rushdie's death. In Britain, the secretary of the Bradford Council of Mosques, said: "Muslims here would kill him, and I would willingly sacrifice my own life and that of my children to carry out the ayatollah's wishes should the opportunity arise." At one meeting, Kalim Siddiqui demanded, "I would like every Muslim to raise his hand in agreement with the death sentence on Salman Rushdie. . . . [Muslims] are rapidly coming to the conclusion that they will have to fight to defend Islam in Britain."[5]

While it is easy to dismiss such remarks as empty rhetoric, they do indicate a fundamental conflict over the acceptable limits of speech, with most Europeans regarding the casual death threats with just as much horror as Muslim activists regarded *The Satanic Verses*—or at least, regarded reports of it: surely none of them ever read the book. Henceforward, many secular Europeans began to question older assumptions about the possibility of living easily alongside Islam and indeed asked worrying questions about Islam itself, at least in its contemporary political manifestation. Put crudely, the Rushdie affair raised questions about the presumed equality of religions and whether some might be actively harmful or dangerous. In the stark words of Melanie Phillips, from this point onward, "the promotion of Islam in Britain became fused with an agenda of murder."

Cartoon Jihad

More recently, clashes between mainstream European values and Muslim sensitivities have been highlighted by the ferocious controversy over the cartoons published in the Danish regional newspaper *Jyllands-Posten*. In 2005, a children's book author complained that he could not find an artist willing to illustrate a work about Muhammad. In response, editor Flemming Rose was shocked by the general atmosphere of fear and self-censorship, and he accordingly commissioned and printed the famous twelve cartoons, the most notorious of which depicted the prophet with his turban in the form of a bomb. Initially, the affair attracted only local resentment, until one Danish activist—Ahmed Abu Laban—took the matter worldwide. Abu Laban himself is a Palestinian with ties to the Muslim Brotherhood. Adding some still more shocking images as if they were part of the original package, Abu Laban began a tour of Muslim nations and institutions, provoking increasing rage. His activism must be understood against a background of growing Islamist radicalism in Denmark itself. Confrontations with the Danish government had also been growing since 2001, when a new conservative regime showed itself determined to encourage integration among Denmark's Muslim immigrants.[6]

By the end of 2005, protests were erupting in Europe and around the Muslim world, as several Muslim nations demanded that the Danish government apologize. One agenda item here was that nations like Egypt and Syria were trying to burnish their Muslim credentials while averting international criticisms for various misdeeds. Muslim nations launched a boycott of Danish goods. In some nations, such as Nigeria, the conflict spawned open violence, causing dozens of deaths. The Danish cartoonists were directly targeted, with the youth organization of the Pakistani Jamaat-e-Islami offering a bounty of 7,000 euros for their deaths.[7]

Some protesters in Europe itself overtly threatened armed violence. By no means all protesters acted thus, and many of the demonstrations were calm and dignified, but some of the activists were spoiling for a fight. In Britain, protesters waved placards proclaiming, among other things, "Behead those who insult Islam"; "Europe you will pay— your 9/11 is on its way"; "You'll come crawling when the mujahedeen come roaring"; or "Remember, Remember the Eleventh of September"— a parody of the popular ditty sung on Guy Fawkes Day. Such comments had a special impact in a country still recovering from the July 7 subway bombings. One slogan threatened, "Europe you will pay, the Fantastic Four are on their way," a direct reference to the subway bombs. Interestingly, these protests were condemned by most shades of Muslim opinion, even including Hizb ut-Tahrir. The most outrageous demonstrations were orchestrated by Al-Ghurabaa', the offshoot of the banned Mujahiroun.[8]

This controversy focused critical divisions between Muslim and non-Muslim perceptions. One of course is the extreme sensitivity about the representation of the Prophet Muhammad, especially in an insulting context, involving violence, fanaticism, or promiscuous sexuality. American conservatives described the event as the "cartoon jihad," implying that launching a holy war over such a cause was cartoonish in the sense of extreme, bizarre, and even comical: the best-known American cartoons are probably those associated with the series Looney Tunes. But the prime difference here is not a matter of Christianity versus Islam but rather one of date and context: it has not been long since a comparably insulting representation of Jesus would have been found horrifying. (In 1922, a British man received nine months' hard labor for comparing Jesus to a circus clown.) Of course, Muslim demands in the Danish controversy went much further in terms of protecting religious sensibilities than were customary in most European nations, and Europeans were appalled by the threats of violence.[9]

Almost as startling was the unanimity that the protests demonstrated. For years, cautious scholars had stressed the critical differences that separated Europe's Muslim communities, emphasizing that their grievances were chiefly economic or social in nature. Watching the protests on their streets, Europeans found it easy to conclude that Islam was after all the core issue, and that the Umma— the universal brotherhood of Muslims, regardless of nationality—was a tangible reality. The protesters' demands also made illuminating assumptions about the relationship of private and public spheres. Muslim demands for a state apology presupposed a situation familiar in most Middle Eastern nations, in which the media serve the government, which decides the tone and content of material published. The idea that Danish newspapers might be wholly independent of the state was rarely admitted, and the implication was that press freedom was as notional a concept as in Egypt or Algeria.

Learning to Be Silent

Although the cartoon affair attracted most public attention, it was by no means the only confrontation of its kind. Over the past decade, Muslim activists have challenged images and art works carrying a cultural and historical significance far beyond that attached to the Danish cartoons. Given the long tradition of conflict between Christianity and Islam, cultural and intellectual as well as military, it is not surprising to find many monuments in Europe commemorating a deep-rooted suspicion of Muhammad and his religion. A medieval fresco of the Last Judgment in Bologna cathedral depicts Muhammad being thrown into Hell, naked, with a snake wrapped around his body and attended by a demon. Such a depiction has naturally served as a focus for Italian Muslim protesters. They further demand that schools with large immigrant populations not be required to read Dante's *Inferno*, which not only consigns Muhammad to deepest Hell but imagines him being regularly disemboweled and reassembled through the rest of eternity. For Dante, being split in this way was the only proper judgment for a heretic who had so grievously divided the church. Spain's Muslims have protested statues of Saint James the Moor-Slayer, Santiago Matamoros, a figure long central to Spanish concepts of national identity and cultural pride. In 2004, authorities at Santiago de Compostela finally agreed to remove paintings depicting a warrior James triumphing over defeated and slaughtered Moors.[10]

More contemporary art has also proved vulnerable. In 2000, a Dutch company planned to stage the opera *Aisha and the Women of Medina*, based on a novel by prestigious Algerian author Assia Djebar. Though the work contained nothing vaguely as shocking as the *Satanic Verses*, the opera was canceled under threats of provoking a new

Rushdie affair. French activists have mobilized to suppress the reading of Voltaire's play *Fanaticism, or Mahomet the Prophet*. Muslim challenges to artistic freedom suggest deep hostility to several cherished values of modern Europe, including the role of the state, the independence of the media, the right to artistic self-expression, the virtue of individual dissent, and the role of the collective as against the individual.

Yet the threat of violence demands that Muslim concerns be heard, even to the point of accepting quite rigid self-censorship. One of the theatrical triumphs of London's 2005 season was a production of Christopher Marlowe's *Tamburlaine*, but most of the audience failed to realize that they were seeing a slightly abridged version. Gone was the scene in which the tyrant burned the Quran, or declared that Muhammad "remains in hell." The director made the changes without any pressure from Muslim organizations. Indeed, the media secretary of the Muslim Council of Britain (MCB) saw little risk of controversy, arguing that "in the context of a fictional play, I don't think it will have offended many people." The following year, Berlin's Deutsche Oper canceled a planned run of Mozart's opera *Idomeneo*, which culminated with a display of the severed heads of religious leaders, including Muhammad. In this instance, the opera company's director caved in not to actual protests, but to a police analysis that warned of possible disturbances. German Chancellor Angela Merkel accurately condemned the decision as "self-censorship out of fear."[11]

Regulating Speech

Responding to these events, and especially to the cartoon affair, some European thinkers and policy makers have demonstrated a remarkable willingness to concede that Muslim protesters did indeed have a point. Günter Grass, for instance, saw the cartoons as "reminiscent of the famous newspaper of the Nazi era, the *Stürmer*, which published anti-Semitic cartoons of a similar style. . . . Where does the West come by all this arrogance in dictating what is right and wrong?" European officials, meanwhile, have made every effort to be conciliatory. After the newspaper *France-Soir* published the cartoons, the French embassy in Algeria issued something close to an apology. (The newspaper's owner, a Coptic Christian, fired its editor.) The statement asserted that France was as "deeply attached to the spirit of tolerance and to respect of religious belief as we are to the principle of freedom of the press. In this light, France condemns all those who hurt individuals in their beliefs or religious convictions." Bill Clinton denounced the cartoons as "appalling" and "outrageous."[12]

Pressure to expand hate speech laws moved to the global stage. Members of the Organization of the Islamic Conference asked the United Nations to support enhanced protection for religion, and the issue surfaced in debates over the new Human Rights Council. The UN's Commissioner for Human Rights, Louise Ardour, declared that the Danish cartoons constituted "an unacceptable disrespect" to Islam, and she appointed a special investigator to examine Danish Islamophobia.[13]

While formally acknowledging a right of free speech, Islamists are correct to point out that the modern European legal and political tradition has always recognized the necessity of restraint. As Sheikh al-Qaradawi notes, European laws enforce tight limits in some areas, especially in the matter of Holocaust denial, and he was writing before historian David Irving found himself imprisoned in Austria for this very offense. Germany and other nations are ferocious in prohibiting the display or possession of Nazi symbols or regalia, while even devoted adherents of free speech rights acknowledge the justice of suppressing anti-Semitic comments. Al-Qaradawi argued,

> The Jews are protected by laws . . . and nobody can say even one word about the number [of victims] in the alleged Holocaust. Nobody can do so, even if he is writing an M.A. or Ph.D. thesis, and discussing it scientifically. Such claims are not acceptable. . . . We want laws protecting the holy places, the prophets, and Allah's messengers.

In 2006, the French Parliament criminalized the act of denying the Armenian genocide of 1915. Superficially, then, framing Muslim demands as a call for equal treatment of minority religions could prove attractive.[14]

But in the face of a frontal attack on free speech, conciliatory gestures looked like an unacceptable bow to repression. The European Union's foreign policy and security chief Javier Solana assured Arab nations that "you can be sure we will do our utmost to prevent such a thing [the Muhammad cartoons] from happening again." Yet such an assurance could scarcely be made in the context of free media and rather suggested a regime of state control. Franco Frattini, the EU commissioner for Justice, Freedom and Security, specifically proposed that media submit to a voluntary code of conduct. By doing so, "the press will give the Muslim world the message: we are aware of the consequences of exercising the right of free expression, we can and we are ready to self-regulate that right." Many observers found such promises terrifying, and not surprisingly, the nations most reluctant to consider such compromises were those eastern European states only recently emerging from Communism.[15]

Some European nations considered responding to calls to respect religious sensitivities by reviving long dormant blasphemy laws. In Britain, a celebrated trial as recently as 1977 showed that the ancient law against blasphemous libel still had teeth, at least in the specifically Christian context. In this case, the newspaper *Gay News* was successfully prosecuted for publishing a poem portraying Jesus as a promiscuous homosexual and thereby spreading "contemptuous, reviling, scurrilous or ludicrous matter relating to God." In the Netherlands, following the battle over the film *Submission,* the justice minister proposed reviving and enforcing a 1932 law prohibiting "scornful blasphemy." The goal, he added, was not to protect religion but rather to prevent political turmoil and destabilization. "It is not about religion specifically, but any harmful comments in general." Italian authorities have dusted off the old law, dating from the fascist era, which penalizes "whoever offends the state's religion by defaming it." The law's protections now extend to "any religion acknowledged by the state," which includes Islam. Even Denmark still has a blasphemy law, though authorities decided not to invoke it against the cartoons.[16]

It would not take much ingenuity to apply such laws to something like the cartoons, and the laws probably would pass legal muster at both national and European levels. In 1989, the British Board of Film Censors banned the film *Visions of Ecstasy,* which luridly portrayed St. Teresa receiving an erotic vision of the crucified Christ. The director protested that the existence of a blasphemy law was an absurd anachronism, but the European Court of Human Rights decided that freedom of speech also demanded "a duty to avoid as far as possible an expression that is, in regard to objects of veneration, gratuitously offensive to others and profanatory." Nor, in light of recent demographic trends, does it seem logical to confine such a privilege to Christian "veneration" alone. In Britain, 58 percent of Muslims surveyed agreed with the statement that, despite the right to free speech, people who insult Islam should face criminal prosecution.[17]

Legality apart, the cartoon conflict has de facto reinstated sanctions against blasphemy in Europe, in the sense that force and the threat of force have succeeded completely in preventing offensive images being shown and in deterring any possible future repetition of the conduct. In practice, European media responded by accepting exactly the kind of self-censorship advocated by European bureaucrats, and already adopted by theaters. In a little-noticed aftermath to the cartoon affair, an Anglican paper in Wales published a mild cartoon featuring Muhammad. On realizing the potential for conflict, the proprietors immediately withdrew the offending item and apologized profusely to Muslim authorities. Meanwhile, the Rotterdam film festival canceled a screening of *Submission* that was to be included as part of a season of censored films. Also canceled was a showing in the EU assembly's press center in Brussels, a venue that should have come within the protection of the European parliament.[18]

Some observers see in the restrictions on religious criticism not just a simple curtailing of free speech but also a newly privileged role for the faith of Islam. After all, Christianity and Islam differ in terms of projecting their views in the wider society. Christianity emphasizes the conversion of individuals, who might as a group have the ability to affect wider values, or in biblical terms, to serve as the leaven that permeates the whole loaf. Islam's traditions, in contrast, are communal and collective, and so is the act of conversion. Islam dates its calendar from the creation of the first Muslim state and society, at Madinah in A.D. 622. Through history, Muslims have sought to create states and legal systems that are in accordance with Islam and Islamic law, presuming that mass conversions will follow gradually, perhaps over centuries—and their expectations have repeatedly been justified. In the meantime, faithful Muslims believe they have a duty to remove laws and customs flagrantly at variance with Islam. From this perspective, if a society conforms itself to Muslim legal and social norms, then it is already on the way to conversion. Of course, Ayaan Hirsi Ali had little time for anti-cartoon protests. Rejecting appeals to "religious sensitivities," she declares that "demanding that people who do not accept Muhammad's teachings should refrain from drawing him is not a request for respect but a demand for submission."[19]

Free Speech and Hate Speech

Together with several related conflicts, the cartoon war has suggested a sharp conflict between basic liberties, between free speech and the right to exercise one's religion. A revival of blasphemy laws faced the difficulty that the offense sounded so archaic, but other efforts to limit speech used much more current justifications. In the name of preventing "hate speech" against particular religions, European states have extended laws originally intended to fight incitement to violence, and have expanded their scope to cover attacks on religions or religious doctrines. This tendency has resulted in draconian prosecutions for what look like forceful arguments rather than "fighting words," as in American constitutional doctrine.

The attempt to regulate intemperate speech has produced results that alarm European secularists and would trouble many Americans. If an American political leader denounced some particular race or religion, that act would probably blight his or her public career and perhaps lead to protests, but it would not be a matter for official intervention. Evangelist Franklin Graham faced no criminal charges for characterizing Islam as "a very evil and wicked religion." In England, in contrast, promoting racial or religious hatred can be a criminal offense. In 2006, BNP leader Nick Griffin was tried (though ultimately acquitted) for asserting, among other things, that Asian Muslims were trying to conquer the United Kingdom, and for describing Islam as "this wicked, vicious faith" that "has expanded from a handful of cranky lunatics about 1,300 years ago."[20]

Other recent cases involve the prosecution of major writers, rather than gutter journalists, for remarks on Islam that should be seen as trenchant and polemical rather than abusive. Italian journalist Oriana Fallaci was prosecuted for her attacks on Islam after 9/11, in her book *The Rage and the Pride*. In this work, she attacked "arrogant . . . Albanians, Sudanese, Bengalis, Tunisians, Algerians, Pakistanis, Nigerians who with much fervor contribute to the commerce of drugs and prostitution." Muslims "breed like rats." She also found Pope John Paul II too soft on the Muslim danger, asking: "Your Holiness, why in the name of the only God, don't you take them into the Vatican? On the condition that they don't smear with shit the Sistine Chapel." In a follow-up volume, *The Force of Reason,* she warned of Europe's descent into a barbarous Eurabia: "Europe becomes more and more a province of Islam, a colony of Islam. In each of our cities lies a second city: a Muslim city, a city run by the Koran. A stage in the Islamic expansionism." Yet despite their harshness, Fallaci's opinions struck a chord: *The Force of Reason* sold 800,000 copies in Italy alone.[21]

Another controversial figure was French novelist Michel Houellebecq, who was tried (and acquitted) for inciting hatred when he denounced Islam as "the dumbest religion" ("la religion la plus con") in an interview with the magazine *Lire*. He added that "when you read the Koran, it's appalling, appalling." Official interventions in such cases herald a kind of ultra-sensitive group libel law radically different from anything in U.S. experience.[22]

The conflict between different concepts of liberties arose in acute form in Great Britain, which since 1976 has enforced severe restrictions on speech directed against racial minorities. This category was taken to include Jews and Sikhs but did not include Muslims, since Islam is not a racial label. In 2005–2006, the British government tried to expand these protections under a Racial and Religious Hatred Bill that would make it a criminal offense to incite "religious hatred through threatening words, actions and insults." A broad coalition of intellectuals and libertarians complained that the new law would severely restrict serious debate over religion. The campaign found an effective face in comedian Rowan Atkinson, best known through his role in the BBC shows *Mr. Bean* and *Blackadder*. In 2006, opponents achieved a rare example of a victory over Tony Blair's substantial parliamentary majority, forcing the government to water down the law. Under the revised version, anyone accused under the law could invoke freedom of speech safeguards to show that the words had no "hateful" intent.[23]

Despite this victory, it is remarkable that a liberal society could come so close (one vote in parliament) to passing a law that would probably have been used to suppress virtually any unflattering reference to Islam. To indicate the possible outcome, some British Muslim leaders had threatened to take action against uses of the term "Muslim terrorists," since that linkage demeaned the religion. This approach has won the sympathy of EU authorities, whose recent guidelines urge member states to eschew terms like "Islamic terrorist," preferring "terrorists who abusively invoke Islam."[24]

At the same time, European governments long proved themselves uncertain about how to respond to various forms of hate speech by Muslim activists themselves when the words were delivered in the form of religious exhortations. Matters have changed, however, following the recent terrorist upsurge, and the furious incitements to armed terrorism delivered by Britain's Abu Hamza did indeed lead to his imprisonment. Interestingly, the rabid extremism of some of the cartoon protests themselves forced European governments to reexamine what had seemed their limitless tolerance of loud-mouthed dissent. In Britain, the overt celebrations of the subway bombings and the open threats of repetition were sufficiently maddening to force official intervention, and several protesters were charged with "using words or written material to stir up racial hatred." One of those charged was a leader of al-Ghurabaa'. Muslim protests in Britain were also counterproductive in other ways, in persuading enough members of parliament to vote against the proposed new law against religious hatred. Another law that actually did pass in 2006 criminalized any action or speech that "glorifies the commission or preparation" of acts of terrorism, a concept that undoubtedly will lead to intense legal debate in years to come. Given the very broad definitions that some writers have applied to "terrorism," there is no reason the law should not be used to penalize commemorations of the American, French, or Irish revolutions. British authorities are now contemplating an unprecedented ban on publicly burning the national flag.

Though prosecuting seditious speech by some Muslim activists, European governments have not hitherto intervened forcefully as they might against other rhetoric not openly directed against the state. Although Muslim activists demanded stricter speech codes and hate crime laws, they faced the obvious paradox that the cartoon portrayals of Muhammad were nothing like as offensive as the outrageous portrayals of Jews and Jewish themes that are a staple of Islamist pamphlets and periodicals, both domestically and internationally. At the height of the cartoon controversy, the hit film in Turkey was *Valley of the Wolves* (*Kurtlar Vadisi Irak*), an exposé of Jewish and American plots in which an American-Jewish doctor harvested the organs of prison inmates for wealthy patients in New York, London, and Israel. The film was a sensation in Turkish areas of Germany, and Berlin audiences responded to scenes of the defeat and killing of Americans with cries of "Allahu Akbar!" While demanding that Denmark apologize for the misdeeds of its media, Muslim nations have not offered their own regrets for such eruptions.[25]

Against Multiculturalism

In the 1970s, the idea that non-European immigrants could not be assimilated into white Christian societies was the familiar currency of the extreme right, of political movements that shaded into neo-fascist and neo-Nazi ideologies. Since 2001, though, such views have become increasingly common in respectable politics, even on the left. After years of regarding figures like Enoch Powell as political lepers, Europeans with solid left-liberal credentials found themselves asking urgently whether radical forms of Islam might indeed provide the kind of ideology that really could generate "rivers of blood." In 2002, the very liberal German Foreign Minister Joschka Fischer asked whether Islamic traditions and teachings were compatible with the values of modern Western societies. Radical Islamists contributed to this reassessment by adopting positions and political styles that, for Europeans, brought back the worst memories of the 1930s. It was not difficult to find a convenient political label for a movement that preached anti-Semitism, burned books, and used paramilitary groups to dominate the streets.[26]

While there was agreement that many Muslims were failing to integrate into European societies, it was more difficult to specify what exactly immigrants are expected to assimilate *to*. What exactly were the core European values, the fundamental tenets of Britishness or Frenchness? Many European countries traditionally defined their citizenship in terms of birth or blood, making it difficult for outsiders to join the national community, although they might well be welcomed as guests. Becoming Danish, say, is not an easy or natural process if one is not born in Denmark. Some more heterogeneous countries like France or Britain offered the possibility of joining in common loyalty to an overarching national state, in loyalty to crown or flag, but even these national loyalties have also been undermined in recent years. Since the 1940s, most European countries have consciously tried to move away from national identification and to encourage a new European consciousness, largely leaving the potent symbols of patriotism to the lower classes, or to the far right.

Sporting events offer virtually the only acceptable forms of patriotic expression. When the leader of the MCB is asked about his patriotism, he replies that he loves soccer, and that "when England plays, we always fly the flag." The high point of racial integration in modern France probably occurred in 1998 when Zinedine Zidane scored the two goals that won the World Cup for France, becoming a national hero to all French people of whatever religion or ethnicity. After years of deep embarrassment about tokens of nationalism, it was only during the 2006 World Cup that Germans finally felt confident enough to fly their black, red, and gold flag. And in a trend that surprised pessimists, German Muslims were among the most dedicated fans of the national team.[27]

Sport aside, though, immigrants are offered little in the way of national identity to which they can or should develop loyalty, however much they may want to. In all the depressing surveys suggesting that minorities of European Muslims reject their new countries, we should not forget that majorities do in fact identify with France, Britain, or Germany and hope that their children will be even more assimilated. But assimilated to what? Muslim feminist Neclá Kelek remarked reasonably enough that "someone once asked me if Germany was my homeland. I could only say that not even Germans consider Germany their homeland. How are we supposed to integrate in a place like that?" Critically, European loyalties are not linked to principles of rights or values in the way that they are in the United States. For all some Americans despair about the state of their melting pot, Europeans regard the modern American experience with integration as an exemplary success in contrast to their own failures. To quote a writer in the French *Libération*, immigrants in the United States threw themselves wholeheartedly into "the American Dream": in contrast, "there is no French, Dutch or other European dream. You emigrate here to escape poverty and nothing more."[28]

America's strong sense of national identity owes much to what is still a broad underlying consensus about rights and values. In the United States, a person who advocates undemocratic or intolerant views is condemned as un-American and violating the principles of the Constitution to which all swear allegiance. Even Americans with very little education have a good general idea of the terms and principles of the Bill of Rights. Europe offers nothing comparable and shows no signs of doing so. Though its proposed Constitution includes noble sentiments about rights and values, they are lost amid the bureaucratic verbiage. If, then, someone wishes to assert liberal values, he or she cannot do so simply by citing the traditional principles of Europe or its constituent states. Arguably, if a "mainstream" set of values can be deduced from the last 150 years or so of European history, they would be authoritarian, military, and hyper-nationalist, rather than pluralist and liberal.

In recent years, though, the urgency of the religious confrontation has forced European thinkers to define their beliefs far more explicitly and to specify the core values that newcomers should accept, however implausibly these can be presented as "fundamentally European." Apart from free speech and tolerance, values of gender equality and sexual freedom also occupy a central role. Inherent to this process of definition is the belief that liberal values are not just good in themselves, equal to those of other intellectual traditions, but they are actually superior. Wouter Bos, leader of the Dutch Labor Party, declared that "unlimited migration and failing integration are a serious threat to solidarity and to the degree of welfare sharing we are proud of as social democrats." He continued,

Those who favor more economic migration into western societies—and even those who simply consider it inevitable—will only be politically credible if they are also credible on the core contract of our society. It requires all citizens to accept civil liberties—including freedom of expression, the equal treatment of men, women, heterosexuals and homosexuals, the separation of church and state, the principle of democratic government and the rule of law.[29]

The idea of a "core contract" was widely cited. German novelist Peter Schneider remarked that Europe was now

challenged to defend its values and principles both at home and abroad. The inner lines of conflict which we are seeing in current discussions on integration, forced marriage, the "Muslim Test" and the cartoon conflict display three broad themes: equality and sexual self-determination of women and homosexuals; freedom of opinion and the press; and the rights of the secular vis-à-vis the sacral world. In a nutshell, the conflict puts in question some of the major achievements of the Enlightenment, the foundation of secular Western societies. The West can only negotiate these questions at the risk of repudiating its soul.

Angela Merkel agreed that "the notion of multiculturalism has fallen apart. Anyone coming here must respect our constitution and tolerate our Western and Christian roots."[30]

Criticism of multiculturalism has been acute in Great Britain. To quote Salman Rushdie, "Multiculturalism . . . has all too often become mere cultural relativism, a much less defensible proposition, under cover of which much that is reactionary and oppressive—of women, for example—can be justified." Another powerful voice is Trevor Phillips, a popular black broadcaster who chairs Britain's Commission for Racial Equality. He has "warned that the country is 'sleepwalking towards segregation,' with society ever more fragmented by ethnicity and religion. Using remarkably frank language, Phillips added that parts of some cities will soon be 'black holes into which no one goes without fear.' "[31]

Some left and liberal thinkers now use an argument that for years has been the preserve of the political right, namely, that multiculturalism seemed to mean the glorification of every society and tradition in the world except the mainstream, which was consistently denigrated. York's Archbishop Sentamu called for a new pride in English cultural identity, complaining that multiculturalism had "seemed to imply, wrongly for me, 'let other cultures be allowed to express themselves but do not let the majority culture at all tell us its glories, its struggles, its joys, its pains.' "[32]

Seeing Muslims

The attack on multiculturalism raises other issues about the by now well-established methods used to integrate new ethnic communities.

To take one question that has emerged forcefully, should western European states see Muslims at all? The question seems absurd, given the undeniable presence of some 15 million residents who nominally have some connection to that faith. But should states react to them primarily according to their religious credentials, as opposed to some other status that they may possess? Following the multicultural model, European states have since the 1990s responded to Muslims as Muslims, as part of a community with a distinctive religious and cultural leadership. In recent years, however, concern about radicalized Islamic politics has provoked a frontal attack on this aspect of multicultural politics. While Europeans initially failed to appreciate the religious and cultural distinctiveness of their new immigrants, they have arguably over-compensated for this in later years.

Most states agree that the best way to prevent violence or disaffection is to ensure that Muslims are conscious of having a voice in democratic society. France has failed dismally in this regard, as the nation's large Muslim communities have no representation whatever in that nation's Chamber of Deputies. In other countries, though, including Belgium, prominent Muslims have succeeded in entering the political mainstream. Since the late 1980s, Britain too has its parliamentary cohort of Asian origin, now with several members of Pakistani background, though the number still falls short of what it should be if it reflected the Muslim share of the population as a whole. The fact that a constituency elects an individual Muslim to represent it leaves no doubt about that person's credentials to speak for at least part of his or her community. More difficult though is the question of recognizing community and religious organizations to serve as voices of Islam, and that has been a controversial question in recent years.

The logic of seeking out moderate and responsible groups is convincing, especially as a means of heading off Islamic extremism. If in fact rioters or terrorists are motivated by religious zeal, then in theory they should pay some heed to official condemnation; and if militants are recalcitrant, then they would find themselves isolated in their communities. (Both theories have proved dubious in practice.) Moreover, the fact that a visibly Muslim body is negotiating with the senior levels of a European government would give ordinary Muslims a sense that they had a voice in national affairs. The practice fits splendidly with the goals of multiculturalism, of acknowledging the different values and interests of communities. Unfortunately, it has also promoted the role of very conservative Muslim activists who on some occasions are themselves scarcely less radical and anti-assimilationist than the extremists they are meant to counterbalance.

Despite its commitment to absolute secularism, to *laicité*, the French government has long pursued a policy of identifying and cultivating moderate Muslim leaders, usually clergy. In 2003, France promoted a new governing body of French Islam, the Conseil Français du Culte Musulman, CFCM, under the leadership of Dalil Boubakeur, imam of Paris's Great Mosque. When two journalists were kidnapped in Iraq in 2004, Interior Minister Dominique de Villepin went to the Great Mosque to join Muslims in prayer for their release. British authorities, likewise, have long cultivated the MCB, and have made every effort to draw distinctions between "ordinary" Muslims, of presumed moderation, and extremists or terrorists. In the aftermath of the July 7 subway attacks, British police ordered officers to wear green ribbons in order to show solidarity with Islam. The government, moreover, persuaded a group of distinguished Muslim "moderates" to serve as conveners for a Home Office task force intended to combat extremism among young Muslims and to join a speaking tour. In 1992, the five hundredth anniversary of the conquest of Moorish Spain, a new Spanish government recognized the Comisión Islámica de España as the official representative of Spain's Muslims, with whom it signed a detailed agreement of Muslim rights and privileges—in effect, a Concordat, much like those agreed between nation-states and the Catholic Church.[33]

The multicultural strategy underlying the "moderate" offensive has much to recommend it, but European nations are only beginning to realize the dilemmas of confessional politics. By seeking to respond to religious minorities, governments are in effect recognizing particular clerical and religious groups as the official representatives of their communities, treating people not as individuals and citizens but as members of collective religious/cultural entities, holding group rights. The policy thus tends toward *communautarisme*, communalism, which successive French governments have regarded as a kind of ultimate political evil. Also, as Christopher Caldwell notes, the incentives offered by the strategy

> drive community representatives toward radicalism. Strident political voices are not just admitted to conversation—they are the preferred voices, because they are seen as more "authentic." If the government's top priority is finding people with the street credibility to dissuade potential terrorists, then the ideal Muslim interlocutor is someone who shares the terrorists' goals while publicly condemning their means.[34]

Moreover, populations of Muslim background are by definition seen as Muslims and presumed to operate under religious and clerical authority. While that assumption might not initially be correct, it could easily become so over time. The media assist this process when reporting on ethnic communities through the lens of religious leaders and organizations, who naturally have their own interests in presenting particular viewpoints. Ethnic issues are thus reported as religious problems, and viewers and readers tend to see them in that guise. This danger is all the greater since many Muslim migrants come from homelands in which religious authority is inextricably bound up with state mechanisms, exercised through ministries or directorates of religious affairs. On European soil, in contrast, immigrants found an environment of religious freedom in which religious creativity and experiment were now possible. It would be all too easy to revert to older ideas, however, to the controlled patterns prevailing in Morocco or Egypt.

By consigning individuals to a religiously defined status, governments are precluding other options. Journalist Nick Cohen reports hearing an imam deliver a reactionary lecture on gender roles at an East London Muslim Center, funded by British and European government money. As he notes, "For the purposes of official classification, they weren't British or British-Asians or English or working class or Londoners or Bengalis or women. They were Muslims and their religious leaders must have a large say in how they lived."[35] As we have seen, Europe's Muslims represent a huge diversity of practice and devotional styles. Treating all under the single label of "Islam" tends to encourage exactly the sense of supranational religious identity that runs flat contrary to goals of assimilation. It also, literally, consecrates the role of religious leadership within those communities. Could the Muslim Brotherhood have designed things more to their purpose?

Incidentally, these official attitudes also have a direct and positive impact on Christian populations. If "immigrant problems" are defined in terms of religion, but more specifically of assimilating Muslims, far less attention is paid to Christian migrants, who in many official classifications are lumped in with old-stock whites. No agency is contemplating erecting government-sponsored Christian Centers, nor are they likely to: who knows, they might practice exorcism? This differential approach to immigrant faiths could accelerate the integration of some sections of the population, by placing African or east Asian migrants in the desirable mainstream category of non-Muslims.

At an extreme end of multiculturalism, we even find the development of a kind of millet model of confessional religious governance. The word millet stems from Ottoman Turkish practice, in which each minority religious/cultural community—Jews, Armenians, Orthodox Christians—enjoyed considerable autonomy to manage its own affairs, subject to the overarching authority of the Ottoman regime. While minorities enjoyed far fewer rights than those accorded to Muslims, the system worked effectively for centuries. While no serious leader has suggested the revival of the millet in contemporary Europe, a significant minority has indeed demanded that Muslim communities be allowed to operate under their own law codes. A 2006 poll of British Muslims found 40 percent in favor of applying sharia law in "predominantly Muslim" areas of the country, and other surveys report a solid majority. In practice, this would involve the establishment of courts operating on sharia principles, chiefly in matters of family and personal law, in divorce, custody, and inheritance, "so long as the penalties did not contravene British law." The Swedish Muslim Association has formally proposed the introduction for separate legal provisions in that country. Amir Taheri suggests that

> in some parts of France, a de facto millet system is already in place. In these areas all women are obliged to wear the standardized Islamist hijab while most men grow their beards to the length prescribed by the sheikhs. The radicals have managed to chase away French shopkeepers selling wine and alcohol and pork products, forced "places of sin" such as dancing halls, cinemas and theaters to close down, and seized control of much of the local administration often through permeation. A reporter who spent last weekend in Clichy and its neighboring towns of Bondy, Aulany-sous-Bois and Bobigny heard a single overarching message: The French authorities should keep out!

When in 2006 the British Home Secretary visited East London, extremist leader Abu Izzadeen heckled him, demanding, "How dare you come here to a Muslim area?"[36]

The prospect of sharia law operating in Europe appalls liberal critics, partly because sharia is commonly associated with brutal physical penalties for crimes. But most find even a modified civil form unacceptable and a reversal of centuries of state-building and progress toward a rule of law. Trevor Phillips has urged Muslims who want to see sharia law to return to their countries of origin, since they simply do not understand British or European values.[37]

The Quest for Moderates

A primary reason for acknowledging the power of religious organizations is to curb the appeal of radicalism and to bolster moderates. In practice, though, these goals have proved elusive, as religious organizations and national federations remain dominated by representatives of a hard-line, conservative Islam. European governments thus give a kind of established status to the kind of Islam associated with the Muslim Brotherhood and its south Asian counterparts, a strand of the religion that is far more conservative and overtly political than that prevailing among ordinary believers. Conservative and reactionary groups have actually increased their strength in the various Muslim federations in recent years. In France, the CFCM was explicitly intended to take Islam out of the cellars and garages that served as semi-clandestine mosques, but its most rapidly growing component is the UOIF, a conservative grouping aligned to the Muslim Brotherhood. So is the most visible Italian organization, the UCOII, a fact that has made Italian governments nervous about including it in dialogue schemes.

Critically, what is a moderate in the context of contemporary Islam? An individual might denounce terrorism and call for Muslims to be loyal citizens of the nations in which they live but could still hold unacceptably radical views on many sensitive issues. In Britain, MCB media secretary Inayat Bunglawala served as a prominent member of the post–7/7 "road-show" intended to denounce extremism. Bunglawala condemns terrorism and declares that Omar Bakri and Hassan Butt "are known for their lunatic opinions and are utterly repudiated by the Muslim community." Yet Bunglawala through the years has left a lengthy paper trail of distinctly nonmoderate comments. In the early 1990s he praised American Islamist Sheikh Omar Abdul Rahman, and before 9/11, he circulated the writings of "freedom fighter" Osama bin Laden. Bunglawala has also denounced the mainstream British media as Zionist-controlled.[38]

The former secretary general of the MCB was Sir Iqbal Sacranie, who in 1989 responded to the *Satanic Verses* controversy by opining that "death is perhaps too easy" for Salman Rushdie. Even so, Tony Blair's government secured a knighthood for him a decade later. Responding to the film *Submission,* Sir Iqbal asked, "Is freedom of expression without bounds? Muslims are not alone in saying 'No' and in calling for safeguards against vilification of dearly cherished beliefs." He has since described Hamas guerrillas and suicide bombers as "freedom fighters, in the same way as Nelson Mandela fought against their apartheid, in the same way as Gandhi and many others fought the British rule in India." Virtually no European Muslim leader of any stature or credibility denies the right of armed resistance to besieged Muslim communities in Palestine, Chechnya, Bosnia, or Kashmir, and many would approve the practice of suicide bombing in such desperate situations. As we have seen, Muslim leaders unhappy with the MCB have defected to new and more liberal organizations such as the British Muslim Forum, so that the British government now canvasses a wider range of opinion than hitherto.[39]

In the aftermath of 9/11, European political leaders recognized the urgency of developing dialogue with "moderate" Muslims thinkers, but often, the quest for such individuals proved difficult. One of Britain's best-known leftists is "Red Ken" Livingstone, mayor of London, who in 2004 was involved in sponsoring a conference on the wearing of the hijab in schools. As part of the event, he invited Sheikh al-Qaradawi, whose condemnation of the September 11 attacks made him seem a representative of mainstream, moderate Islam. In Livingstone's words, he preached "moderation and tolerance to all faiths around the world." Al-Qaradawi's views, however, attracted bitter criticism from various constituencies. He denounced Jews and homosexuals, and supported suicide bombings in Israel. In his view, "It's not suicide, it is martyrdom in the name of God. . . . The Israelis might have nuclear bombs but we have the children bomb and these human bombs must continue until liberation."[40]

On occasion, Muslim leaders use different rhetoric in their statements for public consumption in the West and in lectures or sermons
directed at a Muslim audience in the Middle East or Pakistan. As we
have already seen in the case of Tariq Ramadan, figures touted as moderate in one context appear less so in other settings. Now, one's verdict
on Ramadan may ultimately be more favorable, but the story does suggest the difficulty of choosing Muslim "dialogue partners," whether at
national or international levels.

Whatever other qualms we might have about recent European attempts at defusing extremism, it is far from certain that they actually
work. Even if "moderates" do speak out against violence, such intervention has not yet shown much hope of success. For an analogy, European nations might look back at the various phases of the IRA's
struggle against Britain from the 1930s onward, when the Catholic
Church condemned and even excommunicated revolutionary activists,
but to little avail. In modern times, similarly, France's Muslim clergy
made little obvious impact by their attempt to quell the riots of November 2005; nor have MCB statements done much to quell extremist
support among British Muslim youth. Worse, by appearing to be coopted by the government, moderate leaders can actually harm their
influence within the community, presenting themselves as collabora-
tors. The activist International Crisis Group suggests that through their
excessive willingness to support government initiatives, moderate clergy
in France and elsewhere have actually contributed to the growth of
extremism: "The exhaustion of political Islamism has coincided with
the growth of Salafism."[41]

Expanding Europe

The problems with existing strategies toward Muslim minorities are all
too clear, though to say that existing multicultural policies are flawed
does not mean that they should be given up altogether. Governments
should cooperate with Muslim organizations, though with a much
sharper awareness of their political coloring and of the dangers of actively promoting a kind of Islamism Lite. And European societies
might indeed need to reconsider public portrayals of religion in what is
now authentically a multifaith society.

Nor should we see such policies in a social or economic vacuum.
Multiculturalism might work better than *laicité* in some settings, or
vice versa, but we should never forget the crucial role of economics in
all these debates. Grievances about religion become acute for people
whose social and economic conditions have left them desperate. People who are prosperous and employed have much longer fuses about
social and religious grievances than those who see no hope within the
present order. One great reason for the relative American success with

assimilation has been the country's ability to produce jobs, especially through service industries, which are so prolific in generating entry-level positions. The free market in labor means that most people gain at least a rung on the social ladder, with the potential to rise. In contrast, Europe presently has a daunting total of 19 million unemployed, most with little hope of moving from welfare to work. The greatest contribution to creating an open and generous Euro-Islam might be the wholesale liberalization of EU economic policies, in itself a difficult task. In 2006, a French administration that tried to liberalize youth employment law came close to being overthrown by massive street protests.

Whatever the outcome of economic debates, Europe's secular assumptions are being subject to huge challenges that would have seemed inconceivable just a decade ago, and devoutly secular European policy makers still have very little idea of how to respond to the situation they face. In some ways, the situation is likely to grow more acute, as the question of expanding the membership of the European Union revives debates over the nature of European cultural and particularly religious identity. Put simply, a Europe that is floundering with the problem of integrating its present Muslim population appears close to admitting a significantly larger Muslim minority.

As we have seen, the project of European unity owed much to Catholic thinkers, and although religious justifications faded with the decades, through the 1980s there was never any practical likelihood that the prospective nations of the expanded community would be anything other than predominantly Christian. The main debate, in fact, was whether prospective nations could meet European norms in terms of democratic structure and values, and whether they had a realistic prospect of catching up with the levels of wealth that characterized older core members such as Germany and the Netherlands. When the communist bloc collapsed in 1989, some Europeans feared that admitting new eastern nations too precipitously would create pools of cheap labor that would depress living standards across Europe. By the late 1990s, however, most such fears were allayed, and the European Union seemed set within a decade or two to incorporate most of the continent into a community that was democratic, free, and prosperous.

And then there was Turkey. Turkey, which still retains a sliver of European territory, was officially recognized as a candidate for EU membership in 1999. In 2004, all twenty-five heads of state and government agreed unanimously that Turkey was eligible to join and that serious talks should begin forthwith. This was after all a nation pledged to democracy, with an official secularism as strict as that of France, while Turkey had produced such contemporary movements as the moderate "Turkish Islam" preached by Sufi leader Fethullah Gülen. Bringing Turkey into the European club would be useful for Turkey itself, but also for the wider Islamic world. In the words of Joschka Fischer, "To modernize an Islamic country based on the shared values of Europe would be almost a D-Day for Europe in the war against terror. It would be the greatest positive challenge for these totalitarian and terrorist ideas." The EU would strike a blow for democracy and peace across the Muslim world.[42]

As negotiations proceeded, debate about Turkish membership aroused passions quite different from those encountered by other poorer nations, though the reasons for hostility were rarely explored with any sympathy. For most mainstream political parties, and for much of the media, opposition to Turkish membership was largely framed in terms of nativism or racism, and it was not therefore a respectable form of political discourse. Hence the depths of popular concern did not become obvious until the referenda over the proposed European Constitution held in 2005, when worries about Turkish entry emerged as a smoldering theme in opinion polls. European elites were amazed, and appalled, when the first critical referenda in France and the Netherlands showed heavy majorities against the new constitution. While Turkey was not the only reason for opposition to the current directions of the EU, it was a strong background issue, and these referenda occurred in the two west European nations that already possessed the highest proportions of Muslims.[43]

Trying belatedly to explain the populist reaction, European leaders made little allowance for the reality about concerns over Turkish admission, beyond despairing groans at the continuing power of irrational Islamophobia. But this case more than perhaps any illustrates the chasm of perceptions that separates leaders and led in matters of religion. European elites acknowledged that admitting millions of Turks would change the ethnic balance of a greater Europe but paid virtually no attention to the vast religious implications. While Turkish admission would not create Eurabia—Turks, of course, are not Arabs—it would amount to a radical reconstitution of European society.

Demographic pressures are critical. Turkish birth rates have declined substantially in recent years, largely as a result of the number of women entering the workforce, and the fertility rate now stands at 1.9, comparable to that of France or Ireland. Even so, Turkey is a nation of 70 million, a figure that could be approaching 90 million by 2025: over a quarter of the population is under the age of fourteen. If Turkey were admitted to the EU, it would soon be the most populous member of the European club, overtaking Germany before 2015. The country is almost entirely Muslim, since successive governments have over the past century killed or forced out virtually all their Christians. Turkish accession would immediately change the overall percentage of Muslim Europeans from 4.6 percent to almost 16 percent, and that proportion would rise sharply in the coming two decades, even setting aside future immigration from other regions. EU labor law means that Turks would also have the right to live and work anywhere within Europe, and millions from poorer regions would probably exercise that right.

The presence of ethnic Turks would not of itself transform Europe's religious identity, but the militant secularism of Turkey's long-entrenched military and political elites masks deep-rooted Muslim activism, accompanied by anti-Christian sentiment. The nation has not begun to come to terms with the genocide of its (Christian) Armenian population in 1915. In 2005, when writer Orhan Pamuk complained to a Swiss newspaper that "thirty thousand Kurds and a million Armenians were killed in these lands and nobody but me dares to talk about it," he faced a criminal trial for "publicly denigrating Turkishness." (Charges were later dropped, under international pressure.) In Germany, pressure from the Turkish government as well as from local Turkish communities means that textbook publishers largely refuse to discuss the Armenian genocide, and most schools find the subject too sensitive to confront. During the furor over the Danish cartoons, simmering anti-Christian sentiment in the media reached violent new heights, and a teenager crying "Allahu Akbar!" assassinated Catholic priest Andrea Santoro in the Turkish city of Trabzon.[44]

Also, openly Muslim religious politics have revived in Turkey. In a recent poll, three-fifths of respondents opposed the prospect of their child marrying a non-Muslim, and a third favored boys and girls being educated separately in school. An election in 2002 brought to power the Islamist Justice and Development Party (AKP). The AKP is by no means extremist and describes itself as "Islamic in the same sense that Christian Democratic parties in Western Europe are Christian," which is an effective dig at the pallid religious sentiment of those Western parties. But the AKP is committed to moderating the classic separation of mosque and state, for instance, by allowing headscarves in public schools and colleges. In a traumatic event in a supposedly secular state, in 2006 a self-described soldier of Allah assassinated a Turkish judge who had ruled against the rights of a woman teacher who wore the headscarf. Thirty years of experience in western Europe strongly suggest that once freed of state constraints, Turkish communities overseas sometimes adopt more strongly Muslim identities.[45]

Though it is a more distant prospect, some European political leaders assume that Moroccan admission to the Union is only a matter of time. The country's initial application was rejected on geographical grounds, but Morocco has subsequently developed ever-closer commercial and business links with Europe. Moroccan adherence would expand Europe's Muslim population by at least 30 million. Based on a reasonable analysis of religious and demographic trends, we can hardly avoid the conclusion that Turkish and/or Moroccan entry to the EU would substantially change the cultural identity of the continent, and it is not difficult to see why such a prospect should concern ordinary European citizens and voters.

What is striking about the expansion debates is that European political leaders should show themselves so tone-deaf to popular concerns, so unwilling to recognize the validity or even the existence of religious issues. In their view at least, to quote Giscard d'Estaing, "religion does not play an important role" in European affairs. Yet that assertion, if it was ever true, is rapidly losing force. While European states have been trying to accommodate and include the new presence of Islam, they have unwittingly revived a series of issues that affect Christianity as well, demanding a rewriting of the rules of engagement between church and state.

11

Transforming Faith

Perhaps God is using the Muslims to bang our Christian heads together.

Jobst Schoene

Unless the liberal state is engaged in a continuing dialogue with the religious community, it loses its essential liberalism.

Rowan Williams

Europeans of most political shades would now admit that they face a Muslim Problem, in the sense of deciding how to deal with social, cultural, and political views that seem barely compatible with those of the liberal mainstream. Yet perhaps the issue is not so much a Muslim problem as a religion problem, a systematic failure by European elites to understand religious thought and motivation. In much of the recent discussion about Islam, commentators are understandably anxious to avert the dangers of extremism and terrorism, to persuade Muslims to absorb virtues of tolerance and pluralism. Yet often the underlying assumption is that religion itself is a problem, at least in anything like its historic forms. In the words of one of the best contemporary authorities on European Islam, Jocelyne Cesari, liberal Europeans seem to be asking Muslims, "Why do you need religion? Why can't you live like us?" As Ian Buruma notes, some of the fear of Islam arises from European historical amnesia: Muslim expansion

> causes considerable anxiety among the non-Muslim majority, not only because Islam is the traditional enemy of Christendom, or because political Islam is espoused by terrorists, but precisely because it runs counter to our newly acquired secularism. Forgetting how recently most Europeans abandoned their own religions, people regard Muslim devotion as deeply

"un-European". Americans, still more attached to their own faiths, have less of a problem with others' devotion to theirs.[1]

This blinkered secularist perception affects the solutions that European commentators propose to their religion problem. When they imagine an idealized future Euro-Islam, they portray a deeply secularized faith, which has little by way of orthodoxy, preaches no morality that conflicts with secular assumptions, and does not try to impose its views on the "real world." It should also cease teaching its superiority to other religions since, as rational people are assumed to realize, all religions are equally invalid. And God forbid (so to speak) that it should preach any kind of moral standards, social or sexual. This Islam would in short be a variant of the most pallid and shrinking forms of liberal Christianity, and we might well ask why exponents of any religion would want to see their faith develop in this way.

This model is what is implied when writers envisage an Islamic Reformation, a phrase that reveals little knowledge of the passionate, dogmatic, moralistic, and utterly politicized Christianity of the European Reformation. Even Salman Rushdie, who is not historically naïve, falls prey to this illusion when he writes, "The Islamic Reformation has to begin here, with an acceptance of the concept that all ideas, even sacred ones, must adapt to altered realities." That sentence reads oddly when we think of the career of John Calvin, a revolutionary who established a repressive theocratic regime in Geneva, with moral and religious orthodoxies enforced by the full force of state power.[2]

Both Islam and Christianity will change radically in coming decades, through the experience of living in Europe's social and cultural environment but also from the fact of living side by side and having to interact with each other in a multifaith setting. Yet perhaps neither faith will settle down to the happy accommodation with secularism that European commentators seek. Arguably, instead of fading peacefully away, both religions face increasing conflicts with states, as Christians discover the full implications of laws originally designed to accommodate Muslim sentiments. When we take account of new forms of Christianity, especially in the immigrant context, European societies could yet see repeated cultural and political clashes between religious belief and the secularism that has virtually established itself as the official ideology of the united continent.[3]

Reshaping Christianity

People define themselves by considering what they are not. The very concept of Europe as a cultural rather than geographical expression emerged in the eighth century, during the conflicts between *us*—Latin Christian Europeans—and *them*, namely, African and Asian Muslims.

The battle of Poitiers in 732 was hailed as a victory for the *Europenses,* then a novel description for the people of Latin Europe. In the contemporary world too, the proximity of other religions will reshape European ideas, and not necessarily in confrontational or embattled terms.

Let us imagine a probable near future Europe in which Muslims make up perhaps 10 percent of the continental population, a figure rising to 20 percent of some leading nations. In such a society, Muslims would be a commonplace presence, whether we define Muslims in terms of religious adherence or cultural identity. Even under the most benevolent scenarios, European societies would have to make accommodations for cultural minorities of that strength. But surely, the attitudes of Christians would also change, for example, in their concept of self-identity, much as occurred to Muslims. In the 1950s, for instance, Moroccans or Pakistanis saw Islam as part of the normal background of social and family life. As they moved to non-Muslim societies, they came to see their religion in new ways and redefined their sense of what it meant to be Muslim. In the Europe of the 1950s, similarly, most Italians or Dutch or English adhered to a general Christian identity that was part of the familiar cultural ambience, a set of common assumptions shared by the wider community. In a religiously mixed Europe, such an assumption cannot be held. Alongside the growth of Euro-Islam, we would also see new religious forms to which we might apply the name Euro-Christianity.

Of course, old-stock Europeans might continue their progress toward secularism, with Christian practice declining virtually to nothing, but the contact with Islam could also inspire a rethinking of Christian roots and identity. As we have seen, support for religious schools continues strong in many nations, and the more specifically Christian ideas and institutions are challenged, the more need there would be to justify and defend these, to think more (say) about why Catholic schools maintained the crucifixes on their walls. This is what happened in Italy when the UCOII demanded that Muslims receive the teachings of their own faith in the time set aside for Catholic religious instruction in the schools. Though some Catholic leaders were sympathetic, others forcefully reasserted the Catholic nature of Italian culture, restating the Concordat that proclaimed "that the principles of Catholicism are part of the historic patrimony of the Italian people." Cardinal Camillo Ruini, president of the Italian bishops' conference, urged the state to recognize that Catholicism was still the religion of the overwhelming majority of Italians, "to say nothing of the demand to conserve and reinforce our roots, that's strongly present in the Italian people." Pope Benedict himself uses calls for religious tolerance to reassert the Christian presence in public life, remarking that "I would not ban any Muslim woman from wearing the headscarf. But far less will we allow the cross, which is the public sign of a culture of reconciliation, to be banned!"[4]

Recent terrorist outrages have also caused some Europeans to reevaluate their stances. Utrecht's Catholic cardinal Adrianis Simonis complained that while Europe had "disarmed in the face of the Islamic danger," an event like the Van Gogh killing would lead the Netherlands in particular to rediscover its identity and tradition.[5] After the cartoon controversy, individuals in various countries were heard wondering whether the next step would be a ban on going to church—not that concern about church had ever been much of a motivating force in the past. In Denmark, home of the Distant Church, Muslim protests gave a clear sign that the days of unquestioned Christian monopoly were clearly at an end. If few Danes cared noticeably about the People's Church, most deeply resented the challenge to its role in national life. And some asked why Danish high schools required pupils to read the Quran but not the Bible. Such a decision arguably made sense if nominally Christian pupils encountered the Bible in their churches or homes, but the vast majority clearly did not.

A rediscovery of "Christian values" can take many forms, including aggressive racism. In Britain, the ultra-right British National Party has recently got religion, using the slogan "Defend Our Christian culture." BNP leader Nick Griffin asserts that he is no longer a racist, but has become a "religionist." The British far Right has received an unexpected symbolic bonus in recent years, as the growing independence of the different components of the United Kingdom has encouraged a new sense of *English* identity, using as its flag not the old Union Jack, but the Red Cross of St. George. Meanwhile, just over the past decade or so, St. George's Day, April 23, has returned as a popular celebration, with reenactments of medieval pageantry, and a great deal of strictly nonpolitical drinking. (Adding to its patriotic cachet, this is also Shakespeare's birthday). Although few English people currently use the new cult as an explicit token of religious confrontation, extremists try to exploit its Crusader associations. The English fondness for St. George dates back to the great wars against Islam, when the saint reportedly appeared to Christian forces during the siege of Antioch in 1098. Not surprisingly, the BNP promotes the wider celebration of St. George's Day.

The churches, of course, utterly reject such manifestations, and some clergy want to displace George as England's patron saint precisely because his image potentially offends Muslims: they would rather venerate the native-born martyr St. Alban. Yet the churches too have become more forthright about reminding Europeans of the roots of their culture, challenging the simplistic notion of a multifaith society in which all denominations are equal. Anglican Bishop Michael Nazir-Ali declares that "almost everything you touch in British culture, whether it's art, literature or the language itself has been shaped by the Judaeo-Christian tradition, by the Bible, by the churches' worship and belief." In a 2006 report, the normally very liberal Church of England challenged the whole multifaith concept and the "privileging" of Islam. The authors stressed that "the contribution of the Church of England in particular and of Christianity in general to the underlying culture remains very substantial. . . . It could certainly be argued that there is an agenda behind a claim that a five per cent adherence to 'other faiths' makes for a multifaith society." A new awareness of Christian claims was evident in 2006, when Pope Benedict offered a fulsome apology to Muslims offended by his perceived insult to Islam. Many Europeans were just as offended by the pope's apology, and felt that Muslims had at least an equal obligation to respect the religious traditions of the countries to which they had migrated.[6]

Secular thinkers too worry about the religious heritage that is being lost. Following the London subway bombings, historian Niall Ferguson recalled the phrase attributed to G. K. Chesterton, who reportedly wrote that when people lose their belief in God, it is not true that they believe in nothing, but rather that they believe in anything:

> Over the past few weeks we have all read a great deal about the threat posed to our "way of life" by Muslim extremists . . . but how far has our own loss of religious faith turned this country into a soft target—not so much for the superstition Chesterton feared, but for the fanaticism of others?

His essay was entitled "Heaven knows how we'll rekindle our religion, but I believe we must." As historian Michael Burleigh observes,

> in coming years, more and more Europeans will say they are cultural Christians—as even such figures as novelist Umberto Eco or veteran leftist Régis Debray are doing—as a means of self-assertion against reactionary Islam. In other words, while Europe may continue to be godless, it may see a great deal more religion than anyone bargained for.

In a series of recent essays that astonished his admirers, venerated leftist philosopher Jürgen Habermas proclaims that "Christianity, and nothing else, is the ultimate foundation of liberty, conscience, human rights, and democracy, the benchmarks of Western civilization. To this day, we have no other options [to Christianity]. We continue to nourish ourselves from this source. Everything else is postmodern chatter." Habermas declares himself "enchanted by the seriousness and consistency" of the theology of St. Thomas Aquinas,

> a spiritual figure who was able to prove his authenticity with his own resources. That contemporary religious leadership lacks an equally solid terrain seems to me an incontrovertible truth. In the general leveling of society by the media everything seems to lose seriousness, even institutionalized Christianity. But theology would lose its identity if it sought to uncouple itself from the dogmatic nucleus of religion, and thus from the religious language in which the community's practices of prayer, confession, and faith are made concrete.

He continued, "Recognizing our Judaeo-Christian roots more clearly not only does not impair intercultural understanding, it is what makes it possible."[7]

In other ways too, the presence of Islam has caused Europeans to rediscover aspects of religious life that they had cared little about previously. One recent study of Muslim interactions with the state in Britain, France, and Germany produces findings that appear counterintuitive. Generally, the authors find that legal problems are fewest in Britain, worst in France, with Germany in between. So pernicious, in fact, are relations in France that school controversies and debates over the hijab consume virtually all the attention of Muslim organizations, who are prevented from confronting other critical issues. The authors find that the chief variable is each nation's attitude to the establishment of religion. In Britain, with its old-established national church, religious schools are a familiar quantity, with Catholics long allowed to run their own system parallel to the official Anglican framework. It needs little effort to add Muslims to the list of faith traditions permitted to operate their own institutions. At the opposite extreme, we find the wholly secular model of France, which has little experience with religious schools of any tradition. Countries accustomed to including religious education in public schools should in theory have no difficulty in building Islamic education into the process: German schools already permit the Central Council of Jews to educate children of that faith, so a comparable Muslim body could take on a like responsibility for Muslim children. The advantages of accommodating Muslim children in the public school are obvious, since the practice reduces any need for unsupervised or unlicensed private madrassas, which could easily develop a radical and propagandist coloring.[8]

The authors conclude with high praise for a "mild establishment" as a factor in promoting cultural integration. The irony is apparent: "It took the arrival of Muslims, religious newcomers and a community that took its faith very seriously, to expose the degree to which the established church in Britain remained vital to the politics of various issues." Thirty years ago, few people apart from the most reactionary Anglicans had a good word to say for the principle of establishment.[9]

In thinking about the impact on Christianity of recent controversies, we should also take account of one grim event that has not occurred yet, but that very probably will within the next few years. Briefly, unless political circumstances change radically, there will soon be a major attack on an iconic symbol of European Christianity. To assert this demands no gifts of prophecy. For years, the most extreme segments of radical Islamism have uttered direct threats against Christian belief and practice, and it is immaterial whether such condemnations are in conflict with supposed Quranic calls for tolerance and *convivencia*. Terrorist groups have already targeted Christian individuals and institutions, with a view to achieving the maximum shock effect. In 1995, an Arab group based in the Philippines planned to assassinate Pope John Paul II on his visit to that nation, as a means of distracting attention from a related plot against U.S. airliners. (Though a Turk actually did shoot the same pope in 1981, he was not acting on behalf of Islamist causes.) And when Benedict made his controversial Regensburg speech in 2006, al-Ghurabaa' organized protests outside Westminster Cathedral, England's preeminent Catholic church, as spokesman Anjem Choudary warned that execution awaited anyone who insulted Islam. Cathedrals and great churches have featured among the aborted list of targets planned by Islamist cells. Strasbourg and Cremona cathedrals were among the best-known targets of these thwarted attacks, and threats have been directed against the great cathedral of Bologna, with its controversial murals of Muhammad. Local churches have also been targeted in urban riots such as the notorious outbreaks in France in 2005, though few would see these incidents as part of any concerted conspiracy.

What would be the cultural effect of an attack that would devastate a cherished building such as Westminster Abbey or Notre Dame, Santiago de Compostela or the Duomo of Florence, or St. Peter's in Rome itself? The immediate response, undoubtedly, would be grief and fury, and Muslim leaders would be among the first to condemn the attack, and with utter sincerity. Economic consequences would also be vast, with the shock to tourism. Since an attack would also lead to dramatically increased and even militarized security around other churches, it would promote a sense of religious confrontation and even encourage a rhetoric of crusade and jihad. But such an event would also have its religious impact, galvanizing old-stock European Christians to a new awareness of their culture and heritage, to a newly discovered sense of what they had always taken for granted. The Vatican initially described the London subway attacks of 2005 as "anti-Christian," but withdrew the comment when it was attacked as inflammatory. In other circumstances though, anti-Christian motives might be impossible to conceal.

The Christian-Muslim Encounter

Quite apart from such a possible catastrophe, the substantial presence of Islam within Europe promises to change Christian thought and belief in many ways. For two centuries, many of the intellectual debates within European Christianity have been shaped by the encounter with secularism and skepticism, as Christians attempted to make their faith credible and relevant in the face of modernity. But what happens when the main interlocutors in religious debate operate from assumptions quite different from those of secular critics, when the rivals assume as a given the existence and power of a personal God who intervenes directly in human affairs, and seek rather to clarify the nature of His revelation? In the early decades of immigration, Christian churches often treated Muslims sympathetically, feeling the need to act generously toward the poor and marginalized; but matters will change when the faith of Islam is acknowledged as a full neighbor, wholly resident on European soil.

Though the analogy is not close, we think how American Christianity has been changed over the past century or so by the encounter with a numerically small Jewish presence that never amounted to more than 2 percent of the overall population. Particularly since the 1940s, American Christians have striven to avoid language that would give offense to Jews or seek to exclude their religious heritage, and the term "Judeo-Christian" has become the mandatory characterization of the roots of Western culture. Many Christian clergy and intellectuals try to eliminate language suggesting that their faith has in any sense superseded or supplanted Judaism, so that the Old Testament is commonly referred to as the Hebrew Bible. For many grassroots evangelicals, a love affair with Judaism has spawned a dedicated Christian Zionism, a passionate support of the state of Israel far exceeding even that espoused by many Jews.

Despite their long struggles, Christianity and Islam have influenced each other through the centuries. In the case of Islam, it is scarcely adequate merely to speak of influences, since the religion at its inception drew so heavily on Christian thought and practice. If one single motif dominates the whole Quran, it is an awe-inspiring vision of Judgment and the afterlife that would have been immediately recognizable to Christians (or Jews) of the sixth and seventh centuries. The institution of Ramadan reflects the Christian practice of Lent as it would have existed in Syria at this very time. Christians, in turn, were inspired by Muslim piety. In the eighth century, partly spurred by the Quranic rejection of images and idolatry, a powerful movement in the Orthodox church urged the destruction of virtually all visual depictions of holy figures, provoking the bloody Iconoclast controversy. When Russian Orthodox Christians repeat the Jesus Prayer thousands of times in order to create a trancelike state of devotion, they are doing exactly what Sufi Muslims do worldwide with the declaration of faith in Allah, though in this case it is difficult to tell which practice inspired the other.[10]

In coming decades, European Christians will have no alternative but to look closely at Islam, and they will find there much that is familiar, and that is inspiring. At the synod of European Catholic bishops in 1999, Belgian Cardinal Godfried Danneels praised the Islamic emphasis on "the transcendence of God, prayer and fasting, and the impact of religion on social life." We might quote an essay authored by

Italian priest Fr. Andrea Santoro, who was himself murdered by a Turkish Muslim during the 2006 cartoon controversy. Yet he had been frank in his admiration for Islam. As he had "discovered the face of Islam in practice," he found much that could serve as a basis for fruitful dialogue:

> an instinctive sense of God and His providence; spontaneous welcome of His word and His will; trusting abandonment to His guidance; daily prayer in the middle of one's activity; certainty about the afterlife and the resurrection; the sacredness of the family; the value of simplicity, of the essential things, of welcome and of solidarity.

Islam preserves potent religious practices long familiar to Christianity but largely abandoned in modern times, especially the discipline of sustained fasting. As Tariq Ramadan observes, "The real question is about spirituality. If the presence of Muslims leads Europeans to think about who they are and what they believe in, that has to be positive."[11]

But the presence of Islam also raises acute questions for Christians. Most fundamentally, is Islam a separate religion, as distinct from Christianity as Shinto or Hinduism, or are the two religions sisters separated at birth and raised in different family settings? The medieval Christian view, dating back to St. John Damascene in the eighth century, saw Islam as a Christian deviation, the heresy of the Ishmaelites; and St. John had far better firsthand knowledge of Islam than virtually any of the later Christian controversialists over the next millennium. Dante portrayed Muhammad as a grand and sinister heresiarch, one of the *"seminator di scandalo e di scisma,"* the sowers of scandal and schism. Muslims themselves, of course, see Muhammad as the last and greatest of prophets, and the Quran as God's final and definitive revelation to humanity.[12]

Islam, even in its more liberal forms, scarcely allows for neutrality. A Christian well-wisher might praise the "Prophet Muhammad" and believe that he was in some sense inspired by God, making the Quran a magnificent spiritual document that has spawned one of the world's great faiths. But that is nowhere near enough for Muslims, who believe that Muhammad himself had precisely no input or role in the making of the Quran, which was divinely dictated through angelic mediation. For a Muslim, it is a deadly falsehood to say that Muhammad founded a religion: Islam is as old as the Creation, and Adam, Jesus, and Moses were Muslims.

Once you speak of the "Prophet" Muhammad, you are acknowledging that he did indeed bear prophetic status and that his revelation supersedes all others. But if you do accept the divine authorship of the Quran, no logical reason stands in the way of your total acceptance of Islam. Catholic thinker Alain Besançon has condemned the thoughtless politeness with which some Christians have tried to incorporate Islam into a Christian schema, with the Quran as a sacred book "rooted in Biblical Revelation." This approach "is syncretism in the guise of ecumenism," and its advocates are unwittingly acting *De Propaganda Fide Islamica*. But what alternative is open? If you do believe Muhammad played any role in composing the text, subject to the constraints of his time and social setting, you are issuing a deadly frontal challenge to the whole structure of that religion. If there is a third course—to accept some prophetic status for Muhammad while maintaining belief in the Christian scriptures and the church—it is not yet apparent. In coming decades, though, Europe's Christian thinkers urgently need to formulate some such synthesis, which is irenic without offering total submission to Muslim claims.[13]

In addressing the Muhammad Problem, Christians would also need to consider the role of continuing prophetic revelation, subsequent to the closure of the canonical biblical text. Are the credentials of a scripture to be decided solely by its numerical following, so that prophecy can be taken as genuine when its followers reach a set number, say 100 million? Other questions abound. Let us assume, for example, that Christian evangelism toward Muslims is possible, putting aside questions of both legality and prudence. Are Muslims members of a distinct religion, in need of receiving the Christian revelation, or do they already possess the truth in sufficient measure to make such efforts unnecessary and undesirable? Many Christian churches in Europe and North America, especially of liberal inclination, have already decided against the propriety of evangelizing Jews, since to do so would be to condemn the Jewish Covenant as invalid and obsolete. But do Muslims too have a valid path to God? What, in short, is Islam?

To take another issue, we have already seen the close and usually friendly relationship that Christians and Jews have formed in the United States, and Jewish-Christian relations have generally been close in postwar Europe, subject to periodic strains, particularly over Middle Eastern politics. But in Europe at least, such cooperation might be hard to sustain, as the Jewish presence diminishes while Muslims grow in numbers. Presently, western Europe has perhaps a million Jews, compared to 15 million Muslims, and that disparity will grow steadily. The easiest way for Christians to build bridges to Muslims is to take Muslim political grievances seriously, and high on that list would be the abuses attributed to the state of Israel. For many Europeans, of course, the two causes, Muslim and Jewish, are not comparable, given Europe's special historic debt toward the Jews. Recent demands that Muslim organizations in Italy and elsewhere reject extremism often require recognition of the legitimacy of the state of Israel, which is presented as a fundamental principle of liberal democratic belief. But if only in terms of realpolitik, Muslim issues also demand recognition, however dubious American Christians would be about any European opening toward Islam that neglected Jewish or Israeli interests. In decades to come, attitudes to Islam and Judaism could well form a growing division between Christianity as practiced in Europe and North America.[14]

The Great Division

Yet for all the obvious forces pushing European Christians toward a rapprochement with Islam, the potential divisions are still daunting. Given its dominant position within European Christianity, the attitudes of the Roman Catholic Church are critical for future interactions between the faiths. Both at the Vatican level and within individual nations, we can see a continuing conflict between very different attitudes to Islam. Under John Paul II, the church demonstrated a real openness to Muslims as believers, and as allies in struggles against Western secularism. On several occasions, the Pope spoke of his Muslim "brothers." In 1985, he urged that "we have to respect each other and stimulate each other in good works upon the path indicated by God. . . . believers should foster friendship and union among humanity and the people who comprise a single community on earth." John Paul was also the first pope to enter a mosque, in Damascus in 2001.[15]

At the same time, the Church's global dimension gave its leaders an acute awareness of rising Muslim extremism and intolerance, reflected in conflicts and persecutions around the world. For some years, the Pontifical Council for Interreligious Dialogue was headed by Cardinal Francis Arinze, whose Nigerian background prevented him from succumbing to easy illusions about interfaith collaboration. After the high praise he accorded to Islamic virtues, Fr. Santoro carried on to note the obvious "shadows":

> the fear of true liberty; the limits placed on a more interpersonal and intimate relationship with God, seen as too majestic to come down among human beings; an image of women still very much to be discovered and given value; an individual and public practice of the faith that has to be more thoroughly linked with interior life; and an overly fearful attitude concerning dialogue between cultures and religions.[16]

In 2000, Bologna's Cardinal Giacomo Biffi created a national outcry when he argued that while Italy definitely needed immigrants, a significant Muslim presence would simply be too likely to promote long-term conflict. Preference should be given to people of Catholic background. "And there are many," he said, "Latin Americans, Filipinos and Eritreans."[17]

Intensifying Catholic concern was the growing Muslim presence in Italy itself, symbolized by the sumptuous Saudi-funded Great Mosque of Rome. Opened in 1995, this mosque was at the time the largest in western Europe. From the late 1990s, Catholic churchmen became more public in their expressions of concern about the possible limits of Muslim ambition on European soil. After all, several of the greatest cathedrals of southern Europe—Toledo, Seville, Córdoba, Palermo—stand on the sites of ancient mosques, which Islamist radicals have pledged to see rebuilt. Even Mansur Escudero, president of the moderate FEERI, has requested the right of Muslims to pray in the area around what was once the great mosque of Córdoba. Responding to this request, Michael Fitzgerald, president of the Pontifical Commission for Interreligious Dialogue, noted tactfully that "the Vatican has always been very careful not to ask for similar rights with regard to mosques which once were churches."[18]

Over the past decade, gatherings of European Catholic leaders have witnessed repeated conflicts between hard and soft approaches to Islam. Citing the expansion of Muslim communities in Europe, with evangelistic efforts fueled by Arab petrodollars, one Italian archbishop asked, "How can we ignore in all this a program of expansion and re-conquest?" Alain Besançon warned, "History teaches us that peaceful cohabitation between Islam and Christianity is precarious."[19] Church leaders have demanded greater concern over the plight of Christians in Muslim nations and suggested a degree of reciprocity. In their view, Muslims could scarcely demand complete religious freedom throughout Europe if Christians were allowed limited rights of worship in Islamic lands, and even relatively liberal Muslim nations never accepted a Christian right to evangelize Muslims. As John Allen summarizes the view of leading churchmen,

> If the Saudis can spend $65 million to build the largest mosque in Europe in Rome, in the shadows of the Vatican, then Christians ought to be able to build churches in Saudi Arabia. Or, if that's not possible, Christians should at least be able to import Bibles, and the Capuchin priests who serve the Arabian peninsula ought to be able to set foot off the oil industry compounds or embassy grounds in Saudi Arabia without fear of harassment by the *mutawa,* the religious police. The bishop in charge of the Catholic Church in that part of the world recently described the situation in Saudi Arabia as "reminiscent of the catacombs."[20]

Conservative lay politicians strongly echoed such views.

However important, pleas for religious toleration in Muslim lands have made little impact on secular policy makers, even as they debate the potential EU membership for Turkey and other mainly Muslim states. In 2003, a high-level advisory group commissioned by the EU examined relationships between Europe and the wider Mediterranean world, which in practice meant the Muslim states of north Africa and the Near East. The group found that

> these changes clearly require the EU and its Member States to rethink their relationship, still all too often problematic, with the closest Other.

Europe's relationship with its neighbors within determines its relationship with its neighbors without, and vice versa. Of course the Euro-Mediterranean partners must also make an equivalent effort with their Jewish and Christian minorities.

Given the actual circumstances of toleration in most nations, that "of course" reads almost humorously.[21]

Though Vatican policies can be opaque to outsiders, the papacy of Benedict XVI favors a harder line toward Islam. When Father Santoro was murdered in 2006, the crime was widely seen as an act of martyrdom. Cardinal Ruini expressed his certainty that "in the sacrifice of Fr. Andrea are present all the constitutive elements of Christian martyrdom." The Cardinal also spoke forcefully on Muslim demands for an equal role in the Italian school system, alongside Catholics. In principle, this could be granted, but

> there must not be any conflict in the content of that teaching with respect to our Constitution, for example regarding civil rights, starting with religious liberty, or equality between men and women, or marriage. . . . Further, it would be necessary to ensure that teaching the Islamic religion would not give way to a socially dangerous kind of indoctrination.

Benedict himself created a stir in Bavaria in 2006 when, in a speech directed mainly against European secularism, he quoted one of the last Byzantine emperors Manuel II Paleologus, from a debate in which he rejected the claims of Islam. Manuel reportedly asked a Muslim thinker, "Show me just what Muhammad brought that was new, and there you will find things only evil and inhuman, such as his command to spread by the sword the faith he preached." The speech was mainly concerned with stressing the roots of Christian thought in Greek philosophy and the fundamental importance of Reason, a linkage that could not be reconciled with forcible conversion. "To convince a reasonable soul, one does not need a strong arm, or weapons, or any other means of threatening a person with death." Yet the view of Islam was unflattering, as was the historical context. Adding to the power of the reference, Manuel was defending the Christian faith in the last days before the Ottoman Turks would destroy and annex his empire. In contemporary Germany, such words become evocative, and even threatening, while they have obvious implications for debates over Turkish claims to European status. International Muslim protests against the Regensburg speech recalled the Danish cartoon affair, and some protests turned violent. In Somalia, Islamist thugs murdered a 66-year-old nun.[22]

Preaching Morality

For all their divisions, though, Christians and Muslims potentially have much to learn from each other, in the practical realm as much as the theological. Muslims can certainly learn from Christian forms of accommodation with the secular world, from pluralism. But Christians too recognize that absolute separation of religion and state has its problems. In 2005, the Community of Sant'Egidio organized a meeting to address the question "Is Europe at Its End?" As the ever-thoughtful Archbishop Rowan Williams observed at this gathering,

> Europe's distinctive identity, then, is a "liberal" identity, in the broadest meaning of the word: a political identity which assumes that argument and negotiation, plural claims adjudicated by law, suspicion of "positivist" notions of political power, are all natural, necessary features of a viable and legitimate communal life in society. But the crucial point for the Christian is the conviction that this "liberal" identity is threatened if it does not have, or is unaware of, that perpetual partner which reminds it that it is under a higher judgment. Unless the liberal state is engaged in a continuing dialogue with the religious community, it loses its essential liberalism. It becomes simply dogmatically secular, insisting that religious faith be publicly invisible; or it becomes chaotically pluralist, with no proper account of its legitimacy except a positivist one (the state is the agency that happens to have the monopoly of force).[23]

While Williams was not advocating any kind of religious-based state, his words do indicate the inevitable conflicts between Christian values and those of the secular European state. We should recall this contrast when we hear pleas for Muslims to accept the legitimacy of the nation-states in which they live and to abjure beliefs in a supranational religious cause. As far as they go, such calls are reasonable and desirable, but many would argue that an Islam that is not political is not Islam, at least not in any recognizable historical sense. To say this is not to denounce Islam for fanaticism: arguably the most ancient and pristine forms of the Christian faith were themselves radically apocalyptic, antisocial and antiworldly. But Western observers are over-optimistic if they believe that the alternative to Wahhabi fanaticism is a pallid liberal Islam akin to American mainline churches. Muslims, like Christians, also possess a historical vision that transcends states. Both recall that their religions existed before any nation-state now existing in the world, and will outlive them.

Muslims can learn from Christians the countless advantages of living in a pluralistic state with what Williams terms a liberal identity. Muslims can also remind Christians of the religious values that precede and outlast states, and which produce a healthy suspicion of the idolatry that sometimes surrounds official ideologies. Bruce Bawer argues that "It must become impossible for children growing up in Western Europe to be raised to see their religious affiliation as the be-all and end-all of their identity." Based on Europe's experiences during the twentieth century, many would rather rewrite that sentence to replace "religious affiliation" with the words "national loyalty" or "state ideology." Thus edited, such a sentence would be a welcome reaffirmation of what we might call the Dietrich Bonhoeffer principle.[24]

The sense that Christians and Muslims share common perceptions has already had significant effects in the international arena. At major global meetings in the 1990s, the Vatican cooperated with Islamic nations and interest groups to combat liberal proposals over abortion and contraception, much to the horror of Western feminists. Vatican officials sympathized with Muslim contempt for Western decadence and secularism. In 1997, then-Cardinal Ratzinger declared, "In the face of the deep moral contradictions of the West and of its internal helplessness—which was suddenly opposed by a new economic power of the Arab countries—the Islamic soul reawakened." Muslims understandably felt that "the Western countries are no longer capable of preaching a message of morality, but have only know-how to offer the world."[25]

Christians, like Muslims, teach moral standards that conflict with secular values, though of late, many have been reticent about preaching these too publicly. In 2006, Archbishop Williams himself issued an official plea urging English football fans to behave well when visiting Germany for the World Cup tournament. The new head of the Muslim Council of Britain, Muhammad Abdul Bari, agreed with the statement as far as it went but was disappointed that Williams had not gone much further. "The Archbishop of Canterbury should give guidance; he should be promoting moral issues." Implausibly, Abdul Bari recommended that English families should consider arranged marriages, but more realistically, he urged religious leaders to cooperate in fighting the widespread abuse of alcohol, as well as gambling and sexual immorality. The alcohol issue is an interesting example. While few advocate prohibition, many secular commentators agree that drink culture in Britain has become uncontrollable and dangerous, a serious incentive to violence and sexual assault, and that much greater restraint is needed. Yet the Anglican church has not spoken powerfully on the issue, largely because it does not want to be seen interfering in personal morality. Historically, such reticence is very new, and it could well fade if and when Christians and Muslims do make common cause.[26]

Clashing Values

While Christians face conflicts with Muslims, they also encounter severe tensions with secular societies, tensions that are only gradually becoming apparent. As European states have tried to come to terms with their Muslim populations, they have attempted where possible to adopt policies that accommodated Muslim needs and concerns. Yet policy makers have paid little attention to the effects on other religious groups, whose views might be quite similar to those of Muslims. If religions are to coexist successfully, governments and official agencies must avoid any impression of favoring one over the other, of granting one special privileges. If, then, any one religion receives particular protection, or suffers special disabilities, all other faiths should in theory receive equal treatment.[27]

Such an approach produces worrying consequences for conservative Christians, who at many points share religious or moral beliefs with Muslims. These issues have surfaced in the context of the tests devised by some European nations and regions to winnow out those potential immigrants or citizens whose religious and cultural values run flat contrary to mainstream Western assumptions. As we have seen, Europeans differ from Americans in that they cannot rely on a broadly accepted definition of values and rights intimately linked to national identity, and states have had to make some rough-and-ready decisions about the supposed "European ideology" to which migrants must subscribe. These decisions often make bold assumptions about the nature of the social consensus. The Dutch government produced a video in which potential immigrants were shown the realities of the contemporary Netherlands, including men kissing in public and topless women on beaches. Foreigners are warned, "You have to start all over again. You have to realize what this means before you decide to come here." Other European governments have formulated various kinds of "Muslim Test," which range from the perceptive to the downright silly. Among the worst are those that demand knowledge of minutiae of national history and culture that would daunt most native-born citizens. Would-be Austrian citizens are expected to know "In which Upper Austrian town are there two famous winged altars?" For Americans, these trivial pursuit examinations recall the literacy tests by which the segregationist South arbitrarily excluded minority voters.[28]

Other tests, though, delve more deeply into ideology. The German Land (state) of Baden-Württemberg has created a thirty-item citizenship test that asked, among other things, how respondents felt about theories blaming the Jews for the attacks of September 11. Were these attacks—or those in Madrid—the work of terrorists or freedom fighters? What did respondents think about criticisms of a religion or its institutions? What should be an appropriate response? What about laws mandating gender equality? (No less than seventeen of the questions concerned women's rights). What would they think if a married man left Germany for his home country and returned with a second wife? How would a man feel if his wife or adult daughter wanted to dress like regular Germans? Would he try to stop them? If so, how? Should children be allowed to participate in school sports? In its own lengthy citizenship examination, the state of Hesse asks candidates how they feel about the statement that "A woman should not be allowed to move freely in public or travel unless escorted by a close male relative."[29]

Such questions would certainly bring out radical Islamist tendencies, and all but the hardest-core libertarians would favor excluding potential immigrants who declared sympathy for the mass murder of civilians. But other questions would be a real obstacle for groups far removed from the radicals, for political moderates who are conservative on moral and gender issues, who do not support wide-ranging ideas of gay rights, or who have serious qualms about public nudity. This would certainly be true among Muslims but also those Christians or Jews for whom acceptance of full homosexual equality would constitute an acid test. Now, most European Christians have little difficulty accepting gay rights, especially among those cultural Christians who are not closely affiliated with institutional religion of any kind. Some believers, though, have much less sympathy. Contentious questions include, "Suppose that your adult son came to you and told you he was homosexual and wanted to live with another man. How would you react?" In the context of the citizenship test, the only answer that is correct and acceptable is that the parent should totally accede to his son's decision and not oppose the idea of gay marriage, which is anathema to a large proportion of Christians and Jews.[30]

Many old-stock Europeans would have difficulty in giving their honest opinion about openly homosexual politicians, if a hostile answer disbarred them from residency or citizenship. In practice, of course, old-stock residents are not required to undergo such an inquisitorial process. If they did, Christians would suffer disproportionately from such a winnowing, and immigrant Christians from the global south worst of all. These new Christian churches include some of the most passionate voices protesting homosexual rights and gay marriage.[31]

It would be fascinating to see a sample of American Christians respond to the survey, especially to the questions about gay marriage, which remains fiercely contentious. And apart from a couple of conspicuous exceptions, the United States has very few openly gay politicians at the national level. By the Baden-Württemberg standard, the United States is already a nation of Islamist fanatics.

The Limits of Morality

In the aftermath of recent terrorist violence, European leaders have shown themselves much more determined than hitherto to define and defend their values, the "core contract" of tolerant democratic societies, and to resist subversion by Islamist extremists operating through religious institutions. Radical imams have been prosecuted or deported, some countries exercise surveillance over sermons, and Germany is considering demands that preachers use German, rather than Arabic or Turkish. Some Muslim leaders themselves have praised such restraints as a means of driving out the radicals who poach their followers.

Moneir Mahmoud, imam of Spain's prestigious M30 mosque, has praised government proposals to limit what can be preached in religious gatherings, whether Muslim or Catholic.[32]

American observers have praised what they see as a long-overdue assertiveness and a refusal to let exaggerated concerns about religious freedom permit the spread of revolutionary propaganda. If you parade dressed like a suicide bomber in a city just attacked by similar means, that is an overwhelmingly powerful form of symbolic speech that amounts to a direct threat or incitement to kill. In American legal terms, it is equivalent to shouting "Fire" in a crowded theater, and no religious motivation excuses the action. But as we see from the citizenship tests, west European states especially believe the core contract includes elements that are unsettling to conservative believers across the religious spectrum. As Utrecht cardinal Adrianis Simonis complains, "Political leaders ask whether the Muslims will accept our values. I ask, 'What values are those? Gay marriage? Euthanasia?' "

If the state regulates criticism of these new concepts of rights, we could potentially see serious clashes between church and state, even when religious groups are not advocating violence or subversion. In many countries, the concept of full homosexual equality means the legal prohibition of discrimination, while denunciations of homosexuality are forbidden as a form of hate speech. And while homosexuality is currently the most pressing issue, other themes could be very contentious in the future, especially in matters of reproductive technologies and genetic engineering. In 2006, Vatican officials proposed the excommunication of scientists involved in stem cell research involving human embryos.[33]

To date, courts in different jurisdictions have generally recognized a religious freedom exemption in hate speech cases. In 2001, for instance, the Dutch Justice Ministry prosecuted Islamist preacher Khalil el-Moumni for his aggressive denunciations of homosexuality. The prosecution failed because the court found a religious exception, namely that el-Moumni could indeed ground his views in the Quran and other sacred texts. The Swedish Supreme Court ultimately recognized a similar defense for Pentecostal preacher Ake Green who in 2004 had been sentenced to a month in prison for a sermon denouncing homosexuality. Calling homosexuality "a horrible cancerous tumor in the body of society," he argued that it led to other perversions such as pedophilia, and that tolerating such behavior could call down divine wrath upon the whole nation. In the view of prosecutors, not only did the religious setting not exempt the words from categorization as hate speech but "collecting Bible cites on this topic . . . does make this hate speech."[34]

As in the Muslim instance, nothing in Green's sermon would have seemed exceptional for conservative religious believers in the United States just half a century ago, when quite similar cancer analogies appeared in mainstream media. In that very short time though, gay rights have in Europe at least achieved the status of fundamental human values, to be rigorously defended by law. Far from this trend showing any signs of moderating, the determination to enforce Europe's supposed core values appears all the greater. Powers to exercise surveillance over Muslim preachers to track subversive sentiments, to detect anti-gay or anti-feminist views, could easily be used to unearth reactionary opinions among Christian or Jewish congregations. And if the state insists that Muslim clergy be citizens of the European countries in which they preach, surely the same principle must be applied to other faiths, including Christians, a policy that would have far-reaching effects on immigrant Christian communities. If governments regulate or suppress transnational evangelists like the Tablighi Jamaat, they could equally well exclude charismatic African-based churches.

The nature of potential conflicts is apparent in Britain, where in 2006 the government proposed new regulations that would outlaw all discrimination on the grounds of sexual orientation in any facilities serving the general public, including stores, social clubs, hotels, and bed and breakfasts. It would penalize shops that refused to offer wedding registries for same-sex matches, while schools would have to offer full equality of treatment and coverage. Churches would be required to rent meeting rooms to gay groups, and according to some interpretations, forced to perform gay marriages. The law naturally posed difficulties for religious believers who hold that homosexuality is of its nature sinful, and Anglican leaders like Bishop Michael Nazir-Ali asked that exemptions to be granted on religious grounds. The church received the strong support of Muslim groups like the Islamic Medical Association, which entirely agreed that "the right to hold deep faith convictions that affect the way people think and behave in every aspect of life is sacrificed in these regulations." The government was, however, reluctant to allow exemptions, for fear of undermining the whole principle of the legislation.[35]

Another emotive area of likely conflict between church and state involves children, as concepts of children's rights and child protection have expanded enormously in recent years, almost as ambitiously as gay rights. While no one claims a religious exemption in cases of sexual abuse, newer ethnic communities sometimes adhere to concepts of physical abuse and discipline very different from those in contemporary Europe, and those traditional concepts are often rooted in religion. The clash between religious and social values was evident in the recent British hysteria over the alleged maltreatment of children in exorcism rituals. It is absolutely legitimate for a society to prevent children from being harmed in religious services or rituals, always assuming that legislators are accurately informed about the nature of those services—which, in the British case, they were not. But the response went beyond mere attempts to prevent abuse or violence, as activists targeted practices like exorcism, which are a well-established part of the spiritual warfare doctrine characteristic of charismatic Christianity. In the recent British scandals, a spokesman for the National Society for the Prevention of Cruelty to Children remarked, "Any belief system that leads to the abuse of children is not acceptable." That goes far beyond a simple regulation of abusive practices, but strikes at the core of religious belief. By 2006, charitable groups called for "the establishment of a registration and monitoring system to regulate the faith sector and ensure anyone who wants to set up any place of worship is vetted to ensure they are fit to do so."[36]

The Limits of Evangelism

In other matters too, applying policies designed to respond to Muslims produces potential conflicts between other religious believers and the state. One pending legal crisis concerns religious evangelism and conversion. If European states preach complete freedom of religion, then states should claim no role whatever in decisions to change religion or attempts to promote such conversions. But of its nature, evangelism or proselytizing usually means asserting the superiority of one religious tradition over another, and in the process, disparaging other religions. Now, conversion is big business in contemporary Europe, and both Christians and Muslims engage enthusiastically in the practice.[37] This trend has enormous potential for enhancing religious grievances and even provoking violence, since notoriously, a Muslim who deserts his or her faith is worthy of the death penalty. As recently as 2004, "moderate" Muslim leaders in the United Kingdom urged Prince Charles and other Christian figures not to appeal for an end to the threat of capital punishment in apostasy cases. Yet Britain has flourishing Asian Christian fellowships that work among both Hindus and Muslims, and Bishop Nazir-Ali's parents converted from Shia Islam. African Christians are equally committed to the evangelistic Great Commission.[38]

The basic legal issue remains: can a Christian be permitted to condemn Islam and its Prophet in order to make a convert? Laws against religious hate speech in practice become anti-proselytization measures. Issues of evangelism and conversion proved central to the recent British debates over new laws prohibiting "religious hatred," which could be taken to outlaw Christian proselytizing. Christians and specifically evangelicals were among the main critics of the proposed measure and celebrated its defeat as a religious victory. In the words of evangelical activist Andrea Minichiello Williams, "A new political constituency has been awakened." Together with gay rights issues, and the limits placed on public displays of Christian religious symbols, the restriction of evangelism alarmed conservative Christians. In a lengthy report entitled *Faith and Nation,* Britain's Evangelical Alliance discussed just how far Christians should go in resisting threats to religious liberty. The authors concluded that "the use of defensive force may become a necessary and legitimate remedy for Christians." In theory, at least—and nobody was discussing such ideas as serious prospects—"active resistance" might include "disobedience to law, civil disobedience, involving selective, non-violent resistance or, ultimately, violent revolution."[39]

Also working against religious liberty is the strong European tradition of anti-cult or anti-sect laws that proliferated during the cult scares of the 1990s. Such measures were driven by notorious events like the mass murder-suicides associated with the occultist Solar Temple in France, Switzerland, and elsewhere in 1994–1995. A French law passed in 2000 proposed prison sentences for religious "proselytizers" undertaking "mental manipulation" of the public, the offense being to "exercise serious and repeated pressure on a person in order to create or exploit a state of dependence." The law was arguably well intentioned, and the justice minister spoke of "giving a democratic state the legal tool to efficiently fight groups abusing its core values." But such a law comes close to regulating which religious traditions can be practiced within a nation, suppressing controversial Christian or esoteric movements. France's official list of dangerous sects includes groups such as Jehovah's Witnesses, Scientologists, and Unificationists, but there is no reason it should not extend to virtually any sufficiently enthusiastic evangelical group that "manipulates" people by pointing out that they face hellfire if they do not receive Christ. And that extended definition is by no means fanciful. In 2004, the *Nouvel Observateur* ran a hysterical cover story entitled "Evangelicals: The Cult That Wants to Conquer the World." Exhibit A for cult behavior was President Bush, "a devotee of a weird church, Protestant, expansionist, millenarian and apocalyptic: George Bush is a Born Again Christian."[40]

Religious restrictions are still more marked in countries such as Greece and Russia in which entrenched church establishments are desperately anxious to combat possible upstart rivals. Sunday Adelaja has complained of the chilly attitude his church encounters from Ukrainian authorities: "They treat us as a disgrace of Ukraine. This is the opinion of the government; they consider us a thorn in the flesh." The potential for legal and cultural clashes in coming decades is immense.[41]

Blasphemy

The evangelism issue is above all a matter of consistency. It is scarcely reasonable for Muslim publications to boast at length of the number of converts to that faith while demanding laws that would make Christian missions more difficult. Equally, protections extended to Muslims should in theory apply to all other faiths, yet presently, they are not. If they were, this would be one area where Christians would actually gain more rights than they have presently.

This is especially true in terms of hostile representations of religious themes, and many recent examples illustrate the profound disparity of treatment, and of the official response. The controversies over the Danish cartoons and the film *Submission* taught European media harsh lessons about the limits of presenting controversial themes in the area of Islam, and overwhelmingly, they have responded with self-censorship. Other religious activists have also enjoyed great success in preventing the presentation of unflattering themes. In 2004, Britain experienced a debate quite as unsettling as the cartoon affair, when Birmingham Rep Theatre produced the play *Behzti* (Dishonor). The work, which was written by a young Sikh woman, Gurpreet Kaur Bhatt, depicted sexual abuse and murder in the context of a Sikh temple. Furious militants mounted protests and threatened to storm the theater. Giving credence to the threats was the presence among the protesters of members of aggressive Sikh militias and street gangs with long records of violence, some of which had already been proscribed under British anti-terrorism laws. After consultation with the police, theater authorities withdrew the play, handing the militants a resounding victory. The case proved that the religious sensibilities of Sikhs, like Muslims, must be regarded as sacrosanct.[42]

Such episodes stand in obvious contrast to recent fictional productions offering profoundly hostile or scurrilous portrayals of Christianity, or of Christian churches. One example of course is the vastly popular *Da Vinci Code*, which has as its foundation the theory that all Christian doctrine is founded on error, misrepresentation, or fraud, concocted by sinister clergymen and sustained through the centuries by an evil and deceptive church. Its supporters can of course claim that it was exploring important religious themes through the guise of fiction, though that defense did not protect the equally imaginative *Satanic Verses* or *Behzti*.

In 2005, Britain produced a blatant example of anti-Christian propaganda in *Jerry Springer–The Opera*, in which a sleazy (and gay) Jesus appears on the famous talk show, in a work marked by hundreds of examples of profanity. The show was televised on the BBC, a channel funded by a license fee that serves as a tax on all owners of television sets, whether or not they ever watch the BBC. The show drew tens of thousands of protests, the largest number ever recorded for a British television production. Critics carried placards denouncing the "Blasphemous Broadcasting Corporation." Far from conceding error, though, BBC authorities stressed that the work was a legitimate work of art and the decision to show it a proper exercise of free speech, a decision strongly supported by the left and liberal media, who took the opportunity to denounce critics for their bigotry and philistinism.[43]

The difference in response is striking, but the reasons are obvious. However incensed they became, Christian critics never threatened actual violence or even unruly demonstration. Archbishop Sentamu has denounced the BBC for its consistent display of religious double standards: "They can do to us what they dare not do to the Muslims. We are fair game because they can get away with it. We don't go down there and say, 'We are going to bomb your place.' That is not in our nature." The lesson for filmmakers or broadcasters is clear: when choosing religious topics to cover, only offend those groups who will respect legality. Might, in this instance, assuredly does make right, or at least the right to offend. A cynic might comment that critics of *Jerry Springer* could have ended the work overnight simply by allying with Muslims, who regard Jesus as one of the most venerated prophets, and by enlisting the publicity machine of an Abu Laban. In 1999, Omar Bakri Mohammed had indeed issued a fatwa against Terrence McNally's play *Corpus Christi*, which presented a flagrantly homosexual Jesus.[44]

Another difference separating works of art dealing with Christian themes is that they fit well into an old-established tradition by which Europeans mock their own culture, while attacks on Islam or Sikhism constitute an insult to ethnic minorities. In the cartoon affair, for instance, Rowan Williams complained that Europe's apparent "peacefulness and enlightenment seems to include license to express some very unpeaceful and unenlightened attitudes to minorities of various kinds. Just what kind of 'civility is this' the newcomer could ask?" That defense will wear increasingly thin as European Christianity acquires more of an immigrant cast and the protesters denouncing a future *Jerry Springer* are themselves "newcomers," African and Asian. If Christianity is a predominantly African and Asian religion, does it then deserve protection from public mockery?[45]

While incidents like the cartoon controversy have been reported in terms of the position of Islam, they also raise important questions about the treatment of other religious themes, particularly when there is deliberate attempt to shock. As European states, and the EU, consider the expansion of hate speech codes to cover acts of religious offense, changes cannot fail to have their effects on other religions, including Christianity.

Putting these various issues together, we can envision a near-future Europe that is anything but uniformly secular. While Muslims engage in critical debates about their relationship with modernity and argue how far their faith can be reconciled with national ideologies, Christians will also be redefining their faith and its public role. Though Christian numbers will decline, Christians will continue to organize in groups and movements that are if anything far more committed and activist than for many years past and will constitute more identifiable interest groups. We can reasonably expect a new sensitivity to depictions of religion and sacred themes. Religion will play a more intense role in public debate, especially when this is fueled by court decisions on critical and emotive questions concerning sexuality and gender, family and children, death and the shifting definition of life. "God's Continent" still has more life in it than anyone might have thought possible only a few years ago.

12

Europe's Religions Tomorrow

If you are the type of person who buys stocks and bonds, I'd buy
Christianity. The price now is very low . . . it has to go up.

Odon Vallet

American writers have made much use of Europe's modern encounter
with Islam, often seeing the possible cultural and religious transformation as a horrible warning for their own society. Some of these projections are much more plausible than others. But even if Europeans experienced a fairly benevolent transition to a multifaith society, that
change would still have substantial consequences for the United States,
and for the Atlantic alliance that has long been fundamental to American foreign policy. For ordinary citizens too, European religious developments offer important lessons about the nature of the great faiths
and of the changing faces of Christianity.

The United States versus Europe

Over the past few years, I have on several occasions talked with well-
informed Europeans who are baffled by U.S. concerns over immigration and border control. While not dismissing the problem entirely,
they believe that Americans faced nothing as severe as Europe's difficulties because of the nature of the would-be migrants. More than
once, I have heard the envious remark that the United States has only
to cope with Mexicans, while the Netherlands (or Denmark, or France,
as the case may be) has Moroccans. While I challenge the hostile picture such a contrast offers of Moroccans, the observation does include

a significant truth about the differential nature of immigration in the United States and Europe. While European immigration has been predominantly Muslim, the United States has followed a quite different course.

Immigration to the United States has been predominantly Christian, with only small representation from other religions, chiefly Buddhism and Islam. Muslims today make up barely 1.5 percent of the U.S. population, some 4 million people, in contrast with around 14 percent who claim Latino roots. While Muslim numbers will likely grow in the near future, the figure will continue to be dwarfed by the Latino presence. (Though the media periodically discover the phenomenon of Latinos who convert to Islam, the numbers involved are relatively tiny.) By 2050, Latinos will make up about a quarter of the national population, including 50 to 60 million Americans of Mexican descent. The vast majority of these come from Christian backgrounds, however firm or lax their individual religious beliefs or practices. Christians are also well represented among the Asians and Pacific Islanders who represent the other fastest-growing component of the American people. By 2050, Asians and Latinos combined will comprise a third of the U.S. population and most will probably follow varieties of the Christian faith.

Entirely due to geographical and historical factors rather than to official policy, American immigration over the past forty years has bolstered Christian numbers in a country that was already home to the world's most populous Christian communities. Immigration is if anything making the United States more Christian, in the same years that new arrivals have radically diversified the religious face of western Europe. And no plausible event on the horizon can prevent this transatlantic divergence from becoming still more marked in coming decades.

If we accept the most pessimistic Eurabian visions, then the Euro-American division becomes a daunting cultural wall, as Christian America confronts an Islamicized Europe. As I have argued, such a future is wildly unlikely, but even the more modest changes that will occur still have their consequences. Let us imagine the consequences of this religious division as it might develop over the next twenty to thirty years, as a predominantly Christian United States develops its relationship with a European Union with a Muslim minority of perhaps 10 percent.

Some of the concerns are disturbing, though these are probably of short-term significance. Observers draw attention to the security consequences of changing European conditions, in light of the growth of Islamist extremism in Britain and elsewhere. The September 11 plot was rooted in Europe, and more recent Islamist radicals are likely to carry European citizenship, which would make it more difficult to regulate their entry into the United States. While the United States could plausibly place special restrictions on citizens of particular countries entering its territory or boarding its aircraft, it would be much more difficult to differentiate between European citizens solely on the grounds of their religion or of their names. Had he so chosen, Mohammad Sidique Khan could easily have used his British passport to enter the United States, and perhaps to undertake a suicide attack on the subway system of New York City rather than London. Terrorism experts Peter Bergen and Paul Cruickshank argue that on these grounds, "it can now be argued that the biggest threat to U.S. security emanates not from Iran or Iraq or Afghanistan—but rather from Great Britain, our closest ally."[1]

Assume, though, that the terrorist menace fades within a few years, just as the seemingly perpetual crisis of the 1970s evaporated in its time. Even so, cultural and religious differences between the United States and Europe are still critical, all the more so given Europe's continuing economic heft. For all the excitement over the coming of an Asian Century, the European Union still constitutes a major engine of the global economy, with a combined GNP not far short of the U.S. figure. When *Fortune* magazine surveys the world's largest corporations, European nations still today provide around a third of the total, much as they have since the 1950s, with France, Germany, Britain, and the Netherlands strongly in the lead. Europe matters, economically and politically, and the changing nature of domestic constituencies will affect how that power is used. Within a decade or two, not only will European nations have more Muslims, but these Muslims are vastly more likely to be citizens with voting rights. When he pledged U.S. support to the creation of the state of Israel in 1948, President Harry Truman made the joking comment that he had never heard of an election being swung by the Arab vote, and in most of the United States, that continues to be true. In European nations, however, Muslim voters could well become a critical voting bloc, who at least for the foreseeable future will retain close connections with Arab and Muslim states.[2]

The impact on Middle Eastern affairs could be substantial. Most Americans, whether liberal or conservative, have a strong and largely uncritical view of the state of Israel, in marked contrast to the coolness and sometimes hostility that exists across much of Europe. Explanations for this intercontinental divide are not immediately obvious. Certainly, Europe has larger Muslim minorities than the United States and is more dependent on Middle Eastern oil, but religious factors also play a role. While the U.S. media have accused Europeans (and especially the French) of a continuing anti-Semitism, we might equally point to the strong American tradition of philo-Semitism, which grows naturally from the nation's roots in the Old Testament, and in apocalyptic.

At least on this side of the water, it seems only natural that an overwhelmingly Christian country should see its fate intimately bound up with that of the Jewish state. These attitudes shape responses to the

Middle East conflict, especially during outbreaks of violence. In the words of a *New York Times* report, "Where Europeans see dead Palestinians, Americans tend to see terrorized Israelis."[3] European attitudes may be shifting somewhat, as incidents of violence on European soil create a new sense of sympathy for Israeli sufferings; but the rise of Muslim communities will also force European governments at least to appear to act in a more even-handed way. And although European governments might intervene militarily in Muslim nations, it is difficult to imagine them doing so quite as readily as the British did in Iraq in 2003. The odds of a united transatlantic front in these areas will become even smaller than they are today.

Further dividing the two sides is the rhetoric that each chooses to characterize outside problems. Americans respond naturally to a religious-based language of evil and good, of a kind that makes Europeans cringe. Witness the radically different attitudes to the political rhetoric of Ronald Reagan in the 1980s or President George W. Bush, who famously identified an Axis of Evil. This of course is far more than a matter of terminology. A society that truly believes its enemies are evil is far more likely to demand the deployment of maximum force against them, to seek their utter elimination, rather than to compromise or negotiate: no conditional surrenders are possible. This contrast becomes all the more marked as European leaders insist on public secularism, while Americans feel less restraint about invoking religion.[4]

In other matters of pressing concern to Americans, religion might play a divisive role. For a decade now, U.S. administrations have declared the promotion of religious freedom worldwide a major policy goal, and this cause has drawn enthusiastic support from evangelical Christians as well as Jews. Yet the cause of religious freedom in west Africa, say, or Indonesia, is unlikely to receive the support of European nations, if that policy threatens to involve intrusions into the domestic affairs of Muslim states, and in the process offending Muslim pride within France or Germany.

Other issues of rights and freedoms could directly affect American policy makers. As we have seen, issues of religious freedom are currently a matter of lively debate in European legislatures and, more important, in the courts, which are called to decide critical issues concerning proselytism and free speech, discrimination, and the place of religious symbols in public space. Making these controversies still more significant, they come at a time when Europe is embarking on a program of legal federalism, with the European Court occupying a role reminiscent of the U.S. Supreme Court, with the right to overrule national jurisdictions.

The reshaping of European law has a double impact on the United States, where in recent years the Supreme Court has demonstrated a controversial tilt toward accepting European decisions as guiding principles in matters such as sodomy law and capital punishment, if not as actual precedents. In the 2005 case of *Roper v Simmons*, the Court ruled against executing offenders who were younger than eighteen when their crimes were committed, and one factor in its decision was the overwhelming consensus of European nations against such a practice. Justice Ruth Bader Ginsburg has said that "our island or lone-ranger mentality is beginning to change," as justices "are becoming more open to comparative and international law perspectives." American and European courts could soon find themselves in dialogue over matters of religious freedom, and if they do, European decisions about accommodating Islam could have a wider impact. The cartoon controversy showed European authorities surprisingly willing to accommodate Muslim sensitivities in free speech debates and even to support international moves to regulate offensive or blasphemous speech. Though U.S. administrations would surely never support such measures, they could find themselves increasingly isolated in international debates, as European states align with Muslim nations.

Changing Religions

But while legal and political issues could have their impact, the most significant developments promise to be in the specifically religious realm, as changes in contemporary Europe affect members of different faith groups around the world. Muslims of course run the greatest risks in the short term and should benefit most in the longer perspective. For many Muslims, the encounter with Europe has produced a sudden and often shocking immersion in modernity and has, in addition, created a hothouse atmosphere of controversy and free speech. Though the resulting intellectual and spiritual turmoil contributes to political extremism, the long-term pressures are likely to create an ever-more adaptable form of faith that can cope with social change without compromising basic beliefs. Whether or not we call it Euro-Islam, such a development would be of immense benefit not just to European societies but to neighboring regions of Africa and the Near East as well. The United States would gain immensely from a decline of religious tensions in these regions.

However counterintuitive this may seem, the advent of Islam might also be good news for European Christianity, in an era when those two words were beginning to sound increasingly like an oxymoron. As European states redefine their attitudes to one religion, they have no choice but to take account of the far more numerous presence of Christianity. From a grassroots level too, the immense attention paid to religious concerns and Europe's heritage in the past few years probably will drive more Europeans to take a renewed interest in their Christian roots, to rediscover what it is that so many academic experts seem to be consigning to oblivion. As mainstream Europeans rethink the religious roots of their society, some at least will be led to take that religious dimension more seriously. We know that a broad interest in religion and Christian spirituality survives in Europe, while more focused movements are cultivating new forms of devotion and instruction intended for contemporary societies. It would take a bold prophet to speak of a widespread Christian revival in near-future Europe, but we can see surprising portents of recovery, however localized.[5]

Contrary to expectation, then, Christianity is surviving amid European secularism and often achieving far more than mere survival. That fact has potent implications for other parts of the world facing secularization in the future, not least perhaps in areas of the United States. The changes have a special impact for Roman Catholics, who continue to represent the world's largest single religious institution. European Catholics face severe challenges to their traditional position and must adapt to a world of falling vocations and declining clerical prestige, of a new minority status even in countries familiarly regarded as quintessentially Catholic, while church-state tensions grow. Each issue poses real problems, which demand a rethinking of the nature of church loyalties, the relationship between religion and national identity, and the proper role for the laity. If, though, the European Church can adapt successfully to the role of "creative minority," that augurs well for the fate of churches facing similar problems elsewhere. If the Catholic Church can survive contemporary Europe, it can survive anything.

The church's strong European roots mean that tactics and movements that originate here are likely to spread to other parts of the world, so that as in earlier centuries, European Catholicism provides a creative laboratory of faith. The opportunities to interact with Islam give lessons learned in Europe still wider applicability. And the presence of so many Christian immigrants makes it all the more probable that solutions devised in Europe will spread round the world.

Indeed, the recent despair over the fate of "God's continent" finds a good many historical precedents. Viewed over the centuries, perhaps the best indicator that Christianity is about to expand or revive is a widespread conviction that the religion is doomed or in its closing days. Arguably the worst single moment in the history of west European Christianity occurred around 1798, with the Catholic Church under severe persecution in much of Europe, and skeptical, deist, and unitarian movements in the ascendant across the Atlantic world. Among other horrors, that was the year that French revolutionary armies seized Pope Pius VI and carried him into exile, an event that many took to mark the end of the papacy, and (yet again) the terminal crisis of the Catholic Church. That particular trough in Christian affairs also turned into an excellent foundation, from which various groups built the great missionary movement of the nineteenth century, the second evangelical revival, and the Catholic devotional revolution. Nothing drives activists and reformers more powerfully than the sense that their faith is about to perish in their homelands and that they urgently need to make up these losses farther afield, whether overseas or among the previously neglected lost sheep at home. Quite possibly, the current sense of doom surrounding European Christianity will drive a comparable movement in the near future. Death and resurrection are not just fundamental doctrines of Christianity; they represent a historical model of the religion's structure and development.

Abbreviations

LAT   *Los Angeles Times*
MEQ   *Middle East Quarterly*
NCR   *National Catholic Reporter*
NYT   *New York Times*
WP   *Washington Post*
WS   *Weekly Standard*
WSJ   *Wall Street Journal*

Notes

Introductory Note

1. *Mapping the Global Future: Report of the National Intelligence Council's 2020 Project*, at www.dni.gov/nic/NIC_globaltrend2020_s3.html.

Chapter 1

1. Malise Ruthven, *A Satanic Affair* (London: Chatto and Windus, 1990).

2. Timothy Garton Ash, "Christian Europe, RIP," *Guardian*, April 21, 2005, at www.guardian.co.uk/Columnists/Column/0,,1464758,00.html.

3. Bruce Bawer, *While Europe Slept* (New York: Doubleday, 2006), 34. Bardot is quoted from Joel S. Fetzer and J. Christopher Soper, *Muslims and the State in Britain, France, and Germany* (Cambridge: Cambridge University Press, 2005), 130.

4. Philip Jenkins, *The Next Christendom*, 2nd ed. (New York: Oxford University Press, 2007).

5. Hilaire Belloc, *The Great Heresies* (New York: Sheed & Ward, 1938).

6. Lewis is quoted from *Die Welt*, July 28, 2004. Michel Gurfinkiel, "Islam in France," *MEQ*, 4(1)(1997) at www.meforum.org/article/337. Among recent authors quoting Belloc on Islam, see Patrick Buchanan, "An Idea Whose Time Has Come?" June 23, 2006, at http://news.yahoo.com/s/uc/20060623/cm_uc_crpbux/pat_buchanan20060623.

7. Silvia Taulés, *La nueva España musulmana* (Barcelona: Debolsillo, 2004), 11. Bolkestein is quoted from Christopher Caldwell, "Islamic Europe?" *WS*, October 4, 2004; Bassam Tibi is also quoted from this same article. For the liberation of Vienna, see Paul Reynolds, "Analysis," at http://news.bbc.co.uk/2/hi/europe/

3719418.stm. Compare Tony Blankley, *The West's Last Chance* (Chicago: Regnery, 2005).

8. Bat Ye'or, *The Decline of Eastern Christianity under Islam* (Madison, NJ: Fairleigh Dickinson University Press, 1996); Bat Ye'or, *Eurabia: The Euro-Arab Axis* (Madison, NJ: Fairleigh Dickinson Press, 2005). For the concept of dhimmitude, see also http://jihadwatch.org/dhimmiwatch/. Mark Steyn, "It's the Demography, Stupid," *New Criterion*, 24(2006), www.newcriterion.com/archives/24/01/its-the-demography/; and see also Mark Steyn, *America Alone* (Chicago: Regnery, 2006). Weigel is quoted from Tom Hundley, "A Crucible for Secularism," *Chicago Tribune*, June 19, 2006.

9. Joachim Güntner, "Albträume vom Minderheitendasein im eigenen Land," *Neue Zürcher Zeitung*, February 27, 2006. This passage is translated at www.signandsight.com/intodaysfeuilletons/630.html.

10. Mark Steyn, "Early Skirmish in the Eurabian Civil War," *Daily Telegraph*, November 8, 2005; Claire Berlinski, *Menace in Europe* (New York: Crown Forum, 2006).

11. Ali Laïdi and Ahmed Salam, *Le jihad en Europe* (Paris: Seuil, 2002); Udo K. Ulfkotte, *Der Krieg in unseren Städten* (Frankfurt Am Main: Eichborn, 2003); René Marchand, *La France en danger d'Islam: entre jihâd et reconquista* (Lausanne: Age d'Homme, 2003); Berndt Georg Thamm, *Terrorbasis Deutschland: Die islamistische Gefahr in unserer Mitte* (München: Diederichs, 2004); Ian Buruma, *Murder in Amsterdam* (New York: Penguin Press, 2006); Karen Jespersen and Ralf Pittelkow, *Islamister og Naivister* (Copenhagen: People's Press, 2006).

12. Matthew W. Maguire, "Is Paris Turning?" *Touchstone*, April 2006; Morten Messerschmidt is quoted from Jamie Glazov, "Europe's Suicide?" *FrontPageMagazine.com*, April 26, 2006, www.frontpagemag.com/Articles/ReadArticle.asp?ID=22204. The Europe 2015 map is widely available, but see, for instance, Antonio C. Abaya, "Europe in 2015," at www.manilastandardtoday.com/?page=antonioAbaya_feb21_2006; Rob Long, "National Review Travel Experience," *National Review*, March 13, 2006.

13. Niall Ferguson, *The War of the World* (London: Allen Lane, 2006); Charles Krauthammer, "The Iran Charade," *WP*, January 18, 2006. Patrick Buchanan, *The Death of the West: How Dying Populations and Immigrant Invasions Imperil Our Country and Civilization* (New York: Thomas Dunne, 2002).

14. Philip Longman, *The Empty Cradle* (New York: Basic Books, 2004); Günter Grass, *Headbirths* (New York: Harcourt Brace Jovanovich, 1982); Eli Berman, Laurence R. Iannaccone, and Giuseppe Ragusa, "From Empty Pews to Empty Cradles" (2006), at http://dss.ucsd.edu/~elib/pews.pdf.

15. Martin Walker, "Europe's Mosque Hysteria," *The Wilson Quarterly*, Spring 2006, 14–22.

16. Longman, *The Empty Cradle*; Ben J. Wattenberg, *Fewer* (Chicago: Ivan R. Dee, 2004).

17. Steyn, "It's the Demography, Stupid."

18. *Report of the High-Level Advisory Group Established at the Initiative of the President of the European Commission: Dialogue between Peoples and Cultures in the Euro-Mediterranean Area*, Euromed Report 68 (2003).

19. Fouad Ajami, "The Moor's Last Laugh," *WSJ*, March 22, 2004.

20. Philip Longman, "The Return of Patriarchy," *Foreign Policy*, March–April 2006, www.foreignpolicy.com/story/cms.php?story_id=3376&page=3.

21. Qaddafi is quoted from www.sojo.net/index.cfm?action–ews.display_article&mode=s&NewsID=5401; "Iraqi Ansar Al-Islam Commander Mullah Krekar in Norway," April 6, 2006, MEMRI Special Dispatch Series, 1134, at http://memri.org/bin/articles.cgi?Page=archives&Area=sd&ID=SP113406.

22. George Weigel, *The Cube and the Cathedral* (New York: Basic, 2005).

23. Michael Novak, "Troubled Continent" (2006), at www.michaelnovak.net/Module/Article/ArticleView.aspx?id=156.

24. Ferguson, *The War of the World;* Schoene is quoted from Uwe Siemen-Netto, "Faith: Islam's Third Run for Europe" (2002), at www.islamawareness.net/Fastest/third.html.

25. G. K. Chesterton, *The Flying Inn* (London: Methuen, 1914); Ibn Khaldun, *The Muqaddimah* (Princeton, NJ: Princeton University Press, 2005).

26. Lothrop Stoddard, *The Rising Tide of Color against White World-Supremacy* (New York: Scribner's, 1920).

27. Belloc, *The Great Heresies.*

28. Chesterton, *The Flying Inn.*

29. Rod Dreher, "Murder in Holland," *National Review,* May 7, 2002.

30. "Dutch Muslims kept that society" is quoted from Bawer, *While Europe Slept,* 2–3; "the main reason" is from ibid, 33. "Most people of non-Dutch origin" is quoted from Bruce Bawer, "Tolerating Intolerance," *Partisan Review* 69 (2002), www.bu.edu/partisanreview/archive/2002/3/bawer.html.

31. "If European governments" is quoted from Jamie Glazov, "While Europe Slept," *FrontPageMagazine.com,* May 23, 2006, at www.frontpagemag.com/Articles/ReadArticle.asp?ID=22563. Fallaci is quoted from Margaret Talbot, "The Agitator," *New Yorker,* June 5, 2006, 59–67; Morgens Camre is quoted from Jeffrey Fleishman, "Rage over Cartoons Perplexes Denmark," *LAT,* February 9, 2006; Bat Ye'or, *Eurabia: The Euro-Arab Axis;* Michael Gove, *Celsius 7/7* (London: Weidenfeld & Nicolson, 2006). For Mathias Döpfner, see Brian Moynahan, "Putting the Fear of God into Holland," *Sunday Times* (London), February 27, 2005.

32. Berlinski, *Menace in Europe,* 21.

33. Lowell Ponte, "Goodbye Europe," *FrontPageMagazine.com,* March 28, 2006, www.frontpagemag.com/Articles/ReadArticle.asp?ID=21820.

34. For more optimistic views of the European situation, see Walker, "Europe's Mosque Hysteria"; and "Look Out, Europe, They Say" and "Tales from Eurabia," both in *Economist,* June 22, 2006.

35. For reliable figures on Muslim populations in Europe, see Shireen T. Hunter, ed., *Islam, Europe's Second Religion* (Westport, CT: Praeger, 2002); Brigitte Maréchal, Stefano Allievi, Felice Dassetto, and Jørgen Nielsen, eds., *Muslims in the Enlarged Europe* (Leiden: Brill, 2003); Jørgen S. Nielsen, *Muslims in Western Europe* (Edinburgh: Edinburgh University Press, 2004).

36. Bawer is quoted from Glazov, "While Europe Slept."

37. For "potential Muslims," see, for instance, Justin Vaisse, "Unrest in France, November 2005," January 12, 2006, at www.brook.edu/views/testimony/fellows/vaisse20060112.htm.

38. Callum G. Brown, *The Death of Christian Britain* (London: Routledge, 2001); Grace Davie, *Europe: The Exceptional Case* (London: Darton, Longman and Todd, 2002).

39. "The Great Divide," Pew Global Attitudes Project (Washington, DC: Pew Research Center, 2006), accessible via http://pewglobal.org/reports/display.php?ReportID=253.
40. Roel Meijer, ed., *Alienation or Integration of Arab Youth* (Richmond, UK: Curzon, 2000).
41. Stefano Allievi, *Islam Italiano* (Turin: Einaudi, 2003); Chantal Saint-Blancat, ed., *L'Islam in Italia* (Roma: Edizioni Lavoro, 1999).
42. Philip Jenkins, *The New Anti-Catholicism* (New York: Oxford University Press, 2003).
43. Philip Jenkins, *Hoods and Shirts* (Chapel Hill: University of North Carolina Press, 1997).
44. Compare Leo Lucassen, *The Immigrant Threat* (Urbana: University of Illinois, 2005).
45. Jytte Klausen, *The Islamic Challenge* (New York: Oxford University Press, 2005), 3, 7.

Chapter 2

1. "Among Wealthy Nations US Stands Alone in Its Embrace of Religion," Pew Global Attitudes Survey (Washington, DC: Pew Research Center 2002), http://pewglobal.org/reports/pdf/167.pdf. The 2004 British survey is taken from the YouGov/Daily Telegraph Survey, at www.yougov.com/archives/pdf/STI040101003_2.pdf. For nonreligious responses in France, see Brigitte Maréchal, Stefano Allievi, Felice Dassetto, and Jørgen Nielsen, eds., *Muslims in the Enlarged Europe* (Leiden: Brill, 2003).
2. Stephen Bates, "Decline in Churchgoing Hits C of E Hardest," *Guardian*, April 14, 2001; Tim Radford, "Study Refutes Faith in Silent Majority," *Guardian*, August 16, 2005; Matt Barnwell and Amy Iggulden, "Religious Belief Falling Faster than Church Attendance," *Daily Telegraph*, August 17, 2005; Steve Bruce, *Religion in Modern Britain* (New York: Oxford University Press, 1995).
3. Carol Summerfield and Baljit Gill, eds., *National Statistics: Social Trends, 35*, 2005 edition (London: Palgrave Macmillan, 2005).
4. Much of what follows is drawn from Wil Arts, Jacques Hagenaars, and Loek Halman, *The Cultural Diversity of European Unity* (Leiden: Brill, 2003); Wil Arts and Loek Halman, eds., *European Values at the Turn of the Millennium* (Leiden: Brill, 2004); and Loek Halman, Ruud Luijkx, and Marga van Zundert, eds., *Atlas of European Values* (Leiden: Tilburg University, 2005); and additional data at www.gesis.org/za. Christie Davies, *The Strange Death of Moral Britain* (New Brunswick, NJ: Transaction, 2004). For recent British figures, see Ruth Gledhill, "Church Seeks Spirituality of Youth . . . and Doesn't Like What It Finds," *Times* (London), May 8, 2006. British confirmation figures are from Niall Ferguson, "Heaven Knows How We'll Rekindle Our Religion, But I Believe We Must," *Daily Telegraph*, July 31, 2005. For the English Church Census, see Jonathan Petre, "Migrants Fill Empty Pews as Britons Lose Faith," *Daily Telegraph*, September 18, 2006.
5. Callum G. Brown, *The Death of Christian Britain* (London: Routledge, 2001); Danny Kruger, "There's Plenty of Life Left in the Churches," *Daily Telegraph*, October 13, 2005; Carey is quoted from Kate Fox, *Watching the English*

(London: Hodder and Stoughton, 2004), 354. For Murphy-O'Connor, see Gill Donovan, "Cardinal Says Christianity Is Almost Vanquished," *NCR,* September 14, 2001.

6. For Switzerland, see Hugh McLeod, "The Crisis of Christianity in the West," in Hugh McLeod, ed., *Cambridge History of Christianity: World Christianities 1914–2000* (Cambridge: Cambridge University Press, 2006), 324.

7. Hanna Diskin, *The Seeds of Triumph* (Budapest/New York: Central European University Press, 2001).

8. For the Czech Republic, see Jeffrey Fleishman, "Where Nothing Is Sacred," *LAT,* July 14, 2003.

9. Maurilio Guasco, *Chiesa e cattolicesimo in Italia, 1945–2000* (Bologna: EDB, 2001); Alissa J. Rubin, "Troubles at Home," *LAT,* April 24, 2005; Peter L. Berger, "Religion and the West," *The National Interest,* Summer 2005, 112–119; David O'Reilly, "When Faithful Flee," *Philadelphia Inquirer,* June 5, 2006. The comparative study cited is Eli Berman, Laurence R. Iannaccone, and Giuseppe Ragusa, "From Empty Pews to Empty Cradles" (2006), at http://dss.ucsd.edu/~elib/pews .pdf. Beck is quoted from "Western Europe's Demographic Decline," at www .eurotopics.net/en/presseschau/archiv/aehnliche?likearticle=5916.

10. Peter Hebblethwaite, *The Runaway Church* (New York: Seabury Press, 1975); Peter Hebblethwaite, *The New Inquisition?* (San Francisco: Harper & Row, 1980).

11. For France, see Michel Gurfinkiel, "Islam in France," *MEQ,* 4(1)(1997), at www.meforum.org/article/337. Meisner is quoted at John L. Allen, Jr., "The Word from Rome," *NCR,* March 17, 2006. Barbara Thériault, *"Conservative Revolutionaries"* (New York: Berghahn Books, 2004).

12. The Dublin man is quoted in Noelle Knox, "Religion Takes a Back Seat in Western Europe," *USA Today,* August 10, 2005. Martin A. Convey, *Keeping the Faith in a Changing Society* (Blackrock, Ireland: Columba Press, 1994); Tom Inglis, *Moral Monopoly* (Dublin: University College Dublin Press, 1998); Louise Fuller, *Irish Catholicism since 1950* (Dublin: Gill and Macmillan, 2002).

13. "Annuarium Statisticum Ecclesiae 2003," *L'Osservatore Romano,* www .ewtn.com/library/CHISTORY/annu2003.HTM.

14. The Normandy example is from Elaine Sciolono, "Europeans Fast Falling Away from Church," *NYT,* April 19, 2005. For Cahors, see Robert Pigott, "Losing the Faith in France," http://news.bbc.co.uk/2/hi/programmes/ from_our_own_correspondent/4149645.stm. Sandy Tippett-Spirtou, *French Catholicism* (New York: St. Martin's Press, 2000); Martine Sevegrand, *Vers une église sans prêtres* (Rennes, France: Presses Universitaires de Rennes, 2004).

15. For St. Sulpice, see Sciolino, "Europeans Fast Falling Away from Church"; John Daniszewski, "Catholicism Losing Ground in Ireland," *LAT,* April 17, 2005.

16. Berman, Iannaccone, and Ragusa, "From Empty Pews to Empty Cradles."

17. John Fulton, Teresa Dowling, Anthony M. Abela, Irena Borowik, Penny Long Marler, and Luigi Tomasi, *Young Catholics at the New Millennium* (Dublin: University College Dublin Press, 2000).

18. Laurie Goodstein and Alessandra Stanley, "As Scandal Keeps Growing, Church and Its Faithful Reel," *NYT,* March 17, 2002; Sonya Yee, "Sex

Scandal Stuns Austria's Catholics," *LAT,* July 14, 2004. The Nolan Report (*Review on Child Protection in the Catholic Church in England and Wales*) can be found at www.nolanreview.org.uk/. For Ampleforth, see Ian Cobain, "Silence and Secrecy at School Where Child Sex Abuse Went On for Decades," *Guardian,* November 18, 2005.

19. Chris Moore, *Betrayal of Trust* (Dublin: Marino, 1995); Iseult O'Doherty, *Stolen Childhood* (Dublin: Poolbeg, 1998); Helen Goode, Hannah McGee, and Ciarán O'Boyle, *Time to Listen* (Dublin: Liffey Press, 2003). Tom Hundley, "How Catholicism Fell from Grace in Ireland," *Chicago Tribune,* July 9, 2006.

20. Alison O'Connor, *A Message from Heaven* (Dingle, Ireland: Brandon, 2000); Francis Murphy, Helen Buckley, and Laraine Joyce, *The Ferns Report,* presented to the Minister for Health and Children (Dublin: Government Publications, 2005). Archbishop Diarmuid Martin, "Will Ireland Be Christian in 2030?" at www.zenit.org/english/visualizza.phtml?sid=74415.

21. Joachim Güntner, "Wer Kirchengebäude retten will, muss umnutzungen tolerieren," *Neue Zürcher Zeitung,* April 24, 2006.

22. Kevin Sullivan, "A Spirited Attempt to Save Churches," *WP,* December 25, 2005. Robin Gill, *The Empty Church Revisited,* 2nd ed. (Burlington, VT: Ashgate, 2003).

23. Jeffrey Fleishman, "Where Nothing Is Sacred."

24. Shmuel Trigano, *L'avenir des juifs de France* (Paris: Grasset, 2006).

25. Todd M. Endelman, *The Jews of Britain, 1656–2000* (Berkeley: University of California Press, 2002).

26. Uwe Siemen-Netto, "Faith: Islam's Third Run for Europe" (2002), at www.islamawareness.net/Fastest/third.html.

27. "Text of Draft Preamble for Future European Constitution," www .zenit.org/english/visualizza.phtml?sid=36354; "European Politicians in Unholy Row over God's Place in Constitution," Episcopal News Service, March 19, 2003, www.ecusa.anglican.org/3577_19743_ENG_HTM.htm.

28. George Weigel, *The Cube and the Cathedral* (New York: Basic, 2005).

29. Joseph Ratzinger (Pope Benedict XVI) and Marcello Pera, *Without Roots* (New York: Perseus Books, 2006), 77.

30. Stephanie Holmes, "Profile" (2004), at http://news.bbc.co.uk/2/hi/europe/3718210.stm.

31. Andrew Pierce, "Kelly Questioned over View on 'Sin' of Homosexuality," *Times* (London), May 10, 2006.

32. Callum Brown, "Best Not to Take It Too Far," 2006, at www .opendemocracy.net/globalization-aboutfaith/britain_religion_3335.jsp. For Buttiglione, see Don Feder, "Facing the Population Bust," *FrontPageMag.com,* May 31, 2006, at www.frontpagemag.com/Articles/ReadArticle.asp?ID=22692; Bruton is quoted from Frank Bruni, "Faith Fades Where It Once Burned Strong," *NYT,* October 13, 2003.

33. Michael Burleigh, *Earthly Powers* (New York: HarperCollins, 2006); Sheridan Gilley and Brian Stanley, eds., *Cambridge History of Christianity: World Christianities 1815–1914* (Cambridge: Cambridge University Press, 2005); Hugh McLeod, *Secularisation in Western Europe, 1848–1914* (New York: St. Martin's Press, 2000); Hugh McLeod and Werner Ustorf, eds., *The Decline of Christendom in Western Europe, 1750–2000* (New York: Cambridge University Press, 2003).

34. Kay Chadwick, ed., *Catholicism, Politics and Society in Twentieth-century France* (Liverpool: Liverpool University Press, 2000); Gérard Cholvy and Yves-Marie Hilaire, *Religion et société en France: 1914–1945* (Toulouse: Privat, 2002); Gérard Cholvy and Yves-Marie Hilaire, *La France religieuse: 1945–1975* (Toulouse: Privat, 2002); Michael Snape, *God and the British Soldier* (London: Routledge, 2005); Hugh McLeod, ed., *Cambridge History of Christianity: World Christianities 1914–2000*. For Spain's tradition of mystical Catholic politics, see William A. Christian, Jr., *Visionaries* (Berkeley: University of California, 1996).

35. Michael Burleigh, *Sacred Causes* (London: HarperPress, 2006); Nicholas Atkin and Frank Tallett, *Priests, Prelates and People* (New York: I. B. Tauris, 2003). For Catholicism in the Netherlands, see Walter Goddijn, Jan Jacobs, Gérard van Tillo, et al., *Tot Vrijheid Geroepen* (Baarn, Netherlands: Ten Have, 1999).

36. Jonathan Luxmoore and Jolanta Babiuch, *The Vatican and the Red Flag* (London: Geoffrey Chapman/Continuum, 1999); Carolyn M. Warner, *Confessions of an Interest Group* (Princeton, NJ: Princeton University Press, 2000); Norbert Trippen, *Josef Kardinal Frings*, Vol. 1 (Paderborn: Ferdinand Schöningh, 2003); Ellen Ueberschär, *Junge Gemeinde im Konflikt* (Stuttgart: Verlag W. Kohlhammer, 2003); Dianne Kirby, ed., *Religion and the Cold War* (New York: Palgrave Macmillan, 2003); Mark Edward Ruff, *The Wayward Flock* (Chapel Hill: University of North Carolina Press, 2005); Burleigh, *Sacred Causes*. For the European flag, Weigel, *Cube and the Cathedral*, 194–195.

37. The definition of modernity is from Loek Halman and Ole Riis, eds., *Religion in Secularizing Society*, 1. For secularization theory, see Steve Bruce, *God Is Dead* (Oxford: Blackwell, 2002); David Martin, *On Secularization* (Aldershot, England: Ashgate, 2005). Jonas Pontusson, *Inequality and Prosperity* (Ithaca, NY: Cornell University Press, 2006). Paul Heelas and Linda Woodhead, with Benjamin Seel, Karin Tusting, and Bron Szerszynski, *The Spiritual Revolution* (Oxford: Blackwell, 2004). For rural decline, see Geert Mak, *Jorwerd: The Death of the Village in Late Twentieth-Century Europe* (New York: Harvill Press, 2001).

38. Diarmaid Ferriter, *The Transformation of Ireland 1900–2000* (London: Profile Books, 2004); Luca Diotallevi, *Religione, chiesa e modernizzazione* (Roma: Borla, 1999); Guido Verucci, *Cattolicesimo e laicismo nell'Italia contemporanea* (Milan: Francoangeli, 2001); Paul Ginsborg, *Italy and Its Discontents: 1980–2001* (London: Penguin, 2003). For Spain, see Audrey Brassloff, *Religion and Politics in Spain* (New York: St. Martin's Press, 1998); Josep M. Piñol, *La Transición democrática de la iglesia católica española* (Madrid: Editorial Trotta, 1999).

39. Tracy Wilkinson, "Southern Europe Seeing a Breakup Boom," *LAT*, May 21, 2006.

40. Summerfield and Gill, eds., *National Statistics: Social Trends, 35*, 2005 edition.

41. Renwick McLean, "In Spain, the 40% Solution," *International Herald Tribune*, May 5, 2006.

42. Berman, Iannaccone, and Ragusa, "From Empty Pews to Empty Cradles."

43. For Ferrara, see Frank Bruni, "Persistent Drop in Fertility Reshapes Europe's Futures," *NYT*, December 26, 2002; Alissa J. Rubin, "Troubles at Home," *LAT*, April 24, 2005.

44. Rüdiger Safranski, "Die Hüllen, die uns schützen," *Stuttgarter Zeitung*, March 18, 2006, at www.stuttgarter-zeitung.de/stz/page/detail.php/1119175.

45. Claire Berlinski, *Menace in Europe* (New York: Crown Forum, 2006), 239.

46. Grace Davie, *Europe: The Exceptional Case* (London: Darton, Longman and Todd, 2002).

47. Alexis de Tocqueveille, *Democracy in America*, book 1, chapter 17.

48. Rodney Stark, and Larry Iannaccone, "A Supply-Side Reinterpretation of the Secularization of Europe," *Journal for the Scientific Study of Religion* 33(1994): 230–252; Massimo Introvigne and Rodney Stark, "Religious Competition and Revival in Italy," at www.bepress.com/cgi/viewcontent.cgi?article=1001&context=ijrr.

49. Jørgen Jensen, *Den Fjerne Kirke* (Copenhagen, 1995); Viggo Mortensen, *Kristendommen Under Forvandling* (Højbjerg, Denmark: Forlaget Univers, 2005).

50. William J. Callahan, *The Catholic Church in Spain, 1875–1998* (Washington, DC: Catholic University of America Press, 2000); Vicente Cárcel Ortí, *Historia de la iglesia en la España contemporánea* (Madrid: Palabra, 2002); Juan José Tamayo, *Adiós a la Cristianidad* (Barcelona: Ediciones B, 2003).

51. Adrian Hastings, *A History of English Christianity, 1920–2000*, 4th ed. (London: SCM Press, 2001); Doreen Rosman, *The Evolution of the English Churches, 1500–2000* (Cambridge: Cambridge University Press, 2003); B. G. Worrall, *The Making of the Modern Church*, 3rd ed. (London: SPCK, 2004).

52. Chadwick, ed., *Catholicism, Politics and Society in Twentieth-century France.*

53. Martin E. Marty, "Ethnicity: The Skeleton of Religion in America," *Church History* 41(1972): 15–21.

Chapter 3

1. For the eruv's proponents, see www.nwlondoneruv.org/. "Jewish Eruv Set for London," August 9, 2002, http://news.bbc.co.uk/1/hi/england/2182994.stm.

2. Claire Berlinski, *Menace in Europe* (New York: Crown Forum, 2006), 7. For Christian numbers worldwide, see www.gordonconwell.edu/ockenga/globalchristianity/resources.php.

3. "International Religious Freedom Report 2005," at www.state.gov/g/drl/rls/irf/2005/51555.htm.

4. Luke Harding, "Poland Is Bucking the Europe-Wide Decline in Vocations, and Its Priests Are in Demand," *Guardian*, March 15, 2006; compare Tom Hundley, "Poland Digs In against Tide toward Secularism," *Chicago Tribune*, May 23, 2006.

5. Andrew M. Greeley, *Religion in Europe at the End of the Second Millennium* (New Brunswick, NJ: Transaction Publishers, 2003).

6. Thomas Fuller, "East Europeans Crowd through Britain's Wide-Open Door," *NYT*, October 23, 2005. "We used to celebrate" is from Terry Kirby, "750,000 and Rising: How Polish Workers Have Built a Home in Britain," *Independent* (London), 11 February 2006. For the age structure of British Poles, see Helen Pidd and Luke Harding, "Why Would You Leave a Place like Wroclaw?" *Guardian*, July 21, 2006.

7. Luke Harding, "Poland Is Bucking the Europe-Wide Decline in Vocations"; Timothy A. Byrnes, *Transnational Catholicism in Post-Communist Europe* (Lanham, MD: Rowman and Littlefield, 2001).

8. Juan José Tamayo, *Adiós a la Cristianidad* (Barcelona: Ediciones B, 2003), 207–260; www.somosiglesiaandalucia.org/.

9. Michael Hornsby-Smith, ed., *Catholics in England, 1900–2000* (London: Geoffrey Chapman, 1999); Michael Hornsby-Smith, *Roman Catholic Beliefs in England* (New York: Cambridge University Press, 1991); Martine Sevegrand, *Vers une église sans prêtres* (Rennes, France: Presses Universitaires de Rennes, 2004).

10. Davie is quoted in Matthew Schofield, "In Increasingly Secular Europe, Outpouring for Pope Surprising," Knight Ridder Newspapers, April 8, 2005, at www2.ljworld.com/news/2005/apr/08/in_increasingly_secular/.

11. James P. Gannon, "Is God Dead in Europe?" *USA Today*, January 8, 2006, www.usatoday.com/news/opinion/editorials/2006-01-08-faith-edit_x.htm.

12. Mary Lee Nolan and Sidney Nolan, *Christian Pilgrimage in Modern Western Europe* (Chapel Hill: University of North Carolina Press, 1989); Victor Turner and Edith Turner, *Image and Pilgrimage in Christian Culture* (New York: Columbia University Press, 1978), 203–230. For the functions of pilgrimage, see Simon Coleman and John Eade, eds., *Reframing Pilgrimage* (London: Routledge, 2004).

13. Ellen Badone, ed., *Religious Orthodoxy and Popular Faith in European Society* (Princeton, NJ: Princeton University Press, 1990); Ellen Badone and Sharon R. Roseman, eds., *Intersecting Journeys* (Urbana: University of Illinois Press, 2004). Europe's contemporary pilgrimage sites are discussed in several of the essays in Jill Dubisch and Michael Winkelman, eds., *Pilgrimage and Healing* (Tucson: University of Arizona Press, 2005). For Santiago, see Conrad Rudolph, *Pilgrimage to the End of the World* (Chicago: University of Chicago Press, 2004).

14. For Sarsina, see Tracy Wilkinson, "Collar Holds Blessing, Believers Say," *LAT*, August 29, 2005.

15. Olivier Clement, *Taizé: A Meaning to Life* (Chicago: GIA Publications, 1997).

16. Donal Foley, *Understanding Medjugorje* (Nottingham, UK: Theotokos Books, 2006).

17. Benjamin Forest, Juliet Johnson, and Marietta Stepaniants, *Religion and Identity in Modern Russia* (Burlington, VT: Ashgate, 2005).

18. Wil Arts and Loek Halman, eds., *European Values at the Turn of the Millennium* (Leiden: Brill, 2004); Loek Halman, Ruud Luijkx, and Marga van Zundert, eds., *Atlas of European Values* (Leiden: Tilburg University, 2005).

19. Grace Davie, *Religion in Britain since 1945: Believing without Belonging* (Oxford: Blackwell, 1994); Philip Richter and Leslie J. Francis, *Gone but Not Forgotten* (London: Darton, Longman and Todd, 1998). Grace Davie, *Religion in Modern Europe: A Memory Mutates* (New York: Oxford University Press, 2000).

20. Martin Schwartz-Lausten, *A Church History of Denmark* (Aldershot, England: Ashgate, 2002).

21. Compare Joseph F. Byrnes, *Catholic and French Forever* (University Park: Penn State University Press, 2005); John T. S. Madeley and Zsolt Enyedi, eds., *Church and State in Contemporary Europe* (London: Frank Cass, 2003).

22. Rachel Harden, "Pews Fuller for the Long Christmas," www.cofe.anglican.org. For Hanover, see "Germany Rediscovers Religion," *Deutsche Welle*, May 26, 2005, at www.dw-world.de/dw/article/0,,1596298,00.html?maca=en-bulletin-433-html. For Italian nuns, see John Thorne, "New Fervor among Young Italian Catholics," *Christian Science Monitor*, March 1, 2006.

23. Compare Tamayo, *Adiós a la Cristianidad*, 103–140; Madeley and Enyedi, eds., *Church and State in Contemporary Europe*.

24. Marie Parker-Jenkins, Dimitra Hartas, and Barrie Irving, *In Good Faith* (Aldershot, England: Ashgate, 2004).

25. "Divided Church Awaits Benedict in Catholic Poland," Yahoo News, May 19, 2006, http://asia.news.yahoo.com/060519/3/2krwl.html. Genevieve Zubrzycki, *The Crosses of Auschwitz* (Chicago: University of Chicago Press, 2006).

26. Elizabeth Rosenthal, "Antiabortion Effort in Europe, with U.S. Money, Widens Its Conservative Agenda," *NYT*, August 14, 2005; Nicholas Watt, "EU Challenges Vatican's Draft Abortion Treaty," *Guardian*, January 5, 2006. For conflicts between Catholicism and emerging European ideals, see Timothy A. Byrnes and Peter J. Katzenstein, eds., *Religion in an Expanding Europe* (Cambridge: Cambridge University Press, 2006).

27. Carolyn M. Warner, *Confessions of an Interest Group* (Princeton, NJ: Princeton University Press, 2000).

28. Heather Widdows, *Women's Reproductive Rights* (London: Palgrave Macmillan, 2005).

29. Joseph Ratzinger, "Above All, We Should Be Missionaries," 2000, http://tcrnews2.com/genratzinger.html; John L. Allen, Jr., *The Rise of Benedict XVI* (New York: Doubleday, 2005). For a Protestant perspective, compare Jonathan Bartley, *Faith and Politics after Christendom* (London: Authentic Media, 2006).

30. Jonathan Luxmoore and Jolanta Babiuch, *Rethinking Christendom* (London: Gracewing, 2005).

31. George Weigel, *Witness to Hope*, updated edition (New York: Harper Perennial, 2005).

32. "The great and promising flowering" is from Gordon Urquhart, *The Pope's Armada* (London: Bantam, 1995), 5; Tony Hanna, *New Ecclesial Movements* (London: St. Pauls, 2006). All the movements have a lively presence on the web. See for instance www.schoenstatt.de/; www.regnumchristi.org/; Communion and Liberation can be found at www.clonline.org/; the Community of Sant'Egidio at www.santegidio.org/en/index.html.

33. Tamayo, *Adiós a la Cristianidad*, 149–176; John L. Allen, Jr., *Opus Dei* (New York: Doubleday, 2005); Noam Friedlander, *What Is Opus Dei?* (London: Collins & Brown, 2005).

34. Tamayo, *Adiós a la Cristianidad*, 141–148. John Allen has reported on the Neocatechumenate in several of his "Word from Rome" columns in the *NCR*, e.g., December 23, 2005. The account of the meeting with Pope Benedict is from the column of January 13, 2006.

35. Chris Morgan, ed., *Communion and Liberation* (London: Catholic Truth Society, 2002). Guido Verucci, *Cattolicesimo e laicismo nell'Italia contemporanea* (Milan: Francoangeli, 2001); Davide Rondoni, ed., *Communion and Liberation* (Montreal: McGill-Queen's University Press, 2000).

36. Chiara Lubich, *May They All Be One* (New York: New City Press, 1984); Jim Gallagher, *A Woman's Work* (London: Fount, 1997); Chiara Lubich, *The Cry* (Hyde Park, NY: New City Press, 2001); Frank Johnson, *The Focolare Movement* (London: Catholic Truth Society, 2002).

37. www.rns-italia.it/default2.htm; Bishop Paul Josef Cordes, *Charisms and New Evangelization* (New York: Hyperion Books, 1996); Bishop Paul Josef

Cordes, *Call to Holiness* (Collegeville, Minn.: Michael Glazier Books, 1997); Peter Zimmerling, *Die charismatischen Bewegungen* (Göttingen: Vandenhoeck and Ruprecht, 2001).

38. http://emmanuelcommunity.com/newsite/aboutfounder.html; "We had the feeling" is quoted from www.zenit.org/english/archive/9808/zw980823.html.

39. www.newdawn.org.uk/introduction.htm.

40. www.cho.cz/www/index.php; www.martindom.sk/; I am grateful for information on these movements from Daniel Novotny of the University of Buffalo, and for translation work by Catherine Jenkins.

41. "Fanatical personality cults" is from Urquhart, *The Pope's Armada*, viii.

42. For the leadership of RnS, see www.rns-italia.it/ORGANISM/organism.htm.

43. "Manipulated mass hysteria" is from Urqhart, *Pope's Armada*, 197; "a well-nigh feverish and frenetic cult" is from Peter Fuchs, writing in *Frankfurter Rundschau*, August 19, 2005. This passage is translated from http://signandsight.com/intodaysfeuilletons/316.html.

44. Gary Hamel and C. K. Prahalad, *Competing for the Future* (Cambridge, MA: Harvard Business School Press, 1994).

45. Jan-Peter Graap, "Doubt and Amazement: ProChrist2006 in Europe," at www.lausanneworldpulse.com/worldreports/320/05-2006.

46. Quoted in F. Dean Lueking, "Liturgical Evangelism," *Christian Century*, June 13, 2006.

47. Lueking, "Liturgical Evangelism"; Jeff Chu, "O Father, Where Art Thou?" *Time*, June 11, 2003, at www.time.com/time/europe/html/030616/story.html.

48. Andrew Chandler, *The Church of England in the Twentieth Century* (Woodbridge, UK: Boydell Press, 2006). For the different shades of evangelical and charismatic opinion, see Graham Kings, "Canal, River and Rapids," *Anvil* 20(3)(2003): 167–184, at www.fulcrum-anglican.org.uk/docs/docs.cfm?fname=watercourses&format=pdf&option=inline.

49. For Holy Trinity Brompton, see www.htb.org.uk; The account of mid-size communities is from www.st-andrews.org.uk/mid-size-communities.php.

50. www.springharvest.org/; David W. Bebbington, *Evangelicalism in Modern Britain* (London: Routledge, 1988); William K. Kay, *Pentecostals in Britain* (Carlisle, UK: Paternoster Press, 2000).

51. The quote is from www.freshworship.org/about.html; Eddie Gibbs and Ryan Bolger, *Emerging Churches* (London: SPCK, 2006); www.churchnext.net/.

52. David Pytches, *Living at the Edge* (Bath: Arcadia, 2002); www.soulsurvivor.com/; www.new-wine.org/.

53. Rudolph Brown, "Evangelical Alliance: A Model Organization," *Jamaica Gleaner*, July 1, 2006; www.eauk.org/. For the house churches, Paul A. Welsby, *A History of the Church of England 1945–1980* (Oxford: Oxford University Press, 1984), 245.

54. George Carey, *The Church in the Market Place* (Eastbourne: Kingsway, 1984); Stephen Bates, *A Church at War* (New York: I. B. Tauris, 2004); "Evangelical Alliance Criticised for Slur against Same-Sex Couples," May 31, 2006, www.ekklesia.co.uk/content/news_syndication/article_060531horses.shtml.

55. David Pytches, *Come Holy Spirit*, 2nd ed. (London: Hodder & Staunton, 1995); David Pytches, *Healing Ministry and Pastoral Prayer Ministry* (London: New Wine International, 1999). The testimonies are from www.st-andrews .org.uk/testimonies_healingtestimonies.php.

56. Pytches is quoted from David W. Virtue, "Pytches Pitches Renewal for Ailing Church of England" at http://listserv.episcopalian.org/scripts/wa.exe? A2=ind0104b&L=virtuosity&H=1&P=2036.

57. Philip Jenkins, *Intimate Enemies* (Hawthorne, NY: Aldine de Gruyter, 1992). For the anti-Satanic theories of the time, see Toyne Newton, *The Demonic Connection* (Poole: Blandford Press, 1987); Kevin Logan, *Paganism and the Occult* (Eastbourne, Sussex: Kingsway, 1988); Audrey Harper and Harry Pugh, *Dance with the Devil* (Eastbourne, Sussex: Kingsway, 1990); Russ Parker, *Battling the Occult* (Downers Grove, IL: InterVarsity Press, 1990).

58. Nicky Gumbel, *How to Run the Alpha Course*, new ed. (Eastbourne: Kingsway Communications, 2004); http://alphacourse.org/itv/nickygumbel/.

59. Paula Dear, "Alpha Feeds Modern Spiritual Hunger," August 4, 2005, at http://news.bbc.co.uk/go/pr/fr/-/2/hi/uk_news/4721569.stm.

60. Jon Ronson, "Catch Me If You Can," *Guardian*, October 21, 2000.

Chapter 4

1. "New Archbishop of York Calls for Return to Life-Changing Christianity," *Christian Today*, December 1, 2005, at www.christiantoday.com/news/ church/new.archbishop.of.york.calls.for.return.to.life.changing.christianity/910 .htm; Sentamu's address can be found at www.africanecho.co.uk/africane-chonews3-dec16.html.

2. www.godembassy.org/en/embassy.php.

3. www.kicc.org.uk/. "A very—shall I say—atheistic Europe" is from Wendy Griffith, "A Harvest Sown by Generations Past," at www.cbn.com/spirituallife/ ChurchAndMinistry/ChurchHistory/HarvestSown.asp. Philip Jenkins, *The Next Christendom* (New York: Oxford University Press, 2002), 98–99, 207.

4. Ashimolowo is quoted from Griffith, "A Harvest Sown by Generations Past"; Rosie Murray-West, "Indian Tribe Sends a Missionary to Tackle Spiritual Void in Wales," *Daily Telegraph*, March 6, 2006.

5. "Les églises africaines se développent en Europe," *Religioscope*, January 19, 2003, www.religioscope.info/article_41.shtml; Gerrie ter Haar, *African Christians in Europe* (Nairobi, Kenya: Acton, 2001); Gerrie ter Haar, "African Christians or Christian Africans in Europe?" in James L. Cox and Gerrie ter Haar, eds., *Uniquely African?* (Trenton, NJ: Africa World Press, 2003); Khalid Koser, ed., *New African Diasporas* (New York: Routledge, 2003). For El Shaddai, see Katharine L. Wiegele, *Investing in Miracles* (Honolulu: Hawaii University Press, 2004). Websites of the individual churches can be found at www.rccg .org/; www.igrejauniversal.org.br/.

6. For the French diocese, see Robert Pigott, "Losing the Faith in France," http://news.bbc.co.uk/2/hi/programmes/from_our_own_correspondent/ 4149645.stm. The quote is from Michel Gurfinkiel, "Islam in France," *MEQ*, 4(1)(1997) at www.meforum.org/article/337.

7. Robert Beckford, *Jesus Is Dread* (London: Darton, Longman and Todd, 1998). Damian Thompson, *Waiting for Antichrist* (New York: Oxford University

Press, 2005); Afe Adogame and Cordula Weisskoeppel, eds., *Religion in the Context of African Migration* (Bayreuth, Germany: Bayreuth African Studies Series, 2005); Roswith Gerloff, "The African Diaspora in the Caribbean and Europe from Pre-Emancipation to the Present Day," in Hugh McLeod, ed., *Cambridge History of Christianity: World Christianities 1914–2000* (Cambridge: Cambridge University Press, 2006), 219–135.

8. "London, the cynical capital" is from Leo Benedictus, "From the Day We're Born till the Day We Die, It's the Church," *Guardian*, January 21, 2005.

9. For early British hostility to black Christians, see Oluwole A. Abiola, "African Churches in Europe," www.religiousfreedom.com/conference/Germany/abiola.htm. For the English Church Census, see Jonathan Petre, "Migrants Fill Empty Pews as Britons Lose Faith," *Daily Telegraph*, September 18, 2006. John Beya, "The Francophone Presence in Britain Revisited," in Gerrie ter Haar, ed., *Strangers and Sojourners* (Leuven: Peeters, 1998); Patrick Kalilombe, "Black Christianity in Britain," in ibid, 173–194. For Edwards, see Rudolph Brown, "Evangelical Alliance: A Model Organization," *Jamaica Gleaner*, July 1, 2006.

10. "I take the train" is from Bernard Coyault, "Christianisme: Radioscopie des Églises d'expression africaine en France," February 24, 2005, www.bethel-fr.com/afficher_info.php?id=12897.72; Xavier Ternisien, "Les Églises Afro-Chrétiennes font de la France une terre d'évangélisation," *Le Monde*, January 3, 2001. Jean-Paul Gourévitch, *La France africaine* (Paris: Pré Aux Clercs, 2000).

11. For the Congolese diaspora in Europe, see Célestin Kibutu Ngimbi, "Comment devient-on pasteur en République Démocratique du Congo?" www.congovision.com/science/marasme21.html. Marc Spindler, "Églises étrangères en Europe," at www.protestants.org/textes/protestantisme_europe/acteurs_spindler.htm; Coyault, "Christianisme: Radioscopie des Églises d'expression africaine en France." For the Communauté des Églises d'expressions africaines de France, see www.eglises.org/types/ceaf/.

12. www.eglises.org/france/93/.

13. For the Evangelical Assembly of the Pentecost, see Elisabeth Eaves, "Is France Getting Religion?" *Slate*, http://slate.msn.com/id/2112962/, February 1, 2005. The *Église Protestante Evangélique* is described in Agnieszka Tennant, "The French Reconnection," *Christianity Today*, March 2005, online at www.christianitytoday.com/ct/2005/003/20.28.html.

14. Michael Mewshaw, "In Churches, a Mosaic of Cultures," *NYT*, June 27, 2004.

15. Benjamin Simon, "Christian Pluralism and the Quest for Identity in African Initiated Churches in Germany," www.cesnur.org/2001/london2001/simon.htm. See also Gerrie ter Haar, "African Christians in the Netherlands," in Gerrie ter Haar, ed., *Strangers and Sojourners* (Leuven: Peeters, 1998), 153–172; J. A. B. Jongeneel, R. Budiman, and J. J. Visser, *Gemeenschapsvorming van Aziatische, Afrikaanse en Midden-en Zuidamerikaanse Christenen in Nederland* (Zoetermeer: Boekencentrum, 1996).

16. For the Christian Church Outreach Mission, see "Les Églises africaines se développent en Europe." For the pastors, see www.ccomi.org/pastors.html.

17. Immigrant churches are the subject of a rapidly growing literature, in both North America and Europe. For U.S. conditions, see Helen Rose Ebaugh

and Janet Saltzman Chafetz, eds., *Religion and the New Immigrants* (Walnut Creek, CA: Altamira Press, 2000); Tony Carnes and Anna Karpathakis, eds., *New York Glory* (New York: New York University Press, 2001); Russell Jeung, *Faithful Generations* (New Brunswick, NJ: Rutgers University Press, 2004); Su Yon Pak, Unzu Lee, Jung Ha Kim, and Myungji Cho, *Singing the Lord's Song in a New Land* (Louisville, KY: Westminster John Knox Press, 2005).

18. Philip Jenkins, *The New Faces of Christianity* (New York: Oxford University Press, 2006).

19. Nicholas van Hear, *New Diasporas* (Seattle: University of Washington Press, 1998); Östen Wahlbeck, *Kurdish Diasporas* (New York: St. Martin's Press, 1999); Steven Vertovec, *The Hindu Diaspora* (New York: Routledge, 2000); Stefano Allievi and Jørgen Nielsen, eds., *Muslim Networks and Transnational Communities in and across Europe* (Leiden: Brill, 2003).

20. Hebrews 13:14.

21. Richard Hoskins, *Sacrifice* (London: Little, Brown, 2006); Antony Barnett, Paul Harris, and Tony Thompson, "Human Flesh on Sale in London," *Observer,* November 3, 2002. For Combat Spirituel, see Vikram Dodd, "Police Investigate Religious Links after Witchcraft Abuse of Child, 8," *Guardian,* June 4, 2005.

22. David Batty and Agencies, "Children Abused in Exorcism Rites," *Guardian,* February 25, 2005; Andrew Alderson and Chris Johnston, "Dozens of African Children Beaten, Abused and Accused of Witchcraft, Say Detectives," *Daily Telegraph,* May 6, 2005; Vikram Dodd and Tony Thompson, "Churches Blamed for Exorcism Growth," *Observer,* June 5, 2005; Lucy Ward, "Abuse Stories Isolating African Communities," *Guardian,* July 21, 2005; Jack Grimston, "'Witch Child' Abuse Spreads in Britain: 50 Cases Suspected in London Alone," *Sunday Times* (London), June 25, 2006; Richard Edwards, "Child Sacrifices in London," *Evening Standard,* 16 June 2005; Afe Adogame "Engaging the Rhetoric of Spiritual Warfare," *Journal of Religion in Africa,* 34(2004): 493–522.

23. "I traveled to Africa" is from www.kcl.ac.uk/phpnews/wmview.php?ArtID=1209. "A new Frankenstein religion" is from Richard Hoskins, "Torment of Africa's 'Child Witches,'" *Sunday Times,* February 5, 2006. Hoskins, *Sacrifice.*

24. Lucy Ward, "Churches to Attend Ritual Abuse Summit," *Guardian,* July 12, 2005.

25. "Churches Unite to Condemn BBC Attack on African Christianity," April 18, 2006, www.ligali.org/article.php?id=444.

26. Before his involvement in the domestic sacrifice controversy, all Hoskins's work on African themes had appeared in the form of conference presentations and encyclopedia pieces, chiefly on Kimbanguism. Though for several years Hoskins listed as "forthcoming" a book on this movement, the current status of the project is unknown. His other book publication is on a non-African topic, *The Doctrine of the Trinity in the Works of John Richardson Illingworth and William Temple, and the Implications for Contemporary Trinitarian Theology* (Lewiston, Maine: Edwin Mellen Press, 1999). See also now Hoskins, *Sacrifice.* For Hoskins's background, see www.kcl.ac.uk/ip/moiralangston/RH.html. He currently holds the position of Visiting Senior Research Fellow at King's College, London.

27. Ian Cobain and Vikram Dodd, "How Media Whipped Up a Racist Witch-Hunt," *Guardian,* June 25, 2005.

28. Marie Fatayi-Williams, *For the Love of Anthony* (London: Hodder and Stoughton, 2006).

29. Philip Jenkins, "The Politics of Persecuted Religious Minorities," in Robert A. Seiple and Dennis R. Hoover, eds., *Religion and Security* (Lanham, MD: Rowman and Litlefield, 2004), 25–36.

Chapter 5

1. Fouad Ajami, "The Moor's Last Laugh," *WSJ,* March 22, 2004.
2. Innocenzo Siggillino, et al., eds., *L'Islam nelle città* (Milano: F. Angeli, 2001); Stefano Allievi, *Islam italiano* (Turin: Einaudi, 2003). Minou Reeves, *Muhammad in Europe* (New York University Press, 2001). Emran Qureshi and Michael A. Sells, eds., *The New Crusades* (New York: Columbia University Press, 2003).
3. Allievi, *Islam Italiano;* Stephen O'Shea, *Sea of Faith* (New York: Walker & Company, 2006); César Vidal Manzanares, *España frente al Islam* (Madrid: Esfera de los Libros, 2004).
4. L. P. Harvey, *Muslims in Spain, 1500 to 1614* (Chicago: University of Chicago Press, 2005); Benjamin Ehlers, *Between Christians and Moriscos* (Baltimore: Johns Hopkins University Press, 2006); James Reston, *Dogs of God* (London: Faber and Faber, 2006).
5. Edward W. Said, *Orientalism* (New York: Pantheon, 1978).
6. Rollin S. Armour, *Islam, Christianity, and the West* (Maryknoll, NY: Orbis Books, 2002).
7. Andrew G. Bostom, ed., *The Legacy of Jihad* (Amherst, NY: Prometheus, 2005). For a more benevolent view of Muslim hegemony in India, see William Dalrymple, *The Last Mughal* (London: Bloomsbury, 2006).
8. Caroline Finkel, *Osman's Dream* (New York: Perseus Books, 2006).
9. Hilaire Belloc, *The Great Heresies* (New York: Sheed & Ward, 1938); Nabil I. Matar, *Islam in Britain 1558–1685* (New York: Cambridge University Press, 1998); Nabil I. Matar, *Turks, Moors and Englishmen in the Age of Discovery* (New York: Columbia University Press, 1999); Jack Goody, *Islam in Europe* (New York: Polity Press, 2003). Ibrahim Kalin, "Western Perceptions of Islam," online at www.masnet.org/contempissue.asp?id=253.
10. Bat Ye'or, *The Decline of Eastern Christianity under Islam* (Madison, NJ: Fairleigh Dickinson University Press, 1996); Efraim Karsh, *Islamic Imperialism: A History* (New Haven: Yale University Press, 2006); Alan G. Jamieson, *Faith and Sword* (New York: Reaktion, 2006).
11. Robert D. Crews, *For Prophet and Tsar* (Cambridge, MA: Harvard University Press, 2006); Nicholas Griffin, *Caucasus: Mountain Men and Holy Wars* (New York: Thomas Dunne, 2003).
12. Robert Irwin, *For Lust of Knowing* (London: Allen Lane, 2006).
13. Benjamin Stora and Mohammed Harbi, eds., *La guerre d'Algérie* (Paris: R. Laffont, 2004).
14. Rozina Visram, *Ayahs, Lascars and Princes* (London: Pluto Press, 1986); Humayun Ansari, *The Infidel Within* (London: C. Hurst, 2004).
15. Bat Ye'or, *Eurabia: The Euro-Arab Axis* (Madison, NJ: Fairleigh Dickinson, 2005); Oriana Fallaci, *The Force of Reason* (New York: Rizzoli, 2006).
16. Roger Ballard, ed., *Desh Pardesh* (London: South Asia Books, 1996). For the Muslim presence in various nations, see Shireen T. Hunter, ed., *Islam, Europe's Second Religion* (Westport, CT: Praeger, 2002); Stefano Allievi, *Musulmani d'Occidente* (Rome: Carocci, 2002); Brigitte Maréchal, Stefano Allievi,

Felice Dassetto, and Jørgen Nielsen, eds., *Muslims in the Enlarged Europe* (Leiden: Brill, 2003); Jørgen S. Nielsen, *Muslims in Western Europe* (Edinburgh: Edinburgh University Press, 2004); Ahmed Al-Shahi and Richard Lawless, *Middle East and North African Immigrants in Europe* (London: Routledge/Curzon, 2005).

17. Joel S. Fetzer and J. Christopher Soper, *Muslims and the State in Britain, France, and Germany* (Cambridge: Cambridge University Press, 2005), 62. Nielsen, *Muslims in Western Europe.* Mohammed Arkoun, ed., *Histoire de l'Islam et des musulmans en France du moyen age à nos jours* (Paris: Albin Michel, 2006).

18. Richard Derderian, *North Africans in Contemporary France* (New York: Palgrave Macmillan, 2004); Sylvestre Tchibindat, *Le Logement des algériens en France* (Paris: L'Harmattan, 2005).

19. Stefano Allievi and Jørgen Nielsen, eds., *Muslim Networks and Transnational Communities in and across Europe* (Leiden: Brill, 2003); Marfa Heimbach, *Die Entwicklung der islamischen Gemeinschaft in Deutschland seit 1961* (Berlin: Klaus Schwarz, 2001); Nico Landman, "Islam in the Benelux Countries," in Shireen T. Hunter, ed., *Islam, Europe's Second Religion;* Wolfgang Zank, *The German Melting-Pot* (New York: Palgrave, 2002); Eva Østergaard-Nielsen, *Transnational Politics* (New York: Routledge, 2003).

20. John Rex, "Islam in the United Kingdom," in Shireen T. Hunter, ed., *Islam, Europe's Second Religion.*

21. Alain Boyer, *L'Islam en France* (Paris: Presses Universitaires de France, 1998); Christopher Caldwell, "The Crescent and the Tricolor," *Atlantic Monthly,* November 2000; Dounia Bouzar, *L'Islam des banlieues* (Paris: Syros, 2001); Xavier Ternisien, *La France des mosquées* (Paris: Albin Michel, 2002); Remy Leveau and Shireen T. Hunter, "Islam in France," in Shireen T. Hunter, ed., *Islam, Europe's Second Religion;* Yves Charles Zarka, Sylvie Taussig, Cynthia Fleury, Alexandre Adler, Fadela Amara, and Rochdy Alili, eds., *L'Islam en France* (Paris: Presses Universitaires de France, 2004).

22. Daniele Joly, *Britannia's Crescent* (Aldershot, UK: Avebury, 1995); Tahir Abbas, ed., *Muslim Britain* (New York: Zed Books, 2005).

23. W. A. R. Shadid and P. S. van Koningsveld, eds., *Islam in Dutch Society* (Kampen, Netherlands: Kok Pharos, 1992); Sophie Body-Gendrot and Marco Martiniello, eds., *Minorities in European Cities* (New York: St. Martin's Press, 2000); Jocelyne Cesari, et al., *Islam in European Cities* (Paris: 2001), online at http://euro-islam.info/pages/cities.html.

24. Klaus Kreitmeir, *Allahs deutsche Kinder* (München: Pattloch, 2002); Faruk Sen and Hayrettin Aydin, *Islam in Deutschland* (München: C. H. Beck, 2002); Alexandre Escudier, Brigitte Sauzay, and Rudolf Von Thadden, eds., *Der Islam in Europa* (Göttingen: Wallstein, 2003).

25. For Chirac, see Thomas Deltombe, *L'Islam imaginaire* (Paris: Editions La Découverte, 2005); Andreas Goldberg, "Islam in Germany," in Shireen T. Hunter, ed., *Islam, Europe's Second Religion.*

26. Christopher Caldwell, "A Swedish Dilemma," *WS,* February 28, 2005; Brian Moynahan, "Putting the Fear of God into Holland," *Sunday Times* (London), February 27, 2005.

27. Ravil Bukharev, *Islam in Russia* (New York: Palgrave, 2000); Yaacov Ro'I, *Islam and the Soviet Union* (New York: Columbia University Press, 2000); Hilary Pilkington and Galina Yemelianova, eds., *Islam in Post-Soviet Russia* (New York: RoutledgeCurzon, 2003); Shireen T. Hunter, with Jeffrey L. Thomas and

Alexander Melikishvili, *Islam in Russia* (Armonk, NY: M. E. Sharpe, 2004); Marlène Laruelle and Sébastien Peyrouse, *Islam et politique en Ex-URSS* (Paris: L'Harmattan, 2005).

28. H. T. Norris, *Islam in the Balkans* (Columbia: University of South Carolina Press, 1994); Gerrie ter Haar, "African Christians in the Netherlands," in Gerrie ter Haar, ed., *Strangers and Sojourners* (Leuven: Peeters, 1998), 153–172; H. T. Norris, *Popular Sufism of Eastern Europe* (London: RoutledgeCurzon, 2006).

29. Stefano Allievi, *Islam italiano* (Turin: Einaudi, 2003); Stefano Allievi, "Islam in Italy," in Shireen T. Hunter, ed., *Islam, Europe's Second Religion;* Chantal Saint-Blancat, ed., *L'Islam in Italia* (Roma: Edizioni Lavoro, 1999).

30. Siggillino, et al., eds., *L'Islam nelle città,* 8.

31. Siggillino, et al., eds., *L'Islam nelle città.*

32. Fetzer and Soper, *Muslims and the State in Britain, France, and Germany.*

33. Brigitte Maréchal, "Mosques, Organization and Leadership," in Brigitte Maréchal, Stefano Allievi, Felice Dassetto, and Jørgen Nielsen, eds., *Muslims in the Enlarged Europe* (Leiden: Brill, 2003), 80–81.

34. "Mosque Signals Muslims' Return to Spain," July 10, 2003, http://news.bbc.co.uk/1/hi/world/europe/3055377.stm.

35. Arthur Wesley Helweg, *Sikhs in England,* 2nd ed. (Delhi: Oxford University Press, 1986); Rohit Barot, "Hindus and Hinduism in Europe," in Sean Gill, Ursula King, and Gavin D'Costa, eds., *Religion in Europe* (Grand Rapids, MI: William B. Eerdmans, 1993): 68–85; Steven Vertovec, *The Hindu Diaspora* (New York: Routledge, 2000).

36. Rainer Liedtke and Stephan Wendehorst, eds., *The Emancipation of Catholics, Jews and Protestants* (Manchester: Manchester University Press, 1999).

37. The estimate of 1.4 million immigrants a year is from Niall Ferguson, *The War of the World* (London: Allen Lane, 2006); for the National Intelligence Council, see www.dni.gov/nic/NIC_globaltrend2020_s3.html#page83.

Chapter 6

1. Brigitte Maréchal, Stefano Allievi, Felice Dassetto, and Jørgen Nielsen, eds., *Muslims in the Enlarged Europe* (Leiden: Brill, 2003). Roy is quoted from Tom Hundley, "A Crucible for Secularism," *Chicago Tribune,* June 19, 2006.

2. Amir Khan is quoted from Pat Jordan, "The Great British-Pakistani-Muslim Hope," *NYT Magazine,* March 19, 2006; the Moroccan man is from Farhad Khosrokhavar, *L'Islam dans les prisons* (Paris: Balland, 2004), 52–53.

3. For prospects for a new Euro-Islam, see Felice Dassetto, *La construction de l'Islam européen* (Paris: L'Harmattan, 1996); Jørgen S. Nielsen, *Towards a European Islam* (New York: St. Martin's Press, 1999); Olivier Roy, *Vers un Islam européen* (Paris: Esprit, 1999); John L. Esposito and François Burgat, eds., *Modernising Islam* (London: C. Hurst, 2002).

4. Karima Rhanem, "Witchcraft in Morocco," *Morocco Times,* May 7, 2006, www.moroccotimes.com/paper/article.asp?idr=11&id=14614; Abdellah Hammoudi, *The Victim and Its Masks* (Chicago: University of Chicago Press, 1993); Vincent J. Cornell, *Realm of the Saint* (Austin: University of Texas Press, 1998); Lawrence Rosen, *The Culture of Islam* (Chicago: University of Chicago Press, 2002).

5. Brigitte Maréchal, "Mosques, Organization and Leadership," in Brigitte Maréchal, Stefano Allievi, Felice Dassetto, and Jørgen Nielsen, eds., *Muslims in the Enlarged Europe* (Leiden: Brill, 2003), 113–115.

6. Stefano Allievi and Jørgen Nielsen, eds., *Muslim Networks and Transnational Communities in and across Europe* (Leiden: Brill, 2003), 43–44; Galina Yemelianova, "Transnational Islam v Ethnic Islam in Eastern Europe," in Allievi and Nielsen, eds., *Muslim Networks and Transnational Communities in and across Europe*, 243–280.

7. Alexandre Bennigsen and S. Enders Wimbush, *Mystics and Commissars* (Berkeley: University of California Press, 1985).

8. Ron Geaves, *The Sufis of Britain* (Cardiff, Wales: Cardiff Academic Press, 2000); Stefano Allievi, *Islam italiano* (Turin: Einaudi, 2003), 223; David Westerlund, ed., *Sufism in Europe and North America* (New York: RoutledgeCurzon, 2004); Jamal Malik and John Hinnells, eds., *Sufism in the West* (New York: Routledge, 2006); H. T. Norris, *Popular Sufism of Eastern Europe* (London: RoutledgeCurzon, 2006).

9. Galina Yemelianova, "Transnational Islam v Ethnic Islam in Eastern Europe," 243–280.

10. Olivier Roy, *Globalized Islam* (New York: Columbia University Press, 2004). "The religion of their parents" is from Olivier Roy, "Born Again to Kill," August 4, 2005, at www.signandsight.com/features/296.html. Felice Dassetto, Brigitte Maréchal, and Jorgen Nielsen, eds., *Convergences musulmanes* (Paris: l'Harmattan, 2001).

11. Shermy Larent, "Brigitte Bardot Unleashes Colourful Diatribe against Muslims and Modern France," May 12, 2003, at www.indybay.org/newsitems/2003/05/12/16103761.php. Roy is quoted from "Born Again to Kill." For issues arising from the legal accommodation of religious minorities, see, for instance, Jonas Alwall, *Muslim Rights and Plights* (Lund, Sweden: Lund University Press, 1998); Roberta Aluffi Beck-Peccoz and Giovanna Zincone, eds., *The Legal Treatment of Islamic Minorities in Europe* (Leuven: Peeters, 2004).

12. Allievi and Nielsen, eds., *Muslim Networks and Transnational Communities.*

13. Larry Poston, *Islamic Da'wah in the West* (New York: Oxford University Press, 1992); Gilles Kepel, *The Revenge of God* (University Park: Pennsylvania State University Press, 1994); Gilles Kepel, *Jihad: The Trail of Political Islam* (Cambridge, MA: Belknap Press, 2003); Brigitte Maréchal, "Mosques, Organization and Leadership," 126–143; Lars Pedersen, *Newer Islamic Movements in Western Europe* (Aldershot, England: Ashgate, 1999); Barbara Daly Metcalf, "Traditionalist Islamic Activism," online at www.ssrc.org/sept11/essays/metcalf.htm; Alex Alexiev, "Tablighi Jamaat: Jihad's Stealthy Legions," *MEQ*, 12(2005), at www.meforum.org/article/686.

14. www.ahlehadith.co.uk/.

15. Allievi and Nielsen, eds., *Muslim Networks and Transnational Communities;* Jørgen S. Nielsen, *Muslims in Western Europe* (Edinburgh: Edinburgh University Press, 2004).

16. Randeep Ramesh, "Something Old, Something New," *Guardian*, August 18, 2006; Syed Abul 'Ala Maudoodi, *The Islamic Movement* (London: Islamic Foundation, 1984).

17. Felice Dassetto, "After September 11," in Brigitte Maréchal, Stefano Allievi, Felice Dassetto, and Jørgen Nielsen, eds., *Muslims in the Enlarged Europe*

(Leiden: Brill, 2003), 489–530; Olivier Roy and Mariam Abou Zahab, *Islamist Networks* (New York: Columbia University Press, 2004); Emmanuel Razavi, *Frères musulmans* (Paris: Jean Cyrille Godefroy, 2005); Sylvain Besson, *La conquête de l'Occident* (Paris: Edition Seuil, 2005).

18. Quintan Wiktorowicz, *Radical Islam Rising* (Lanham, MD: Rowman and Littlefield, 2005).

19. Ray Takeyh and Nikolas K. Gvosdev, *The Receding Shadow of the Prophet* (Westport, CT: Praeger, 2004); "Van Dawa tot Jihad" (Den Haag: Ministerie van Binnenlandse Zaken en Koninkrijksrelaties, 2004), at www.aivd.nl/contents/pages/10835/notavandawatotjihad.pdf.

20. Melanie Phillips, *Londonistan* (London: Encounter Books, 2006); Takeyh and Gvosdev, *The Receding Shadow of the Prophet*.

21. Tony Judt, *Postwar* (New York: Penguin, 2005). Roy is quoted from Craig S. Smith, "Europe's Muslims May Be Headed Where the Marxists Went Before," *NYT*, December 26, 2004; Farhad Khosrokhavar is quoted from Craig S. Smith, "In Europe's Jails, Neglect of Islam Breeds Trouble," *NYT*, December 8, 2004.

22. Salman Rushdie, "What This Cultural Debate Needs Is More Dirt, Less Pure Stupidity," *Times* (London), December 10, 2005; Delwar Hussain, "Bangladeshis in East London," July 7, 2006, at *www.opendemocracy.net/democracy-protest/bangladeshi_3715.jsp*.

23. Jonathan Laurence, "Managing Transnational Islam in Western Europe" (2004) at www.lisproject.org/immigration/papers/laurence.pdf.

24. Afzal Khan is quoted in Christopher Caldwell, "After Londonistan," *NYT Magazine*, June 25, 2006. The leader from Villeurbanne is from Henri Astier, "French Struggle to Build Local Islam," November 14, 2005, http://news.bbc.co.uk/go/pr/fr/-/2/hi/europe/4430244.stm.

25. The M30 complex is described in Yoni Fighel, "Swiss Authorities Thwart Plot to Down El Al Passenger Plane," www.ict.org.il/spotlight/det.cfm?id=1143. For Kazan, see Susan B. Glasser, "Muslims Test Russia's Tolerance," *WP*, September 9, 2002; Niall Ferguson, "The March of Islam," *Daily Telegraph*, May 21, 2006. For Stockholm, see Christopher Caldwell, "Islam on the Outskirts of the Welfare State," *NYT Magazine*, February 5, 2006.

26. Hanri Astier, "French Struggle to Build Local Islam."

27. Paul A. Silverstein, *Algeria in France* (Bloomington: Indiana University Press, 2004); Laurence, "Managing Transnational Islam."

28. Hanri Astier, "French Struggle to Build Local Islam."

29. Charles Bremner, "Stoned to Death," *Times* (London), December 4, 2004.

30. Magdi Allam, *Bin Laden in Italia* (Milan: Mondadori, 2002).

31. "Spain and Islam," www.fides.org/eng/dossier/2005/espana_islam05.html. For extremism in Spain, see Pedro Canales y Enrique Montánchez, *En el nombre de Alá* (Barcelona: Planeta, 2002). For Germany, Werner Schiffauer, *Die Gottesmänner* (Frankfurt am Main: Suhrkamp, 2000). The IGMG website is found at www.igmg.de/index.php?module=ContentExpress&func=display&ceid=1.

32. Jørgen S. Nielsen, *Muslims in Western Europe* (Edinburgh: Edinburgh University Press, 2004); www.mcb.org.uk/. For the older stress on ethnic rather than racial identity, see Stephen Castles, with Heather Booth and Tina Wallace, *Here for Good: Western Europe's New Ethnic Minorities* (London: Pluto

Press, 1984). For the growing realization of the distinctively Islamic presence in the late 1980s, see, for instance, Felice Dassetto and Albert Bastenier, *Europa: nuova frontera dell'Islam* (Rome: Edizioni Lavoro, 1988); Tomas Gerholm and Yngve Georg Lithman, eds., *The New Islamic Presence in Western Europe* (London: Mansell, 1988).

33. Magdi Allam, *Bin Laden in Italia*; for the Muslim Brotherhood in the West, see Sylvain Besson, *La conquête de l'Occident* (Paris: Edition Seuil, 2005).

34. For the Ligue Française de la Femme Musulmane, see www.lffm.org/. For the UOIF, see www.uoif-online.com/. "Openly bankrolled by the Algerian government" is from Henri Astier, "French Struggle to Build Local Islam"; Glen Feder, "The Muslim Brotherhood in France," at www.inthenationalinterest .com/Articles/September%202005/September2005FederPFV.html.

35. The remark about the Ahmadiyyas is from Jytte Klausen, *The Islamic Challenge* (New York: Oxford University Press, 2005), 36. "A Question of Leadership," August 21, 2005, news.bbc.co.uk/go/pr/fr/-/1/hi/programmes/panorama/4171950.stm.

36. Silvia Taulés, *La nueva España musulmana* (Barcelona: Debolsillo, 2004); "Interview with Dr. Mansur Abdussalam Escudero," www.islamfortoday.com/escudero.htm.

37. Henri Astier, "French Struggle to Build Local Islam."

38. Nasr Abu Zaid and Esther R. Nelson, *Voice of an Exile* (Westport, CT: Praeger, 2004). Tahhan is quoted from "Muslim Intellectual Calls for 'Protestant Islam,'" MEMRI Special Dispatch Series, 1198, July 6, 2006, at http://memri.org/bin/articles.cgi?Page=archives&Area=sd&ID=SP119806. Kanan Makiya, *The Rock* (London: Constable, 2002). The comment about Makiya is from Nick Cohen, "A Question of Faith," *Observer*, May 12, 2002.

39. For al-Qaradawi and the controversies surrounding him, see for instance "Sheik Yusuf al-Qaradawi: Theologian of Terror," August 1, 2005, at www.adl.org/main_Arab_World/al_Qaradawi_report_20041110.htm?Multi_page_sections=sHeading_2.

40. The quote is from http://service.spiegel.de/cache/international/0,1518,329784,00.html; Bassam Tibi, *The Challenge of Fundamentalism* (Berkeley: University of California Press, 1998); Bassam Tibi, *Der Islam und Deutschland* (München: Deutsche Verlags-Anstalt DVA, 2000); Bassam Tibi, *Islamische Zuwanderung* (München: Deutsche Verlags-Anstalt, 2002); Bassam Tibi, *Islam Between Culture and Politics*, 2nd ed. (London: Palgrave Macmillan, 2005). For another widely read reformer, see Ziauddin Sardar, *Desperately Seeking Paradise* (Cambridge: Granta Books, 2004).

41. Paul Donnelly, "Tariq Ramadan: The Muslim Martin Luther?" *Salon*, http://dir.salon.com/story/people/feature/2002/02/15/ramadan/index_np.html.

42. Antoine Sfeir, *Les réseaux d'Allah* (Paris: Plon, 2001). Recent exposés include Caroline Fourest, *Frère Tariq* (Paris: Grasset, 2004); Lionel Favrot, *Tariq Ramadan dévoilé* (Lyon: Lyon Mag' Hors Serie, 2004); Paul Landau, *Le sabre et le Coran* (Paris: Editions du Rocher, 2005); Ralph Ghadban, *Tariq Ramadan und die islamisierung Europas* (Berlin: Verlag Hans Schiler, 2006); Besson, *La conquête de l'Occident*. For the saga of the Munich mosque, see Ian Johnson, "Ex-Nazis Spark Radical Islam," *WSJ*, July 12, 2005; Lorenzo Vidino, "The Muslim Brotherhood's Conquest of Europe," *MEQ* 12(1)(2005), at www.meforum.org/article/687/.

43. Tariq Ramadan, *Western Muslims and the Future of Islam* (New York: Oxford University Press, 2003), 26.

44. "Muslim identity is a response," is from Ramadan, *Western Muslims and the Future of Islam*, 93. "In my memories" is from Martin Beglinger, "Under Suspicion," February 8, 2006, at www.signandsight.com/features/586.html. Tariq Ramadan, "Europeanization of Islam or Islamization of Europe?" in Shireen T. Hunter, ed., *Islam, Europe's Second Religion*. "In medieval Europe" is quoted from Innocenzo Siggillino, et al., eds., *L'Islam nelle città* (Milano: F. Angeli, 2001), 73.

45. Beglinger, "Under Suspicion."

46. Ramadan, *Western Muslims and the Future of Islam*, 4

47. Joachim Güntner, "Interview with Zafer Senocak," www.qantara.de/webcom/show_article.php/_c-478/_nr-226/i.html; Zafer Senocak "Ganze Stadtteile Verwandeln Sich in Anatolische Provinznester," *Die Welt*, April 18, 2006.

48. Soheib Bencheikh is quoted from "Islam and Secularism" at www .qantara.de/webcom/show_article.php/_c-478/_nr-130/i.html. Soheib Bencheikh, *Marianne et le prophète* (Paris: Bernard Grasset, 1998).

49. Samantha M. Shapiro, "Ministering to the Upwardly Mobile Muslim," *NYT Magazine*, April 30, 2006. The reference to the *nahda* is from Lindsay Wise, "Amr Khaled: Broadcasting the Nahda," *TBS Journal*, 13(2004) at www .tbsjournal.com/Archives/Fall04/wiseamrkhaled.html.

50. "Sudanese Scholar Hassan Al-Turabi Elaborates on His Revolutionary Fatwa on Muslim Women," www.memritv.org/Transcript.asp?P1=1112; Jörg Lau, "Keine Gewalt," *Die Zeit*, July 6, 2006. See also Tariq Ramadan, "Die Gesellschaft des 'Wir,' " *Financial Times Deutschland*, September 7, 2006, at *www .ftd.de/meinung/kommentare/110966.html*.

51. Marvine Howe, *Morocco: The Islamist Awakening and Other Challenges* (New York: Oxford University Press, 2005).

Chapter 7

1. *Report of the Official Account of the Bombings in London on 7th July 2005* (London: Her Majesty's Stationery Office, 2006). For his final speech, see "London Bomber: Text in Full," September 1, 2005, at http://news.bbc.co.uk/1/hi/uk/4206800.stm. Crispin Black, *7–7: The London Bombings* (London: Gibson Square Books, 2006).

2. Salman Rushdie, "The Right Time for an Islamic Reformation," *WP*, August 7, 2005.

3. For the Netherlands, see Brian Moynahan, "Putting the Fear of God into Holland," *Sunday Times* (London), February 27, 2005; "The War of the Headscarves," *Economist*, February 5, 2004.

4. Robert S. Leiken, "Europe's Angry Muslims," *Foreign Affairs*, July/August 2005.

5. These issues have attracted keen political and academic attention in recent years. One prolific writer in this area is Jocelyne Cesari: see, for instance, her *Être musulman en France aujourd'hui* (Paris: Hachette, 1997); idem, *Musulmans et républicains* (Brussels: Editions Complexe, 1998); idem, *Islam and the West* (New York: Palgrave Macmillan, 2004); idem, *When Islam and Democracy Meet* (New York: Palgrave Macmillan, 2004). Jocelyne Cesari, et al., "European

Muslims and the Secular State in a Comparative Perspective" (NOCRIME, Network of Comparative Research on Islam and Muslims in Europe, Final Symposium, 2003), available via http://euro-islam.info/pages/pubs.html.

6. For some of the leading British residents of Pakistani origin, see www.101pakistanis.com/; for Ridouan, see www.audionautes.net/. *Emel*, the "Muslim Lifestyle Magazine," targets Britain's upwardly mobile Muslims (www .emelmagazine.com/).

7. Tony Judt, *Postwar* (New York: Penguin, 2005).

8. For the "città invisibili" see Innocenzo Siggillino, et al., eds., *L'Islam nelle città* (Milano: F. Angeli, 2001). Christopher Caldwell, "Islam on the Outskirts of the Welfare State," *NYT Magazine*, February 5, 2006.

9. "An Underclass Rebellion," *Economist*, November 14, 2005. For the emergence of a European underclass as a consequence of globalization, see Gabor Steingart, *Weltkrieg um Wohlstand* (Munich: Piper, 2006).

10. Gilles Kepel, *Les banlieues de l'Islam* (Paris: Hachette, 1987).

11. Elaine Sciolino, "Europe Meets the New Face of Terrorism," *NYT*, August 1, 2005. Compare "Young Muslims and Extremism," draft report produced for the British Home Office and Foreign Office, available online at www.global security.org/security/library/report/2004/muslimext-uk.htm; Bill Powell, "Generation Jihad," *Time*, September 25, 2005.

12. www.asianrichlist.co.uk/.

13. Daniel Binswanger, "La grande détonation," *Die Weltwoche*, November 10, 2005. For "Ali and Rachid," see Henri Astier, "French Muslims Face Job Discrimination," November 2, 2005, at http://news.bbc.co.uk/go/pr/fr/-/2/hi/ europe/4399748.stm; Henri Astier, "France's Disaffected Muslim Businessmen," November 4, 2005, at http://news.bbc.co.uk/go/pr/fr/-/2/hi/europe/ 4405790.stm.

14. Farhad Khosrokhavar, *L'Islam dans les prisons* (Paris: Balland, 2004); Hans Werdmolder, *A Generation Adrift* (Dordrecht, Netherlands: Kluwer, 1997); Muzammil Quraishi, *Muslims and Crime* (Aldershot, England: Ashgate, 2005).

15. Farhad Khosrokhavar, *L'Islam dans les prisons*; James A. Beckford, Daniele Joly, Farhad Khosrokhavar, *Muslims in Prison* (London: Palgrave Macmillan, 2005); James A. Beckford and Sophie Gilliat, *Religion in Prison* (Cambridge, UK: Cambridge University Press, 2005). For Bollate, see Tracy Wilkinson, "In a Prison's Halls, the Call to Islam," *LAT*, October 4, 2005.

16. Boris Thiolay, "Vingt ans après la marche des beurs," *L'Express*, November 20, 2003.

17. Craig S. Smith, "Europe's Muslims May Be Headed Where the Marxists Went Before," *NYT*, December 26, 2004; Gilles Kepel, *Jihad, the Trail of Political Islam* (Cambridge, MA: Belknap Press, 2002).

18. Peter Schneider, "The New Berlin Wall," *NYT Magazine*, December 4, 2005; Hind Fraihi, *Undercover in Klein-Marokko* (Leuven: Van Halewyck, 2006); for Bawer, see Lowell Ponte, "Goodbye Europe," FrontPageMagazine.com, March 28, 2006.

19. Hisham Aidi, "Let Us Be Moors," at www.columbia.edu/cu/ccbh/ pdfs/Souls.Let_Us_Be_Moors.pdf; Adam Sage, "Profile of an Extremist," *Times* (London), September 28, 2001.

20. Farhad Khosrokhavar, *L'Islam des jeunes* (Paris: Flammarion, 1997); Nikola Tietze, *Islamische Identitäten* (Hamburg: Hamburger Edition, 2001); Hans-

Ludwig Frese, *Den Islam Ausleben* (Bielefeld: Transcript, 2002); Viola G. Georgi, *Entliehene Erinnerung* (Hamburg: Hamburger Edition, 2003); Neclá Kelek, *Islam im Alltag* (Münster: Waxmann, 2002).

21. Brigitte Maréchal, Stefano Allievi, Felice Dassetto, and Jørgen Nielsen, eds., *Muslims in the Enlarged Europe* (Leiden: Brill, 2003), 17.

22. "The Great Divide," Pew Global Attitudes Project (Washington, DC: Pew Research Center, 2006), accessible via http://pewglobal.org/reports/display.php?ReportID=253.

23. "Hizb ut Tahrir," August 27, 2003, at http://news.bbc.co.uk/1/hi/programmes/newsnight/3182271.stm.

24. Sharon Waxman, "True Believers," *WP*, November 23, 2001.

25. For languages, see Brigitte Maréchal, et al., eds., *Muslims in the Enlarged Europe*, 37; Patrick Barkham, "Journey through Britain's Muslim Divide," *Guardian*, July 16, 2005.

26. Elaine Sciolino, "Europe Meets the New Face of Terrorism."

27. "People recruiting for Islamic Jihad" is from Scott MacMillan, "Holland in Flames," *Slate*, November 11, 2004, www.slate.com/id/2109523/; "Adrift from both" is from "The Enemy Within," *Economist*, July 14, 2005. Olivier Roy, *Globalized Islam* (New York: Columbia University Press, 2004). Brian Moynahan, "All doors close" is from "Putting the Fear of God into Holland." "Van Dawa tot Jihad" (Den Haag: Ministerie van Binnenlandse Zaken en Koninkrijksrelaties, 2004), at www.aivd.nl/contents/pages/10835/notavandawatotjihad.pdf. Zachary Shore, *Breeding Bin Ladens* (Baltimore: Johns Hopkins University Press, 2006).

28. "He emerged from jail" is from Leiken, "Europe's Angry Muslims." "The breeding grounds" is from Brian Moynahan, "Putting the Fear of God into Holland." Emerson Vermaat, *De Hofstadgroep, Portret van een Radicaal-Islamitisch Netwerk* (Soesterberg, Netherlands: Aspekt Publishers, 2005). Ian Buruma, *Murder in Amsterdam* (New York: Penguin Press, 2006). Meghnad Desai, *Rethinking Islamism* (New York: I. B. Tauris, 2006). For a British account of radicalization, see Moazzam Begg, *Enemy Combatant* (London: Free Press, 2006).

29. Mark Juergensmeyer, *Terror in the Mind of God*, 3rd ed. (Berkeley: University of California Press, 2003).

30. Patrick Barkham, "Journey through Britain's Muslim Divide."

31. Dan Bilefsky, "Cartoons Ignite Cultural Combat in Denmark," *International Herald Tribune*, January 1, 2006.

32. Schneider, "The New Berlin Wall." For the Netherlands, see Brian Moynahan, "Putting the Fear of God into Holland."

33. Rosie Cowan, "Mock Suicide Bomber Back in Jail for Breaching Parole," *Guardian*, February 8, 2006.

34. Magdi Allam, *Bin Laden in Italia* (Milan: Mondadori, 2002); Elizabeth Poole, *Reporting Islam* (London: I. B. Tauris, 2002); Thomas Deltombe, *L'Islam imaginaire* (Paris: Editions La Découverte, 2005); Elizabeth Poole and John E. Richardson, eds., *Muslims and the News Media* (New York: I. B. Tauris, 2006).

35. "The Great Divide," Pew Global Attitudes Project (Washington, DC: Pew Research Center, 2006), accessible via http://pewglobal.org/reports/display.php?ReportID=253.

36. Wilhelm Heitmeyer, Joachim Müller, and Helmut Schröder, *Verlockender Fundamentalismus* (Frankfurt am Main: Suhrkamp, 1997). For reactions

to the Van Gogh murder, see Charles Bremner, "Stoned to Death," *Times* (London), December 4, 2004.

37. www.yougov.com/archives/pdf/TEL050101030_1.pdf. For the 2006 poll, see Hélène Mulholland, "We Must Defeat Ideas of Extremists, Says Blair," *Guardian*, July 4, 2006. For the rejection of British identity, see David Goodhart, "It's Paranoia, not Islamophobia," *Guardian*, July 15, 2005.

38. "British Muslims in Eye of Storm," at www.islamonline.net/English/News/2006-07/07/01.shtml.

39. Peter Riddell, "Poll Shows Voters Believe Press Is Right not to Publish Cartoons," *Times* (London), February 7, 2006.

40. The reference to "satellite city" is from Leiken, "Europe's Angry Muslims." For Hind Fraihi, see "Undercover in Klein-Marokko," April 4, 2006, at http://islamineurope.blogspot.com/2006_04_01_islamineurope_archive.html.

41. www.yougov.com/archives/pdf/TEL050101030_1.pdf. Dilwar Hussein, "The Impact of 9/11 on British Muslim Identity," in Ron Geaves, et al., eds., *Islam and the West Post–September 11th* (Burlington, VT: Ashgate, 2005).

42. Pierre-Andre Taquieff, *Rising from the Muck* (Chicago: Ivan R. Dee, 2004).

43. Dalil Boubakeur and Bernard Kanovitch, *L'Appel au dialogue* (Paris: Editions 1, 2003). "The Great Divide," Pew Global Attitudes Project (Washington, DC: Pew Research Center, 2006), accessible via http://pewglobal.org/reports/display.php?ReportID=253.

44. David Pryce-Jones, *Betrayal* (New York: Encounter, 2006); "Hizb ut Tahrir."

45. "The Great Divide," Pew Global Attitudes Project.

46. "Report: Blair Advisers Urge That U.K. Cancel Holocaust Day," *Ha'Aretz*, September 11, 2005; Theodore Dalrymple, "A Wiser Holland," *National Review*, January 30, 2006.

47. Peter Riddell, "Poll Shows Voters Believe Press Is Right not to Publish Cartoons."

48. Caroline Glick, "Ilan Halimi and Israel," *Jerusalem Post*, February 24, 2006.

49. Glick, "Ilan Halimi and Israel." "The children of blacks" is from Craig S. Smith, "Torture and Death of Jew Deepen Fears in France," *NYT*, March 5, 2006. Matthew Kaminski, "Barbarians inside the Gate," *WSJ*, February 25, 2006, at http://online.wsj.com/article/SB114083643710283317.html.

50. Caroline B. Glick, "From 1933–1945, the Enemy Was Nazi Germany. Today, It's Political Islam," *Jewish World Review*, February 27, 2006, at www.jewishworldreview.com/0206/glick022706.php3.

51. For the train attack, see Kaminski, "Barbarians inside the Gate."

52. Amir Khan is quoted from Pat Jordan, "The Great British-Pakistani-Muslim Hope," *NYT Magazine*, March 19, 2006; Philip Lewis, *Islamic Britain* (New York: I. B. Tauris, 2002); Tariq Modood, *Multicultural Politics* (Minneapolis: University of Minnesota Press, 2005).

53. Caldwell, "Islam on the Outskirts of the Welfare State."

54. Thomas Grofl, "The Motivation Bomb," May 18, 2006, at www.signandsight.com/features/762.html. For the emergence of a conservative Muslim youth culture in Germany, see Julia Gerlach, *Zwischen Pop und Dschihad* (Berlin: Christoph Links, 2006).

55. Marie-Agnès Beau, "Hip Hop and Rap in Europe," in Paul Rutten, ed., *Music, Culture and Society in Europe* (Brussels: European Music Office, 1996); Tony Mitchell, ed., *Global Noise* (Middletown, CT: Wesleyan University Press, 2001); Ayhan Kaya, *Sicher in Kreuzberg* (Bielefeld, Germany: Transcript Verlag, 2001); Alain-Philippe Durand, *Black, Blanc, Beur* (Lanham, MD: Scarecrow Press, 2002).

56. http://comp.uark.edu/~tsweden/IAM.html. Abd Al Malik, *Qu'Allah bénisse la France* (Paris: Albin Michel, 2004).

57. Ted Swedenburg, "Islamic Hip-Hop vs. Islamophobia: Aki Nawaz, Natacha Atlas, Akhenaton," in Tony Mitchell, ed. *Global Noise*; http://comp.uark.edu/~tsweden/IAM.html.

58. Quoted in Paul A. Silverstein and Chantal Tetreault, "Postcolonial Urban Apartheid," http://riotsfrance.ssrc.org/Silverstein_Tetreault/. I have altered their translation somewhat.

59. www.danielpipes.org/blog/34. I have altered the translation somewhat ("On se fou" is better translated as "Screw France" than the more aggressively obscene "Fuck France").

60. For FranSSe, see Olivier Guitta "Homegrown Gangstas " *WS*, September 23, 2005. For Alpha 5.20, see Hugh Schofield, "French Rappers' Prophecies Come True," November 16, 2005, at http://news.bbc.co.uk/1/hi/world/europe/4440422.stm.

61. This discussion is synthesized from a wide range of European and U.S. news coverage in November–December 2005.

62. Hugh Schofield, "La Haine: Schools, Synagogues and Hundreds of Cars Burn," *Independent*, November 6, 2005; Mark Steyn, "Early Skirmish in the Eurabian Civil War," *Daily Telegraph,* November 8, 2005; Olivier Guitta, "Paris When It Sizzles: The Intifada Comes to France," *WS,* November 14, 2005.

63. Joel Mowbray, "Deadly Denial," *FrontPageMagazine.com,* November 9, 2005 http://frontpagemag.com/Articles/ReadArticle.asp?ID=20100.

64. "France and Its Muslims," at www.islamonline.net/English/European Muslims/PoliticsCitizenship/2006/07/01.shtml.

65. The fatwa is discussed in Robert Spencer, "Jihad in Europe?" *FrontPageMagazine.com,* November 8, 2005, www.frontpagemag.com/Articles/Printable.asp?ID=20107; "We don't feel represented" is from George Neumayr, "The Vichy Solution," *American Spectator,* November 9, 2005; Jocelyne Cesari, "Ethnicity, Islam, and Les Banlieues," http://riotsfrance.ssrc.org/Cesari/.

66. Schofield, "La Haine"; Jim Wolfreys, "Interview with Faïza Guène," *Socialist Review,* May 2006 at www.socialistreview.org.uk/article.php?article number=9736. Jean-Eric Boulin, *Supplément au Roman National* (Paris: Editions Stock, 2006).

67. For the 1981 riots, see "Britain '81: Rebellion and Repression," special issue of *Race and Class* 23 (2–3) 1981–1982; Martin Kettle and Lucy Hodges, *Uprising!* (London: Pan, 1982); *The Brixton Disorders, 10–12 April 1981: Report of an Inquiry by the Rt. Hon. Lord Scarman* (London: Her Majesty's Stationery Office, 1982). For the 2001 riots, see *Oldham Independent Review: Panel Report, 11 December 2001,* at http://image.guardian.co.uk/sys-files/Guardian/documents/2001/12/11/Oldhamindependentreview.pdf. Christopher Allen, *Fair Justice* (London: Forum against Islamophobia and Racism, 2003). Gautam Malkani's novel *Londonstani* (London: Fourth Estate, 2006) portrays a world of British

Asian gangs involved in faction fights and petty crime, though in this case the participants are Hindu and Sikh rather than Muslim.

68. Jennifer Ehrlich and Tom Vandyck, "Belgian 'Malcolm X' Seeks Office," *Christian Science Monitor,* May 16, 2003; www.arabeuropean.org/vision.php.

Chapter 8

1. Anne Sofie Roald, *Women in Islam* (New York: Routledge, 2001); see also the essays in Jacqueline Andall, ed., *Gender and Ethnicity in Contemporary Europe* (New York: Berg, 2003).

2. Robert Orsi, *Thank You, Saint Jude* (New Haven, CT: Yale University Press, 1996).

3. From a rapidly expanding literature on women, gender, and Islam, see, for instance, Yvonne Yazbeck Haddad and John L. Esposito, eds., *Islam, Gender, and Social Change* (New York: Oxford University Press, 1998); Saba Mahmood, *Politics of Piety* (Princeton, NJ: Princeton University Press, 2004).

4. Ghada Hashem Talhami, "European, Muslim and Female," *Middle East Policy,* 11(2)(2004): 152–168. See also Shireen T. Hunter, ed., *Islam, Europe's Second Religion* (Westport, CT: Praeger, 2002); Brigitte Maréchal, Stefano Allievi, Felice Dassetto, and Jørgen Nielsen, eds., *Muslims in the Enlarged Europe* (Leiden: Brill, 2003); Jørgen S. Nielsen, *Muslims in Western Europe* (Edinburgh: Edinburgh University Press, 2004).

5. Fadela Amara and Sylvia Zappi, *Ni putes ni soumises* (Paris: La Découverte Poche, 2004); Trica Danielle Keaton, *Muslim Girls and the Other France* (Bloomington: Indiana University Press, 2006).

6. "The Enemy Within," *Economist,* July 14, 2005.

7. Jamie Glazov, "Europe's Suicide?" *FrontPageMagazine.com,* April 26, 2006, at www.frontpagemag.com/Articles/ReadArticle.asp?ID=22204. From a large literature on recent debates about multiculturalism, see Ruud Koopmans and Paul Statham, *Challenging Immigration and Ethnic Relations Politics* (New York: Oxford University Press, 2000); Adrian Favell, *Philosophies of Integration* (Basingstoke: Palgrave, 2001); Brett Klopp, *German Multiculturalism* (Westport, CT: Greenwood Press, 2002); Ralph Grillo and Jeff Pratt, eds., *The Politics of Recognizing Difference* (Aldershot, England: Ashgate, 2002); Rémy Leveau, Khadija Mohsen-Finan, and Catherine Wihtol de Wenden, eds., New *European Identity and Citizenship* (Aldershot, England: Ashgate, 2002); Roberta Aluffi Beck-Peccoz and Giovanna Zincone, eds., *The Legal Treatment of Islamic Minorities in Europe* (Leuven: Peeters, 2004); Ruud Koopmans, Paul Statham, Marco Giugni, and Florence Passy, *Contested Citizenship* (Minneapolis: University of Minnesota Press, 2005).

8. Review of Neclá Kelek, *Die fremde Braut* (Köln: Kiepenheuer und Witsch Verlag, 2005), at http://print.perlentaucher.de/buch/20151.html.

9. "France's Polygamy Problem," *Deutsche Welle,* July 31, 2005, www.dw-world.de/dw/article/0,1564,1664241,00.html.

10. Muhammad Asad, ed., *The Message of the Quran* (Bristol, UK: The Book Foundation, 2003), 127. "A Reappraisal of the Position of Women in Islam," www.qantara.de/webcom/show_article.php/_c-478/_nr-462/i.html?PHPSESSID=5869.

11. "Spain and Islam," www.fides.org/eng/dossier/2005/espana_islam05.html.

12. Samira Bellil, *Dans l'enfer des tournantes* (Paris: Gallimard, 2003); Sharon Lapkin, "Western Muslims' Racist Rape Spree," *FrontPageMagazine .com*, December 27, 2005, www.frontpagemag.com/Articles/ReadArticle.asp?ID= 20646.

13. The Danish scholar is quoted from "Immigrant Rape Wave in Sweden," December 12, 2005, http://fjordman.blogspot.com/2005/12/immigrant-rape-wave-in-sweden.html; for al-Qaradawi, see Lapkin, "Western Muslims' Racist Rape Spree."

14. Mark Rice-Oxley, "Britain Examines Honor Killings," *Christian Science Monitor*, July 7, 2004, www.csmonitor.com/2004/0707/p06s02-woeu.html. "Two Jailed for Life over Brutal Honour Killing," *Guardian*, July 14, 2006. Peter Popham, "Murder of Muslim Girl 'Rebel' by Her Father Shocks All Italy," *Independent*, August 20, 2006.

15. "Divorced the Turkish cousin" is from Jody K. Biehl, "The Whore Lived Like a German," *Der Spiegel*, March 2, 2005, www.spiegel.de/international/ 0,1518,344374,00.htm; /www.papatya.org/. Interview with Neclá Kelek, April 10, 2006, http://signandsight.com/features/695.html.

16. For al-Qaradawi, see www.islamonline.net/servlet/Satellite?page name=IslamOnline-English-Ask_Scholar/FatwaE/FatwaE&cid=1119503543886; Frank Bruni, "Doctor in Italy Tries to Ease Pain of an African Tradition," *NYT*, February 1, 2004.

17. El-Moumni is quoted from http://en.wikipedia.org/wiki/Khalil_ el-Moumni; the Spanish imam is cited from "Spain and Islam." For Sacranie, see George Weigel, "Europe's Two Culture Wars," *Commentary*, May 2006, 29–36 at www.commentarymagazine.com/article.asp?aid=12105031_1.

18. Khaled El-Rouayheb, *Before Homosexuality in the Arab-Islamic World, 1500–1800* (University of Chicago Press, 2005). "Tunisian Weekly *Réalités* Dedicates Series of Articles to Homosexuality in Tunisia," May 24, 2006, http:// memri.org/bin/articles.cgi?Page=archives&Area=sd&ID=SP117006; For Imaan, see www.imaan.org.uk/. For Candela, see "Españolas – por Alá" at www .el-mundo.es/magazine/m73/textos/islam1.html.

19. Patrick Barkham, "Gay Magazine in Race Row after Calling Islam a Barmy Doctrine," *Guardian*, January 2, 2006.

20. Ayaan Hirsi Ali, *The Caged Virgin* (New York: Free Press, 2006); Ayaan Hirsi Ali, "Aus Freiheit wächst Integration," *Der Tagesspiegel*, September 7, 2006.

21. Though not commercially available, the film can be viewed at www .ifilm.com/ifilmdetail/2655656?htv=12. Ian Buruma, *Murder in Amsterdam* (New York: Penguin Press, 2006).

22. Christopher Caldwell, "Holland's Deadly Tolerance," *WS*, November 22, 2004.

23. For the "despicable" Prophet and "Mohammed is, by our," see Deborah Scroggins, "The Dutch-Muslim Culture War," *Nation*, June 27, 2005, at www.thenation.com/doc/20050627/scroggins/2. "They are afraid" is from Sebastian Rotella, "Shaking Pillars of Islam," *LAT*, November 7, 2005; Andrea Seibel, "Der Staat Mufl mehr verlangen," *Die Welt*, October 17, 2005, www .welt.de/data/2005/10/17/789959.html.

24. Biehl, "The Whore Lived Like a German."

25. Mariam Lau, "Stepping out of the Fire," at www.signandsight.com/ features/937.html.

26. Rotella, "Shaking Pillars of Islam."

27. Quoted from Peter Schneider, "The New Berlin Wall," *NYT Magazine*, December 4, 2005.

28. Seyran Ateš, *Grosse Reise ins Feuer* (Berlin: Rowohlt, 2003); Neclá Kelek, *Die fremde Braut* (Köln: Kiepenheuer und Witsch Verlag, 2005); Neclá Kelek, *Die verlorenen Söhne* (Köln: Kiepenheuer und Witsch, 2006). For Ateš's withdrawal from activism, see Lau, "Stepping Out of the Fire." Emel Algan is discussed in Andrea Seibel, "Mein Kopf gehört mir," *Die Welt*, December 19, 2005.

29. For the Vitry-sur-Seine case, see Charles Bremner, "Stoned to Death," *Times* (London), December 4, 2004; www.niputesnisoumises.com/mouvement .php?section=accueil; Fadela Amara with Sylvia Zappi, *Shattering Silence* (Berkeley: University of California Press, 2006); Talhami, "European, Muslim and Female." For the concept of gender jihad, see Alfred Hackensberger, "Emanzipation im namen des Islams," *Neue Zürcher Zeitung*, July 12, 2006. "The struggle against" is quoted from Giles Tremlett, "Muslim Women Launch International 'Gender Jihad,'" *Guardian*, October 31, 2005.

30. www.papatya.org/.

31. Marlise Simons, "Muslim Women in Europe Claim Rights and Keep Faith," *NYT*, December 29, 2005. Nadine B. Weibel, *Par-delà le voile* (Brussels: Complexe, 2000).

32. Deirdre Fernand, "Go and Live in Saudi Arabia, Mad Mullahs," *Sunday Times* (London), February 19, 2006; Saira Khan, *P.U.S.H. for Success* (London: Vermilion, 2006).

33. Faiza Guene, *Kiffe Kiffe Tomorrow* (New York: Harvest Books, 2006). Caitlin Killian, *North African Women in France* (Stanford, CA: Stanford University Press, 2006). For divorce statistics, see Simons, "Muslim Women in Europe Claim Rights and Keep Faith."

34. Simons, "Muslim Women in Europe Claim Rights and Keep Faith."

35. Dounia Bouzar and Saïda Kada, *L'Une voilée, l'autre pas* (Paris: Albin Michel, 2004).

36. Craig Whitlock, "How a Town Became a Terror Hub," *WP*, November 24, 2005.

37. Wilders is quoted from http://challenge.visualessence.nl/C1339780254/ E20051221233911/index.html; For Djavann, see Bruce Bawer, "Crisis in Europe," *The Hudson Review*, Winter 2006, 577–598. For Candela, see "Españolas— por Alá."

38. Andrew Anthony, "The Big Cover-Up," *Observer*, November 20, 2005. Amel Boubekeur, *Le Voile de la Mariée* (Paris: L'Harmattan, 2004).

39. Ghada Hashem Talhami, "European, Muslim and Female"; Joel S. Fetzer and J. Christopher Soper, *Muslims and the State in Britain, France, and Germany* (Cambridge: Cambridge University Press, 2005); Keaton, *Muslim Girls and the Other France.*

40. For the historical background of French secularism, see Christopher Clark and Wolfram Kaiser, eds., *Culture Wars* (Cambridge: Cambridge University Press, 2003). Robert Bistolfi et François Zabbal, eds., *Islams d'Europe: intégration ou insertion communautaire?* (La Tour d'Aigues: Editions de l'Aube, 1995); Abderrahim Lamchichi, *Islam et musulmans de France* (Paris: Harmattan, 1999); Adrian Favell, *Philosophies of Integration* (Basingstoke: Palgrave, 2001);

Rémy Leveau, Khadija Mohsen-Finan, and Catherine Wihtol de Wenden, *L'Islam en France et en Allemagne* (Paris: La Documentation Française, 2001); Rachid Kaci, *La République des lâches* (Paris: Syrtes, 2003); Jean-Loup Amselle, *Affirmative Exclusion,* 2nd ed. (Ithaca, NY: Cornell University Press, 2003); Antoine Sfeir and René Andrau, *Liberté, égalité, Islam* (Paris: Tallandier, 2005); Jonathan Laurence and Justin Vaisse, *Integrating Islam* (Washington, DC: Brookings Institution Press, 2006); Jocelyne Cesari and Sean McLoughlin, eds., *European Muslims and the Secular State* (Burlington, VT: Ashgate, 2006).

41. Fetzer and Soper, *Muslims and the State in Britain, France, and Germany; Commission de Réflexion sur l'Application du Principe de Laïcité dans la République* (Paris: Présidence de la République, 2003), at www.ladocfrancaise.gouv.fr/brp/notices/034000725.shtml. Stéphanie Giry, "France and Its Muslims," *Foreign Affairs,* September/October 2006, 87–104. John R. Bowen, *Why the French Don't Like Headscarves* (Princeton University Press, 2006).

42. Christopher Caldwell, "A Swedish Dilemma," *WS,* February 28, 2005; Susan B. Glasser, "Muslims Test Russia's Tolerance," *WP,* September 9, 2002.

43. Fetzer and Soper, *Muslims and the State in Britain, France, and Germany;* Sarah Lyall, "Britain Upholds School Ban on a Muslim Gown," *NYT,* March 23, 2006. Alan Cowell, "Blair Says Muslim Veil Is a Mark of Separation," *NYT,* October 17, 2006.

44. Lisa Nimmervoll, translated at www.eurotopics.net/en/presseschau/archiv/calender/NEWSLETTER-2006-05-15.

45. Phinehas is described in Numbers 25; women are advised about hair covering in 1 Cor. 11.

46. Susan Brownmiller, *Against Our Will* (London: Secker and Warburg, 1975).

47. "Sudanese Scholar Hassan Al-Turabi Elaborates on His Revolutionary Fatwa," www.memritv.org/Transcript.asp?P1=1112. For changing gender attitudes in the Arab world, see Allegra Stratton, *Muhajababes* (London: Constable & Robinson, 2006).

Chapter 9

1. Raymond Whitaker and Francis Elliott, "Intelligence Chiefs Warn Blair of Home-Grown 'Insurgency,'" *Independent,* August 7, 2005. Compare "Young Muslims and Extremism," draft report produced for the British Home Office and Foreign Office, available online at www.globalsecurity.org/security/library/report/2004/muslimext-uk.htm.

2. Much of the following is based on Philip Jenkins, *Images of Terror* (Hawthorne, NY: Aldine De Gruyter, 2003).

3. Gilles Kepel, *A l'Ouest d'Allah* (Paris: Editions du Seuil, 1994); Hassane Zerrouky, *La nébuleuse islamiste en France et en Algérie* (Paris: Editions 1, 2002); Gilles Kepel, *Jihad: The Trail of Political Islam* (Cambridge, MA: Belknap Press, 2003); Christophe Deloire and Christophe Dubois, *Les islamistes sont déjà là* (Paris: Albin Michel, 2004); Guillaume Bigot and Stéphane Berthomet, *Le jour où la France tremblera* (Paris: Ramsay, 2005); Lorenzo Vidino, *Al Qaeda in Europe* (Amherst, NY: Prometheus Books, 2006).

4. "60 percent returned" is from Magdi Allam, *Bin Laden in Italia* (Milan: Mondadori, 2002), 21. For the impact of the Balkan wars, see Evan Kohlmann,

Al-Qaida's Jihad in Europe (Oxford, England: Berg Publishers, 2004); Jürgen El-sässer, *Wie der Dschihad nach Europa kam* (St. Polten, Vienna: NP Buchverlag, 2005). For the GICM, see Elaine Sciolino and Hélène Fouquet, "Belgium Wres-tles with Counterterrorism Efforts," *NYT*, October 9, 2005; Mark Townsend, John Hooper, Greg Bearup, Paul Harris, Peter Beaumont, Antony Barnett, Mar-tin Bright, Jason Burke, and Nick Pelham, "The Secret War," *Guardian*, March 21, 2004.

5. Elaine Sciolino, "Complex Web of Madrid Plot Still Tangled," *NYT*, April 12, 2004.

6. *Report of the Official Account of the Bombings in London on 7th July 2005* (London: Her Majesty's Stationery Office, 2006). Crispin Black, *7–7: The London Bombings* (London: Gibson Square Books, 2006).

7. Sandra Laville, "Terror Trial Hears Tapes of Plot to Blow Up Club," *Guardian*, May 26, 2006; compare Anthony McRoy, *From Rushdie to 7/7: The Radicalisation of Islam in Britain* (London: Social Affairs Unit, 2005).

8. Emerson Vermaat, *De Hofstadgroep, Portret van een Radicaal-Islamitisch Netwerk* (Soesterberg, Netherlands: Aspekt Publishers, 2005); Bouyeri is quoted from "Van Gogh Murderer: Prophet Justifies My Deed," www.nisnews.nl/public/030206_1.htm.

9. "Violent Jihad in the Netherlands" (Den Haag: Ministerie van Binnen-landse Zaken en Koninkrijksrelaties, 2006), at www.aivd.nl/contents/pages/65582/jihad2006en.pdf. Theodore Dalrymple, "A Wiser Holland," *National Re-view*, January 30, 2006; Robert S. Leiken, "Europe's Angry Muslims," *Foreign Affairs*, July/August 2005.

10. Jenkins, *Images of Terror*; for the "Titanic" plot, see "Italy: Algerian Suspects Allegedly Planned to Kill 10,000," *La Stampa*, November 18, 2005, at www.adnki.com/index_2Level.php?cat=Terrorism&loid=8.0.230427816&par =0. For the nuclear threat, see Vikram Dodd, "Al-Qaida Plotting Nuclear At-tack on UK, Officials Warn," *Guardian*, November 14, 2006.

11. The police statement can be found at "Killer Jailed over Poison Plot," April 13, 2005, http://news.bbc.co.uk/go/pr/fr/-/1/hi/uk/4433709.stm.

12. Alex Alexiev, "Tablighi Jamaat: Jihad's Stealthy Legions," *MEQ*, 12(2005), at www.meforum.org/article/686. "Van Dawa tot Jihad" (Den Haag: Ministerie van Binnenlandse Zaken en Koninkrijksrelaties, 2004), at www .aivd.nl/contents/pages/10835/notavandawatotjihad.pdf.

13. The group's website can be found at www.hizb-ut-tahrir.org/english/english.html.

14. Michael Whine, "The Mode of Operation of Hizb-ut-Tahrir in an Open Society," February 20, 2004, at www.ict.org.il/articles/articledet.cfm? articleid=515; Shiv Malik, "The Radical Islamic Group That Acts as 'Conveyor Belt' for Terror," *Independent*, August 7, 2005.

15. www.hizb-ut-tahrir.org/english/definition/messages.htm.

16. Tony Corn, "World War IV as Fourth-Generation Warfare," *Policy Re-view*, January 2006, www.policyreview.org/000/corn.html; for Abdul Latif, see Dan Bilefsky, "Cartoons Ignite Cultural Combat in Denmark," *International Herald Tribune*, January 1, 2006.

17. Andrew Nott, "I Want to Be a Martyr Says Activist," *Manchester Evening News*, April 6, 2004, at www.manchestereveningnews.co.uk/news/s/86/86545_i_want_to_be_a_martyr_says_activist.html.

18. Michael Whine, "Al-Muhajiroun," May 21, 2003, at www.ict.org.il/articles/articledet.cfm?articleid=484; "Al-Muhajiroun," April 29, 2004, http://news.bbc.co.uk/1/hi/programmes/newsnight/3670007.stm; Aaron Klein, "Brit Arrested in Iraq Tied to U.S. Group," January 8, 2005, at http://worldnet daily.com/news/article.asp?ARTICLE_ID=42296. Neil Doyle, *Terror Base UK* (London: Mainstream, 2006).

19. Rosie Cowan, Duncan Campbell, Richard Norton-Taylor, and Giles Tremlett, "Bus Bomb Clues May Hold Key to Terror Attack," *Guardian*, July 11, 2005.

20. Andrew Nott, "I Want to Be a Martyr Says Activist"; "UK 'Terror Target' Claim Dismissed," January 7, 2002, http://news.bbc.co.uk/1/hi/uk/1746454.stm.

21. David Cohen "Terror on the Dole," April 20, 2004, www.thisislondon.co.uk/news/londonnews/articles/10329634?version=1; "Most of our people" is from Aatish Taseer, "A British Jihadist," *Prospect,* August 2005, www.prospect-magazine.co.uk/article_details.php?id=6992.

22. Richard Bernstein, "What Is Free Speech, and What Is Terrorism?" *NYT*, August 14, 2005.

23. Craig S. Smith, "Where the Moors Held Sway, Allah Is Praised Again," *NYT*, October 21, 2003; Mark McCallum, "Muslim Call to Thwart Capitalism," July 12, 2003, http://news.bbc.co.uk/1/hi/world/europe/3061833.stm.

24. Terry McDermott, "Moroccan Preacher Said to Have Met with 9/11 Plotters," *LAT*, July 6, 2005; Mark Townsend, et al., "The Secret War."

25. Peter Finn, "Hamburg's Cauldron of Terror," *WP*, September 11, 2002; Desmond Butler, "Sept. 11 Plotter Reportedly Sent Terror Funds Flowing through Dutch Town," *NYT*, September 22, 2002.

26. "Muslim Suspect in Slaying Was Student," *NYT*, November 8, 2004. For Saudi influence, see "Saoedische Invloeden in Nederland, Verbanden Tussen Salafitische Missie, Radicaliseringsprocessen en Islamistisch-Terrorisme," AIVD, 2004, at www.minbzk.nl/contents/pages/8931/rapportsaoedischeinvloe den.pdf.

27. The Finsbury Park saga has been a leading story in the British media over the past decade, and Abu Hamza has been the subject of countless profiles. Sean O'Neill and Daniel McGrory, *The Suicide Factory* (London: Harper-Perennial, 2006); Doyle, *Terror Base UK.*

28. Steven Erlanger and Chris Hedges, "Terror Cells Slip through Europe's Grasp," *NYT*, December 28, 2001.

29. Sebastian Rotella, "Wooing Next Wave of Holy Warriors," *LAT*, March 2, 2003.

30. Sifaoui is quoted in Jamie Campbell, "Why Terrorists Love Britain," *New Statesman*, August 9, 2004. See also Mohamed Sifaoui, *Inside Al Qaeda* (New York: Thunder's Mouth Press, 2004); Mohamed Sifaoui, *La France, malade de l'islamisme* (Paris: Cherche Midi, 2002).

31. Antony Barnett, Jason Burke, and Zoe Smith, "Terror Cells Regroup—and Now Their Target Is Europe," *Observer*, January 11, 2004.

32. "An Underclass Rebellion," *Economist*, November 14, 2005. For Belgium, see Ambrose Evans-Pritchard, "Arab Racist Sparked Riot in Antwerp, Say Belgians," *Daily Telegraph,* November 29, 2002.

33. J. Millard Burr and Robert O. Collins, *Alms for Jihad* (Cambridge: Cambridge University Press, 2006); Dominic Casciani, "Muslims Fight On over

Banned Charity," September 11, 2003, http://news.bbc.co.uk/1/hi/uk/3100452.stm.

34. "The recruiting has got out of control," statement by Abdul Haqq Baker of the Brixton Mosque. "Hizb ut Tahrir," at http://news.bbc.co.uk/1/hi/programmes/newsnight/3182271.stm; Sifaoui is quoted in Jamie Campbell, "Why Terrorists Love Britain."

35. Nicolas Sarkozy, "Notre stratégie est la bonne," *Le Monde*, November 5, 2005, at www.lemonde.fr/web/article/0,1-0@2-3232,36-706906@51-704172,0.html; "Although hoodlums" is from Hisham Aidi, "Let Us Be Moors," at www.columbia.edu/cu/ccbh/pdfs/Souls.Let_Us_Be_Moors.pdf.

36. For el-Faisal, see Jamie Doward, "Cleric Who Urged Jihad to Be Freed from Prison," *Observer*, August 20, 2006.

37. Sebastian Rotella, "Fragmented Europe Invites Terrorism," *LAT*, April 26, 2004; Olivier Roy, "Born Again to Kill," August 4, 2005, at www.signand sight.com/features/296.html; Bill Powell, "Generation Jihad," *Time*, September 25, 2005.

38. Ali Köse, *Conversion to Islam* (London/New York: Kegan Paul 1996); Stefano Allievi, *I nuovi musulmani* (Rome: Edizioni Lavoro, 1999); Jonathan A. Romain, *Your God Shall Be My God* (London: SCM, 2000); Anne-Sofie Roald, *New Muslims in the European Context* (Leiden: Brill, 2004); Mark Sedgwick, *Against the Modern World* (New York: Oxford University Press, 2004); Karin van Nieuwkerk, ed., *Women Embracing Islam* (Austin: University of Texas Press, 2006).

39. Silvia Taulés, *La nueva España musulmana* (Barcelona: Debolsillo, 2004). "We've come to offer" is from Craig S. Smith, "Where the Moors Held Sway, Allah Is Praised Again," *NYT*, October 21, 2003.

40. Quoted in Sebastian Rotella, "Al Qaeda's Stealth Weapons," *LAT*, September 20, 2003.

41. Quoted in "Al Muhajiroun," http://news.bbc.co.uk/1/hi/programmes/newsnight/3670007.stm.

42. Quoted from "Al Muhajiroun."

43. Sirri is quoted from Fouad Ajami "The Moor's Last Laugh," *WSJ*, March 22, 2004. For Hakimi, see Elaine Sciolino and Hélène Fouquet, "Belgium Wrestles with Counterterrorism Efforts"; Bigot and Berthomet, *Le jour où la France tremblera*.

44. "Iraqi Ansar Al-Islam Commander Mullah Krekar in Norway," April 6, 2006, MEMRI Special Dispatch Series, 1134, at http://memri.org/bin/articles.cgi?Page=archives&Area=sd&ID=SP113406. Butt is quoted from David Millward, "Radical Muslim Questions Tactics of Bombers," *Daily Telegraph*, July 30, 2005.

45. Thomas Joscelyn, "The Algerian Plague," *WS*, January 19, 2006.

46. Brian Moynahan, "Putting the Fear of God into Holland," *Sunday Times* (London), February 27, 2005; Christopher Caldwell, "After Londonistan," *NYT Magazine*, June 25, 2006.

Chapter 10

1. Jean Raspail, *Le Camp des saints* (Montréal: Editions du Jour, 1973); Stephen Castles, with Heather Booth and Tina Wallace, *Here for Good: Western Europe's New Ethnic Minorities* (London: Pluto Press, 1984).

2. For the BNP see Jeremy Seabrook, "Where Islam Is Popery and Muslims the Enemy Within," *Guardian*, May 1, 2004; Zig Layton-Henry and Czarina Wilpert, eds., *Challenging Racism in Britain and Germany* (New York: Palgrave Macmillan, 2003). Castles, et al., *Here for Good.*

3. Christopher Allen and Jørgen S. Nielsen, *Islamophobia in the EU after 11 September 2001: Summary Report* (Vienna: European Monitoring Centre on Racism and Xenophobia, 2002); Barry van Driel, eds., *Confronting Islamophobia in Educational Practice* (Stoke-on-Trent: Trentham, 2004); Christopher Allen, "Endemically European or a European Epidemic?" in Ron Geaves, et al., eds., *Islam and the West Post–September 11th* (Burlington, VT: Ashgate, 2005); David Goodhart, "It's Paranoia, not Islamophobia," *Guardian*, July 15, 2005.

4. Elisabeth Badinter, Johannes von Dohnanyi, Cornelia Filter, Wilhelm Heitmeyer, Robin Morgan, and Alice Schwarzer, *Die Gotteskrieger und die falsche Toleranz* (Köln: Kiepenheuer and Witsch 2002); Renzo Guolo, *L'Islam è compatibile con la democrazia?* (Roma: Laterza, 2004).

5. Melanie Phillips, *Londonistan* (London: Encounter Books, 2006).

6. Paul Belien, "Denmark's Intifada," *American Conservative*, March 13, 2006, 6–9.

7. *Muslimsk-Dansk Dagbog: 19 Dagbøger fra Muhammad-Krisen* (Copenhagen: Informations—Forlag, 2006); David Trads, *Islam i Flammer* (Copenhagen: Host and Son, 2006).

8. Jamie Doward, Mark Townsend, Bartle Bull, and Gaby Hinsliff, "Embassies Ablaze as Muslim Anger Spreads," *Observer*, February 5, 2006.

9. Olivier Guitta, "The Cartoon Jihad," *WS*, February 20, 2006.

10. Richard Owen, "Muslims Say Fresco Must Be Destroyed," *Times* (London), June 29, 2001. Dante, *Inferno*, Canto xxviii.

11. Dalya Alberge, "Marlowe's Koran-Burning Hero Is Censored to Avoid Muslim Anger," *Times* (London), November 24, 2005.

12. Günter Grass, "Kein Kampf der Kulturen, sondern zweier Un-Kulturen," *Die Welt*, February 10, 2006, at www.welt.de/data/2006/02/10/843397.html; this translation is from www.signandsight.com/features/590.html. Craig S. Smith and Ian Fisher, "Firestorm over Cartoon Gains Momentum," *NYT*, February 2, 2006.

13. Belien, "Denmark's Intifada."

14. "Sheik Yousef Al-Qaradhawi Responds to Prophet Muhammad's Caricature," http://memritv.org/Transcript.asp?P1=1026.

15. "EU Moves to New Media Rules on Religion," February 9, 2006, www.eupolitix.com/EN/News/200602/83041a0d-8b56-484d-99c8-8ac53d84235e.htm.

16. Ambrose Evans-Pritchard, "Blasphemy Law Revival Upsets the Dutch Elite," *Daily Telegraph*, August 18, 2004. For Italy, see Margaret Talbot, "The Agitator," *New Yorker*, June 5, 2006, 59–67.

17. Mark Kermode, "It's Not Just Muslims Who Lay Down the Law on Blasphemers," *Observer*, February 12, 2006.

18. "Security Concerns Cancel Another Van Gogh Screening," April 20, 2005, www.cbc.ca/story/arts/national/2005/04/20/Arts/submissioncancel050420.html.

19. Ayaan Hirsi Ali, "The Right to Offend," www.welt.de/z/plog/blog.php/the_free_west/the_free_wests_weblog/2006/02/10/the_right_to_offend.

20. "BNP Leader Warned of Multiracial Hell Hole," *Guardian*, January 19, 2006; Soumaya Ghannoushi, "Religious Hatred Is No More Than a Variety of Racism," *Guardian*, November 13, 2006.

21. Oriana Fallaci, *The Rage and the Pride* (New York: Rizzoli, 2002); Oriana Fallaci, *The Force of Reason* (New York: Rizzoli, 2006).

22. "Michel Houellebecq: The Sex Export," *Independent*, August 21, 2005.

23. Rob James, "After Shocking Defeat for U.K. 'Hate' Bill, Debate Goes International," March 14, 2006, at www.christianitytoday.com/ct/2006/111/23.0.html.

24. David Rennie, " 'Islamic Terrorism' Is Too Emotive a Phrase, Says EU," *Daily Telegraph*, April 12, 2006.

25. "Anti-Semitic Film Cheered with Cries of 'Allah Is Great,' " *WorldNet-Daily.com*, February 26, 2006, www.worldnetdaily.com/news/article.asp?ARTICLE_ID=49005.

26. "Dim Drums Throbbing in the Hills Half Heard," *Economist*, Aug 8, 2002.

27. For the head of the MCB, see Alice Thomson, "British Should Try Arranged Marriages," *Daily Telegraph*, June 10, 2006.

28. Kelek is quoted from www.signandsight.com/features/740.html; *Libération* is quoted from Charles Bremner, "Stoned to Death," *Times* (London), December 4, 2004. For a Turkish-German affirmation of pride in German identity, see, for instance, Feridun Zaimoglu, "Mein Deutschland," *Die Zeit*, April 12, 2006. Rémy Leveau, Khadija Mohsen-Finan, and Catherine Wihtol de Wenden, eds., *New European Identity and Citizenship* (Aldershot, England: Ashgate, 2002).

29. Wouter Bos, "Europe's Social Democrats, Solidarity and Muslim Immigration," *Globalist*, December 09, 2005. www.theglobalist.com/DBWeb/print StoryId.aspx?StoryId=4976. For debates over multiculturalism, see Krzysztof Michalski, ed., *Religion in the New Europe*, vol. 2 of *Conditions of European Solidarity* (Budapest/New York: Central European University Press, 2006).

30. Peter Schneider, "Das Versprechen der Freiheit," *Der Tagesspiegel*, February 23, 2006, at www.tagesspiegel.de/kultur/archiv/23.02.2006/2371175.asp; Merkel is quoted in Lawrence Solomon, "Cultures Collide," *Financial Post*, February 17, 2006, www.canada.com/nationalpost/news/story.html?id=34cbfbb7-eb95-4e77-a155-3904297e45de.

31. The passage about Phillips is quoted from Leo McKinstry, "Dis-United Kingdom: Multiculturalism Isn't Working," *WS*, December 5, 2005.

32. Ruth Gledhill, "Multiculturalism Has Betrayed the English, Archbishop Says," *Times* (London), November 22, 2005.

33. Jonathan Laurence and Justin Vaisse, *Integrating Islam* (Washington, DC: Brookings Institution Press, 2006); www.mosquee-de-paris.net/home.html. The Spanish treaty can be found at www.mju.es/asuntos_religiosos/ar_n08_e.htm; Silvia Taulés, *La nueva España musulmana* (Barcelona: Debolsillo, 2004).

34. Christopher Caldwell, "After Londonistan," *NYT Magazine*, June 25, 2006.

35. Nick Cohen, "Belief Isn't Everything," *Observer*, August 14, 2005.

36. Amir Taheri, "France's Ticking Time Bomb," *Arab News*, November 5, 2005; www.benadorassociates.com/article/18823; Ian Johnson and John Carreyrou, "As Muslims Call Europe Home, Dangerous Isolation Takes Root,"

WSJ, July 11, 2005. For Britain, see Marcel Berlins, "Sharia Law? Don't Even Think about It," *Guardian,* February 20, 2006; "War Torpedoes Labour's Muslim Backing," *Asian News,* March 30, 2006, at www.theasiannews.co.uk/heritage/ s/191/191543_war_torpedoes_labours_muslim_backing.html. For the millet, see Benjamin Braude and Bernard Lewis, *Christians and Jews in the Ottoman Empire* (New York: Holmes & Meier, 1982). For Abu Izzadeen, see Philip Johnston, "The Shadow Cast by a Mega-Mosque," *Daily Telegraph,* September 25, 2006.

37. Trevor Phillips, "Muslims 'Must Accept' Free Speech," February 26, 2006, http://news.bbc.co.uk/1/hi/uk/4752804.stm.

38. Inayat Bunglawala, "It's Getting Harder to Be a British Muslim," *Observer,* May 19, 2002; Alasdair Palmer, "Top Job Fighting Extremism for Muslim Who Praised Bomber," *Daily Telegraph,* August 21, 2005.

39. Palmer, "Top Job Fighting Extremism for Muslim Who Praised Bomber"; "A Question of Leadership," August 21, 2005, http://news.bbc.co.uk/ go/pr/fr/-/1/hi/programmes/panorama/4171950.stm.

40. This and other harrowing remarks can be found in "Sheik Yusuf al-Qaradawi: Theologian of Terror," August 1, 2005, at www.adl.org/main_ Arab_World/al_Qaradawi_report_20041110.htm?Multi_page_sections= sHeading_2.

41. "France and Its Muslims," at www.islamonline.net/English/European Muslims/PoliticsCitizenship/2006/07/01.shtml.

42. Fischer is quoted in Robert Kagan, "Embraceable E.U.," *WP,* December 5, 2004. For Fethullah Gülen, see http://en.fgulen.com/; "Does Muslim Turkey Belong in Christian Europe?" National Press Club, January 13, 2005, at http://pewforum.org/events/index.php?EventID=66.

43. Gerhard Frey, ed., *Halbmond über Deutschland? (*München: FZ-Verlag, 2004); Olivier Roy, ed., *Turkey Today* (London: Anthem Press, 2005).

44. "Publisher, Writer Face Trial in Turkey," www.pen.org/page.php/ prmID/1017. Bruce Clark, *Twice a Stranger* (Harvard University Press, 2006).

45. "Poll: Turks Oppose Headscarf Ban, Back Religion," Reuters story, June 14, 2006.

Chapter 11

1. Cesari is quoted in Esther Pan, "Europe: Integrating Islam," www.cfr .org/publication/8252/europe.html; Ian Buruma, "Cross Purposes," *Guardian,* January 7, 2006.

2. Salman Rushdie, "The Right Time for an Islamic Reformation," *WP,* August 7, 2005.

3. Jytte Klausen, *The Islamic Challenge* (New York: Oxford University Press, 2005).

4. John L. Allen, Jr., "The Word from Rome," *NCR,* March 24, 2006, at http://nationalcatholicreporter.org/word/word032406.htm. Benedict is quoted from Timothy Garton Ash, "Christian Europe RIP," *Guardian,* April 21, 2005 at www.guardian.co.uk/Columnists/Column/0,,1464758,00.html. John T. S. Madeley and Zsolt Enyedi, eds., *Church and State in Contemporary Europe* (London: Frank Cass, 2003); Marco Impagliazzo, ed., *La nazione cattolica* (Milano: Guerini e Associati, 2004). Joseph F. Byrnes, *Catholic and French Forever* (University Park: Penn State University Press 2005).

5. Brian Moynahan, "Putting the Fear of God into Holland," *Sunday Times* (London), February 27, 2005.

6. Nazir-Ali is quoted from Michael Burleigh, "Future Generations Will Hear Far More about God and Politics," *Daily Telegraph*, November 7, 2006. The 2006 Report is described in Jonathan Wynne-Jones, "Drive for MultiFaith Britain Deepens Rifts, Says Church," *Daily Telegraph*, October 8, 2006.

7. Niall Ferguson, "Heaven Knows How We'll Rekindle Our Religion, But I Believe We Must," *Daily Telegraph*, July 31, 2005; Michael Burleigh, "Godless Europeans Turn to Cultural Christianity," *The Australian*, June 2, 2006, www .theaustralian.news.com.au/story/0,20876,19331121-7583,00.html. Michael Burleigh, *Sacred Causes* (London: HarperPress, 2006); Sandro Magister, "The Church Is under Siege," at *www.chiesa.espressonline.it/dettaglio.jsp?id=20037&eng=y.* Jürgen Habermas, *Time of Transitions* (New York: Polity Press, 2006).

8. Joel S. Fetzer and J. Christopher Soper, *Muslims and the State in Britain, France, and Germany* (Cambridge: Cambridge University Press, 2005).

9. Fetzer and Soper, *Muslims and the State in Britain, France, and Germany*, 60.

10. Richard Bulliet, *The Case for Islamo-Christian Civilization* (New York: Columbia University Press, 2004).

11. Danneels is quoted from John L. Allen, Jr., "Europe's Muslims Worry Bishops," *NCR*, October 22, 1999. Fr. Santoro is quoted from John L. Allen, Jr., "The Word from Rome," *NCR*, February 10, 2006, at http://nationalcatholic reporter.org/word/word021006.htm. Ramadan is quoted from Nicholas Le Quesne, "Trying to Bridge a Great Divide," *Time*, www.time.com/time/innovators/ spirituality/profile_ramadan.html.

12. For efforts at dialogue, see www.christianmuslimforum.org/; Jørgen S. Nielsen ed., *The Christian-Muslim Frontier* (New York: I. B. Tauris, 1998); Augusto Tino Negri, *I cristiani e l'Islàm in Italia* (Torino: Elledici, 2000); Albert Reiner and Wilfried Dettling eds., *Im Schatten der Politik* (Altenberge: Oros, 2002); Stefano Allievi, "Relations between Religions," in Brigitte Maréchal, Stefano Allievi, Felice Dassetto, and Jørgen Nielsen, eds., *Muslims in the Enlarged Europe* (Leiden: Brill, 2003), 369–414; Bill Musk, *Kissing Cousins* (London: Monarch Books, 2005).

13. The reference to *De propaganda fide Islamica* is from Michel Gurfinkiel, "Islam in France," *MEQ*, 4(1)(1997), at www.meforum.org/article/337. Alain Besancon, *Trois tentations dans l'église* (Paris: Calmann-Levy, 1996).

14. Sandro Magister, "Renato Martino, a Cardinal Out of Control," www .chiesa.espressonline.it/dettaglio.jsp?id=46686&eng=y.

15. "John Paul II and Islam," at www.daughtersofstpaul.com/john paulpapacy/meetjp/thepope/jpislam.html.

16. Fr. Santoro is quoted from John L. Allen, Jr., "The Word from Rome," *NCR*, February 10, 2006, at http://nationalcatholicreporter.org/word/word 021006.htm.

17. "Anti-Muslim Remarks Create a Furor," *San Francisco Chronicle*, September 15, 2000; "Cardinal Asks Italy to Favor Catholic Immigrants," *America*, September 30, 2000.

18. "Spain and Islam," www.fides.org/eng/dossier/2005/espana_islam05 .html. Gustavo de Aristegui, *La yihad en España* (Madrid: La Esfera de los Libros, 2006).

19. Allen, "Europe's Muslims Worry Bishops."

20. John L. Allen, Jr., "The Word from Rome," *NCR*, March 31, 2006, http://nationalcatholicreporter.org/word/word033106.htm.

21. *Report of the High-Level Advisory Group Established at the Initiative of the President of the European Commission: Dialogue between Peoples and Cultures in the Euro-Mediterranean Area, Euromed Report 68* (2003).

22. John L. Allen, Jr., "The Word from Rome," *NCR*, March 24, 2006, at http://nationalcatholicreporter.org/word/word032406.htm. For Benedict's Regensburg speech, see Ian Fisher, "Pope Assails Secularism, Adding Footnote on Jihad," *NYT*, September 13, 2006.

23. "Forum Debate: Is Europe at Its End?" September 12, 2005, www.archbishopofcanterbury.org/sermons_speeches/2005/050912.htm.

24. Bruce Bawer, *While Europe Slept* (New York: Doubleday, 2006), 229.

25. Joseph Cardinal Ratzinger, *Salt of the Earth* (San Francisco: Ignatius Press, 1997); Ian Fisher, "Pope to Sound Theme of Non-Christian Ties at Festival," *NYT*, August 18, 2005.

26. Alice Thomson, "British Should Try Arranged Marriages," *Daily Telegraph*, June 10, 2006.

27. Grace Davie, "Pluralism, Tolerance and Democracy," in Thomas Banchoff, ed., *The New Religious Pluralism and Democracy* (New York: Oxford University Press, forthcoming); Stephen V. Monsma and J. Christopher Soper, *The Challenge of Pluralism* (Lanham, MD: Rowman and Littlefield, 1997); Stephen V. Monsma and J. Christopher Soper, eds., *Equal Treatment of Religion in a Pluralist Society* (Grand Rapids, MI: William B. Eerdmans, 1998).

28. Bruce Mutsvairo, "Dutch Immigrants Must Watch Racy Film," Associated Press story, March 15, 2006.

29. Vera Gaserow, "Was deutsch ist," *Frankfurter Rundschau*, March 24, 2006; Richard Bernstein, "A Quiz for Would-Be Citizens Tests Germans' Attitudes," *NYT*, March 29, 2006; The Hesse test is found at "100 Ways to Become German," March 28, 2006, http://print.signandsight.com/features/675.html; "Baden-Württemberg: Gesprächsleitfaden für die Einbürgerungsbehörden," January 1, 2006, http://islam.de/4401.php.

30. "Baden-Württemberg: Gesprächsleitfaden für die Einbürgerungsbehörden."

31. Juan José Tamayo, *Adiós a la Cristianidad* (Barcelona: Ediciones B, 2003), 177–206.

32. Danny Wood, "Madrid Imam Hails Preacher Curbs," May 5, 2004, http://news.bbc.co.uk/2/hi/europe/3684859.stm. Brian Moynahan, "Putting the Fear of God into Holland," *Sunday Times* (London), February 27, 2005.

33. Simonis is quoted from Brian Moynahan, "Putting the Fear of God into Holland."

34. "Swedish Pastor Sentenced to Month in Prison for Preaching against Homosexuality," July 5, 2004, www.lifesite.net/ldn/2004/jul/04070505.html.

35. Jonathan Petre, "Gay Equality Law Will Undermine Religious Belief, Claims Bishop," *Daily Telegraph*, June 3, 2006.

36. David Batty and Agencies, "Children Abused in Exorcism Rites," *Guardian*, February 25, 2005. For the charitable groups and the vetting of new churches, see "Call for Church Child-Safety Vet," July 6, 2006, http://news.bbc.co.uk/go/pr/fr/-/2/hi/uk_news/5150368.stm.

37. Jonathan A. Romain, *Your God Shall Be My God* (London: SCM, 2000).

38. Sally J. Sutcliffe, ed., *Good News for Asians in Britain* (Cambridge, UK: Grove Books, 1998).

39. Rob James, "After Shocking Defeat for U.K. 'Hate' Bill, Debate Goes International," March 14, 2006, at www.christianitytoday.com/ct/2006/111/23.0.html. Jonathan Wynne-Jones, "Christians Ask If Force Is Needed to Protect Their Religious Values," *Sunday Telegraph*, November 5, 2006; *Faith and Nation* (London: Evangelical Alliance, 2006), at www.eauk.org/media/faith-and-nation-report.cfm.

40. Larry Witham, "French Proposal Targets Proselytizing," *Washington Times*, June 28, 2000, online at www.cesnur.org/testi/fr2k_june7.htm. Danièle Hervieu-Léger, *La religion en miettes, ou la question des sectes* (Paris: Calmann-Lévy, 2001); Danièle Hervieu-Léger, "France's Obsession with the Sectarian Threat,'" *Nova Religio* 4(3), 2001. "Les évangéliques: La secte qui veut conquérir le monde," *Nouvel Observateur*, February 26, 2004.

41. http://old.godembassy.org/2004/inter-en.htm.

42. "Growing British-Sikh Militancy Explored in Radio 4 Doc," AIM, August 22, 2005, www.asiansinmedia.org/news/article.php/radio/1069; Grace Davie, "Pluralism, Tolerance and Democracy," in Thomas Banchoff, ed., *The New Religious Pluralism and Democracy* (New York: Oxford University Press, forthcoming).

43. Paul Bond, "Christian Right Forces Attack 'Blasphemous' British Television Comedy," January 18, 2005, www.wsws.org/articles/2005/jan2005/spri-j18_prn.shtml; John Plunkett, "BBC Defends Cartoon Coverage," *Guardian*, February 6, 2006.

44. For Sentamu, see Jonathan Petre, "BBC Frightened of Criticising Islam, Says Archbishop," *Daily Telegraph*, November 15, 2006. "Fatwa for 'Gay Jesus' Writer," October 29, 1999, at http://news.bbc.co.uk/1/hi/uk/493436.stm.

45. Williams is quoted from Mark D. Tooley, "Consoling the Cartoon Mob," *FrontPageMagazine.com*, March 24, 2006, at http://frontpagemag.com/Articles/ReadArticle.asp?ID=21780.

Chapter 12

1. Peter Bergen and Paul Cruickshank, "London Broil," *New Republic*, August 25, 2006. Compare Gary Younge, "Newspapers Warn of Threat to America from Londonistan," *Guardian*, July 12, 2005. Zachary Shore, *Breeding Bin Ladens* (Baltimore: Johns Hopkins University Press, 2006).

2. For some optimistic projections of a European-dominated future, see T. R. Reid, *The United States of Europe* (Penguin Press, 2004); Jeremy Rifkin, *The European Dream* (New York: Jeremy P. Tarcher, 2004); Mark Leonard, *Why Europe Will Run the 21st Century* (London: Fourth Estate, 2005).

3. Roger Cohen, "Bush's Smiles Meet Some Frowns in Europe," *NYT*, January 22, 2005.

4. Philip Jenkins, *Decade of Nightmares* (New York: Oxford University Press, 2006).

5. Eric Kaufmann, "Breeding for God," *Prospect Magazine*, November 2006, at www.prospect-magazine.co.uk/article_details.php?id=7913.

Index

Lutherans, 49–50, 69, 79, 93. *See also*
 Denmark; Germany; Sweden
Luton, 219
Lyon, 111, 134, 142

Maaseik, 196, 224
Macaulay, Thomas Babington, 72
Macedonia, 114
Maciel, Marcial, 76
Madagascar, 93–94
Madrid, 5, 95, 103, 134, 210–11,
 213, 217–19, 221, 276
Magdeburg, 70
Maguire, Matthew W., 5
Mahmoud, Moneir, 276
Makiya, Kanan, 140–41
Mali, 184
Malmö, 151, 198
Manchester, 111, 133–34, 150, 218
Marche des Beurs, 156
Marlowe, Christopher, 240
Marriages, arranged, 183, 192, 199,
 273
Marriages, forced, 146, 183
Marseille, 109, 111, 144
Martin, Diarmuid, 59
Marty, Martin, 52
Martyrdom: Christian, 71; Islamic,
 160–61, 164, 219
Mary. *See* Virgin Mary
Maududi, Syed Abul Ala, 129
M.C.B. *See* Muslim Council of Britain
Megachurches, 76, 92
Meisner, Joachim, Cardinal, 32
Melilla, 136
Merkel, Angela, 240, 248
Messerschmidt, Morten, 6
Methodists, 36, 50, 69, 77, 93
Mewshaw, Michael, 95
Milan, 155, 223
Millet system, 251–52
Millî Görüs, 137, 193
Monasteries, 33–34
Morocco: Islamist extremism in, 146;
 kingdom of, 105, 135, 138,
 257–58; migrants in Europe, 110,
 134–35, 138–39; religious reform,
 144, 146; terrorism in, 146, 221;
 traditional Islam, 124. *See also*

France; Groupe Islamique
 Combattant Marocain (G.I.C.M.);
 Italy; Netherlands
Mosques: building of, 115–16;
 funding of, 132–39, 269–70;
 numbers of, 104, 116; official
 supervision of, 231, 275–76;
 radical and extremist, 135–39,
 160, 220–25, 228–29
Moussaoui, Zacarias, 157, 210, 222,
 224
Mozart, Wolfgang Amadeus, 240
Muhabbet, 171
Muhammad, 140, 190, 200, 239,
 267–68, 271. *See also* Cartoon
 controversy
Multiculturalism, 182–83, 186–87,
 189–92, 246–52
Multi-faith society, concept of,
 199–200, 263
Munich, 95, 142, 207
Murphy-O'Connor, Cormac,
 Cardinal, 28
Musaala, Anthony, 91
Muslim Brotherhood, 129, 131,
 137–38, 142, 145, 157, 237,
 251–52. *See also* Hamas; Takfir wal
 Hijra
Muslim Council of Britain, 137–39,
 188, 194, 240, 246, 250, 253–54

Naples, 136
National identities, 246–48
Nazir-Ali, Michael, 262, 277–78
Nazis, 42–43, 106–7, 142, 241
Nazi analogies, 13–14, 67, 240, 246
Neocatechumenate, 72–73
Netherlands: churches, 79, 83;
 colonial empire, 107–8; decline of
 religious practice, 12, 34, 44, 57;
 EU Constitution referendum, 256;
 immigrant Christian churches, 88,
 95; integration, debates over,
 247–48; Muslim extremism,
 159–60, 162, 167; Muslim
 organizations, 135; Muslim
 populations, 12, 15, 110–13, 118,
 140, 149, 239, 242; religious
 liberalism, 140; social liberalism,

Lightning Source UK Ltd.
Milton Keynes UK
UKOW03f1433130914

238532UK00001B/1/P